PERSONAL DEBT IN EUROPE

Personal debt remains an important factor in many economic models because it encourages people to finance consumption or the purchase of durable goods. Whether this model is sustainable for individuals or the countries in which they reside is an ongoing question of great complexity and many social and economic implications, not only for the burdened individuals and their countries, but also for the EU as a whole. In *Personal Debt in Europe*, Federico Ferretti and Daniela Vandone examine the 'dark side' of personal debt, or over-indebtedness, in social, economic, and legal terms. They employ cross-country consumer-level data to present the latest empirical studies on the problem, analyse these findings to better understand its nature and causes, and discuss the merits of proposed insolvency legislation and harmonisation initiatives in the EU.

Federico Ferretti is Associate Professor in Economic Law and Financial Markets, Department of Sociology and Economic Law, University of Bologna (Italy) and a member of the Financial Services User Group of the European Commission. He is a qualified lawyer of the High Courts of Italy.

Daniela Vandone is Full Professor of Banking and Finance, Department of Economics, Management and Quantitative Methods, University of Milan. Her research interests are in financial markets and institutions, with a focus on the microeconomics of banking, financial regulation, financial decision-making, household finance, personal debt and over-indebtedness.

Personal Debt in Europe

THE EU FINANCIAL MARKET AND CONSUMER INSOLVENCY

FEDERICO FERRETTI
University of Bologna

DANIELA VANDONE
University of Milan

CAMBRIDGE
UNIVERSITY PRESS

University Printing House, Cambridge CB2 8BS, United Kingdom

One Liberty Plaza, 20th Floor, New York, NY 10006, USA

477 Williamstown Road, Port Melbourne, VIC 3207, Australia

314-321, 3rd Floor, Plot 3, Splendor Forum, Jasola District Centre, New Delhi - 110025, India

103 Penang Road, #05-06/07, Visioncrest Commercial, Singapore 238467

Cambridge University Press is part of the University of Cambridge.

It furthers the University's mission by disseminating knowledge in the pursuit of education, learning and research at the highest international levels of excellence.

www.cambridge.org
Information on this title: www.cambridge.org/9781108445474
DOI : 10.1017/9781108615358

© Federico Ferretti and Daniela Vandone 2019

This publication is in copyright. Subject to statutory exception and to the provisions of relevant collective licensing agreements, no reproduction of any part may take place without the written permission of Cambridge University Press.

First published 2019
First paperback edition 2022

A catalogue record for this publication is available from the British Library

Library of Congress Cataloging in Publication data
NAMES: Ferretti, Federico, author. | Vandone, Daniela, author.
TITLE: Personal debt in Europe : the EU financial market and consumer insolvency / Federico Ferretti, University of Bologna, Daniela Vandone, University of Milan.
DESCRIPTION: Cambridge, United Kingdom ; New York, NY : Cambridge University Press, 2019. | Includes bibliographical references and index.
IDENTIFIERS: LCCN 2018038866 | ISBN 9781108426732 (hardback)
SUBJECTS: LCSH: Consumer credit – Europe. | Loans, Personal – Europe. | Debt – Europe. | Consumer credit – Law and legislation – Europe.
CLASSIFICATION: LCC HG3756.E85 F47 2019 | DDC 332.7/43094–dc23
LC record available at https://lccn.loc.gov/2018038866

ISBN 978-1-108-42673-2 Hardback
ISBN 978-1-108-44547-4 Paperback

Cambridge University Press has no responsibility for the persistence or accuracy of URLs for external or third-party internet websites referred to in this publication, and does not guarantee that any content on such websites is, or will remain, accurate or appropriate.

Contents

1	**Introduction**	page 1
2	**Personal Debt in the Economy**	11
	2.1 The Demand Side of the Personal Debt Market	11
	2.2 Personal Debt in Europe: Size and Growth of the Market	11
	2.3 Factors Shaping the Evolution of the Personal Debt Market	19
	2.4 The Characteristics of Households Holding Personal Debt	21
3	**The Industry of Personal Debt**	29
	3.1 The Supply Side of the Personal Debt Market	29
	3.2 Personal Debt Products	30
	3.3 Innovative Solutions	30
	3.4 Principal Players on the Market	33
	3.5 The Economics of Personal Debt	34
	3.6 A Performance Analysis	39
4	**From Indebtedness to Over-Indebtedness: Multidimensional Causes and Consequences**	51
	4.1 Unmanageable Debt	51
	4.2 Definition of Over-Indebtedness	52
	4.3 Measures of Over-Indebtedness	55
	4.4 Causes of Over-Indebtedness	59
	4.5 An Economic Literature Review on Over-Indebtedness	62
	4.6 An Empirical Investigation into Over-Indebtedness in Europe	66
	4.7 Focus on Consumer Credit	71
	4.8 Behavioural Factors and Over-Indebtedness	71
	4.9 The Relevance of Behavioural Traits in the Effectiveness of Measures to Prevent Over-Indebtedness	76
	4.10 Remarks	85

5	**EU Policy and Law for the Prevention and Management of Over-Indebtedness**	87
	5.1 The Competence of the EU vis-à-vis National Competence	87
	5.2 Prevention: Credit Laws; Responsible Credit and Creditworthiness Assessment	90
	5.3 Responsible Lending, the Responsible Creditor and Private Law	93
	5.4 The Consumer Credit Directive	95
	5.5 The Mortgage Credit Directive	97
	5.6 The Guidelines of the European Banking Authority	104
6	**The Role and Function of Solvency Data and Financial Technologies (Fintech and Big Data)**	107
	6.1 Solvency Data in the Economy	107
	6.2 Solvency Data in the Policy and Legal Context	121
	6.3 The Legal Form and Functions of Credit Bureaus in the EU	125
	6.4 Data Sources	128
	6.5 Cross-Border Exchange of Data and the Integration of Credit Markets	136
	6.6 Competition in the Credit Information Industry	139
	6.7 Big Data and Fintech in the Age of Algorithmic Consumer Finance	141
	6.8 Opportunities and Risks of Algorithmic Finance	146
	6.9 Anacredit	150
7	**Credit Risk Analysis and Creditworthiness in Relation to EU Data Protection Legislation**	156
	7.1 Data Protection and Its Values	156
	7.2 Notice and Legitimate Grounds for Data Processing	159
	7.3 Data Subject's Consent	164
	7.4 Automated Decision-Making and Profiling	168
	7.5 Reliability and Proportionality of Data to Achieve Policy Objectives	170
	7.6 Solvency Data and Big Data as the Gateway of the Economic and Social Life of Consumers	174
	7.7 Alternative Data Protection-Friendly Data Analysis: a Semi-Serious Proposal	177
8	**The Treatment of Over-Indebtedness: Towards a Harmonisation of Personal Insolvency Law in a Fragmented EU?**	180
	8.1 Personal Insolvency Legislation in the EU	180
	8.2 Consumer Protection and the Role of the European Courts	186

	8.3	Testing the Sentiment of Expert Stakeholders	192
	8.4	Over-Indebtedness in Context: the Capital Markets Union and Retail Financial Services in the EU	197
	8.5	A Policy and Legal Analysis	199
	8.6	Inconsistencies in the EU Legal Framework	205
	8.7	The Surfacing of EU Principles?	206
9	**Conclusions and Scope for Further Research**		214
	9.1	Concluding Remarks	214
	9.2	The Way Forward for New Streams of Research	219

Bibliography   225

Index   245

1

Introduction

This book is about personal debt and the over-indebtedness of consumers in the European Union (EU) from the different multidisciplinary perspectives of economics, policy and law.

Personal indebtedness is a topical theme for researchers, regulators, the financial services industry and civil and consumer organisations. This is particularly the case under the current economic model encouraging consumers to use debt to finance consumption and the contemporary policy discussions regarding personal debt's place in the economy. Equally, this is a topic in continuous development for the renovated thrust in the integration of the EU financial market and the ensuing development of new policies and regulatory changes. The latest EU initiatives on the Capital Markets Union (CMU)[1] to improve choice, transparency and competition in retail financial services in a truly integrated EU market are illustrations of this process.[2]

---

[1] European Commission, Green Paper – Building a Capital Market Union, COM(2015) 63 final. The CMU is a plan of the European Commission to mobilise capital in Europe and the creation of a true single market for capital in the EU. The initiative was followed by the adoption of an action plan setting out a list of key measures to achieve a true single market for capital in Europe. See European Commission, Communication from the Commission to the European Parliament, the Council, the European Economic and Social Committee and the Committee of the Regions – Action Plan on Building a Capital Markets Union, COM(2015) 468 final. The European Commission has further updated and complemented the CMU action plan by strengthening existing actions and introducing new measures in response to evolving priorities and challenges. See European Commission, Communication from the Commission to the European Parliament, the Council, the European Economic and Social Committee and the Committee of the Regions on the Mid-Term Review of the Capital Markets Union Action Plan, COM(2017) 292 final.

[2] European Commission, Green Paper on Retail Financial Services. Better Products, More Choice, and Greater Opportunities for Consumers and Businesses, COM(2015) 630 final. The objective of this action is to improve choice, transparency and competition in retail financial services to the benefit of European consumers and how to facilitate true cross-border supply of these services, so that financial firms can make the most of the economies of scale in a truly integrated EU market. The Green Paper is followed by an action plan setting out a strategy to strengthen the EU single market for retail financial services. See European Commission, *Communication from the Commission – Consumer Financial Services Action Plan: Better Products, More Choice*, COM(2017) 139 final.

The focus of the book lies firmly on the social and economic phenomena of the 'dark side' of personal debt, i.e. over-indebtedness. The law and its analysis are treated as policy responses to this problem. The backdrop of the analysis is the recent financial and economic crisis that has transformed and shaped the latest EU policies and law in the financial sector. Over-indebtedness is empirically investigated and quantified using cross-country consumer-level data, and conceptualised through the lenses of the latest findings over its nature and causes.

The topic of this book is a traditionally difficult one to analyse, especially if taken in its European context. Consumer over-indebtedness has been often associated with financial credits, whose cultural approach, use and extension has varied significantly from one Member State to the other. Yet, the integration of EU consumer and mortgage credit markets is crucial for an efficient functioning of the EU financial system, the economy and the internal market. The market for loans available to consumers has grown rapidly across the EU and the industry of personal debt has become increasingly sophisticated. The economics of personal debt, the liberalisation and expansion of credit markets alongside the increased availability of credit and innovative solutions from financial institutions have explained the relatively recent mounting levels of consumer debt across societies. Although, from an economic perspective, it is known that personal debt may guarantee heightened economic welfare by smoothing out consumption over time, the risk exists that if more credit is available and offered to a broader base of consumers, more consumers become indebted and exposed to the risk of becoming unable to meet the contracted obligations.

On the other hand, credit availability and open access to credit markets have meant widening participation and financial inclusion to allow as many consumers as possible without discrimination to participate in the credit society and the consumption model of the market economy. These bases may also suggest why for a long period of time excessive lending or borrowing have been the focus of consumers becoming over-committed and unable to repay their debts, pushing the debate over behavioural issues of creditors or debtors. Irresponsible lending and predatory practices on one side, and irresponsible borrowing decisions, consumption choices and cognitive biases on the other side have so far dominated the attention of scholars and policymakers alike.[3] The emphasis on behavioural causes has often resulted in the attribution of defaults to a responsibility of the creditor or a personal failure of the debtor.

Thus, against the above background, this study examines the state and adequacy of EU policies and law in dealing with the large scale of over-indebted consumers and their insolvency, as well as the legal responses taken within the context of the overall goal of the integration of the EU retail financial market. It ultimately questions their effectiveness and suitability to address a complex multidimensional

---

[3] e.g. see Micklitz (2013a); Ramsay (2012a).

problem that impacts dearly on the lives of those who are affected and carries great social and economic costs for the EU. In analysing all the aspects of the problem, the potential for EU personal insolvency law to stem in the future this 'dark side' of the market will be ultimately evaluated.

An ambition of the research is to take a holistic perspective to 'problem debt'. It discusses the extent to which an integrated but reformed EU personal insolvency regime is necessary. The law has limits in tackling the problems at their roots, but it can play a role in mitigating the effects of the problem. The EU dimension and the fundamental freedoms that it entails need to be taken into account too. This latter aspect is also particularly relevant as the European Commission has currently put forward a legislative proposal on the harmonisation of substantive insolvency law for businesses. It is not limited to legal persons but it extends to natural persons who are entrepreneurs. However, more evidence is needed to weigh up whether an adapted extension of harmonised EU rules of insolvency legislation to consumers is necessary or appropriate.

The warning, in the case of the regulation of over-indebted consumers, is that it is not only a market-related issue but the lives of people are at stake too.

Traditionally, financial services are a key and sensitive sector of the economy. The large majority of consumers and small businesses have dealings with providers of financial services. Access to financial services is increasingly considered as a necessary condition for participation in the economy and society generally. Failures of the financial system, or the way in which financial institutions conduct their businesses, may clearly have devastating effects on the economy and society as a whole, but ultimately on the lives of individuals. As an illustration, the global credit and financial crisis has raised important issues regarding the protection of consumers in financial markets, the scope, intensity and effectiveness of regulation in financial markets, and the need for additional safeguards to stem the social and individual problems that the crisis has caused or exacerbated. With the austerity measures imposed by a large number of Member States as a core strategy to overcome the crisis resulting from the failures of the financial system, non-performing personal and mortgage loans and job losses have increased and have remained at high levels. Ensuing individual and social problems have intensified and they seem to be persisting long after the onset of the crisis.

Therefore, important questions arise as to the rationales and the objectives of financial regulation. Why do consumer financial markets need regulation? Why would personal debt problems need regulation? What should financial regulation aim for?

So far, traditional consumer law theory mostly has followed market economic theory which identifies the main rationale for regulation in market failure. Markets are optimal when they operate in a situation of perfect competition and maximise the welfare of their economic agents because of their efficient allocation of resources. This assumption reflects the view that there is a relative or close equivalence between the pursuit of suppliers' self-interest in the maximisation of profits and the promotion of the general interest, resulting in lower prices for consumers where marginal private benefits equal marginal social benefits, and marginal private costs equal marginal social costs. The traditional assumption of perfect competition is that all market actors act rationally, in their own self-interest, with good and full information, all goods and resources are freely transferable, all markets permit free and easy entry and exit, and prior distribution of wealth and resources does not unfairly impact on competition. In these terms, self-interest always promotes the interest of the community even though this is not part of the original intention.[4]

Here, the relationship between suppliers and consumers assumes a transfer of wealth, not its redistribution.

Market theory recognises that its assumptions practically never hold true in the real world and market failure occurs when there is a failure of one of the conditions for the optimal operation of a competitive market. Thus, the potential failures associated with one of these conditions provide a justification for regulation to correct it. Typical market failures are the obstacles to competition, soundness and safety of products or services, and the imbalance of power between suppliers and consumers.[5]

Thus, in the financial services arena, most of the objectives of consumer regulation are to tackle inefficiencies and externalities to make financial markets more competitive, promote confidence in the use of financial products, and empower consumers as economic agents. Examples are regulations intervening on the competitive behaviour of suppliers, contract terms, mandatory information disclosure, financial education initiatives and product safety.

Clearly, this free market approach is premised on utilitarianism and permeated by neo-liberal ideology that is not universally accepted and open to debate.

At the same time, there are also other more interventionist rationales for regulation which are not primarily justified on economic grounds. These are the non-economic, social rationales for regulation. The promotion of gender equality in financial markets, the mitigation of cultural exclusion, the widening and inclusion of access to products, and the redistribution of wealth are examples of non-economic objectives.

Thus, if the aim is to readjust the position of individuals in society rather than treating them solely as consumers – i.e. the demand side of the market – then wealth maximisation needs to be subordinated to wealth distribution and regulation becomes the tool to achieve it. This may not involve lower prices but policies of consumer protection to spread and shift risks from the consumer to the supplier.

---

[4] Smith (1776); see also e.g. Malloy (2004), esp. ch. 2.
[5] e.g. see Cartwright (2004), esp. ch. 2; Howells and Weatherill (2005), esp. ch. 1; Ramsay (2007), esp. chs. 1–2.

Distributive justice is a social rationale concerned with the distribution of resources and rights on the basis of what is fair rather than what is economically efficient.

Another rationale for regulation is paternalism, which is about state intervention on behalf and in the perceived interest of a person regardless of individual choice and wishes. The preservation or enhancement of community values such as trust, honesty, loss-sharing and fair dealing are other rationales for regulation that aim to address concerns over the type of society that people would like to live in.[6]

Also in this case, these non-economic rationales can be justified on ideological grounds for the achievement of a social market, or the defence or improvement of the welfare state.

To some extent, both the economic and social rationales for regulation of financial markets may coexist and apply at once, and some objectives may also overlap. For example, product safety is an aim of both economic and non-economic rationales. Both rationales, however, do not escape a rigorous cost–benefit analysis and trade-offs premised on a utilitarian calculus.

An underdeveloped and neglected approach to regulation can find its rationale in the respect of the fundamental rights or dignity of individuals as internationally recognised. Ultimately, it draws on the Kantian idea of the centrality of the individual, where the economy is at the service of humankind and not vice versa, and the individual may not be used as a means to social or economic ends.[7] The rights of the individual are treated seriously and trump any conflicting interest or competing consideration. The respect for the individual is at the centre of the attention of the regulator which will intervene to protect or preserve the individual rights at stake, or the means to achieve them. In this perspective, the emphasis is placed on the individual more than the collective. In this light, consumer rights may become rights of the individual instead of rights of a heterogeneous group. Consumers are not a separate group of people, they are human beings, and every consumer is a citizen.[8] The consumer evolves into a market or economic citizen. This vision is likely to attribute a constitutional dimension to consumers and consumer protection, where the rationale of financial regulation becomes the respect for fundamental rights and its objective is the respect for the dignity and freedom of the individual consumer and his/her full participation in society.

There are practical implications in a fundamental rights-led approach to regulation. Participation in the economic and social life of the community where individuals live is already a right recognised in international conventions.[9] The achievement or respect of human dignity already inform and are the objective of human rights legislation. Intervening in the financial marketplace, a right-led approach to regulation may provide

---

[6] Ibid.
[7] Kant (1785).
[8] e.g. see Deutch (1994), esp. p. 537.
[9] e.g. see the 1966 International Covenant on Economic, Social and Cultural Rights (ICESCR) which is binding on all EU Member States.

the necessary preconditions for individuals to participate in the economic and social life of their community. Inclusion and access to financial services become such preconditions. Consumer protection becomes part of the democratisation process where the consumer becomes a market or economic citizen rather than solely an economic or social agent. Financial services develop into services enabling the access of all citizens to affordable high-quality services throughout the community, including cross-border financial services. These include, for example, ad hoc schemes for persons with low income, safety, security and reliability of high-quality products and services, continuity of services, choice, transparency and access to information from providers and regulators. The implementation of these principles generally requires the existence of independent regulators with clearly defined powers and duties, such as powers of supervision and sanction. Other requirements are the provisions for the representation and active participation of consumers/users in the definition and the evaluation of services, the availability of appropriate redress and compensation mechanisms, and the existence of evolutionary clauses allowing terms and conditions to be adapted in accordance with changing objective user and consumer needs or circumstances, including changes in the economic and technological environment.[10] For example, access to a basic bank account or personal data protection become fundamental rights in financial markets necessary to the inclusion of the individual in economic and social life and respect for his/her dignity as a human being.

If the rationale for financial regulation is taken away from the exclusive cost–benefit analysis discourse embedded in market failure and the social rationales for regulation alike, consumer protection may become a right in itself when fundamental rights or constitutional values are at stake and claims need to be rendered justiciable. The consumer grows to be equipped with the tools necessary to take his/her role in the market.

Thus far EU consumer law and policy has served the purpose for the realisation of the internal market and seems to be inclined towards an economic approach to regulation. It has departed from a conception of consumer protection as the object of the law and is directed towards a notion of the consumer as an actor for the completion of the single market.[11]

The financial crisis and the social imbalances that it has caused may have finally offered the opportunity to the EU to intervene with non-economic rationales for regulating the financial market. Interest rate ceilings, measures to tackle the over-indebtedness of European consumers, controls on termination and default penalties and on debt recovery from consumers could be welcome policy initiatives of the EU in this direction.

However, what certainly the sophistication of financial markets and their close link with the lives of individuals have shown is that protection of the individual

---

[10] Szyszczak et al. (2011); see also Morgan (2006), esp. p. 465, taking the example of water.
[11] e.g. see Micklitz (2012b); Weatherill (2013).

consumer is a fundamental part of maintaining human dignity and a necessary precondition for his/her full participation in the economic, social and democratic life of society.

A holistic approach to policies and regulation of personal over-indebtedness may need to take all these rationales into account, especially the consideration that this is not only about market law or national social legislation, but that the dignity and lives of individuals are affected in their roots.

The book is divided into nine chapters.

This Chapter 1 introduces the topic of the book, the conceptual framework and the structure.

Chapter 2 provides an account of the role of personal debt in the modern economy and focuses on the size and the growth of the personal debt market in Europe. To this end, data from the ECRI Statistical Package are analysed over the period 1995–2016, both at aggregate level and by country. The focus is not only on the total amount of debt, but also on relative measures, such as the debt to gross domestic product (GDP) ratio, the debt to income ratio and the per capital amount of debt, in order to draw a picture of the personal debt market in Europe and its evolution over time. The chapter also provides an empirical analysis of the characteristics of indebted consumers using data from the Eurosystem's Household Finance and Consumption Survey. The analysis is framed within the life-cycle theory, which is the traditional economic setting where the characteristics of individuals and households holding debt are analysed. The socio-demographic and economic features of consumers who participate in the debt market are separately investigated for mortgage debt and consumer credit too, in order to shed light on the existing differences between the two groups of borrowers.

Chapter 3 analyses the economics of the personal debt industry in order to shed light on the mechanisms behind the development and growth of the business. In particular, the chapter highlights the variety of personal debt solutions and the innovations in the contractual terms of mortgages and consumer credit products that have contributed over years to diversify the portfolio of personal debt products and reach previously under-served customers, and presents the different types of players on the market, both mainstream, such as banks, specialised personal debt intermediaries and captive companies, and non-mainstream, such as pawnbrokers, doorstep lenders and high-cost short-term credit brokers. Credit providers making use of technologically enabled financial innovation in consumer services (fintech) are also newcomers in the landscape of the industry. The chapter also discusses the economics of personal debt and presents time-series data, from the European Central Bank, on interest rates, annual percentage rate of charges, card payments and non-performing loans, with the aim of focusing on the opportunities and risks of this dynamic industry. An empirical analysis of the performance of a representative sample of consumer credit companies concludes the chapter; data are from Orbis Bank Focus (Bureau Van Dijk) and covers the period 2005–16.

Chapter 4 introduces the topic of over-indebtedness and analyses the phenomenon from an economic perspective to quantify the size and the characteristics of consumers that are over-indebted or at risk of over-indebtedness. The chapter attempts to define over-indebtedness, focuses on the complexity of measuring the phenomenon and illustrates existing indicators aimed at capturing profiles of financial distress. It also discusses and analyses the causes of over-indebtedness, proposes a review of extant empirical literature which highlights the characteristics of over-indebted consumers, and provides an empirical investigation of the dimension of over-indebtedness in Europe and the characteristics of over-indebted households using data from Eurosystem's Household Finance and Consumption Survey. Besides, the chapter specifically focuses on the role played by psychological and personal traits – like impulsivity, myopia or overconfidence – on debt decision-making and risks of over-indebtedness. It investigates the under-studied impact of behavioural traits on the effectiveness of measures to prevent over-indebtedness. An empirical analysis concludes the chapter, with the aim of highlighting the role impulsivity plays in weakening the positive impact of financial literacy on debt decisions.

Chapter 5 further develops the issues raised in the previous chapter, i.e. the move from personal indebtedness to over-indebtedness and its consequences. It introduces the concept of financial fragility or vulnerability, distinguishing between the economic, policy and legal readings of vulnerability. The ensuing feeble dividing line between social and economic matters is addressed, as well as considerations regarding the intertwining of social and economic policies. In this context, a main aim of the chapter is to provide readers with an insight of the extent to which 'problem debt' is – or should be – a matter of national or EU competence in policy and lawmaking. This discussion includes debates about the competence of the EU to deliver social justice, and the policy and legal consequences of this answer. Questions over the private nature of debt relationships and the role attributed to contract and consumer law (including their national and EU dimensions) will also become part of and feed into the discussion over the economic and social attribution of competences. Next, the chapter examines the EU policy measures designed to address the phenomenon of consumer over-indebtedness. The resulting focus is mainly on ex-ante preventive measures – such as financial education, debt counselling, transparent information, arrears management. A substantial part of the chapter concerns responsible lending and borrowing measures, and the assessment of consumer creditworthiness. The emphasis given to policies on the responsible creditor and interferences with private autonomy and private law relationships are scrutinised. Finally, it investigates how EU policies to tackle over-indebtedness are translated into EU law. The key distinction between prevention and cure of over-indebtedness reflects the analysis of the relevant legislation. Within this context, preventive measures addressed in the Consumer Credit Directive and the Mortgage Credit Directive are analysed, alongside the guidelines provided by other relevant institutions (e.g. the European Banking Authority).

Chapter 6 explores the role and function of solvency data and financial technologies (fintech). The assessment of consumer creditworthiness features strongly under the law. Based on the previous chapter, this chapter focuses on the use of credit data, emerging technologies and big data as the tool mostly used by the credit industry for credit-risk analysis, to assess the creditworthiness of consumers and engage with responsible lending, as well as problems of over-indebtedness. However, this is an area which raises controversies and problems hardly addressed by the policies and the law. Unlike for the harmonisation of EU rules on credit to consumers for the creation of the internal market, the underlying consumer data infrastructure remains fragmented at national level, failing to achieve univocal, common or defined policy objectives under a harmonised legal framework. The multiple uses, incoherencies, fragmentation across the EU, and new risks for consumers are analysed to show the policy and legal gaps, which in turn feed into the policies and legal framework of over-indebtedness. Ultimately, the aim of the chapter is to analyse and demonstrate the extent to which the current practices alongside the relevant EU policies and law suffer from poor coordination to the detriment of both European consumers and the completion of the internal market. It is put forward that new solutions are needed. Equally, there is much hype about the potential for fintech and big data to transform and deliver financial services to consumers, which may present new opportunities but also new or incremental risks for consumers and their financial inclusion. Finally, an emerging aspect that the concluding part of the chapter addresses is the extent to which a standardisation of the data necessary to measure creditworthiness and over-indebtedness are starting to develop at EU level and the many obstacles that remain. The establishment of the Banking Union (BU) and the prudential supervision of the Euro-area suggest standardisation and convergence of the data used to measure debt levels, arrears and delinquencies.

Chapter 7, in turn, studies the credit risk analysis and creditworthiness in their legal context, with specific reference to solvency data and big data vis-à-vis the new EU data protection legislation set by the General Data Protection Regulation (GDPR). Fundamental rights and consumer protection concerns arise from the dissemination and sharing of traditional and non-traditional data, as well as from their expanding uses. This is an area of the EU internal market that demands the attention of the EU legislator without further delays. An aim of the Chapter is to analyse, from the perspective of financial inclusion and consumer protection, the extent to which the current EU legal framework set by the GDPR is prepared to respond to the challenges posed by the use of data and innovation in the context of the prospective opportunities and detriment for consumers. Particular emphasis is given to the issues of economic efficiency vis-à-vis consumer exploitation and inclusion – financial, economic and social. It assesses the extent to which the risks are likely to contrast or outweigh the benefits and the degree of protection offered by the GDPR to stem potential consumer detriment. Ultimately, it questions whether the law is fit for purpose or not in consideration of the enactment of brand new legislation in this area.

Chapter 8 studies the treatment of over-indebtedness once this has materialised. Particular regard is given to personal insolvency law and its national dimension. Within a fragmented legal framework in the EU, the chapter analyses how the EU has pursued the route of mutual recognition to ensure engagement between the Member States (Council Regulation 1346/2000 and The Recast Regulation 2015/848) and the extent of their applicability to the insolvency of natural persons. In light of the many problems and risks facing European consumers faced with weak, uncoordinated or under-resourced insolvency laws, this chapter also provides an analysis of the role that the European Courts play in stemming the financial problems of consumers brought by the financial and economic crisis of recent years. By analysing the flourishing case law of recent years, the goal is to show how so far the Courts have supplemented for the deficiencies of policy and law makers. At the same time, the Chapter emphasises the limits of what the Courts can do under the current legal framework. Thus, the chapter brings together the identified policy and legislative weaknesses in ex-post curative measures or debt solutions for the treatment of the problem to analyse the major gaps and inconsistencies that the EU faces and the role of personal insolvency law. It offers a critique of the current EU framework of responsible lending and debt solutions to address a problem that the book identifies as a European one. At the same time, the chapter analyses the extent to which the legal framework and the case law are providing the surfacing of EU principles in the area of debt solutions. The latest legislative initiatives on business insolvency and the extent to which some provisions may apply to natural persons are analysed (e.g. the EU proposal on preventive restructuring frameworks and minimum standards for a second chance for entrepreneurs). The rationale and case for EU harmonisation of personal insolvency law against the latest policy initiatives (Green Paper on Retail Financial Services and Capital Market Union) is finally put forward.

Chapter 9 concludes by bringing together the findings of the previous chapters. It attempts to put forward the main argument that the EU should take the competence to harmonise and legislate in the area of debt solutions for consumers maintaining high levels of consumer protection and respect of fundamental rights enshrined in EU law. At the same time, it advances the ideas that it recognises as the way forward, suggesting the scope for further research and the new frontiers that it believes should constitute the future study of 'problem debt'.

2

Personal Debt in the Economy

2.1 THE DEMAND SIDE OF THE PERSONAL DEBT MARKET

This chapter provides an account of the role of personal debt in the modern economy. In particular, it covers the economic dynamics of national personal debt markets and the importance of debt in the current economic model, and analyses the social, demographic and economic characteristics of individuals in debt.

Section 2.2 focuses on the size and the growth of the personal debt market in Europe. To this end, data from the ECRI Statistical Package are analysed over the period 1995–2016, both at aggregate level and by country. The focus is not only on the total amount of debt, but also on relative measures, such as the debt to GDP ratio, the debt-to-income ratio and the per-capital amount of debt, in order to draw a picture of the personal debt market in Europe and its evolution over time. Section 2.3 focuses on the factors shaping the evolution of the personal debt market, while Section 2.4 provides an empirical analysis of the characteristics of indebted consumers using data from the Eurosystem's Household Finance and Consumption Survey (HFCS). The analysis is framed within the life-cycle theory,[1] which is the traditional economic setting where the characteristics of individuals holding debt are analysed. The socio-demographic and economic features of consumers who participate in the debt market are separately investigated for mortgage debt and consumer credit, to shed light on existing differences between the two groups of borrowers.

2.2 PERSONAL DEBT IN EUROPE: SIZE AND GROWTH OF THE MARKET

In the last twenty years credit to households[2] in Europe had experienced a strong growth until the 2008 crises, a downturn in the following years and an upward trend

---

[1] Modigliani and Brumberg (1954).
[2] In the field of economics, the term 'household' in frequently used in place of the term 'consumer'. This is because the household is the basic unit of analysis in many microeconomic models and micro data

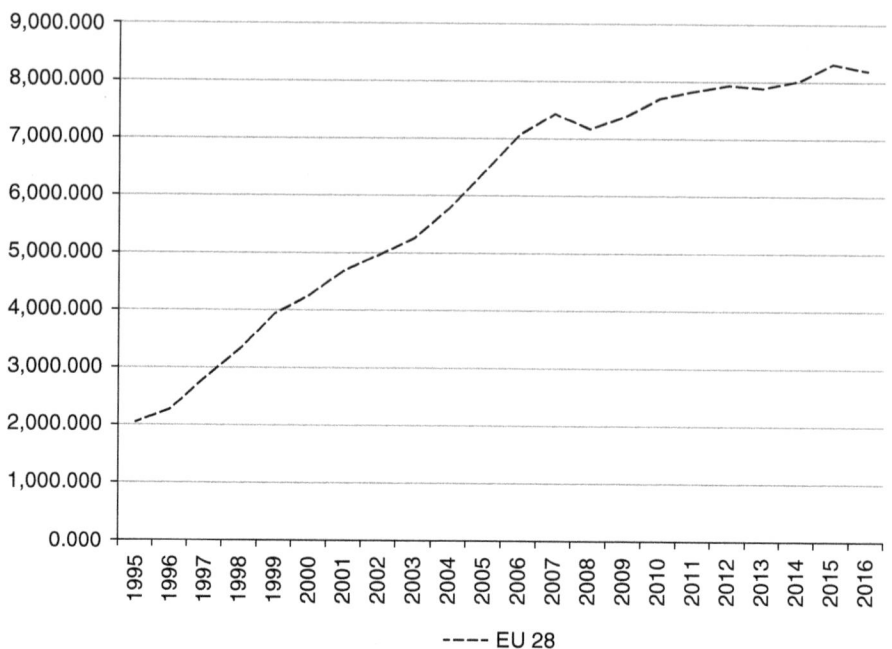

FIGURE 2.1 Total personal debt (€bn, 1995–2016)
Source: authors' elaboration of ECRI Statistical Package

from 2014. On the overall, outstanding credit to households in Europe increases from €2,046 billion in 1995 to €8,192 billion in 2016 (Figure 2.1).[3]

Focusing on relative measures, in 2016 personal debt accounted for 55.6 per cent of GDP, almost 10 percentage point more than in 1995, when personal debt to GDP was 46.7 per cent. The rise is even stronger considering the debt to disposable income ratio, which increased from 70.3 per cent in 1995 to 89.8 per cent in 2016. The main component of credit to consumers is represented by mortgages,[4] although a certain degree of heterogeneity appears among countries (Figure 2.2). Indeed, while on average housing loans represent 77.6 per cent of the total amount of outstanding personal debt in Europe, the percentage is lower in Bulgaria (48.3 per cent) and much higher in the Netherlands (92.2 per cent).

Data on non-mortgage debt[5] highlights similar growth trends (Figure 2.3). Consumer credit expanded very rapidly in Europe prior to the 2008 financial crisis, when it increased from €330 billion in 1995 to €1,019 billion in 2008. Following the crisis, when lenders

produced by central banks and statistic institutes include assets and liabilities of 'one or more people' who live in the same dwelling and also share meals or living accommodation.

[3] The data source is ECRI Statistical Package 2017, 'Lending to households and non-financial corporations in Europe, 1995–2016', August. See www.ceps.eu for detailed information on the database.
[4] Home mortgages and other real estate property mortgages.
[5] The terms 'non-mortgage debt', 'consumer credit', 'unsecured credit' are used as synonyms, indicating all lending to households other than mortgage loans, obtained for the purpose of acquiring or

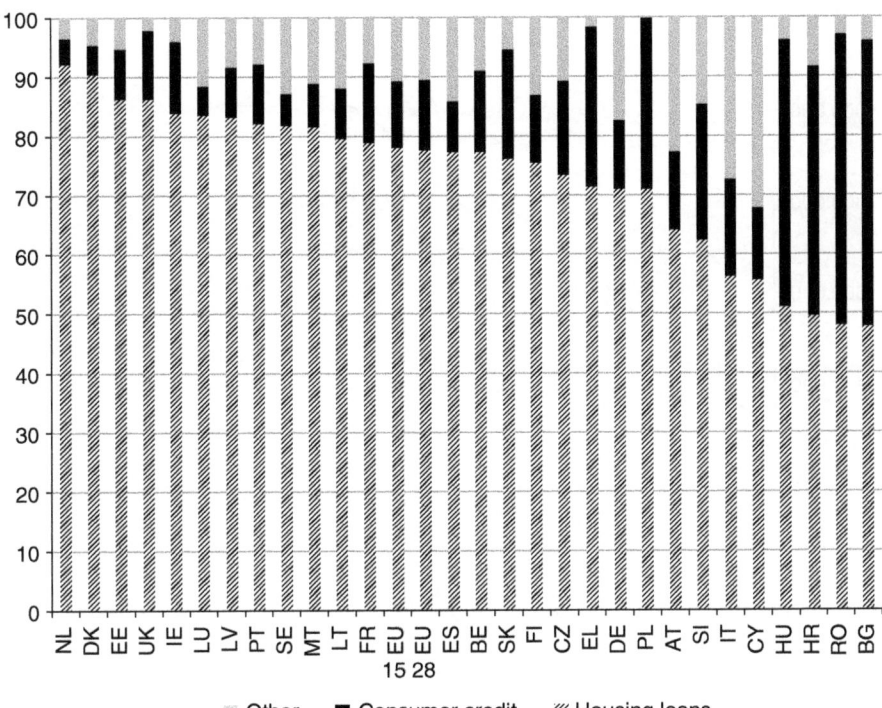

FIGURE 2.2 Total personal debt, by type of product (%, 2016)
Austria (AT), Belgium (BE), Bulgaria (BG), Cyprus (CY), Czech Republic (CZ), Denmark (DK), Estonia (EE), Finland (FI), France (FR), Germany (DE), Greece (EL), Croatia (HR), Hungary (HU), Ireland (IE), Italy (IT), Latvia (LV), Lithuania (LT), Luxembourg (LU), Malta (MT), Netherlands (NL), Poland (PL), Portugal (PT), Romania (RO), Slovakia (SK), Slovenia (SI), Spain (ES), Sweden (SE), United Kingdom (UK)
Source: authors' elaboration of ECRI Statistical Package

reduced their exposures and became cautious in supplying new loans, and consumers became concerned about being exposed to personal debt, unsecured credit decreased to €936 billion in 2013. The recovery momentum began in 2014 with a 1.0% growth, 4.6% in 2015 and 0.3% in 2016, when the outstanding amount was €991 billion.

The aggregate picture masks a great degree of variation across countries in the dynamics of consumer credit outstanding over time. The breakdown highlights that some countries, like the United Kingdom, Italy, Finland, Sweden experienced an increase in consumer credit before and after the 2008 crisis, while others, such as Spain, the Netherlands, Austria and even more Cyprus and Ireland, experienced periods of increased, followed by strong drops (Figure 2.4).

improving a property, such as credit cards, credit lines, overdraft facilities, personal loans and other non-collateralised loans.

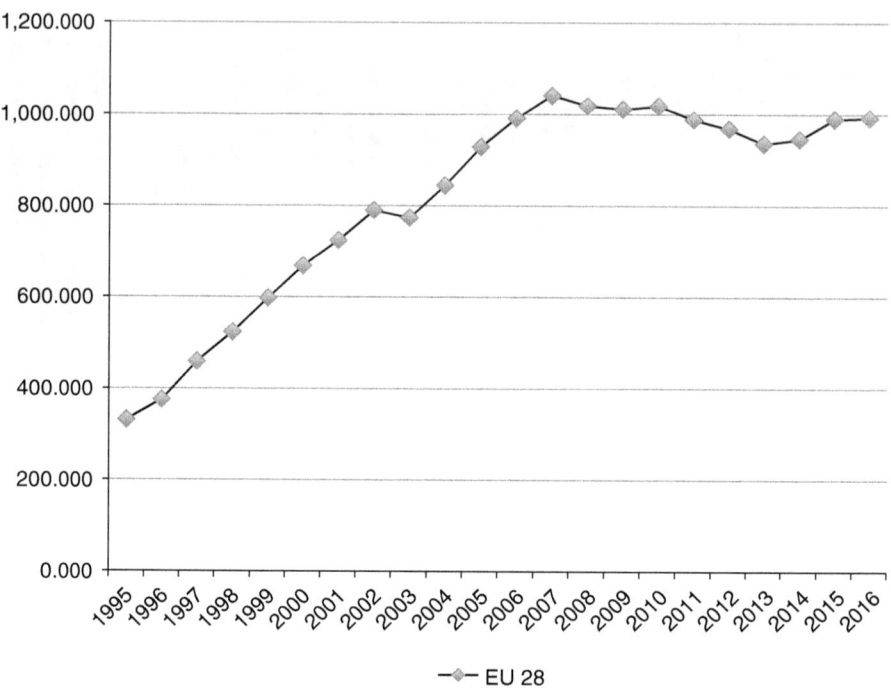

FIGURE 2.3 Consumer credit (€bn, 1995–2016)
Source: authors' elaboration of ECRI Statistical Package

In terms of total amount (Figure 2.5), the largest consumer credit markets are found, as expected, in the largest economies. Specifically, the consumer credit market is dominated by the United Kingdom, with €227 billion of outstanding debt (22.9%), and concentrated in few other markets, that is Germany (18.5%), France (15.3%), Italy (11.1%) and Spain (7.0%). Taken together, these countries account for 75.0% of the unsecured credit outstanding in Europe.

Relative measures are helpful to better highlight the diffusion of debt across countries. Indeed, the consumer credit to GDP ratio highlights uneven levels of development of the consumer credit market in the various European economies (Figure 2.6). Cyprus and Greece have the highest ratio, likely due to the recession which has resulted in a strong drop in GDP, with a total unsecured credit accounting for 14.9% and 13.9% of GDP respectively. At the other extreme, the consumer credit to GDP ratio is lower for Lithuania (1.8% of GDP). The four countries where the majority of outstanding consumer credit is concentrated do not appear among countries with very high levels of consumer credit per GDP ratio. They registered the following consumer credit to GDP ratios: UK 10.0%; France 6.8%; Italy 6.6%; Germany 5.9%. Comparison between 2004 and 2016 suggests that differences between European countries show a certain degree of convergence, and are probably destined

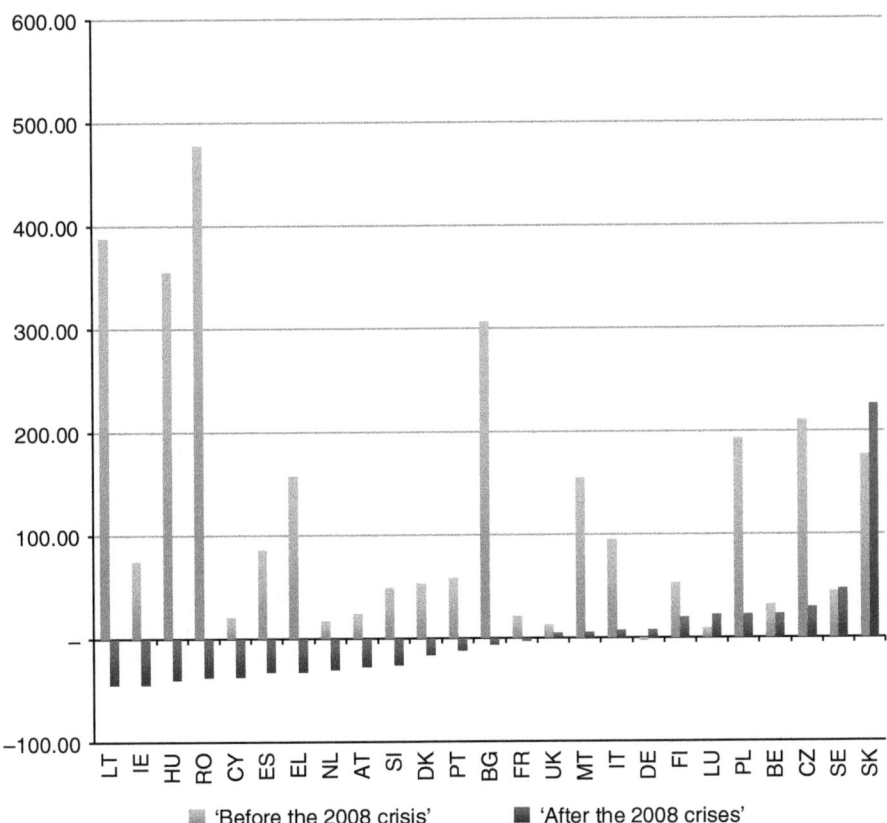

FIGURE 2.4 Changes in consumer credit outstanding before and after the 2008 crisis (€bn)
Austria (AT), Belgium (BE), Bulgaria (BG), Cyprus (CY), Czech Republic (CZ), Denmark (DK), Estonia (EE), Finland (FI), France (FR), Germany (DE), Greece (EL), Croatia (HR), Hungary (HU), Ireland (IE), Italy (IT), Latvia (LV), Lithuania (LT), Luxembourg (LU), Malta (MT), Netherlands (NL), Poland (PL), Portugal (PT), Romania (RO), Slovakia (SK), Slovenia (SI), Spain (ES), Sweden (SE), United Kingdom (UK)
Source: authors' elaboration of ECRI Statistical Package

to narrow in the near future. Growth rates in unsecured credit in less mature markets are high, also due to low initial levels, and continue to move closer to the European average. In Slovakia, for example, consumer credit increased sharply following privatisation of the banking system by foreign groups, which fulfilled potential consumer lending in the country.[6]

In terms of per-capita amounts (Figure 2.7), consumer credit is higher and above average in the United Kingdom (€5,468), Ireland (€2,560), and the Scandinavian countries (€2,766 in Denmark, €2,650 in Finland), as well as in Cyprus (€3,150).

[6] Zavadil and Messner (2014).

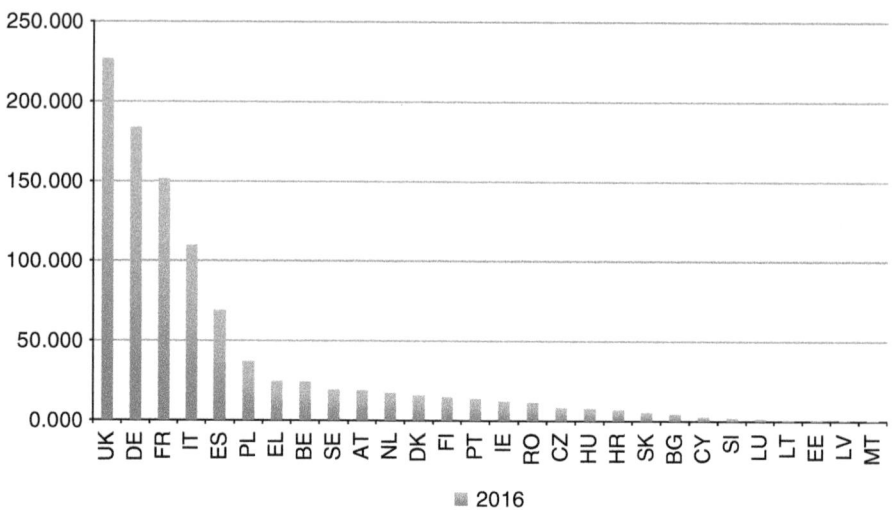

FIGURE 2.5 Consumer credit, by country (€bn, 2016)
Austria (AT), Belgium (BE), Bulgaria (BG), Cyprus (CY), Czech Republic (CZ), Denmark (DK), Estonia (EE), Finland (FI), France (FR), Germany (DE), Greece (EL), Croatia (HR), Hungary (HU), Ireland (IE), Italy (IT), Latvia (LV), Lithuania (LT), Luxembourg (LU), Malta (MT), Netherlands (NL), Poland (PL), Portugal (PT), Romania (RO), Slovakia (SK), Slovenia (SI), Spain (ES), Sweden (SE), United Kingdom (UK)
Source: authors' elaboration of ECRI Statistical Package

Conversely, the amount is lower in Eastern Europe, where it is equal to €244 in Lithuania, €247 in Latvia, €501 in Estonia. The average per-capita amount in Europe is €1,955 (Figure 2.5).[7]

Comparison between 2004 and 2016 highlights that countries in Eastern Europe, starting from comparatively immature credit market conditions, registered a strong increase. More mature markets, like Italy, Finland, Belgium also reported a strong increase in the per-capita amount of non-mortgage credit, pointing out the heightening relevance of this form of credit. Only few markets, already far above the EU-28 average in 2004 – such as the Netherlands, Austria, Ireland and to some extent the United Kingdom – recorded a reduction.

When focusing on the burden of consumer credit (Figure 2.8), measured by the debt-to-income ratio,[8] the picture changes significantly. Countries like Bulgaria, Hungary, Poland that show a per-capita level of consumer credit below the average level in Europe (respectively €620 in Bulgaria, €785 in Hungary, €982 in Poland and

---

[7] ECRI indicators are calculated at aggregate levels, therefore they refer to the overall population rather than to indebted individuals only. Consequently, as a matter of fact, the average per-capita amount of debt is higher for those who are indebted, as pointed out by data reported in section 2.4, which are conversely calculated for indebted individuals only.

[8] See Chapter 4 for a detailed analysis of debt burden ratios and their relevance in measuring over-indebtedness.

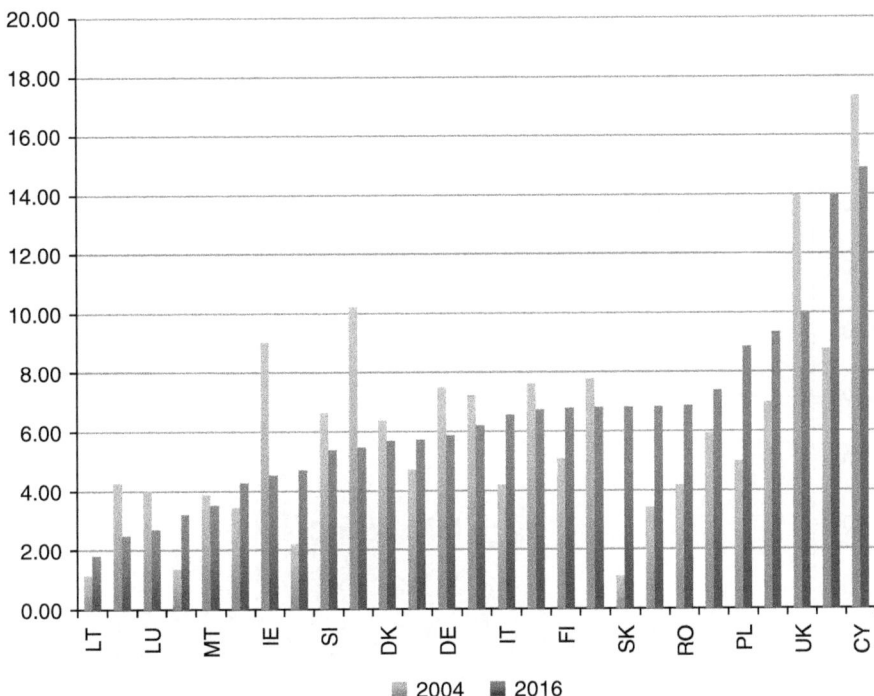

FIGURE 2.6 Consumer credit per GDP, by country (%, 2004 and 2016)
Austria (AT), Belgium (BE), Bulgaria (BG), Cyprus (CY), Czech Republic (CZ), Denmark (DK), Estonia (EE), Finland (FI), France (FR), Germany (DE), Greece (EL), Croatia (HR), Hungary (HU), Ireland (IE), Italy (IT), Latvia (LV), Lithuania (LT), Luxembourg (LU), Malta (MT), Netherlands (NL), Poland (PL), Portugal (PT), Romania (RO), Slovakia (SK), Slovenia (SI), Spain (ES), Sweden (SE), United Kingdom (UK)
Source: authors' elaboration of ECRI Statistical Package

€1,955 in the EU-28), display a much higher incidence of consumer credit to disposable income, equal respectively to 17.8%, 14.7%, 12.2%, against an EU-28 average of 10.8%. More generally, new Member States registered strong trends in the consumer credit to disposable income ratio for years.

Levels of debt burden in Europe are far below those in the US, where the debt-to-income ratio was above 26.0 per cent in 2016 (Figure 2.9).

Overall, the analysis of aggregate data reveals some main trends:

- the total value of the outstanding personal debt increased from €2,046 billion in 1995 to €8,192 billion in 2016. At the end of 2016 the total value of the outstanding personal debt in Europe was 55.6% of GDP, while the debt to disposable income was 89.8%. In 1995 these were equal to 46.7% and 70.3%, respectively;

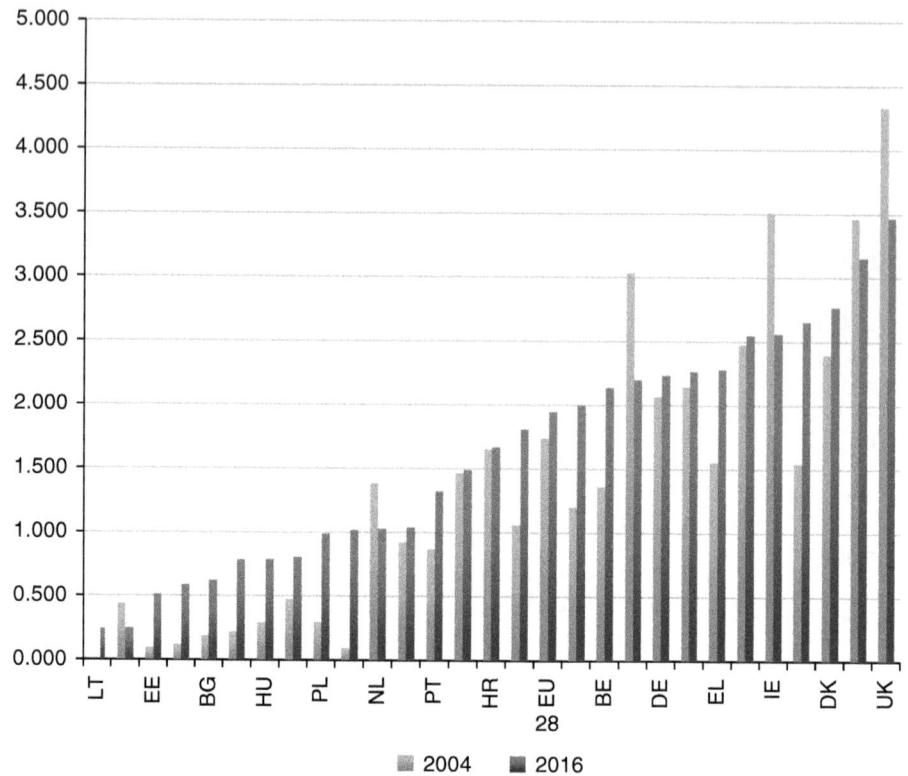

FIGURE 2.7 Consumer credit per capita, by country (€1,000s, 2004 and 2016)
Austria (AT), Belgium (BE), Bulgaria (BG), Cyprus (CY), Czech Republic (CZ), Denmark (DK), Estonia (EE), Finland (FI), France (FR), Germany (DE), Greece (EL), Croatia (HR), Hungary (HU), Ireland (IE), Italy (IT), Latvia (LV), Lithuania (LT), Luxembourg (LU), Malta (MT), Netherlands (NL), Poland (PL), Portugal (PT), Romania (RO), Slovakia (SK), Slovenia (SI), Spain (ES), Sweden (SE), United Kingdom (UK)
Source: authors' elaboration of ECRI Statistical Package

- as for consumer credit, after a reduction following the 2008 crisis, the recovery momentum began in 2014, with a 5.9% growth in 2014–16. In terms of total amount, the largest consumer credit markets are found in the largest economies, the United Kingdom, Germany, France, Italy and Spain. However, when looking at the debt-to-income ratio, the highest levels are shown in countries like Poland, Hungary and Bulgaria;
- there is a significant heterogeneity across countries relative to size and dynamics of the personal debt markets. However, data emphasise that the level of personal debt on a per-capita basis is converging, since it is growing more rapidly in countries with more immature markets. It is also noteworthy that even in more mature markets the growth of personal debt is still ongoing

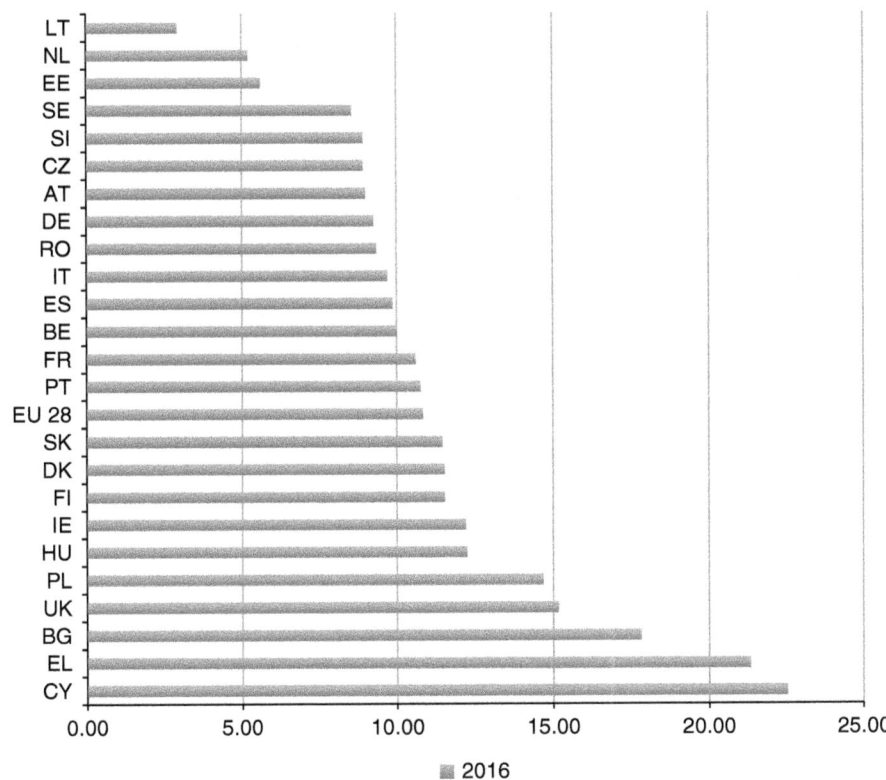

FIGURE 2.8 Consumer credit to disposable income (%, 2016)
Austria (AT), Belgium (BE), Bulgaria (BG), Cyprus (CY), Czech Republic (CZ), Denmark (DK), Estonia (EE), Finland (FI), France (FR), Germany (DE), Greece (EL), Croatia (HR), Hungary (HU), Ireland (IE), Italy (IT), Latvia (LV), Lithuania (LT), Luxembourg (LU), Malta (MT), Netherlands (NL), Poland (PL), Portugal (PT), Romania (RO), Slovakia (SK), Slovenia (SI), Spain (ES), Sweden (SE), United Kingdom (UK)
Source: authors' elaboration of ECRI Statistical Package

at levels higher than those recorded by disposable income and it is coupled with an increasing tendency to spend rather than save.

2.3 FACTORS SHAPING THE EVOLUTION OF THE PERSONAL DEBT MARKET

Over the years, both the supply and demand sides of the market, as well as structural transformations in the economy, have contributed to support the expansion and shape the dynamics of the personal debt market.

On the supply side, aggressive marketing and advertising strategies by banks and financial intermediaries have contributed to expand and encourage the use of consumer credit to finance consumptions. Other factors are market liberalisation, improved

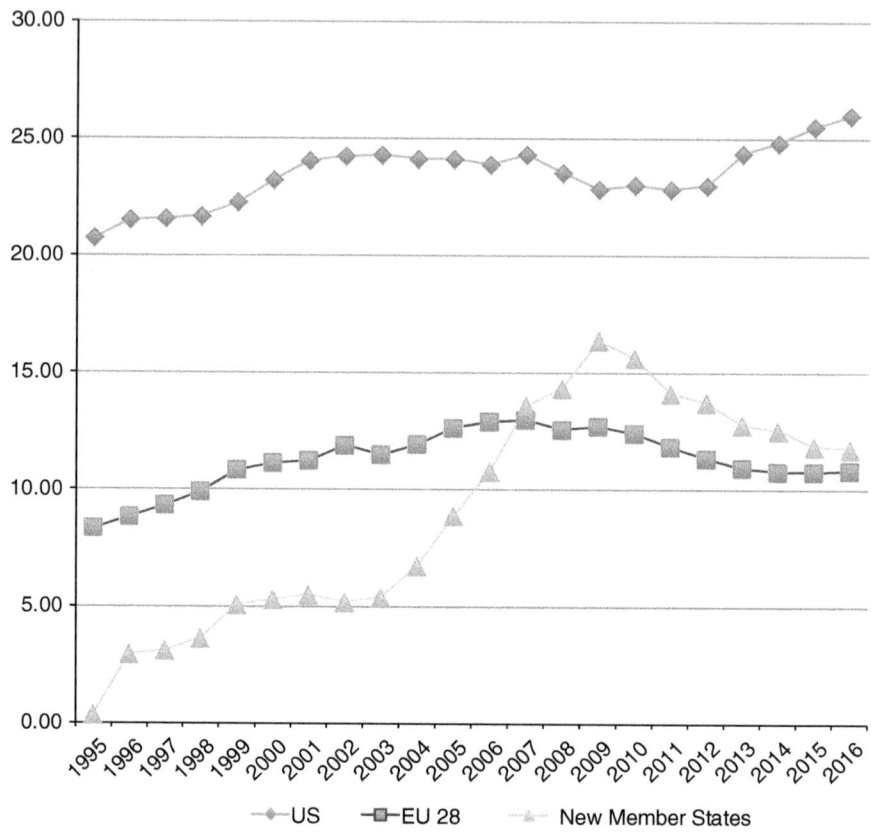

FIGURE 2.9 Consumer credit to disposable income (%, 1995–2016)
Source: authors' elaboration of ECRI Statistical Package

techniques for the measurement and control of credit risk, technological innovation, a widening in the range of products supplied, as well as a generalised easier access to credit. Changing distribution models have also contributed to increased volume of loans distributed online.[9]

On the demand side, personal debt growth has been driven by, among other factors, changes in sociocultural norms and constructions, as well as new spending models that have made personal debt more acceptable, a reduction in intergenerational transfers and a decline in the informal credit market.[10]

Furthermore, the general increase in personal debt can be ascribed to factors related to changes in labour market and social policies. Indeed, rising unemployment, stagnating real wages, proliferation of low-paid and unsecured jobs have increased dependency of wage earners on borrowing. Similarly, the dismantling of

[9] Credit Agricole (2017).
[10] Crook (2006); European Central Bank (2011); Vandone (2009).

public provision of services, such as health, retirement and education are posing further pressures on debt demand.[11]

Likewise, the above-mentioned differences registered between European markets can be ascribed to the nature and level of maturity and complexity of the personal debt industry in each country (e.g. the aggressiveness in offering innovative credit solutions and improved credit-scoring mechanisms), to sociocultural factors which influence saving and spending decisions, as well as to differences in countries' welfare policies, such as the existence and coverage of pension systems, public healthcare and education, and the efficiency of the justice system, which may affect the length and cost of credit recovery.

Overall, the retreat of the welfare state against the expansion of credit in the private sector, as well as the increasing replacement of the former with the latter, has contributed to foster a rising role of personal debt in the economy. The dynamics of the globalisation of financial markets has introduced the concept of the 'financial consumers' and emphasised their economic role and individual responsibility for the risks generated both individually and by the financial markets. In the EU, this individualisation of risk can also be framed in terms of financial and social inclusion of consumers as a tool to foster the internal market. The financialisation of the consumer is designed to include as many more market agents as possible, not only on the demand side of financial services but also as the financial instrument to feed the consumptive model of the broader market for goods and services.

2.4 THE CHARACTERISTICS OF HOUSEHOLDS HOLDING PERSONAL DEBT

Any investigation into the growth of personal debt in the economy should necessarily address the socio-demographic and economic characteristics of those holding debt.

The mainstream economic framework by which the characteristics of individuals holding debt is analysed is the life-cycle theory.[12] According to this model, individuals make their borrowing (and saving) decisions in order to smooth consumption over predictable fluctuation of income, with the aim of guaranteeing a constant marginal utility of consumption over their lifetime. The underlying idea is that income is generally low in the early stages of the individual's life cycle, increases towards retirement and decreases during retirement. Therefore, individuals will borrow at the beginning of their working life in order to raise consumption over the level offered by current income, save in the middle when income is above spending, and spend saving during retirements.

In this section, the characteristics of consumers that are indebted are investigated with the aim of identifying which groups are more likely to use personal debt or

---

[11] Karacimen (2017).
[12] Modigliani and Brumberg (1954).

make greater use of it, also in the light of evidence emerging from existing economic literature analysing indebtedness choices within the above-mentioned theoretical framework. To this end, micro data from Eurosystem's HFCS are used.[13]

The Eurosystem's HFCS,[14] which is a project involving national central banks and statistical institutes, provides household-level data on the asset, liabilities, income and consumption of households, as well as demographic variables such as household size, age, education and employment status of the 'household reference person', defined as the highest income earner in the household. So far, two waves of the HFCS have been conducted and released, respectively, in April 2013 and December 2016. The number of households interviewed in the last wave was more than 84,000. Values are reported for both mortgage debt, and for consumer credit, in order to highlight any difference in the characteristics of consumers holding these two types of loans.

First, the analysis focuses on the size of the participation in the debt market, both in percentage and median value, and then moves to socio-demographic and economic characteristics of indebted households (Table 2.1).

The first interesting aspect that emerges from Table 2.1 is that more than 40.0 per cent of households are indebted, and the participation is higher in the consumer credit segment. Although the participation slightly reduces from the first to the second survey, reflecting the general debt market trend already highlighted in section 2.2, the median value of those that are indebted increases from €24,000 in 2013 to €28,200 in 2016. Such an increase is mainly driven by the mortgage segment of the debt market, where median values rise from €75,600 to €77,600.

Participation in the debt market presents considerable degrees of heterogeneity across countries (Table 2.2).

TABLE 2.1 *Participation in the debt market (2013 and 2016)*

Indebted households	Total debt	Mortgage debt	Consumer credit
% 2013	44.0	23.5	29.4
% 2016	42.4	23.3	28.2
Median value (€, 2013)	24.0	75.6	5.3
Median value (€, 2016)	28.2	77.6	5.0

Source: authors' elaboration of Eurosystem's HFCS

---

[13] Among other surveys that provide information relating to socio-demographic characteristics, income, net wealth and indebtedness from representative samples of households there are, at national level, the Survey of Household Income and Wealth (SHIW) for Italy, the Survey of Household Finances (EFF) for Spain, the British Household Panel Survey (BHPS) for the United Kingdom.
[14] See www.ecb.europa.eu for detailed information about the survey.

TABLE 2.2 *Participation in the debt market, by country (%, 2016)*

Indebted households (%)	Total debt	Mortgage debt	Consumer credit
Austria	34.4	16.7	20.6
Belgium	48.4	34.5	25.2
Cyprus	59.1	42.0	37.0
Estonia	36.8	20.7	25.1
Finland	57.4	35.2	43.9
France	47.2	24.3	33.6
Germany	45.1	20.4	32.8
Greece	27.1	13.3	17.1
Hungary	36.9	20.1	25.5
Ireland	56.8	37.0	41.4
Italy	21.2	10.1	13.9
Latvia	33.5	17.0	23.0
Luxembourg	54.6	35.2	33.9
Malta	37.1	19.1	27.6
Netherlands	63.1	42.0	37.9
Poland	37.0	13.4	28.4
Portugal	45.9	34.7	22.6
Slovakia	36.7	16.2	25.3
Slovenia	38.6	9.1	34.8
Spain	49.3	35.0	27.4

Source: authors' elaboration of Eurosystem's HFCS

At the upper end, the Netherlands, Cyprus and Finland report the highest participation in the credit market, both secured and unsecured, with a percentage of 63.1%, 59.1% and 57.4% respectively. Italy and – to a lesser extent – Greece are at the lower end of participation in the credit market at 21.2% and 27.1% respectively. For more than two-thirds of the countries, participation is higher in the consumer credit market compared to the mortgage segment.

Table 2.3 shows, for several socio-demographic and economic variables, the percentage of households holding personal debt.

Focusing on the first column, which accounts for the participation in the debt market regardless of type of debt, most of the findings are in line with the life-cycle theory and the need on the part of individuals to improve lifestyle by smoothing consumption.

Indeed, the greatest part of personal debt is concentrated in the youngest age of adult life, when the head of the household is between 35 and 44 years old. This is typically the time when households borrow in anticipation of future income growth to buy a home and/or consumer durables. Consistent with Schooley and Drecnik Worden (2010),

TABLE 2.3 *Participation in the debt market, by socio-demographic and economic characteristics (%, 2016)*

Indebted households	Total debt	Mortgage debt	Consumer credit
Household size			
1	27.9	10.5	20.8
2	39.3	20.1	26.9
3	54.2	33.6	32.5
4	62.8	42.8	38.9
5 and more	60.7	38.1	39.7
Age (of the reference person)			
16–34	54.6	23.7	40.7
35–44	60.9	40.2	37.0
45–54	54.9	34.0	34.6
55–64	41.9	21.4	28.6
65–74	24.4	10.2	16.7
more than 75	9.3	3.0	7.1
Education (of the reference person)			
Basic education	29.5	14.0	20.8
Secondary education	46.0	22.5	32.7
Tertiary education	52.5	35.9	30.0
Percentile of income			
0–20	23.5	7.9	17.9
20–39	32.5	12.9	24.1
40–59	42.9	19.9	31.1
60–79	52.5	31.2	33.9
80–100	60.4	44.4	33.9
Percentile of net wealth			
0–20	43.6	7.7	41.3
20–39	36.8	15.6	28.5
40–59	47.0	33.9	26.0
60–79	42.6	29.0	23.8
80–100	41.7	30.0	21.3
Work status (of the reference person)			
Employee	56.6	33.4	36.5
Self-employed	56.0	38.7	33.9
Retired	19.5	7.3	14.1
Other not working	32.8	11.5	25.7

Source: authors' elaboration of Eurosystem's HFCS

Crook (2006) Fabbri and Padula (2004) Del Rio and Young (2006), young people, characterised by expectation of rising income, have a stronger demand for credit than older households, which, over time, drops because income is sufficient to cover spending.

As far as education, the percentage of households with debt is higher among groups with high education, confirming empirical findings which report that a higher level of education is a robust proxy for rising future earnings and greater information-processing skills.[15] Besides, individuals with an higher level of education may have better access to credit markets.[16] Level of education in general can reasonably be seen to have a positive impact on individuals' financial knowledge: the higher this level of knowledge is, the easier it is to access and evaluate financial products and services. Ferri and Simon (2000) use the ratio between cash and financial instruments as a proxy for individuals' educational levels and report that the lower the ratio, the higher the level of financial expertise which, in turn, raises awareness regarding the decision to borrow. In \Chapter 5, however, some criticalities related to the effectiveness on financial education measures are pointed out.

Large families are also more likely to participate in the credit market; while 27.9% of single households report having debt, the number rises to 62.8% for households with four members and 60.7% for households with five or more than five members. This is in line with Fabbri and Padula (2004), who find that the probability of holding debt is higher in the case of large families with children at preschool or school age, and that there is a positive relation between levels of indebtedness and the number of household members. Besides, Del Rio and Young (2006) and Crook (2006) show that married individuals are more likely to have unsecured debt than non-married.

A monotonic function also characterises the income distribution, since the percentage of households holding debt rises with higher income: 60.4 per cent in the last quintile,[17] the one with the highest levels of income, against 27.9 per cent in the first quintile, the one with the lowest levels of income. Indeed, as posited by the life-cycle theory, demand for credit is positively influenced by expectations of increased future receipts: if there are no expectations of increased income in the future, there should be no need to advance spending via debt.[18] As to current income levels, Fabbri and Padula (2004) reveal a positive relation between levels of debt and current income. Del Rio and Young (2006) and Magri (2007) show that for middle-range levels of income, the marginal utility of consumption is high and income rises can generate higher spending and subsequent increased demand for credit. Crook (2006) also shows that high-income individuals have a greater probability of having debt also due to the probability of facing fewer supply side constraints.

---

[15] Del Rio and Young (2006); Dynan and Kohn (2007); Grant (2003); Lusardi and Tufano (2015).
[16] Cox and Jappelli (1993); Crook (2006).
[17] Quintiles are defined by the points that divide income data, or other variables, into five equal groups of households, from the lowest level to the highest level.
[18] Cox and Jappelli (1993); Crook (2005); Ferri and Simon (2000); Khan et al. (2016); Meng et al. (2013).

Conversely, the variation of indebtedness across different levels of net wealth does not display specific trends, consistently with empirical literature which does not report homogeneous findings. In particular, Magri (2007) shows that rises in wealth are tracked by falls in the demand for personal debt as spending can be financed autonomously. However, households with intermediate wealth levels are more likely to participate in the consumer credit market due to increased spending patterns that characterise improvements in lifestyle. Del Rio and Young (2006) focus their analysis on households with a portfolio of financial assets and find that households that do not own such a portfolio have a greater probability of having unsecured debt than those who do.

As to employment status, the percentage of households holding debt is higher for employees and the self-employed. This may reflect easier access to credit, given the guarantee represented by the salary itself, and it is consistent with the theoretical models that consider uncertainty about future income as a factor that reduces borrowing. Empirical evidence shows that demand for personal loans is higher among the employed in comparison to the self-employed, who are subject to greater uncertainty regarding future income. For this reason, recourse to debt on the part of individuals with greater uncertainty regarding their future income, such as individuals with temporary employment contracts, is less than could be expected.[19] The retired have a lower probability of having debt as a result of the age effect, since there are no further expectations of rising future income.[20]

The unemployed are also less likely to participate in the credit market.[21] This finding, which seems in contrasts with the life-cycle theory predicts (i.e. those temporarily without a job should increase their demand for credit in order to maintain a level of consumption) is likely based on liquidity constraints from the supply side of the market, since these households may not have access to the amount of credit needed to smooth consumption.[22]

2.4.1 Differences between Mortgages and Consumer Credit

So far, empirical evidence on HFCS data seems to be in line with the life-cycle theory and the possibility to use future earning to repay the amount owned. However, when focusing on the second and third columns of Table 2.3 and distinguishing between households holding mortgages and households holding consumer credit, there are some interesting differences. Specifically, the socio-demographic and economic features of households holding mortgages are similar to those reported in the previous section. Conversely, consumer credit displays different patterns: the groups that are more likely to hold unsecured credit are younger, less educated, with lower levels of income and wealth. Besides, compared to mortgages, the unemployed and retired are also more likely to hold

---

[19] Crook (2006).
[20] Turinetti and Zhuang (2011).
[21] Del Rio and Young (2006).
[22] Deaton (1992).

consumer credit. The rationale behind different empirical evidence for the two types of debt may be that mortgage debt decisions last for a long time and follow the life cycle, while non-mortgage debt decisions are largely determined by short-run benefits. In fact, several reports and academic studies highlight that consumer credit is increasingly used by certain groups of households to meet daily expenses and to cover gaps in income which turn out to be permanent rather than related to a specific stage of the life cycle.[23] Besides, compared to mortgages, consumer credit decisions are more influenced by behavioural patterns, like impatience, materialism, satisfaction and self-esteem, which may lead the consumer to buy on credit terms, without necessarily being fully aware of the sustainability of the debt. Chapter 4 is dedicated to the analysis of the impact of personal traits on debt decisions and risk of over-indebtedness.

Table 2.3 shows that consumer credit, compared to mortgage debt, is more prevalent among younger households, those between 16 and 34 years (40.7% and 23.7% respectively). At the same time, the percentage of households with more than 65 years holding consumer credit is ten points higher than mortgage debt (23.8% and 13.2% respectively). This evidence is in contrast with the inverse U shape that usually displays the age profile of household debt according to the life cycle. Similarly, as for education, consumer credit is more prevalent in households with a secondary rather than a tertiary education, which probably reflects both demand and supply constraints.

Regarding income, the percentage of low-income households holding consumer credit is much higher than mortgages (17.9% and 7.9% respectively). Although this probably reveals supply constraints on mortgages, it is noteworthy that almost one-fifth of households that belongs to the lower quintile of income are holding non-mortgage debt, and another 24.1% belongs to the second quintile. As will be highlighted in Chapter 4, low-income households are those with the higher probability of being over-indebted.

A monotonic function characterises the net wealth distribution, which is not the case for mortgages. In other words, the percentage of households holding consumer credit is higher for households with low levels of net wealth, and decreases as far as the level of net wealth increases.

The work status of the reference person also displays different patterns compared to mortgages. Indeed, the percentage of not-working households holding consumer credit goes up to 25.7%, while it is less than half for mortgages (11.5%). Besides, 14.1% of retired households are holding consumer credit, whereas only 7.3% hold mortgages. Finally, more than 20.0% of households hold non-mortgage debt in order to cover living expenses (Table 2.4).

This evidence alone does not necessarily conflict with the standard life-cycle intertemporal optimisation, but it certainly draws attention to the fact that parts of outstanding debt contracted through consumer credit are held by individuals aged

---

[23] Bank of England (2010); International Monetary Fund (2012a); Observatoire des crédits aux ménages (2008, 2009).

above 65, typically a period in life when borrowing cannot be justified by expectations of rising future income. Similarly, a group of households exists with lower levels of income and net wealth and less stable financial situations that use consumer credit as a mean of making ends meet. In the event of unexpected negative variation in income, they may find themselves in a situation of over-indebtedness.

Table 2.5 summarises the characteristics of the groups of households that are more likely to hold mortgages and consumer credit solutions.

TABLE 2.4 *Purposes for which consumer credit is used (%, 2016)*

Non-mortgage debt: purpose for which the money was used	
To purchase the HMR	5.0
To purchase another real estate asset	2.0
To refurbish or renovate the residence	14.0
To buy a vehicle or other means of transport	32.0
To finance a business or professional activity	3.8
To consolidate other consumption debts	5.2
For education purposes	7.9
To cover living expenses or other purchases	20.2
Other	6.6
Don't know, no answer	3.4

Source: authors' elaboration of Eurosystem's HFCS

TABLE 2.5 *Characteristics of groups more likely to hold mortgage debt and non-mortgage debt*

	Mortgage debt	Consumer credit
Age	Younger adult	The youngest, but also significantly high percentage for elderly
Education	Higher level of education	Less educated
Household size	Large families	Large families
Income	Higher level of income	High concentration among low-income people
Wealth	High level of net wealth	Low level of net wealth
Work status	Higher concentration among employee and self-employed	High concentration among not working and retired too

Source: authors' elaboration

3

The Industry of Personal Debt

3.1 THE SUPPLY SIDE OF THE PERSONAL DEBT MARKET

The growth of the personal debt market has undoubtedly been driven by an increasing demand for personal debt solutions, further fuelled by structural transformations in the economy and changes in social policies. However, the supply side has also played a significant role in shaping the evolution of the market. Indeed, for years banks and financial intermediaries have widened and refined their portfolio of products and services, by developing innovative products, raising service standard levels, improving credit risk activities and speeding up the approval process, in order to satisfy more effectively existing customer needs and to develop and serve new market niches, such as consumers with thin or no credit history, older age groups and students.

This chapter analyses the economics of the personal debt industry in order to shed light on the mechanisms behind the development and growth of the business.

Sections 3.2 and 3.3 analyses the variety of personal debt solutions and the innovations in the contractual terms of mortgages and consumer credit products that have contributed over years to diversify the portfolio of personal debt products and reach previously under-served customers. Section 3.4 presents the different types of players on the market, both mainstream, such as banks, specialised personal debt intermediaries and captive companies, and non-mainstream, such as pawnbrokers, doorstep lenders and high-cost short-term credit brokers. Fintech credit providers are also newcomers in the landscape of the industry. Section 3.5 analyses the economics of personal debt and presents time-series data, from the European Central Bank, on interest rates, annual percentage rate of charges (APRC), card payments and non-performing loans, with the aim of focusing on opportunities and risks of this dynamic industry. The last section is an empirical analysis of the performance of a representative sample of consumer credit companies. Accounting information are from Orbis Bank Focus (Bureau Van Dijk) and covers the period 2005–16.

The econometric model is a generalised method of moments[1] which includes firm-specific variables, like size, risk, capitalisation of the companies and market-specific variables that capture credit diffusion across countries.

3.2 PERSONAL DEBT PRODUCTS

Personal debt solutions include a vast portfolio of instruments, that range from secured long-term mortgages, to unsecured short-to-medium-term consumer credit products. Mortgages are long-term credit agreements which are secured by an immovable property. They are used to purchase fixed assets, such as buildings or lands, with the loan secured against the assets. Consumer credit products are short-to-medium-term credit agreements for the purchase of consumer goods or to meet personal expenses. They are typically unsecured and therefore bear a higher risk compared to mortgages. According to what the funds are used for, consumer credit products can be further classified into loans linked to a specific purchase, and loans not linked to a specific purchase. The first category refers to car finance and other loans granted at the point of sale for the purchase of goods or services, such as electrical appliances, furniture, high-tech products, catalogue sales, as well as medical care, fitness and travel operators. The credit agreement is signed with the customer directly at the point of sale and the lender is either the captive of the parent company (particularly in the car and retail sectors) or a specialised finance company working in agreement with a merchant or dealer. The second category includes credit products not linked to a specific purchase, like authorised overdraft facilities, direct personal loans, revolving credit. These loans are supplied by banks and specialised financial intermediaries and are used for several purposes, ranging from education, to health and medical care, etc. Among consumer credit products, revolving credit is the largest product category. Data from Eurofinas[2] show that in 2016 revolving credit represented 36% of all new credit, followed by car finance at the point of sale (30%), direct personal loans (25%) and non-automotive credit at the point of sale (from (9%). The amount of credit not linked to a specific purpose is therefore far above the total amount of specific purchase-targeted loans: on average 60% versus 40% over the period 2009–16.

3.3 INNOVATIVE SOLUTIONS

The last two decades have been characterised by several innovations in the contractual terms of mortgages and consumer credit products, and consumers can nowadays choose among a variety of personal debt solutions.

---

[1] Arellano and Bover (1995).
[2] Eurofinas is the association of specialised consumer credit providers in Europe. In 2016 it represented seventeen member associations and almost 50 per cent of the European consumer credit market in terms of outstanding loans (www.eurofinas.org).

As far as secured loans, non-traditional mortgages have been developing alongside traditional products, with more flexible features such as negative amortisation loans, mortgages with high loan-to-value (LTV) ratio, zero down payment loans, maturity longer than thirty years, flexible maturity with constant reimbursement. Besides, new products, which facilitate in situ mortgage equity withdrawal, have become available and rapidly expanded, especially before the global financial crisis. These mortgages allow homeowners to draw down on their housing wealth without having to move. They also offer flexibility in monthly repayments so that financial resources can be stored or resealed as needed over the life cycle. Among these products, home equity lines of credit allow homeowners to use a line of credit to borrow up to a certain age; they often recognise an interest-only monthly repayment while the principal is refunded at the end of the loan term. Other types of home equity extractions are the cash-out refinancing mortgages, which consist in the refinancing of a mortgage if the house value has increased or if the initial mortgage has been reduced, or the closed-end home equity loans, which often take the form of a second mortgage on the same contractual terms of the first mortgage.[3]

Some of these non-traditional mortgages products are specifically addressed to seniors, who may have difficulty accessing traditional mortgages, since they are late in their life cycle, and are constrained by banks because of their age and the level of the debt repayments-to-income ratio they would be expected to pay. The most relevant example of an age-specific product targeted at seniors is the reverse mortgage.[4] Reverse mortgages, or lifetime mortgages, are secured loans in which a homeowner can borrow money against the value of the house, receiving funds in the form of a fixed monthly payment or a line of credit. No monthly repayments of the mortgage are required until the borrower dies or s/he sells the home, and the transaction is structured so that the loan amount does not exceed the value of the home over the life of the loan. Another equity extraction product targeted at seniors who may need to supplement their retirement income or pay for long-term care is the home reversion mortgage, which combines a partial or complete sale of the property, with the homeowner retaining the right to remain in occupation for life. The occupant may also receive a lump sum at initiation and monthly amount thereafter.

Among consumer credit products, several solutions have been designed to increase the customer base and offer products that better suit consumers preferences and needs. Some examples are consumer good leasing, salary/retirement-backed loans and student loans. Leasing and hire purchase are credit agreement with or without the obligation to buy at the end of the contract. The typical examples are car leases and, to a lesser extent, furniture and household equipment. Salary/retirement-backed loans are consumer credit products available to company employees and

---

[3] Moulton et al. (2017).
[4] Bishop and Shan (2008); Haffner et al. (2015).

retired receiving an allowance. Their main feature is that repayments can be no more than one-fifth of the employee's salary or retirement. Student loans are advances offered at favourable conditions and targeted to cover tuition fees, which will be repaid after the completion of education and when the salary exceeds a certain threshold. In fact, the amount to repay each month is based on the income, rather than the amount borrowed. Therefore, if the income changes, the repayment amount changes as well, to reflect increase or reduction in the salary and, if the borrower stops working, the repayment stops until re-employment. The range of consumer credit products is often complemented by other financial products. One example that has become prominent in recent years is that of payment protection insurance, which is an insurance product that enables borrowers to cover debt repayments in case of adverse shocks, such as illness, death or job loss. Loyalty programmes on credit cards also represent a product innovation aimed at entering more easily specific market niches. Consumer credit providers are also taking advantage of advanced innovative technologies, such as big data, artificial intelligence, machine learning, with the aim on the one hand of offering new products, services and distributing channels to satisfy customers' needs or expectations, as well as to reach under-served consumers, and, on the other hand, to reduce credit and operating risk by better-performing core activities, such as credit screening and monitoring, fraud and cybercrime prevention, anti-money laundering, regulatory compliance activities.

Innovation in personal debt products has undoubtedly the potential to remove certain constraints, and therefore increase opportunities to access credit as well as accommodate the heterogeneity of customers' preferences in accessing credit markets.[5] Besides, these products offer a means of buffering unexpected falls in income (e.g. job loss, divorce), or the financial resource to meet acute spending needs at all stages of the life cycle.[6] At the same time, however, personal debt products, especially non-traditional mortgage products, have features that are associated with higher levels of risk, since they are addressed to customers that are not supposed to hold debt according to the core principles of the life-cycle theory (see Chapter 2). They may therefore raise financial fragility and expose economies to higher aggregate level of risk.[7] Similarly, student loan schemes, although they may increase access to university education for economically disadvantaged groups, raise concerns about the current levels of student debt and the impact these may have on young adults in the early stages of their working lives.[8] Likewise, payment protection insurance for years has raised issues related to the high costs and lack of competition, since it is frequently offered by lenders together with the loan granted and consumers are unaware

[5] Rasmussen and Zenios (2007).
[6] Ong et al. (2013).
[7] Acolin et al. (2015); de Silva et al. (2015).
[8] Shen and Ziderman (2009).

they can buy it separately.⁹ A recent study highlights that the cost of the payment protection insurance is very high, especially when the product is sold directly by banks together with the loan product.¹⁰

3.4 PRINCIPAL PLAYERS ON THE MARKET

Personal debt is mainly granted by banks and specialised financial institutions. The first are typically commercial banks which, as part of their traditional banking activity, offer lending products both to corporate and retail customers. They usually provide all kinds of financial products, including consumer credit and mortgages. Conversely, specialised financial institutions focus exclusively on lending to mortgages or consumer credit solutions. A specific type of specialised consumer credit company is represented by captive companies, such as Volkswagen Bank, Honda Bank, GE Money Bank. These intermediaries are fully owned by manufacturing or retail groups and represent the financial arm of a non-financial parent company. They limit their activity to consumer credit, and the amounts advanced are destined exclusively to the purchase of the parent company's product. Captives, in this role, provide dealers not only with a service that can play a crucial role in consumers' purchasing decisions, but also one that creates and consolidates customer loyalty.

Aside from mainstream credit providers, in some local contexts other consumer credit lenders exist, such as pawnbrokers, doorstep lenders, and high-cost short-term credit loans providers (HCSTCs). Pawnbrokers offer short-term loans collateralised by items of personal property (which are 'pawn' to the broker), such as jewels, cameras, televisions, home audio equipment, watches, gold, that are returned to the borrower on repayment of the loan. Doorstep lenders, also known as home lenders, lend and collect repayments door to door. They usually provide unsecured small amounts of loans over short periods of time and collect repayments on a weekly basis. HCSTCs, or payday loans, are similar to doorstep loans but provide credit online or in store. These non-mainstream types of credit are very quick to obtain and are specifically targeted at the sub-prime market, that is individuals who, due to low income and/or low credit rating, find it difficult to access mainstream channels. Therefore, they typically bear higher risk, especially door-to-door loans and HCSTCs, given that they are unsecured, and entail very high borrowing interest rates.¹¹ A recent report from the Association of Chartered Certified Accountants

---

⁹ Britain Competition Commission (2009).
¹⁰ Ivass (2016).
¹¹ To have an idea of the level of interest rate on these type of unsecured lending, see the following advertisement extracted from the website of a payday lender in the UK: 'XXX offers cash loans online and in store, minimum loan terms 3 month, maximum 36 month, minimum APR 49.9%, maximum APR 1287.9%. The representative example on the website is: amount of credit £250.00 for 30 days, total amount payable £310.00, interest £60.00. The interest rate is 292% and the APR 1270%.' In the United Kingdom, since no statutory interest rate ceiling exists, the cost of these types of loans would in other countries be considered as usury. It has to be said, however, that in markets where loans ceilings are in

analyses the business models of payday lending.[12] The focus is on the online market, which bears greater levels of risk compared to the retail market since the first is larger and growing faster than the second. Furthermore, online markets have significantly higher default rates (around 50 per cent), which are borne ultimately by borrowers in the form of high charges and fees, causing relevant detriment often to people who are among the most vulnerable in society. An input to the transformation of this segment of the industry may come from the UK Financial Conduct Authority, which imposed in 2014 a price cap on payday loans to protect borrowers from unfair lending practices and ensure borrowers never pay back more in interest fees than the amount borrowed.

More recently, technology innovation, like machine learning, artificial intelligence, distributed ledger technology, cloud computing, predictive behavioural analytics and data-driven marketing, have also contributed to the development of non-traditional financial services providers, commonly known as fintech credit providers (e.g. Lending Club, Prosper, Sofi, Zopa, Funding Circle, Alibaba, Prêt d'Union). Although the fintech sector is still small in comparison to the size of financially intermediated assets and capital markets, some market observers estimate that a significant portion of banks' revenues will be at risk over the next few years, in particular in retail banking.[13] Policymakers, regulators and international institutions have started exploring this new environment.[14] From an economic perspective, the main key issue is the potential impact of fintech on traditional banks and their business models. Specifically, the debate focuses on whether fintech may disrupt existing structures and business models, blur industry boundaries, facilitate strategic disintermediation and revolutionise how financial firms supply credit and products.[15] Indeed, fintech promises to reshape the financial industry by increasing competition, cutting costs and prices, improving the quality of financial services, increasing accessibility to financial services.[16] However, great opportunities always come with great risks which may trigger widespread instability; this is why in the academic research the balance between costs and benefits of competition in the banking industry is still an open issue.[17]

3.5 THE ECONOMICS OF PERSONAL DEBT

There are several sources of income deriving from personal debt, which can be mainly split into interest and non-interest income. Interest income is the amount of

---

place, borrowers in difficulty with loans owed to formal credit suppliers often resort to informal or illegal lenders, i.e. loan sharks.

[12] McAteer and Beddows (2014).
[13] KPMG (2017); McKinsey (2015).
[14] Bank for International Settlements (2018); European Banking Authority (2017); International Monetary Fund (2017). See also Chapter 6.
[15] Carbò-Valverde (2017).
[16] *The Economist* (2015).
[17] Thakor (2011).

revenues earned by financial intermediaries from lending funds, while non-interest income is the amount of revenues derived primarily from fees from services on loan-related products.

Table 3.1 shows the level of interest rates on loans to households over time, for (1) house purchase, (2) consumption,[18] (3) revolving loans and overdrafts,[19] (4) extended credit card credit.[20]

The level of interest rates charged on personal debt solutions varies according to whether they are collateralised or unsecured, the maturity, the overall riskiness of the counterpart. Interest rates are therefore higher for consumer credit solutions (5.26% for consumption and 7% for revolving and overdraft), compared to loans for house purchase (1.85%), and the level reaches peaks of almost 16% for extended credit cards.

Tables 3.2 and 3.3 report APRC levels for loans to consumers for house purchases and for consumption, respectively. The APRC is the total cost of the credit to the consumer, expressed as an annual percentage of the total amount of credit, which enables the consumer to compare different credit proposals according to the costs of the loan.[21] The APRC is by definition higher than the interest rate on loans since it

---

[18] Loans granted for the purpose of mainly personal use in the consumption of goods and services. It excludes revolving, overdrafts and extended credit card credit, which are separate groups because they experience a large number of inflows and outflows throughout the month (European Central Bank, 2017).

[19] Loans obtained through a line of credit (*ibid.*).

[20] Loans granted to the cardholder for which an interest rate or tiered interest rates usually greater than 0 per cent are charged. Often, minimum instalments per month have to be made, to at least partially repay extended credit (*ibid.*).

[21] The APRC was introduced by the first Consumer Credit Directive (Directive 2008/48/EC of the European Parliament and of the Council of 23 April 2008 on credit agreements for consumers and repealing Council Directive 87/102/EEC, L 133/66). It represented a landmark in the regulation of consumer credit, which for the first time identified consumer protection and a harmonised European consumer credit market as its objectives. To achieve these goals, homogeneous comparatives were needed to evaluate different products offered in different countries often priced on the basis of different methods. Having established the usefulness of reference points such as the 'total cost of credit to the consumer' and the 'annual percentage rate of charge', specific methods adopted to calculate both were to be fixed initially in accordance with the provisions or practices existing in the Member States or, eventually, to be established freely by each of them. In other words, countries were given freedom to regulate the question on the basis of existing approaches and legislation. Efforts to harmonise instruments that were at that time not in widespread use among the majority of EU Member States would not have been justified. At the beginning of the 1990s, the decision to adopt one method in calculating APR represented another step towards harmonisation and the creation of an internal market in which consumers may benefit from high levels of protection. As a result, a single mathematical formula was introduced for calculating the APR and for determining credit cost items to be used in the calculation by indicating those costs which must not be taken into account. Later, in 1998, Directive 98/7/EC reformulated APR as such: 'The annual percentage rate of charge which shall be that rate, on an annual basis which equalizes the present value of all commitments (loans, repayments and charges), future or existing, agreed by the creditor and the borrower, shall be calculated in accordance with the mathematical formula set out in Annex II'; the same directive also made provisions that raised the level of information to be included in the advertising and offer of credit agreements.

TABLE 3.1 *Interest rates on loans to households (new business, %)*

	2010	2011	2012	2013	2014	2015	2016	2017
For house purchase	3.4	3.76	3.18	3.08	2.55	2.28	1.78	1.85
For consumption	6.38	6.72	6.46	6.54	6	5.74	5.38	5.26
Revolving loans and overdrafts	8.55	8.81	8.26	7.92	7.63	7.22	7.07	7
Extended credit card credit	16.58	17.06	16.93	16.92	17.11	16.97	16.69	16.84

Source: authors' elaborations on European Central Bank MFI interest rate statistics

TABLE 3.2 *APRC: loans to households for house purchase (new business, %)*

	2008	2009	2010	2011	2012	2013	2014	2015	2016	2017
Austria	5.66	3.34	3.27	3.57	2.98	2.76	2.52	2.39	2.34	2.17
Cyprus	6.84	4.82	4.97	5.81	5.44	4.93	5.01	3.9	3.35	3.39
Estonia	5.81	3.62	3.77	3.68	2.84	2.9	2.57	2.64	2.5	2.64
Finland	4.25	2.11	2.27	2.68	2	2.15	1.79	1.36	1.2	1.03
France	6.01	4.48	4.07	4.59	4.05	3.83	3.26	3.06	2.51	2.29
Germany	4.96	4.13	3.73	3.57	2.88	2.85	2.17	1.98	1.72	1.86
Greece	5.54	3.56	4.06	4.5	3.25	3.03	3.37	3.03	3.42	3.52
Ireland	4.38	2.8	3.29	3.12	3.61	3.44	3.76	3.42	3.22	3.08
Italy	5.19	3.01	3.18	4.27	3.92	3.8	3.08	2.81	2.32	2.27
Latvia	6.66	4.5	4.15	4.19	3.48	3.35	3.25	3.48	2.86	2.72
Lithuania	5.57	4.19	3.86	3.83	2.53	2.35	2.02	2.02	2.01	2.22
Luxembourg	4.26	2.05	2.32	2.63	2.31	2.21	2.01	1.92	1.75	1.79
Malta	4.35	3.71	3.63	3.6	3.56	3.3	3.58	3.18	3.16	3.05
Netherlands	5.53	4.91	4.37	4.56	4.1	3.66	3.14	2.8	2.42	2.42
Portugal	5.7	2.81	4.08	5.21	4.39	3.96	3.94	3	2.8	2.41
Slovakia	6.83	5.79	5.07	5.27	4.77	4.18	3.21	2.83	2.14	2.02
Slovenia	6.64	3.56	3.63	4.21	3.29	3.58	3.19	2.85	2.58	2.77
Spain	5.83	2.62	2.66	3.66	2.93	3.16	2.64	2.31	2.18	2.05
euro area	5.18	3.63	3.68	4.01	3.4	3.35	2.74	2.55	2.24	2.15

Source: authors' elaborations on European Central Bank MFI interest rate statistics

includes the interest rate and all the other costs, like commissions, taxes and any other kind of fees which the consumer is required to pay in connection with the credit agreement and which are known to the creditor, except for notarial costs. Costs in respect of ancillary services relating to the credit agreement, in particular insurance premiums, are also included if, in addition, the conclusion of a service contract is compulsory in order to obtain the credit or to obtain it on the terms and conditions marketed.

TABLE 3.3 APRC: loans to households for consumption excluding revolving loans and overdrafts, convenience and extended credit card debt (new business, %)

	2008	2009	2010	2011	2012	2013	2014	2015	2016	2017
Austria	7.24	5.35	6.84	6.5	5.92	6.37	6.66	6.72	6.45	6.32
Belgium	8.67	7.27	6.39	6.15	6.95	6.29	5.2	5.54	4.61	4.43
Cyprus	8.21	7.36	7.26	7.39	7.21	6.42	6.05	5.01	4.3	4.7
Estonia	8.81	33.88	36.75	36.31	37.21	36.58	26.48	18.64	18.82	19.59
Finland	6.04	4.52	5.81	6	5.85	6.17	5.73	5.67	5.69	5.82
France	7.96	6.82	6.14	6.85	6.6	6.32	5.27	4.66	4.16	3.82
Germany	7.02	6.06	7.01	6.93	6.41	6.26	6.01	6.03	5.69	5.39
Greece	11.59	11.19	12.33	11.49	10.54	10.77	8.74	9.73	8.79	9.78
Ireland	6.17	4.24	5.46	5.45	6.56	8.19	8.13	7.4	7.67	7.6
Italy	10.01	9.55	8.12	8.93	8.87	8.57	8.11	7.93	7.63	8.05
Latvia	12.84	13.25	18.89	21.14	18.3	31.11	28.73	29.84	22.64	21.94
Lithuania	13.54	12.71	12.42	14.08	22.67	18.61	17.66	16.04	14.14	14.6
Luxembourg	6.56	5.09	4.34	4.8	4.91	4.89	4.26	3.92	2.82	2.73
Malta	6.25	6.09	5.89	5.12	5.64	4.41	5.39	5.21	5.61	5.33
Netherlands	7.31	8.79								
Portugal	11.89	10.49	9.89	11.65	10.97	11.09	10.18	9.28	8.8	8.75
Slovakia	13.02	15.71	15.35	16.8	16.01	15.52	12.89	11.22	9.68	9.11
Slovenia	9.17	7.49	6.8	7.64	7.49	7.97	8.02	7.42	7.55	7.73
Spain	10.99	9.72	7.47	9.11	8.31	9.52	9.1	8.45	8.05	8.27
euro area	8.61	7.58	7.07	7.35	7.05	7.1	6.53	6.25	5.87	5.8

Source: authors' elaborations on European Central Bank MFI interest rate statistics

As shown in Table 3.2, and in line with the different characteristics of the two types of loans, the APRC is lower for loans for house purchase (2.15 per cent in 2017 in the euro area). Besides, differences among countries are small and tend to converge over time. The overall level of the APRC is also reducing over time.

Conversely, as shown in Table 3.3, the level of the APRC on loans for consumption is much higher (5.8% in 2017 in the euro area). There are also strong differences among countries, with a level that ranges from below 5% in Luxembourg, Belgium, France, to levels close to 20% in Estonia and even higher in Latvia (21.94%). Above all, despite the overall decreasing level of interest rates in the economy, in 2017 the APRC of loans to households for consumption in most countries was almost unchanged over time or even higher than ten years before. It has also to be noted that data on the APRC on revolving, overdraft and extended credit cards are not available; given the higher interest rates on these types of credit solutions, the level of APRC reaches very high levels.

The size of the market and the ability to enter new niche segments increases the overall dimension of revenues coming from the business, also in terms of non-interest income.

Aggressive marketing strategies have also been shown to exert various degrees of influence on consumer credit usage, especially as regards credit cards.[22] An example of non-interest revenues that may increase profits for the industry are earnings on the supply of other loan-linked products, such as the payment protection insurance. This form of insurance produces several positive externalities for lenders. First, the sale of the product generates a revenue, in the form of commission fee. Second, it lowers risk levels which, in turn, reduce the likelihood of credit recovery or impairment charges. Third, it acts as an effective vehicle for penetrating relatively high-risk market segments thanks to the fact that the loan granted is fully secured.

Likewise, revolving credit cards generates annual fees, fixed charges, merchant and interchange fees, as well as interest income owed on instalment repayments.[23] By monitoring customer spending, cards also provide useful information for lenders to improve their cross-selling opportunities. Finally, credit cards are suitable for the development of co-branding and rewards agreements, which may include cash-back programmes, discount programmes or points programmes, in which the cardholder can earn points that can be redeemed for things like airline miles, hotel visits, car rentals or merchandise. These agreements are typically aimed at increasing the size of the potential customer base. Table 3.4 shows the number of card payment per capita, while Table 3.5 reports the relative importance of payment services. What emerge from data is an overall increasing relevance in the use of credit cards in all countries in Europe.

The economics of the industry are mainly impaired by non-performing loans, that is loans in default or close to being in default. Table 3.6 reports the ratio of non-performing loans to gross loans in the euro area.

The level of the non-performing loans ratio shows significant differences among countries, which mainly reflect the effect of the global and sovereign crisis on the overall soundness of the different economic and financial systems. It ranges from levels below 5 per cent in the Netherlands, Luxembourg, Finland, Germany, up to levels close or higher than 50 per cent in Greece and Cyprus. According to empirical literature, non-performing loans are also influenced by institutional factors, such as the efficiency of the justice system, which is relevant in taking steps against insolvent consumers and recover non-performing loans, and the extent of information-sharing among financial institutions regarding the level of borrowers' credit risks. As regards formal mechanisms, the more efficient a justice system is, the lower the costs for credit recovery.[24]

The economics of personal debt are therefore a combined set of costs and revenues, which call for a focus on the performance of the industry. This is the core of the next section.

[22] Salina and Siti Rahayu (2016).
[23] Credit cards can be classified as charge or revolving, depending on the method of repayment. Amounts owed on charge cards are settled in one payment, typically in the first days of the following month. No interest is charged in the period between use and repayment. Revolving cards, conversely, are linked to a revolving credit line that allows the card holder to repay in instalments the amounts owed (Vandone 2001).
[24] Bianco et al. (2002); Fabbri and Padula (2004).

TABLE 3.4 *Number of card payments per capita by country (years 2012 and 2016)*

	2012	2016
Austria	53.7	74.3
Belgium	111.0	151.0
Bulgaria	4.5	13.1
Croatia	—	63.8
Cyprus	48.0	59.2
Czech Republic	30.5	70.5
Denmark	223.7	329.5
Estonia	160.3	217.2
Finland	213.4	279.5
France	129.2	164.5
Germany	39.6	49.4
Greece	6.7	28.0
Hungary	27.2	54.2
Ireland	89.2	162.4
Italy	27.0	43.1
Latvia	62.9	123.8
Lithuania	43.8	82.0
Luxembourg	155.5	215.9
Malta	37.7	56.9
Netherlands	157.8	231.7
Poland	31.5	83.3
Portugal	115.6	144.9
Romania	7.9	17.7
Slovakia	31.5	67.2
Slovenia	62.0	78.5
Spain	51.7	74.5
Sweden	230.1	319.1
United Kingdom	165.5	249.7
euro area	71.0	97.1
EU	79.3	116.6

Source: authors' elaboration on European Central Bank payment statistics

3.6 A PERFORMANCE ANALYSIS

The empirical analysis focuses on consumer credit granted by specialised companies. Universal banks are not included in the sample since accounting data are related to the whole banking business rather than consumer credit only and, therefore, are not comparable.[25] The sample consists of 110 European consumer credit companies, and

---

[25] The sample is anyway highly representative of the outstanding consumer credit granted by specialised lenders, accounting for almost 50 per cent of the total consumer credit outstanding at the end of 2016 (Eurofinas 2017).

TABLE 3.5 *Relative importance of payment services (% total number of payments; year 2016)*

	Card payments	Credit transfer	Direct debits	Cheques
Austria	39.1	32.0	25.5	0.1
Belgium	49.4	37.0	12.9	0.3
Bulgaria	20.5	53.3	1.2	0.0
Croatia	38.4	45.7	3.5	0.0
Cyprus	53.2	18.8	9.6	15.2
Czech Republic	30.7	66.5	2.7	0.0
Denmark	81.3	18.7	–	0.0
Estonia	66.3	33.3	–	0.0
Finland	62.8	37.1	–	0.0
France	52.6	17.9	19.0	10.2
Germany	19.0	29.6	50.6	0.1
Greece	47.0	45.4	4.1	1.2
Hungary	45.0	46.6	5.9	0.0
Ireland	62.6	20.7	10.1	3.1
Italy	45.5	24.5	13.8	3.2
Latvia	60.8	39.1	0.0	0.0
Lithuania	51.5	35.6	–	0.0
Luxembourg	5.3	2.5	0.8	0.0
Malta	53.0	24.1	3.0	17.8
Netherlands	54.7	29.2	16.1	0.0
Poland	56.5	43.0	0.5	0.0
Portugal	69.3	13.0	12.4	2.7
Romania	58.4	39.4	1.8	0.3
Slovakia	46.2	47.6	3.6	0.0
Slovenia	42.2	41.4	10.8	0.0
Spain	50.4	15.0	27.9	0.9
Sweden	66.3	27.3	6.3	0.0
United Kingdom	65.1	16.8	16.2	1.9
euro area	42.0	24.5	–	3.2
EU	48.9	25.1	20.4	2.5

Source: authors' elaboration on European Central Bank payment statistics

covers the period 2005–14. Data on the ownership are hand-collected from websites: Eurofinas and various national associations, such as the Association Française des Sociétés Financières (France),[26] the Bankenfachverband (Germany),[27] the Asociacion National de Establecimientos Financieros de Credito (Spain),[28] the Associazione

[26] www.asf-france.com
[27] www.bfach.de
[28] www.asnef.com

TABLE 3.6 *Gross non-performing loans and advances (% total gross loans and advances; loans to households)*

	2014	2015	2016
Austria	7.1	5.6	4.7
Belgium	6.2	5.0	4.2
Cyprus	52.2	55.2	54.5
Estonia	30.0	21.0	12.7
Finland	1.3	0.9	1.1
France	4.4	4.3	4.1
Germany	2.9	2.3	2.0
Greece	38.5	45.9	46.3
Ireland	18.1	15.4	14.4
Italy	12.8	12.9	12.2
Latvia	16.5	14.9	13.1
Lithuania	20.4	15.6	9.7
Luxembourg	2.2	2.1	2.5
Malta	6.2	6.2	5.8
Netherlands	2.0	1.7	1.3
Portugal	9.5	9.6	9.3
Slovakia	6.8	6.6	—
Slovenia	8.2	7.4	4.0
Spain	5.3	4.5	4.5
euro area	6.4	6.1	5.7

Source: authors' elaborations on European Central Bank MFI supervisory and prudential statistics

Italiana del Credito al Consumo (Italy),[29] the Finance and Leasing Association (United Kingdom).[30]

Accounting information is from Orbis Bank Focus.[31] Unconsolidated statements are used to focus on the specificities of consumer credit operations. Specifically, profitability is measured by the return-on-asset (roa) ratio and the return-on-equity (roe) ratio. The first is calculated as net income over total assets and is an indicator of how profitable a firm is relative to its total assets, measuring the net profit generated for each euro of net assets. The second is calculated as net income over total equity and shows how much profit a company earned on each euro invested by its shareholders.[32] The higher the ratios, the higher the level of profitability. Efficiency is measured using the cost-to-income ratio, which is operating costs

[29] www.assofin.it
[30] www.fla.org.uk
[31] See www.bvdinfo.com for detailed information on the database.
[32] The roa and the roe ratios are calculated using the profit before taxes rather than the net income, since the level of taxation is different in each European country.

TABLE 3.7 *Descriptive statistics (average values years 2005–14)*

Variable name	Mean	Median	Std dev
roa	1.48%	1.19%	2.08%
roe	19.53%	12.68%	44.24%
Cost–income ratio	62.31%	57.26%	25.95%
Risk	7.65%	4.84%	7.28%
Income diversification	1.177	1.750	13.910
Capitalisation	12.2%	9.6%	11.7%
Size	5.516	1.441	8.637

Notes
roa=pre-tax income/total assets (%); roe=pre-tax income/total equity (%); cost–income ratio=cost/income (%); risk=impaired loans/gross loans (%); income diversification=net interest income/non-interest income; capitalisation=equity/total assets; size=total assets (€m)
Source: authors' elaboration on Orbis Bank Focus

divided by operating income; the higher the ratio, the lower the level of cost-efficiency. Income diversification (net interest income to non-interest income), capitalisation (equity to total assets) and size (total assets, in €m) are also measured. Variables are treated with a winsorising procedure that replaces values above the 99th percentile and below the 1st percentile respectively with the 99th percentile and the 1st percentile.

3.6.1 Descriptive Statistics

Table 3.7 provides descriptive statistics of the accounting ratios described above. On average, over the period 2005–14 the roa ratio almost equals 1.5% and the roe is around 20%, while the cost-to-income ratio in slightly above 62%. These ratios show more positive values compared to the overall financial sector, which, at the end of 2016, reported the following average ratios: roa 0.21%, roe 3.22%, cost to income 65.79%.[33] The income diversification ratio is above 100%, meaning that income from the provision of services is higher than income from the lending activities, while capitalisation is around 12%. Median values highlight a not irrelevant degree of heterogeneity among consumer credit providers, especially in terms of size.

Table 3.8 reports descriptive statistics for the two periods, before and after the 2008 crisis. In the third column of the table we ran a paired t-test to determine whether there is a statistically significant mean difference between the accounting ratios of the two groups.

[33] European Central Bank (2018).

TABLE 3.8 *Descriptive statistics pre- and post-crisis*

	Mean		
	Pre–2008	Post–2008	Diff
roa	1.83%	1.34%	0.488** (2.962)
roe	27.87%	17.32%	11.549** (3.073)
Cost–income ratio	60.41%	63.06%	−2.652 (−1.397)
Risk	5.37%	8.00%	−2.631** (−2.975)
Income diversification	2.157	0.794	1.363 (1.098)
Capitalisation	10.2%	13.0%	−0.027*** (−3.471)
Size	4.798	5.799	−1.000 (−1.565)

Notes
***, ** and * represent, respectively, 1%, 5% and 10% significance
roa=pre-tax income/total assets (%); roe=pre-tax income/total equity (%); cost–income ratio=cost/income (%); risk=impaired loans/gross loans (%); income diversification=net interest income/non-interest income; capitalisation=equity/total assets; size=total assets (€m)
Source: authors' elaboration on Orbis Bank Focus

As expected, the level of performance is far higher before the 2008 crisis, with a difference statistically significant of almost 0.5% for roa and 11.5% for roe (roa: 95% CI, 0.164 to 0.812, $t = 2.962$, $p < 0.01$; roe: 95% CI, 4.157 to 18.942, $t = 3.073$, $p < 0.01$). In fact, as shown in Chapter 2, after the crisis there has been a strong reduction in the volume of new and outstanding credit, as well as a reduction in net interest margins following the narrowing spreads between average lending and borrowing rates that has likely reduced the overall performance of the consumer credit industry. The performance has also been negatively affected by a worsening in the cost-efficiency levels of consumer credit companies. Conversely, data shows an increase in the levels of capitalisation, which means higher levels of soundness in terms of solvency. In fact, the average solvency ratio has increased from 10.2% before the crisis to 13% after the crisis; a statistically significant increase of 2.7% (95% CI, −0.043 to −0.012, $t = −3.417$, $p < 0.001$).

Differences in the level of accounting measures are also related to the geographical area where consumer credit companies are located, with higher levels of performance in North Europe (Table 3.9). Diversities among areas may be due to uneven levels of development of the consumer credit market and the personal debt

TABLE 3.9 *Descriptive statistics by geographical area (average values years 2005–14)*

Variable name	North Europe		Middle Europe		South Europe		East Europe	
	Mean	Std dev	Mean	Std dev	Mean	Std dev	Mean	Std dev
roa	1.89%	2.560	1.53%	1.802	0.87%	2.103	1.57%	2.028
roe	41.97%	85.442	15.60%	22.276	10.14%	25.432	15.64%	29.125
Cost–income ratio	63.92%	25.732	61.07%	19.129	61.85%	40.139	69.33%	22.700
Risk	6.49%	9.023	7.52%	5.801	8.19%	6.973	12.63%	12.402
Income diversification	1.03	19.138	1.65	10.068	0.38	16.843	0.14	14.155
Capitalisation	10.5%	0.078	11.7%	0.087	13.9%	0.183	16.5%	0.155
Size	3.959	4.831	6.425	9.873	6.620	8.846	0.288	0.294

Notes
The number of companies are distributed by geographic area as follows: North Europe including UK, 23; Middle Europe, 49; South Europe 25; East Europe, 13; roa=pre-tax income/total assets (%); roe=pre-tax income/total equity (%); cost–income ratio=cost/income (%); risk=impaired loans/gross loans (%); income diversification=net interest income/non-interest income; capitalisation=equity/total assets; size=total assets (€m)
Source: authors' elaboration on Orbis Bank Focus

industry across European countries. Indeed, higher levels of maturity and complexity of the consumer credit market – measured, for example, by the consumer credit to GDP ratio – are expected to positively influence performance since consumer credit companies may offer a wider range of products and services dedicated to a more sophisticated demand, with interest rates targeted to different niches of market segments, as well as benefits from higher scale and scope economies.

The Figures 3.1–3.6 report the trend of the main accounting variables over the period under analysis. The roa and roe measures highlight a reduction over years of the levels of performance before the 2008 crisis, from 2% in 2005 down to 1.4% in 2009 (roe: from 34% in 2005 to 13% in 2009), and then more steady levels over years. The cost-to-income ratio is almost stable over time, reflecting unchanged levels of cost-efficiency, while the capitalisation level has increased in recent years due to the need to adjust and improve solvency levels following the crisis. The evolution of the roa reflects strong differences among geographical areas.

3.6.2 *The Econometric Model*

The performance of consumer credit companies is then analysed in a dynamic setting, using the generalised method of moments[34] and the following specification:

---

[34] Arellano and Bover (1995).

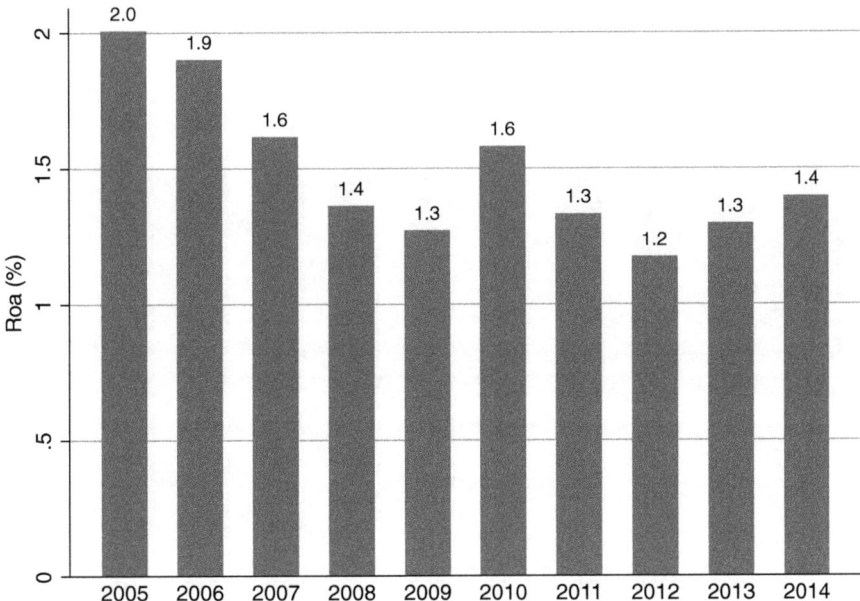

FIGURE 3.1 Return-on-asset ratio (%, years 2005–14)
Source: authors' elaboration on Orbis Bank Focus

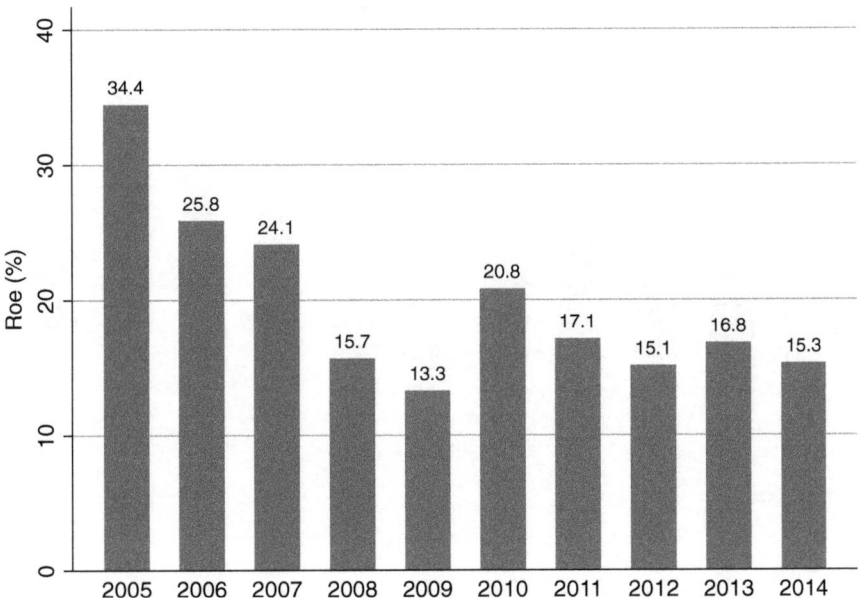

FIGURE 3.2 Return-on-equity ratio (%, years 2005–14)
Source: authors' elaboration on Orbis Bank Focus

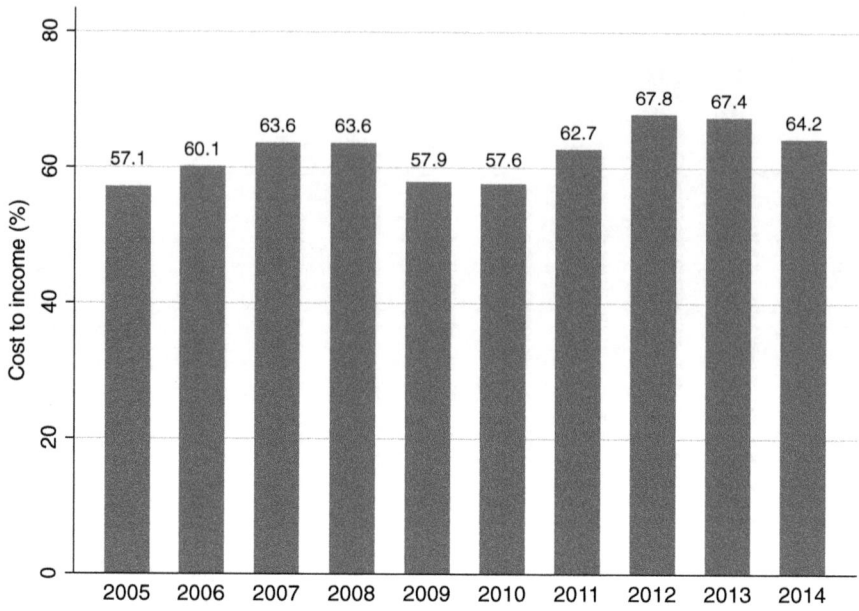

FIGURE 3.3 Cost-to-income ratio (%, years 2005–14)
Source: authors' elaboration on Orbis Bank Focus

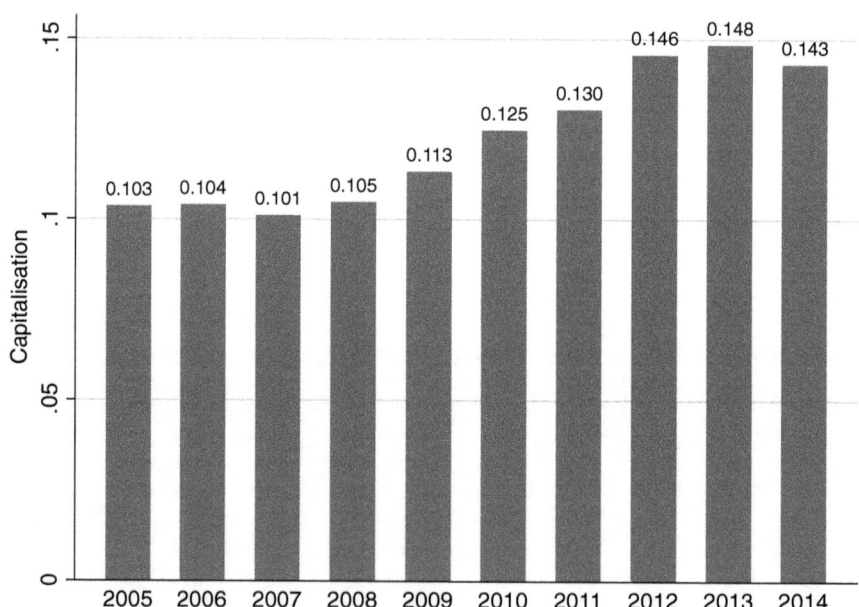

FIGURE 3.4 Capitalisation (%, years 2005–14)
Source: authors' elaboration on Orbis Bank Focus

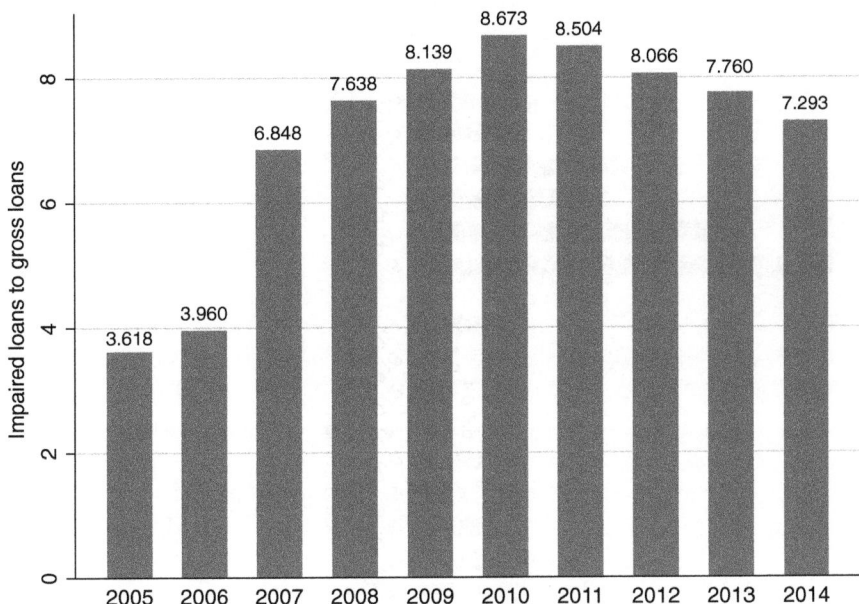

FIGURE 3.5 Impaired loans to gross loans (%, years 2005–14)
Source: authors' elaboration on Orbis Bank Focus

$$Perf_i = a + \beta_1 Perf_{i,t-1} + \beta_2 FS_{i,t} + \beta_3 MS_{i,t} + \mu i \beta \mu \nu \mu_i + \nu_i$$

with i = 1, ..., N and t = 2, ..., T

where the dependent variable is the performance of i-th consumer credit company at time measured by the roa ratio ($Perf_i$) and the regressors are the one year lag of the performance, a vector of firm-specific variables (FS_i); a vector of market-specific variables (MS_i). The βs are the related coefficient, μi controls for cross-sectional variation and νi is the disturbance term.

In line with existing literature on the determinant of the performance of financial intermediaries, the firm-specific variables are size,[35] risk, capitalisation and income diversification.[36] Market-specific variables, which are aimed at capturing the uneven level of maturity of the consumer credit market across Europe, are the credit diffusion, measured by the consumer credit to GDP ratio, and the debt growth ratio among households, measured by the debt-to-income ratio. We also used the GDP per capita to account for difference among countries' economic environment which may influence consumer credit companies' profitability.

[35] To avoid potential endogeneity with the dependent variable, size is proxied using the logarithm of the total equity instead of the total asset. The correlation between the two variables is around 94 per cent.
[36] See e.g. Berger and Mester (2003); Demirguc-Kunt and Huizinga (2000); Molyneux and Thornton (1992).

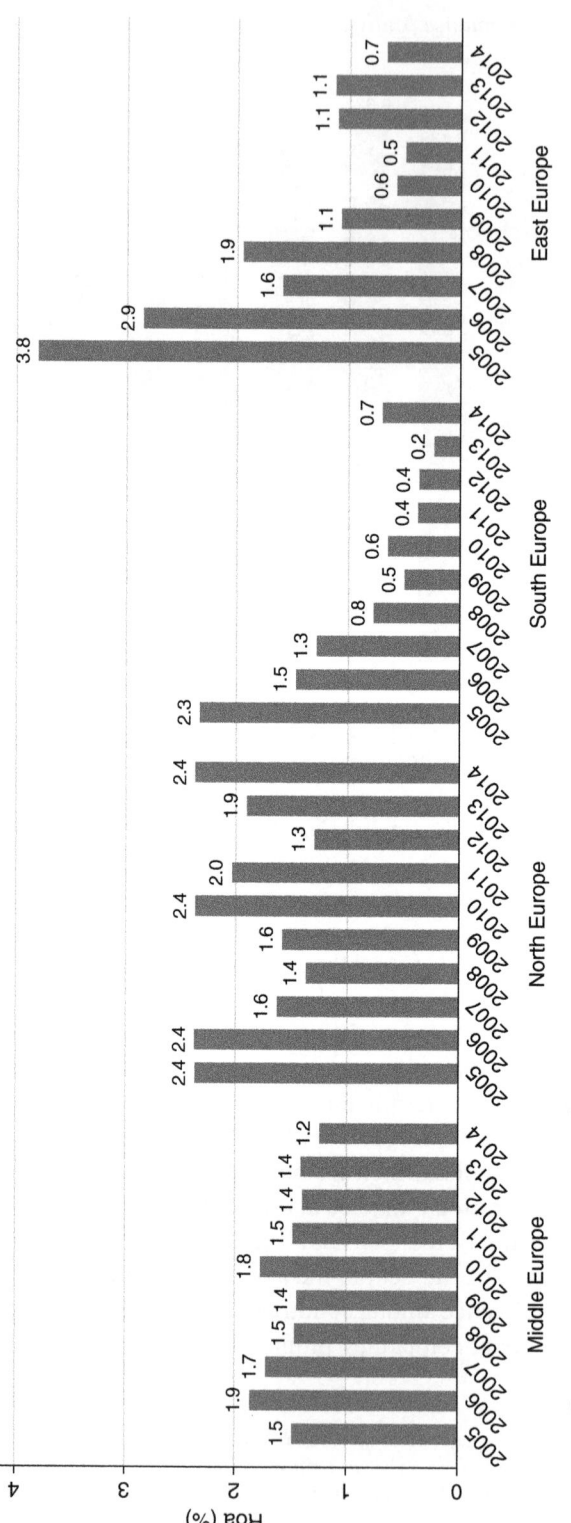

FIGURE 3.6 Return-on-asset ratio geographic area (%, years 2005–14)
Source: authors' elaboration on Orbis Bank Focus

TABLE 3.10 *Dynamic regression results*

	ROA	Cost to income
roa t−1	0.428***	0.103
size	0.580**	1.065***
capitalisation	−0.266	0.535
risk	0.002	−0.083***
diversification	0.016*	0.011
credit diffusion		0.740***
household debt		−0.040***
GDP per capita		0.000
Constant	−6.582*	−15.977***
Walt test for joint significance (p-value)	39.949	51.496
Observations	254	207

Notes
* $p<0.1$; ** $p<0.05$; *** $p<0.01$
Source: authors' elaboration on Orbis Bank Focus

3.6.3 Empirical Results

Table 3.10 presents the results of the GMM dynamic regression analysis.

Empirical estimations highlight that the performance of the consumer credit industry in Europe is driven both by firm-specific and market-specific variables. In particular, among firm-specific variables results highlight that profitability is positively affected by size and negatively by risk. Capitalisation and previous year performance are no longer statistically significant when introducing more specifications in the model. The effect of size on profitability is positive and statistically significant and reflects marginal cost savings and cost reductions due to economies of scale and possible implementation of entry strategies. The impact of credit risk is conversely negative: the higher the level of risk, the higher the accumulation of loan losses which in turn lead to a lower profitability. In case of consumer credit providers, this may in part be related to the growth of consumer credit and the generally easier access to the market which raises the diffusion of this financial solution also among riskier borrowers[37] and stresses the need for a continuous improvement in screening and monitoring policies.

As far as market-specific factors, profitability is positively affected by credit diffusion while it is negatively influenced by the level of personal debt. Credit diffusion can be interpreted as a proxy of the level of maturity of the industry and the dynamic regression result suggests that in a more mature market profitability is higher.

---

[37] Cavalletti et al. (2014); Ottaviani and Vandone (2011); Vandone et al. (2012).

Possible reasons work both on the revenue and the cost side of the profit and losses account. On the revenue side, in a more mature market consumer credit companies may increase market segmentation, offer a wider and more sophisticated range of products with different characteristics for different needs, and benefit from cross-selling. On the cost side, since the volume of the business is bigger, companies may also benefit from economies of scale and scope. The level of personal debt is a proxy of the burden of debt, measured by the debt-to-income ratio; the coefficient is significant and negative. This finding is in line with the empirical literature that shows that an increase in debt burden increases the risk of over-indebtedness and the probability for consumers not to repay their loan, with a negative impact on the profitability of consumer credit providers (see Chapter 4 on over-indebtedness).

Overall, the evidence emerging from the empirical analysis highlights threat and opportunities for the industry. A growing and more profitable consumer credit industry may offer more sophisticated and diversified lending solutions, and therefore target specific market segments or include new customers. Besides, product diversification may clearly represent a competitive advantage in entering national markets with lower levels of maturity. At the same time, the expansion of the personal debt market in Europe is tracked by increasing levels of market complexity and competitiveness, which may leave their mark on earnings margin. This is particularly relevant in a period characterised by the changing competitive landscape which is seeing the entrance of Fintech competitors that can further erode market shares and profitability of traditional consumer credit companies. Given that the industry has a performance on average higher than the overall financial sector, and that the personal debt market is still growing both in mature and more immature economies, it is likely that the personal debt industry will inevitably display a profile of dynamism in the future.

4

From Indebtedness to Over-Indebtedness: Multidimensional Causes and Consequences

4.1 UNMANAGEABLE DEBT

As highlighted in Chapter 2, personal debt is an important part of the economy since it may guarantee individuals heightened economic welfare by providing them greater flexibility over their spending and facilitating lifetime consumption. However, it is also well known that – especially for certain groups of individuals – paying back debt may become problematic.

The 2008 financial crisis and the turmoil in the personal debt market underscored the need to better understand which consumers get into arrears and repayment difficulties and why their debt become unmanageable. This is because over-indebtedness can have multiple negative impacts at micro and macro level on consumer well-being, in terms of reduced standard of living, social exclusion, physical and mental health, on the stability of the financial system, due to potential defaults in debt repayments, on society as a whole, in terms of reduced aggregate demand, employment and growth.

This chapter analyses over-indebtedness from an economic perspective with the aim of quantifying the phenomenon and analysing the characteristics of consumers that are over-indebted or at risk of over-indebtedness. Sections 4.2 and 4.3 define over-indebtedness, focus on the complexity of measuring the phenomenon and illustrate existing indicators aimed at capturing profiles of financial distress. Sections 4.4 and 4.5 analyse the causes of over-indebtedness and provide a review of extant empirical literature which highlights the characteristics of over-indebted consumers. Sections 4.6 and 4.7 provide an empirical investigation into the extent of over-indebtedness in Europe and the characteristics of over-indebted households. Data from Eurosystem's Household Finance and Consumption Survey (HFCS) are used to provide insight into the phenomenon in Europe and at country level. Sections 4.8 and 4.9 specifically focus on the role played by psychological and personal traits – impulsivity, myopia, overconfidence – on debt decision-making and risk of over-indebtedness. It also investigates the under-studied impact of behavioural traits on the effectiveness of measures to prevent over-indebtedness. An empirical analysis concludes, with the aim of highlighting the role that impulsivity plays in weakening the positive impact of financial literacy on debt decisions.

4.2 DEFINITION OF OVER-INDEBTEDNESS

Over the years there have been several attempts to understand and define over-indebtedness at EU level.

The concept derives from that of debt, and the debt–credit connection. Credit and debt can be reconducted to the private law relationship of one party (the creditor) advancing goods or services which will be repaid at a later stage by the other party (the debtor), with or without interest. This creation of longer-lasting (as opposed to instantaneous) contractual relationships notoriously includes loans, i.e. the advancement of money to pay upfront for goods or services, an activity usually done by credit institutions in the credit market, which may take the form of consumer or mortgage credit. The reference to the 'consumer' element indicates that the credit is provided to individuals for personal, domestic or household purposes, differentiating it from business credit.[1]

Cultural approaches or habits regarding the use of financial credit may vary considerably from one Member State to another. Nevertheless, the liberalisation and expansion of credit markets, alongside the consequent increased availability of credit to feed the consumption model of modern society may explain why, traditionally, consumer loans and excessive lending by financial institutions or borrowing by consumers have been associated with over-indebtedness. Market deregulation accompanied by incomplete social safety nets is often recognised as creating structural conditions that lead to an environment hospitable to financial difficulty.[2]

But, if it is undisputed that lending/borrowing gives rise to indebtedness, the extent to which borrowing turns into over-indebtedness and is responsible for it is not straightforward and it remains doubtful.

This is because indebtedness per se is not recognised as being a problem, as pointed out in Chapter 2. On the contrary, from an economic viewpoint consumer borrowing is seen positively to adjust fluctuations in income, address short-term liquidity problems, and give the possibility of improving lifestyle by smoothing consumption over their lifetime and making accessible expensive goods such a property.[3]

The problem arises when, irrespective of the causes, indebtedness becomes such that debtors are unable to meet their contractual obligations, so that indebtedness is

---

[1] In some circumstances, the distinction between consumer and business credit can be blurred when small business is involved. Despite having a common root, the different nature, problems, policies and regulation of business credit are beyond the scope of this work.
[2] Braucher (2006); Micklitz (2013); Ramsay (2012).
[3] Braucher (2006); Ramsay (2012).

excessive vis-à-vis repayment capacity. This is where the first conceptual difficulties emerge about the understanding of the precise moment when the passage from indebtedness to over-indebtedness occurs, as well as the meaning itself of over-indebtedness and the knowledge of it, all of which in turn have major implications for policy and the legal framework

Over time, a growing number of EU-commissioned studies and academic literature have obstinately attempted to define the exact and univocal terms or boundaries of the phenomenon.[4] However, as such efforts have been the result of the observation of national situations characterised by structural or prolonged difficulties in repaying personal debts, a common operational definition or measurement at EU level has not emerged and to a large degree it still does not exist.

The major effort undertaken by the European Commission in its study *Towards a Common European Operational Definition of Over-Indebtedness* has revealed that there is not a uniquely acknowledged definition, and the concept varies across the Member States. Despite attempts to identify common elements, the study unveiled that even if the measurement unit in most cases refers to the 'household', in other cases the focus is on the 'individual debtor'. Or the length of time of the financial difficulty, though present in most jurisdictions, is not universally accepted. Likewise, only half of the studied jurisdictions made a reference to cost-of-living expenses. What perhaps is the most common element in the various jurisdictions is the indication of payment incapacity to honour contractual obligations, but without commonality of type of commitment.[5]

Despite highlighting terminological and conceptual confusions, in its attempt to recognise common elements of over-indebtedness, the study captured the multi-dimensional nature of the problem. This includes an economic dimension of over-commitments, a time dimension over a long period which makes it structural, a social dimension leading to exclusion, and a psychological dimension of stress and health harm.[6]

---

[4] For a complete overview of the studies, see Kilborn (2010). For example, first attempts have differentiated it from the legal term of insolvency for the association of the latter to the stance of the creditor and the impossibility of recovering the due amount because of the negative debt-to-asset ratio or lack of liquidity. Thus, it has been seen it as a social phenomenon and a situation in which consumers will definitely not be able to meet their financial obligations and defined by an overall deterioration of their dependants' economic situation leading to social and economic exclusion. See e.g. Huls et al. (1994); Reifner et al. (September 2003). More recent studies make reference to a situation which occurs when an individual's level of debt cannot be sustained in relation to his or her current earnings or additional resources raised from the sale of his or her assets. See e.g. Group of Specialists on Seeking Legal Solutions to Debt Problems (Cj-S-Debt) (18 January 2007); Niemi (2009); OCR Macro (October 2001); Vandone (2009). For the one EU document on over-indebtedness, see Recommendation CM/Rec (2007)8 of the Committee of Ministers to member states on legal solutions to debt problems (20 June 2007).

[5] OEE Etudes (February 2008).

[6] *Ibid.*

This study has been helpful in understanding the scope of the problem but its multidimensional notion proves difficult for a practical application, especially if it has to be translated into supranational policy and law. In particular, it hardly helps the jurist, who unavoidably needs to identify a sufficiently precise content and its borders to the extent that a legal framework aims at conferring a status to the situation of 'over-indebtedness' and identify the scope of application of its norms.

As acknowledged by recent scholarship, the continuing vacuum of a clear content-based notion of over-indebtedness not only makes the comparison between Member States difficult,[7] but also a European response problematic.

On the other hand, however, EU competence on the matter can be seen as important to the effective operation of the single market to avoid fragmentation between the various national jurisdictions when dealing with the effects generated by the same market in retail financial services.

In addition, the promotion of competition between credit providers or other financial institutions under Articles 3 TFEU[8] and 32 TFEU,[9] as well as requirements of consumer protection under Article 12 TFEU[10] and 169 TFEU,[11] may demand that household over-indebtedness becomes framed in effective Union policy and law.[12]

A new perspective that could become helpful for future concrete EU initiatives is represented by the latest European Commission-commissioned study on the updated mapping of the situation, its nature and its causes.[13]

The study represents an important step forward in the knowledge of the actual social circumstances in which financial difficulty is embedded. It details the type of consumers who are more prone to be in financial distress, the causes and the consequences of debt problems and the national measures in place to identify and alleviate the debt crisis.

For the purpose of this work, the empirical investigation which has been conducted suggests that time may have come to abandon attempts to precisely define

---

[7] Micklitz (2012).
[8] Under Art. 3 TFEU, the EU shall have exclusive competence in the establishing of the competition rules necessary for the functioning of the internal market.
[9] Under Art. 32 TFEU, in carrying out the tasks entrusted to it the Commission shall be guided by developments in conditions of competition within the EU in so far as they lead to an improvement in the competitive capacity of undertakings and ensure rational development of production and an expansion of consumption within the EU.
[10] Under Art. 12 TFEU, consumer protection requirements shall be taken into account in defining and implementing other Union policies and activities.
[11] Under Art. 169 TFEU, in order to promote the interests of consumers and to ensure a high level of consumer protection, the Union shall contribute to protecting the health, safety and economic interests of consumers, as well as to promoting their right to information, education and to organise themselves in order to safeguard their interests
[12] This, for example, was a stance taken by the Economic and Social Committee, *Opinion of the Economic and Social Committee on 'Household over-indebtedness'*, C 149/01 (2002).
[13] Civic Consulting (2014).

a term that the majority of stakeholders find unhelpful – from the industry to civil society organisations and from public authorities to independent experts. Instead, the starting point is that over-indebtedness in practice is about people, who are unable to pay debts and meet essential living expenses, and therefore find themselves in persistent difficult and traumatic situations. Thus, according to the report, the focus could be on identifying the key policy concerns that exist and from there developing reliable indicators to help track them. In so doing, over-indebtedness is broken down into two dimensions:

(a) the type of financial commitment, which in addition to financial borrowing includes all other household commitments including bills or rents; and
(b) the nature of the matter, specified as the excessive level or inability to meet commitments when they fall due.[14]

The relevant indicators of the (a) type of commitment include measures of arrears on mortgages, consumer credit, rent, utility payments, the incapacity to face unexpected expenses and the inability to sustain basic living expenses.[15]

Seen from this angle, the approach becomes more grounded in the real social and financial circumstances of individuals, and is more pragmatic. Over-indebtedness is about people, who have ongoing difficulties with meeting their commitments of any nature, and not just in repaying loans contracted with financial institutions. To some extent, this may have the potential for substantial policy implications in shifting attention away from credit relationship with financial institutions. Equally, this also provides the crucial relevance of the causes of over-indebtedness that are intertwined with (b) the nature of the problem, because they become key determinants for its assessment.

In short, consumers are considered over-indebted if they are having – on an ongoing basis – difficulties meeting (or falling behind with) their commitments, whether these relate to servicing secured or unsecured borrowing or to payment of rent, utility or other household bills. This characterisation is not limited to the issue of debts stemming from financial credits but it includes all consumer essential outgoings, and it is tied to income and other expenditure relating to taxation and cuts in social welfare.[16]

4.3 MEASURES OF OVER-INDEBTEDNESS

The definition of over-indebtedness then is undoubtedly broad in terms and able to capture the multidimensional nature of the phenomenon. However, from an economic perspective, it raises challenges in measurement, since it is difficult to find a unique measure that identifies consumers that are in such a situation. Specifically,

[14] Ibid.
[15] Ibid.
[16] Ibid.

the complexity of measuring over-indebtedness is mainly due to the type of liabilities included and to the identification of the threshold beyond which debt levels become unmanageable.[17]

Over years, a growing number of measures have been set up. They can be grouped into: (1) measures that include among liabilities only financial debt, and (2) more comprehensive measures, that include all types of liabilities, such as utility bills, taxes, rent payments. For some of these measures a threshold has been set up; however, in most cases, they are evaluated within their scale in relative terms.

Measures that account only for financial debts are commonly used by central banks to analyse the impact of household financial fragility on the stability of financial systems when adverse macroeconomic shocks occur, such as increase in interest rates, increase in unemployment rate and house price decrease.[18] The underlying idea is that high levels of debt are not necessarily a problem, as long as consumers are able to service and repay debts. However, when the level of debt is high compared to income and wealth, consumers become less resilient to adverse external economic shocks and debt may become unmanageable.

One of the most commonly used measure of over-indebtedness is the debt-service-to-income ratio, which is defined as the total monthly debt repayment divided by the gross monthly income. The debt-service-to-income ratio is an indicator of the burden that debt holding represents to current income and has a threshold which is normally set at 30 per cent (25 per cent when related only to consumer credit). Beyond this level, debt represent a significant burden for consumers. In order to account for the assets that the household may have and eventually sell to meet debt-servicing obligations, D'Alessio and Iezzi (2016) propose a different version of the debt-service-to-income index, which reduces the total borrowing repayments by an amount proportional to the ratio between the outstanding debt and the value of the household's financial and real assets.

Other indicators used to measure financial vulnerability are the debt-to-asset ratio, which provides information related to the capacity of the total stock of assets to pay back debt, and the debt-to-income ratio, which combines stock and flow variables to provide insights into the extent to which debt can be paid back from the flow of income rather than the stock of assets. For these indicators, the threshold is normally set at 100 per cent and a value above this line signals high insolvency risk.

The above-mentioned indicators are straightforward to calculate, given the availability of data at micro level collected by central banks or national institutes of statistics.[19] Besides, they bear a low level of arbitrariness in defining the variables,

---

[17] Ampudia et al. (2014); Vandone and Anderloni (2016).
[18] Albacete and Lindner (2013); Hlaváč et al. (2013).
[19] In general, one of the main issues related to the possibility of using meaningful data is the availability of appropriate datasets. In Europe, the most complete and publicly available dataset that collects information on sociodemographic and economic variables at households level is the HFCS. As highlighted in Chapter 2, other well-known national datasets are the British Household Panel

and allow meaningful comparisons across countries. However, they may underestimate the size of the phenomenon as they refer only to financial debt while over-indebtedness is a more comprehensive phenomenon. For instance, these measures do not account for consumers that are over-indebted because they are unable to meet other commitments, such as paying utility bills and housing rental, but do not hold debt because, for example, they have no access to financial credit. The dynamic of those ratios may also be misleading. A reduction in the outstanding debt-to-income ratio, instead of being a positive signal of reduction in the risk of over-indebtedness, might be due to a cutback in credit and might be accompanied by a downturn in the economy with a consequent higher exposure to financial vulnerability (like after the 2008 crisis).

Therefore, beyond economic ratios based only on financial debt, other evidence can contribute to measure over-indebtedness and give a more comprehensive picture of the phenomenon. Ampudia et al. (2014) propose a comprehensive indicator, the so-called 'financial margin', defined as the net income and liquid financial assets available after debt payments, taxes and basic living expenses. The threshold is set at zero, meaning that a consumer is in financial distress if the financial margin is null or negative.

There are also subjective indicators of financial vulnerability, such as the inability to make ends meet, to cope with an unexpected expense or to go without specialised medical care. They are usually reported in surveys and represent self-assessments by consumers. Other indicators that capture situations of financial distress, due to financial debt and other types of commitments, are statistics on arrears (e.g. arrears on financial debt, utilities, rent) or statistics on formal debt settlement (e.g. number of debts written off). These indicators, however, are more difficult to compute and their comparability across countries is more limited, because of the level of information required, not always available or comparable over time and space.

Different variables can also be combined to build ratios that account for the multidimensional nature of over-indebtedness. The next section proposes an indicator of financial vulnerability aimed at synthesising different profiles of financial stress.

4.3.1 The Financial Vulnerability Index

The Financial Vulnerability Index is an indicator of financial distress that jointly analyses different features of consumer over-indebtedness.[20] In fact, it comes from the overlap of different components, like expenditure vulnerability, income and saving vulnerability, commercial and financial loan commitments vulnerability. Besides, it includes both self-reported variables, such as the congruence of income

Survey (BHPS – UK), the Survey on Household Finances (EFF – Spain) and the Survey on Household Income and Wealth (SHIW – Italy).

[20] Vandone et al. (2012).

and monthly expenses, the capacity to cope with unexpected expenses, and the decision to go without specialised medical care, and more objective indicators, such as whether over the last twelve months the individual had problems even once in shopping for food, buying essential clothing, paying utility bills, rent, or paying off loans or mortgages and whether such difficulties turned into objectively real problems in the form of late or non-payment.

From a statistical point of view, the implementation of the index requires a reduction process with the aim of checking for a reduced number of appropriate combinations of the original variables that summarise vulnerability from different points of view.[21] Using the quantifications and the factor loadings resulting from the dimensionality reduction process, the Financial Vulnerability Index is calculated as follows:

$$\text{Financial Vulnerability Index} = \sum_{p=1}^{n} a_p X_{pi}$$

where X_{pi} is the standardised value for the p_{th} variable and a_p is its corresponding factor score. For the sake of convenience and immediacy in the interpretation, the indicator is rescaled between 0 (minimum vulnerability) and 10 (maximum vulnerability). Therefore, the higher the value, the higher the level of financial vulnerability.

The empirical application of the Financial Vulnerability Index has been made on a large sample of Italian individuals, and for three different waves of surveys.[22] This highlights that the index is suitable not only for measuring but also for monitoring the evolution of the phenomenon over time. Table 4.1 reports the mean and median values of the Financial Vulnerability index for three periods.

The Index showed a significant deterioration in the financial vulnerability situation of consumers from 2009 to 2013, which is most likely due to the exacerbation of the financial stress conditions following the 2011 sovereign debt crisis. Conversely, in 2016 it confirms, albeit slightly, an easing of negative trends. The average value, in fact, decreased from 3.2 in 2013 to 2.8 in 2016, a value only slightly higher than the initial figure of 2009 which began to capture the first signs of financial fragility following the sub-prime mortgage crisis. Similar considerations apply considering the median of the index, which in 2016 shows lower values than in 2009 and 2013.

It is however to be noticed that the analysis of the data shows that only those households with an index around zero (which are on average less than 20% of the

---

[21] The traditional principal components analysis (PCA) is the standard statistical tool generally used to reduce the dimensionality of a problem. However, most of the theoretical results, including the consistency of the estimates of the factor loadings, are obtained on the assumption of samples from multivariate normal distributions. This, in theory, should considerably limit its field of application, at least when some of the variables are categorical or, even worse, binary (Kolenikov and Angeles 2004). Given the nature of our data, we therefore use a generalisation of the traditional PCA, the nonlinear principal components analysis methodology which leads to an optimal synthesis of observed variables in a reduced space preserving measurement levels of qualitative ordinal data without assuming a priori differences between their categories. The methodology is explained in detail in Vandone et al. (2012).

[22] Results are reported in Vandone et al. (2012, 2014); Vandone and Anderloni (2016).

TABLE 4.1 *Descriptive statistics of the Financial Vulnerability Index (years 2009, 2013, 2016)*

	Mean	Median
Financial Vulnerability Index (year 2009)	2.703	2.172
Financial Vulnerability Index (year 2013)	3.164	2.662
Financial Vulnerability Index (year 2016)	2.750	2.121

Source: Vandone and Anderloni (2016)

sample) are able to make ends meet or meet an unexpected expense easily or very easily and do not have problems in covering expenses or paying bills. Vice versa, the rest of the sample presents elements of vulnerability which are rapidly growing. For example, at the median index value there is already a high percentage of households that have some problems getting to the end of the month, while almost 15 per cent of the households are in no way capable of meeting an unexpected expense.[23]

4.4 CAUSES OF OVER-INDEBTEDNESS

According to the literature, over-indebtedness can mainly be traced back to two main causes: (1) excessive levels of accumulated debt, and (2) changes in circumstances that make the contracted debt no longer sustainable. Earlier literature refers to the first as 'active over-indebtedness' and to the second as 'passive over-indebtedness'.[24]

Active over-indebtedness is generated by excessive levels of debt held by consumers, following decisions to borrow up to a level that is unsustainable on the basis of present or future earnings: consumers overburden themselves with more debt than they can afford. Such decision may be due to individuals' inability to process effectively information available and, as a result, to evaluate the consequences of indebtedness, as well as lack of information transparency that hinders well-informed decision-making. It may also be driven by factors such as low income and illiquid balance sheet or by lifestyle behaviours which lead a consumer to non-optimal consumption and indebtedness choice. Finally, over-indebtedness may come from borrowing choices made knowing that the amount owed will not be repaid (so-called 'strategic default').[25]

---

[23] In the above-mentioned papers related to the empirical application of the Financial Vulnerability Index there is also a multivariate analysis of the determinants of the index, a description of the differences among quintiles of score, and a principal component analysis of groups belonging to different levels of index.

[24] Banque de France (1996); Vandone (2009).

[25] Local financial and judicial institutions may explain cross-country differences and are used in literature as a proxy to capture the differences in punishment for default (Duygan-Bump and Grant 2008). For an analysis of the relationship between debt and crime, see McIntyre (2017).

Passive over-indebtedness is determined by unexpected factors beyond an individual's control, such as changes in personal life conditions (i.e. separation, death or illness) or changes in macroeconomic variables (e.g. interest rate increase, house prices decrease, unemployment increase). These unexpected events, by reducing income and/or increase liabilities, negatively impact repayment capacity and make what was once a manageable liability no longer sustainable.

The financial crisis has enriched the spectrum of factors driving over-indebtedness with politically sensitive elements that were never counted as 'debt' but that were obvious to any ordinary person. These causes include increased level of taxation (now more topical than ever in a number of Member States with austerity measures in place) and cuts in social welfare which require more household outgoings to provide for their cover, as well as basic utilities or daily essential expenditure and low standards of incomes vis-à-vis the cost of living.[26] In a nutshell, all that is needed to make ends meet.

Not surprisingly, most of the above findings find confirmation in another new study on selected countries having in common the intervention of international bail-outs.[27]

The latest studies assume a particular significance for the competence of the EU in the matter and the ensuing policy and lawmaking. For the first time, they establish a clear, though non-exclusive, link between over-indebtedness and poverty or impoverishment in its double face: if it is true that over-indebtedness leads to deprivation and poverty, it is equally factual that low-income or middle-class exposure to financial shocks of any nature is associated with over-indebtedness. They expose what is intuitive, i.e. that most people have to pay for housing (be it rent or mortgage), they need to meet essential living expenditure, they may have some levels of consumer loans which they could afford at the time of contracting, etc. As a consequence, some people may need to take further use of credit to make up for those repayments. But for a substantial number of people who are at the level of floatation a shock in their income or in their outgoings may take them from indebtedness to over-indebtedness under its latest conceptualisation (consumers are considered over-indebted if they are having – on an ongoing basis – difficulties meeting or falling behind with their commitments, whether these relate to servicing secured or unsecured borrowing or to payment of rent, utility or other household bills).[28]

In essence, it is likely that lifetime or macroeconomic events have a direct impact on all existing contractual relations of low- or middle-income families, some of

---

[26] Civic Consulting (2014).
[27] Domurath, Comparato, Micklitz (2014). The study presents the results of empirical research on the effects of the financial crisis in six countries within and outside the eurozone (or the EU-28) which, though in different forms, have been subject to a bail-out: Greece, Portugal, Spain, Romania, Hungary and Iceland.
[28] Civic Consulting (2014). See above in this chapter.

which have been conceptualised by recent scholarship as 'lifetime contracts' (or social long-term contracts).[29]

Of course, there may be those who knowingly or unknowingly mismanage their financial affairs, but the scale of this problem seems limited and it has never really helped to understand the phenomenon. Yet, the problem of failure to repay loans to financial institutions exacerbates the financial situation of the debtor because of the spiralling of debt problems due to the impact of interest, compounded interest, penalties, fees, etc. up to the point when the situation becomes unmanageable or reaches the point of no return. Likewise, aggressive or irresponsible lending practices which clearly exist in the marketplace must not be condoned, as they are unfair and they can make consumers' bad financial situations even worse. This clearly justifies in itself regulation tailored to tackle them. But, as established by previous research, these sorts of lending practices are not the original or principal causes of financial difficulty and in statistical terms they affect only a small number of borrowers.[30]

A convincing reason for becoming over-indebted could be a conjuncture of external events with consumers not adjusting effectively their budgets to these changes.[31] More empirical research would be needed to better understand the extent to which such a conjuncture has a significant bearing on problem debt.

Some Member States have experienced other issues. For example, a number of new Member States have been through structural changes in a relatively short period of time and have common structural characteristics that may have exacerbated the effects of the financial turmoil or have impacted differently on the causes of over-indebtedness (e.g. borrowing in foreign currencies, heavy reliance on influx of foreign capital, transition to market economy and sudden increase in house prices with following severe negative equities).[32]

In any event, in the end the innovative approach taken by the latest reports towards over-indebtedness and their findings opens new routes and challenges to the European jurist as to the policy and legal response that may be offered at EU level.

At first sight, it appears clear that the type of financial commitments and the nature of the problems find their roots in a number of national soils which are beyond the remit or control of the EU legislator and which are far broader than the debt–credit relationship – for example, issues of political economy, taxation, salary levels and cost of living. These are very sensitive national political issues and not much can be expected at the level of policy and law on over-indebtedness, especially under EU law.

Nevertheless, there might be something left for the EU and its future agenda on over-indebtedness. Until now the focus has been exclusively on the internal market

---

[29] Nogler and Reifner (2014).
[30] See e.g. Kempson (2002).
[31] See e.g. Banque de France (September 2014).
[32] See e.g. European Central Bank (January 2005); Farkas (2012); Koyama (2010).

and the empowerment of the reasonably circumspect consumer in the private law relationship between lenders and borrowers,[33] concentrating on the responsible behaviour of the contracting parties and prevention through creditworthiness assessment (see Chapter 5.).

A possible new method of looking at over-indebtedness, however, submits that time may have come to focus more on debt solutions expansive of the private law relationship. Here the suggestion is to explore European measures to a problem that is intertwined with the single market and that can well remain separate from those other wider sensitive political national issues that the phenomenon raises.

4.5 AN ECONOMIC LITERATURE REVIEW ON OVER-INDEBTEDNESS

Several empirical studies have focused on the causes of over-indebtedness and the characteristics of consumers, over-indebted or at risk of insolvency, providing evidence based on micro-level data. Another strand of literature has focused more on the macroeconomic impact of over-indebtedness on the stability of financial systems when adverse macroeconomic shocks occur. The main empirical findings are reported in the following sections.

4.5.1 *Characteristics of Over-Indebted Consumers*

This strand of literature identifies the groups of consumers more at risk of becoming over-indebted. The ultimate goal is to give policymakers evidence to help produce the relevant tools and to plan policy intervention to properly prevent and manage situations of financial difficulty or over-indebtedness.

These studies identify the main statistically significant sociodemographic and economic variables that characterise the most vulnerable groups, such as age, gender, marital status, size of the family, number of income earner, financial and real wealth, level of income, type of occupation.

As for sociodemographic characteristics, the risk of over-indebtedness seems a growing problem among young generations, who incur debt for education, housing and consumption while, at the same time, have to deal with the difficulties of a relatively fragile job market.[34] Oksanen et al. (2015), analysing debt problems in the Finnish population, find that younger age groups have a higher prevalence of debt problems. The International Monetary Fund (2012), focusing on the financial vulnerability of Spanish households, also reports that the share of debt-at-risk is significantly largest in poorer and younger households, although they account only for a small fraction of total personal debt. Del Rio and Young (2006) look at the relationship between household vulnerability and unsecured borrowing using

---

[33] Micklitz (2012, 2013); Ramsay (2010).
[34] Jiang and Dunn (2013); Montgomerie (2013).

microdata from the BHPS. The authors use a self-reported indicator of financial distress and analyse the probability of households who hold unsecured debt, reporting problems with repayment. While the proportion of households reporting debt problems did not change much between 1995 and 2000, they find that there were significant changes in their socio-economic characteristics, specifically an increase in unsecured debt taken on by young households with a high debt–income ratio, which, in turn, made them more vulnerable to potential shocks in their income or to increases in interest rates. Single parents also experience more debt problems,[35] and the number of children may put pressure on the household budget.[36] The role played by unexpected changes in life, such as divorce, sickness, unemployment can also be pivotal,[37] as well as family size, since families with a high number of children have a higher probability of being in financial distress.[38]

As for economic and financial features, Bridges and Disney (2004) focus on the characteristics of low-income families that have problems of arrears and default in loan commitments as well as in other areas, such as payment for housing and utilities. In their analysis, the authors combine the arrears data in order to examine how the aggregate level of arrears is associated with different household characteristics and show that credit use and accumulation of arrears differ between single parents and couples with children, and also between homeowners and renters. They also show that loans from finance companies pose repayment difficulties for almost one in five families, primarily tenants. Zajaczkowski and Zochowski (2007) use data from the Polish Household Budget Survey to analyse the distribution of debt burden ratio across the individuals in Poland and find that low-income households exhibit higher debt-service-to-income ratio. Similarly, Magri et al. (2011), using EU–SILC data for a selection of European countries between 2005 and 2008, analyse the characteristics of households that hold a higher amount of consumer credit. They find that a share of households, ranging from 8 per cent to 16 per cent across countries, who borrow in the consumer credit market are poor in income, which is relevant since they are more at risk of financial fragility given their inability to face unexpected expenses with their income and/or wealth.

Focusing on homeowners and renters, May et al. (2004) investigate the affordability of debt, both in terms of the amount of income that is devoted to servicing debts and households' perceptions of whether their debts are a problem. They find that, while the vast majority of debt is owed by homeowners with mortgages, debt problems are concentrated among renters, who are consistently more likely to report problems servicing their unsecured debt than are homeowners. Moreover, consumers with both high levels of income gearing and high debt in relation to housing assets are more likely to face debt problems.

[35] Patel et al. (2012); Russel et al. (2013).
[36] Brown and Taylor (2005); Keese (2008).
[37] Duygan and Grant (2008).
[38] Vandone et al. (2012).

The debt burden is also a significant driver of situation of over-indebtedness, especially when debt is represented by consumer credit. Albacete and Lindner (2013), using data from the HFCS in Austria, find that having a non-mortgage debt has a positive significant correlation with vulnerability. Besides, households with low income and low wealth, or households with an unemployed reference person are found to be particularly vulnerable. Vandone et al. 2012 find that the level of debt servicing is positively related to financial vulnerability and the effect is stronger for consumers holding consumer credit. Zavadil and Messner (2014) focus on Slovakia and analyse the factors that determine household wealth based on micro data from the HFCS. As for debt, they find that consumer credit, in particular credit card debt and instalment loans, increase instant utility but do not contribute to household wealth in the long run. The detrimental impact on household finances is also due to high interest rates. Conversely, they find that mortgages, as posited by the life-cycle theory, have a positive impact on household net wealth when they are used to buy their main residence. Christelis et al. (2010) analyse the financial fragility of Europeans aged 65 and over and describe how this fragility varies across countries, age groups, health status and other socio-economic variables. They report that the stock of accumulated debt, the time to maturity, the availability of collateral and the weight of instalment payments in disposable income represent an element of financial fragility.

There are also several reports from financial authorities or consumer associations that analyse in detail the characteristics of consumers over-indebted or at risk of over-indebtedness. For example, the Banque de France has been conducting a survey on consumer over-indebtedness since 2001, entitled *Le surendettement des ménages*. The investigation is based on an analysis of the files declared admissible by the Banque de France over-indebtedness commissions (Arts. L. 711–1–L. 712-2, Code de la consommation) during the period under review. Data are analysed at country and regional levels to identify the geographic areas where the phenomenon is more concentrated as well as the sociodemographic and economic characteristics of over-indebted consumers.[39] Similarly, the Money Advice Service periodically estimates over-indebtedness, returning a detailed picture of over-indebtedness in the UK and at regional level. In analysing demographic and lifestyle data, they highlight the more relevant and recurring factors which are linked to over-indebtedness, that is renting the home, having more than three children, having an income below £10,000. According to their studies, younger people and single parents are also more likely to be over-indebted.[40]

Overall, extant literature highlights that there are groups that are more at risk of being over-indebted, such as the younger, single parents, large families, low-income and low-wealth individuals, renters.

---

[39] Banque de France (2016).
[40] Money Advice Service (2016).

More recent interdisciplinary studies in the field of behavioural economics have focused on the role of psychological traits – like impulsivity, materialism, anxiety, optimism – in debt decision and exposure to risk of over-indebtedness. Sections 4.8 and 4.9 focus on the impact of personal traits on the risk of over-indebtedness and policy measures set up to prevent situations of financial vulnerability.

4.5.2 Shocks and the Stability of the Financial System

This body of literature analyses the impact of external adverse shocks, mainly macroeconomic shocks, on the household's financial condition and the probability these shocks switch a situation of indebtedness into a situation of over-indebtedness. Papers are mainly from central banks because the 2008 financial crisis has underscored the need for an in-depth analysis of the risk arising from the household segment, given that it threatened the stability and the resilience of the banking system. Aware of the dangers of this phenomenon, European authorities and national overseers have increased the research activity and the policy tools directed at investigating this issue, by identifying definition and measures of household vulnerability, and evaluating the effect of their vulnerability on the stability of the European financial system and on Member Countries' economic growth.[41]

Ampudia et al. (2014), using the HFCS, analyse the financial vulnerability of households in the euro area to different macro shocks such as those caused by interest rates, house prices and employment. They find that the risk posed to the stability of the financial system by the household sector is generally contained, although there is heterogeneity across countries which depends not only on household composition of wealth (asset, liabilities, income) but also on institutional factors and, especially, the efficiency of the legal system. The International Monetary Fund (2012) conducted a sensitivity analysis to interest rates, unemployment and house price shocks of household indebtedness in Spain and found that the debt at risk not covered by household assets could more than treble under a certain macroeconomic adverse scenario. The impact of shocks is relatively more severe for borrowers, in particular among the poor and the young. Sugawara and Zaluendo (2011) investigated the impact of four macroeconomic shocks – interest rates, unemployment, exchange rate and house prices – on the debt-service-to-income ratio of Croatian households and found an increase in new vulnerable households of almost 6 per cent. In Finland, Herrala and Kauk (2007) reported a similar increase in the percentage of consumers in financial distress when extreme adverse scenarios occurred. Shocks in interest rates have a stronger negative impact since most loans bear variable interest rates.

Hlaváč et al. (2013) developed a framework for stress-testing the household sector and capturing the different impacts of a deterioration in the macroeconomic

---

[41] Albeceite and Lindner (2013); Ampudia et al. (2014); Zavadil and Messner (2014).

environment on different income groups of the Czech population. They found that growth in unemployment, interest rates and inflation led to a rise in the percentage of distressed households. Low-income households were the most vulnerable group. Albacete and Lindner (2013) also estimated the exposure of banks to potentially vulnerable households and found that the risk to financial stability stemming from the debt of vulnerable households seemed to be relatively low; it comes mainly from households holding non-mortgage debt, which however are much lower than mortgage debt. Beck et al. (2012) also highlight that a rapid increase in personal debt determines vulnerabilities that can precipitate a banking crisis.

Overall, these studies point out that in a situation where consumers are already heavily indebted, even moderate shocks can generate a huge amount of defaults which, in turn, can trigger the stability of the financial system.

4.6 AN EMPIRICAL INVESTIGATION INTO OVER-INDEBTEDNESS IN EUROPE

In this section, data from Eurosystem's HFCS are used to provide insight into the scale of over-indebted households in Europe and their characteristics.[42] To this end, the value of the debt–burden ratios is reported for Europe and by country. It follows an analysis of the sociodemographic and economic characteristics of groups of consumers with similar levels of debt burden, with a specific focus on those that are over-indebted.

4.6.1 The Size of Over-Indebtedness

Table 4.2 reports the median value, for Europe and by country, of the most commonly used indicators of debt burden: the debt-to-asset ratio, the debt-to-income ratio and the debt-service-to-income ratio. Data are from the second wave of the HFCS (2016) and refers to indebted households only.

The median value of the debt-to-asset ratio for indebted households is equal to 25.7%, while for the debt-to-income ratio and the debt-service-to-income ratio the median value is 71.8% and 13.5% respectively.

The variation across countries is considerable. As for the debt-to-asset ratio, clear outliers are the Netherlands (49.0%), Ireland (38.5%) and Portugal (37.8%); while at the other end of the distribution are Poland (6.8%), Slovenia (8.6%) and Malta (9.1%). The debt-to-income ratio exceeds 100% in Cyprus (251.0%), Portugal (198.5%), the Netherlands (177.1%), Spain (141.8%), Luxembourg (114.1%) and Ireland (102.1%), while it is below 50% in Poland (15.2%), Slovenia (24.9%), Austria (32.7%), Germany (38.1%), Estonia (38.3%), Slovakia (42.0%) and Latvia (42.8%). The variation across countries is lower for the debt-service-to-income ratio,

---

[42] Eurosystem's HSFC is described in Chapter 2.

TABLE 4.2 *Debt burden indicators, total and by country (conditional on participation; %; year 2016)*

	Debt-to-asset ratio	Debt-to-income ratio	Debt-service-to-income ratio
Austria	20.1	32.7	5.8
Belgium	18.7	79.8	13.4
Cyprus	22.9	251.0	35.7
Estonia	15.3	38.3	9.7
Finland	35.3	76.7	11.3
France	20.4	68.0	18.0
Germany	30.0	38.1	8.9
Greece	17.4	53.3	16.8
Hungary	20.2	60.3	16.4
Ireland	38.5	102.1	14.5
Italy	18.4	69.6	13.3
Latvia	28.2	42.8	11.4
Luxembourg	22.2	114.1	16.5
Malta	9.1	55.3	13.4
Netherlands	49.0	177.1	12.9
Poland	6.8	15.2	9.9
Portugal	37.8	198.5	16.2
Slovakia	12.6	42.0	11.1
Slovenia	8.6	24.9	12.6
Spain	22.6	141.8	19.1
Europe	25.7	71.8	13.5

Source: Eurosystem's HFCS

and there is also a change in the relative position of countries, which mainly reflect the different participation of households in the mortgage market.

The debt burden ratios are in most of the cases well below the threshold usually discriminating situations of over-indebtedness, (100% for the debt-to-asset and the debt-to-income ratio, 30% for the debt-service-to-income ratio – see section 4.2) therefore suggesting low levels of insolvency risk. However, it is relevant to point out that measures of central tendency[43] may mask considerable variation across households. In fact, when moving to the last quintile (i.e. the right tail of the distribution), the distribution of the ratios reflects situations of worrisome financial fragility.

Table 4.3 focuses on the debt-service-to-income ratio, and provides the value of the ratio at different levels of percentile. The focus is on percentiles above the median value, namely the 75th, 90th, 95th and 99th percentile of the distribution,

---

[43] Median values are values lying at the midpoint of a frequency distribution of observed values, such that there is an equal probability of falling above or below it.

TABLE 4.3 *The debt-service-to-income ratio: median and percentiles (conditional on participation; %; year 2016)*

	Debt-service-to-income ratio
Median	13.3
p75	23.2
p90	36.6
p95	52.0
p99	144.8

Source: authors' elaboration on Eurosystem's HFCS

in order to analyse the part of the distribution with higher levels of debt burden and point out whether, in this case, the value exceeds the threshold which identifies situations of over-indebtedness.[44]

For households in the bottom decile (p90), the debt-service-to-income ratio is three times higher than the median, and reaches the value of 36.6%; it means that there is 10% of the population with a debt service to income suggesting very high levels of insolvency risk. At the 95th percentile of the distribution the debt burden is even above 50% and for the last 1% the ratio is more than 100%, signalling no income left for living expensing after paying debt instalments.

4.6.2 *The Characteristics of Over-Indebted Consumers*

To analyse the sociodemographic and economic characteristics of groups of consumers characterised by similar levels of financial vulnerability, the sample is divided into quintiles on the basis of the level of debt-service-to-income ratio (Table 4.4). Each quintile identifies 20 per cent of households in the sample, from the least vulnerable (1st quintile) to the most vulnerable (5th quintile). In addition, the last column shows the values for the households group with a debt service to income higher than 30 per cent and therefore at risk of over-indebtedness.

Across quintiles, data highlight strong differences according to several sociodemographic and economic variables.

Regarding age, in the most vulnerable group (5th quintile) there are relatively more householders between 16 and 44 years (51.8%) compared to the first quintile (42.9%); conversely, the share of householder with more than 65 years is relatively higher. Besides, in the most vulnerable group there is a higher incidence of

[44] The percentile is a value on a scale of 100 that indicates the per cent of a distribution that is equal to or below its percentile in a sentence.

TABLE 4.4 *The debt-service-to-income ratio by quintile (conditional on participation; %; year 2016)*

	Quintile of debt-service-to-income ratio					Debt-service-to-income ratio > 30%
	1	2	3	4	5	
Gender						
Male	68.6	69.4	69.2	68.9	67.4	66.9
Female	31.4	30.6	30.8	31.2	32.6	33.1
Age						
16–34	23.4	15.2	15.2	19.8	20.9	20.6
35–44	19.5	24.3	27.5	32.4	30.9	30.5
45–54	22.7	26.5	28.8	26.3	24.3	24.4
55–64	20.2	21.9	17.5	13.7	15.5	16.5
65–74	9.6	8.8	8.1	6.6	6.2	6.0
over 75	4.5	3.1	2.9	1.2	2.1	1.9
Household size						
1	21.1	17.3	17.5	16.3	22.0	23.1
2	33.1	31.2	28.1	26.6	26.5	27.6
3	19.9	20.8	22.3	24.8	20.6	19.5
4	17.7	22.0	23.1	24.2	21.8	21.4
5 +	8.2	8.6	9.0	8.0	9.1	8.5
Level of education						
Primary	5.2	6.5	7.9	8.2	13.0	14.1
Lower secondary	11.1	11.0	10.3	11.9	15.9	16.7
Upper secondary	53.2	48.0	44.5	43.3	38.4	37.7
Tertiary	30.5	34.5	37.2	36.6	32.7	31.5
Quintile of income						
1	9.2	4.6	5.1	5.6	19.9	24.0
2	14.2	10.3	11.9	11.9	22.3	23.1
3	18.3	20.2	20.3	23.1	22.9	22.1
4	22.5	26.8	29.6	32.1	21.5	19.6
5	35.8	37.9	33.0	27.3	13.3	11.2
Quintile of wealth						
1	23.3	16.4	16.0	14.3	19.2	21.0
2	18.0	16.9	18.1	18.0	21.0	20.1
3	16.2	20.2	21.7	28.9	22.6	20.3
4	19.1	25.0	24.1	21.5	18.7	18.9
5	23.3	21.5	20.1	17.3	18.5	19.9
Work status						
Employee	62.3	70.3	71.6	73.9	57.9	54.5
Self-employed	8.1	8.7	7.6	9.6	16.4	18.9
Retired	17.5	15.7	14.1	9.7	11.8	11.5
Other not working	12.1	5.3	6.6	6.8	13.9	16.0
Expenses higher than income	14.8	15.1	15.7	17.6	26.1	27.5
To meet expenses:						
Sold assets	1.9	10.9	7.1	9.9	5.5	5.9

TABLE 4.4 (continued)

	Quintile of debt-service-to-income ratio					Debt-service-to-income ratio > 30%
	1	2	3	4	5	
Got a credit card/ overdraft facility	18.1	18.7	27.3	30.3	28.6	26.8
Got some other loan	35.3	36.8	36.7	25.9	21.2	22.4
Spent out of savings	53.4	56.1	50.5	57.3	46.6	45.3
Asked help from relatives and friends	25.7	28.9	27.3	23.9	37.6	38.9
Left some bills unpaid	11.2	13.3	17.3	22.1	39.1	42.0
Other	4.0	5.0	4.0	8.1	10.0	9.6
No. of observations	6,626	6,362	6,447	6,425	6,432	5,018 (15.5%)

Source: authors' elaboration on Eurosystem's HFCS

women (32.6%) compared to less vulnerable households in the first quintile (31.4%). In the most vulnerable group there is also a higher incidence of lower-educated households. Indeed, households with only primary or lower education in the last quintile are 42.2% compared to 16.3% in the first group. Households with upper secondary education drop from 53.2% in the first quintile to 38.4% in the last quintile.

As for type of work, the percentage of not-working households is quite similar across quintiles. However, data do not allow to distinguish between those who are unemployed and those who are not working for other reasons.

Regarding the level of income, the table shows very clearly that among the most vulnerable people there is a much higher incidence of low-income individuals. Indeed, among the most vulnerable subjects, the percentage of individuals with very low income (1 quintile) or low (2 quintile) income is 42.2%, against 23.46% among households with low levels of debt burden.

Similar considerations apply when focusing on the quintiles of net wealth. The most vulnerable groups are characterised by a lower level of wealth, while moving towards higher levels of wealth the presence of less vulnerable subjects is greater.

Finally, households with higher levels of debt burden are also those that, to a greater extent, report a level of expenditure higher than income (26.11% against 14.82% for less financially fragile individuals).

The table also highlights that 15.5% of the sample is over-indebted, with a debt-service-to-income ratio higher than 30% (last column). For this group of households, the sociodemographic and economic characteristics already identified for the fifth quintile are further exasperated: younger age, larger family size, lower level of education, lower level of income and wealth. When looking at the way they meet their expenses, it is also clear that they do not have any further access to credit and therefore rely on help from relatives and friends (38.9%) and leave bills unpaid (42%).

4.7 FOCUS ON CONSUMER CREDIT

The debt-service-to-income ratio has been analysed also for consumer credit only, to see if there are specificities in the over-indebted households holding this type of debt (Table 4.5). Data seem to confirm the literature.[45]

Indeed, the table highlights that almost 9% of the sample is over-indebted, with a non-mortgage service to income ratio higher than 25% (last column). In the group of over-indebted households for unsecured credit there is a much higher concentration of low-income individuals and individuals with a lower level of wealth. Almost 40% of households with an unmanageable debt have low levels of income, and 33% have low levels of wealth. There is also a higher concentration of low-educated households (37% with primary or lower secondary school), as well as a much stronger share of not-working individuals (23.7%), which is probably due to a higher incidence of unemployment. These individuals do not have further access to credit (the percentage of households that got a credit card or an overdraft facility is 8% lower compared to the fifth quintile), but rely more on their social networks (35.6% compared to 31.1% in the fifth quintile). The percentage of households not able to pay their bills increases to 40% (compared to 32% in the fifth quintile). Interestingly, data highlight a relevant share of retired households among over-indebted households; this finding is surprising and does not account for the life-cycle theory. Of course, for individuals already in the highest quintile of the distribution even moderate external shocks, due to macroeconomic factor or personal life event, can easily lead to repayment defaults.

4.8 BEHAVIOURAL FACTORS AND OVER-INDEBTEDNESS

Besides sociodemographic and economic variables, recent studies in behavioural economics have made an important contribution in drawing attention to the role played on debt decision-making by personal attitudes, suggesting that several psychological factors affect consumers' debt decisions and risk of over-indebtedness.[46] The underlying idea is that the behaviour of individuals deviates systematically from the assumptions of *homo oeconomicus* behind the life-cycle theory (see Chapter 2), and they may become over-indebted because of behaviours that conflict with traditional notions of economic rationality.[47]

---

[45] Albacete and Lindner (2013); Del Rio and Young (2008); Ottaviani and Vandone (2011); Zavadil and Messner (2014).
[46] Karlsson et al. (2004); Lea et al. (1995).
[47] Rationality as a concept adopted in economic theory consists in a series of hypothetical, regularised preferences on the part of an individual described by their utility function.

TABLE 4.5 *Consumer-credit-service-to-income ratio by quintile (conditional on participation; %; year 2016)*

	Quintile of consumer-credit-service-to-income ratio					Consumer-credit-service-to-income ratio > 25%
	1	2	3	4	5	
Gender						
Male	68.3	68.1	67.1	67.8	67.1	66.9
Female	31.7	31.9	32.9	32.2	32.9	33.1
Age						
16–34	32.9	20.6	22.0	19.6	17.9	18.4
35–44	24.5	25.3	23.1	21.1	24.5	24.9
45–54	19.9	22.3	24.9	24.2	25.6	23.4
55–64	16.3	17.1	20.1	21.1	19.1	21.1
65–74	4.7	10.0	7.0	9.6	10.3	9.2
over 75	1.7	4.5	2.9	4.2	2.5	2.8
Household size						
1	20.0	16.7	18.1	24.3	26.0	28.8
2	31.3	29.5	28.7	30.8	28.9	28.2
3	19.8	23.5	19.1	18.8	17.7	15.7
4	20.2	21.4	24.4	18.0	19.9	19.7
5 +	8.7	8.9	9.5	8.0	7.5	7.6
Level of education						
Primary	3.1	6.5	8.7	11.8	16.8	17.1
Lower secondary	9.1	11.9	10.7	13.5	17.0	20.4
Upper secondary	55.0	48.7	51.8	49.6	44.2	45.6
Tertiary	32.8	32.9	28.7	25.2	22.0	16.9
Quintile of income						
1	12.0	5.0	6.0	9.0	26.1	39.8
2	14.4	12.8	13.1	17.6	23.2	23.0
3	17.7	19.3	24.4	30.7	22.2	18.4
4	23.7	26.5	31.4	26.5	19.2	12.5
5	32.2	36.4	25.1	16.3	9.3	6.3
Quintile of wealth						
1	28.9	22.2	23.6	28.9	31.8	32.5
2	19.9	19.8	23.7	19.5	17.3	17.3
3	20.6	18.8	20.4	17.6	19.2	16.8
4	14.0	19.8	20.6	21.2	17.6	16.4
5	16.3	19.3	11.8	12.8	14.1	17.0
Work status						
Employee	68.4	68.7	70.1	63.9	52.6	37.7
Self-employed	6.1	7.1	8.2	8.45	12.9	20.3
Retired	8.3	18.0	14.5	19.8	17.6	18.2
Other not working	17.2	6.1	7.1	7.7	16.8	23.7
Expenses higher than income	17.3	19.2	19.8	21.4	26.9	30.2

TABLE 4.5 *(continued)*

	Quintile of consumer-credit-service-to-income ratio					Consumer-credit-service-to-income ratio > 25%
	1	2	3	4	5	
To meet expenses:						
Sold assets	2.5	4.9	7.9	5.9	5.0	5.7
Got a credit card/overdraft facility	18.6	28.6	33.1	35.7	32.5	24.5
Got some other loan	34.1	38.6	44.2	41.1	41.3	38.8
Spent out of savings	45.8	47.7	49.8	43.1	39.5	42.9
Asked help from relatives and friends	33.7	26.9	31.9	33.1	31.1	35.6
Left some bills unpaid	18.9	16.4	19.2	23.5	31.9	40.2
Other	3.8	7.6	10.2	7.1	11.5	8.5
No. of observations	3,481	3,474	3,476	3,473	3,472	1,514 (8.7%)

Source: authors' elaboration on Eurosystem's HFCS

There are many psychological factors identified in the literature as inducing consumers to make non-rational borrowing choices, such as perception of risk, personality, materialism, anxiety, optimism and impulsivity.[48] Among those factors, impulsivity appears to play a major role.

From an economic perspective, impulsivity is linked to the concept of hyperbolic discount,[49] which is a psychological bias according to which impulsive individuals tend to systematically overvalue immediate costs and benefits and undervalue those in the future.[50] Therefore, they make decisions motivated more by immediate reward rather than by the potential long-term negative outcomes of their choices.[51]

---

[48] Karlsson et al. (2004); Lea et al. (1995); for a more recent literature review, see Kamleitner et al. (2012).
[49] Franken et al. (2008); Zermatten et al. (2005).
[50] The discounted utility approach states that individuals show a preference for the reward that arrives sooner rather than later. In economics, this process is traditionally modelled in the form of a time-consistent model of discounting. However, a large number of studies have highlighted deviations from the constant discount rate assumed in the model, and the hyperbolic discounting accounts for these deviations. The most important consequence of hyperbolic discounting is that individuals using hyperbolic discounting reveal a strong tendency to make choices that are inconsistent over time; they overestimate the duration of time intervals and, as a consequence, discount the value of delayed rewards more than do self-controlled individuals (Wittmann and Paulus 2008). Steep discounting of delayed rewards denotes impulsivity and impatience, whereas being willing to wait for larger rewards is assumed to reflect self-control. An individual is more likely to purchase a product on credit that he cannot afford because the loss associated with the purchase (in terms of available financial resources) is delayed, and so the costs are discounted.
[51] Martin and Potts (2009).

When it comes to decision to demand for debt, impulsivity pushes individuals, at the time they have to decide whether to purchase on credit terms or not, to opt for immediate purchase. They go for 'buy now, pay later' solutions that bring immediate gratification at a future cost, disregarding the ensuing sustainability of debt.[52] In general, high impulsive individuals are biased towards immediate rewards when evaluating options and are less sensitive to the negative consequences of their choices.[53]

Much empirical evidence supports the view that impulsive individuals have a higher propensity to take on debt, in particular unsecured debt.[54] In an interdisciplinary study, Ottaviani and Vandone (2011) estimated the role of personal factors in determining participation in the debt market on a sample of individuals that underwent the Iowa gambling task while electrodermal responses were recorded. The results revealed the significant influence of individuals' impulsivity in making debt decisions, after controlling for traditional sociodemographic and economic variables. Interestingly, impulsivity predicted consumer credit, but it was not significantly associated with mortgages. As mentioned in Chapter 2, the rationale may be that while mortgage debt decisions are related to large amounts of debt that will be repaid over a long period of time, unsecured debt decisions are largely determined by short-run benefits more influenced by behavioural patterns like impatience, materialism, satisfaction and self-esteem,[55] which may lead the individual to buy on credit terms, without necessarily being fully aware of the sustainability of the debt.

Meier and Sprenger (2010) analyse the time preferences of a sample of US individuals and find that individuals who exhibit a particular desire for immediate consumption have higher probability to borrow and to have higher credit card balances. Achtziger et al. (2015) use a sample of the German population, who underwent the subscale self-discipline with eleven items of the SCS,[56] to explore the link between self-control, compulsive-buying behaviour and debt. The empirical analysis highlights that individuals with low self-control are more at risk to run into debt problems because they are not able either to resist the temptation to buy something they easily desire in a given moment, or to control negative emotions that may induce compensatory responses such as purchases. Consistently, Limerick and Peltier (2014) highlight a positive relation between impulsivity and higher credit card balances on a sample of college students. Similarly, Pirog and Roberts (2007) using survey data from US college students find evidence of the role

---

[52] Meier and Sprenger (2010); Siemens (2007).
[53] Martin and Potts (2009); Potts et al. (2006).
[54] Ibid.
[55] Dittmar and Bond (2010).
[56] Tangney et al. (2004).

that impulsiveness plays in credit card misuse, and empirically highlight the link between failure in self-control, impulsive spending and compulsive buying.

Omar et al. (2014) focus on the relation between personal traits and credit card misuse and find that compulsive-buying behaviour is the more relevant factor driving debt rise and repayment problems. Similar results are in Wang et al. (2011), that find that compulsiveness is associated with higher frequency of revolving credit card use. Shui and Ausubel (2004) report that impulsivity, and therefore time inconsistencies, lead consumers to choose credit cards with lower introductory interest rates to those with higher initial rates, although in the long run the latter is a better choice because the effective interest rates are lower. Using survey data on households, Vandone et al. (2012) and Gathergood (2012) found that low levels of self-control predicted over-indebtedness and increase the risk of being exposed to adverse financial shocks.

Point-of-purchase stimuli, logos, advertisements, discounts, product design, marketing channel innovation and sale promotions constitute examples of efforts to activate impulsive behaviour.[57] Heidhues and Koszegi (2010) also highlight that many features of consumer credit contracts are consistent with individuals' time inconsistent preferences.

Psychological biases other than the hyperbolic discount are identified in the literature as inducing individuals to make non-rational financial choices. Two of them may be relevant in debt decisions, i.e. the overconfidence bias and the availability heuristic, although no empirical studies have specifically analysed the magnitude of the effect. The overconfidence is a bias in which a person's subjective confidence in his or her judgement is reliably greater than the objective accuracy of those judgements, especially when confidence is relatively high. As regards debt decisions, individuals that tend to be over-optimistic about their own exposure to risk may believe that they are capable of managing their level of indebtedness, whatever that may be. As a result, they systematically underestimate the probability of being hit by adverse events (illness, job loss, etc.) that can lead to financial fragility and over-indebtedness and overestimate their capacities in managing household resources. The availability heuristic is a mental shortcut that relies on immediate examples that come to a given person's mind when evaluating a specific topic, concept, method or decision. The more frequent and recent the event occurred, the more likely it is that individuals will overestimate the probability of a similar event happening again; vice versa, the less frequent and more remote in time the event took place, the more likely it is that individuals will underestimate the probability of a similar event's reoccurring. As regards debt, if experiences of certain adverse events, such as liquidity crises, financial difficulties or over-indebtedness, are not available, individuals will tend to underestimate the chances of being affected by

---

[57] Jones et al. (2003); McCall et al. (2004).

such events. What is more, even if the same individuals were regularly exposed to statistics illustrating insolvency rates among other people, the impersonal nature of such information may mean it is not effective.

4.9 THE RELEVANCE OF BEHAVIOURAL TRAITS IN THE EFFECTIVENESS OF MEASURES TO PREVENT OVER-INDEBTEDNESS

Impulsivity and other behavioural traits do not only cause a higher risk of over-indebtedness, but also negatively influence the effectiveness of measures designed to prevent situation of financial distress. Indeed, studies carried out within behavioural economics have highlighted that individuals have little awareness of the existence and consequences these psychological mechanisms have. Furthermore, these studies have shown how deviant behaviour patterns persist even when individuals are aware of the risks they face.[58] Therefore, consumers' incapacity to take corrective steps despite knowing of the dangers of over-indebtedness may have significant repercussions in designing effective policies for the management of situations of indebtedness that are at risk of becoming pathological. In fact, recent studies highlight that behavioural traits may challenge the beneficial impact of financial literacy in reducing the risk of over-indebtedness.

4.9.1 *Financial Education as a Tool to Improve 'Responsible Borrowing'*

Financial literacy is considered a key element in debt decision and a relevant tool in improving 'responsible borrowing', since it contributes to improve individuals' capacity to understand financial information and take informed decisions, help them to choose the right debt product for their need and to plan strategies to reach difficult financial goals and to put into place solutions designed to safeguard the financial future.

In recent years, a growing number of studies have focused on the relevance of financial literacy in improving individuals' capacity to understand financial information and raise awareness about the implications of debt, and have highlighted that the level of financial illiteracy is higher for individuals holding higher levels of debt-to-income and that the same individuals also have higher shares of high-cost credit.[59]

Lusardi and Tufano (2015) specifically focus on debt literacy, defined as the ability to make simple decisions regarding debt contracts and applying basic knowledge about interest compounding to everyday financial choices. They analyse gap in debt literacy for a sample of Americans and find generalised low level of debt literacy

---

[58] Kilborn (2005); Lea et al. (1995); Watson (2009).
[59] Braunstein and Welch (2002); Disney and Gathergood (2013); Lusardi and Tufano (2015); Robb (2011).

across the population. In particular, as for credit card behaviour, the authors find that less knowledgeable cardholders pay higher average charges and fees, and roll over their debt more frequently compared to their benchmark. Besides, those with lower levels of debt literacy report that they have accumulated too much debt or have difficulty in paying off debt, thus signalling a link between debt literacy and over-indebtedness after controlling for several individual characteristics.

Gathergood and Weber (2017) use a sample of UK mortgage holders to investigate the effect of financial knowledge in the choice between different mortgage products with different costs and find that individuals with a lower level of financial literacy are more likely to hold riskier mortgages, such as alternative mortgage products (AMPs) with a linked investment vehicle. Similarly, Moore (2003) highlights that individuals with lower levels of financial knowledge are more likely to hold costly mortgages.

Robb (2011) examines the relationship between financial knowledge and credit card behaviour for a sample of college students, given the strong growth in the availability by financial intermediaries of consumer credit in the form of credit cards among this market segment, and rising concerns related to the consequences of misuse of credit cards and greater debt burden in the long run. Empirical findings highlight that students with higher levels of financial knowledge display more responsible credit card use, since they are less likely to have a card at the maximum limit and are more likely to report always paying off their credit card. Disney and Gathergood (2013) specifically focus on the link between financial literacy and consumer credit and report several findings signalling a link between knowledge and the composition of consumer credit portfolios. In particular, the authors report that households with low levels of financial literacy are less able to interpret information on the cost of credit products and, as a consequence, hold a more costly portfolios of credit. They are also less likely to engage in behaviour which may help them to improve their awareness of the credit market (such as reading the finance-related pages in the news media).

Overall, several factors fuel the urgency surrounding financial literacy – such as the broader spectrum of services by a wider array of providers, predatory lending, high levels of consumer debt, low saving rate – and highlight how financial literacy deficiencies may affect household day-to-day money management and make consumers vulnerable to financial crises.[60]

4.9.2 Financial Education Initiatives in Europe

Given the relevance of the issue, EU regulatory authorities have started devoting efforts and resources to improve households' financial literacy, considered a key driver in softening households' financial vulnerability. Two recent reports provide

---

[60] Braunstein and Welch (2002).

an overview of financial education programmes and best practices in Europe.[61] These initiatives are targeted at the general population as well as at specific target groups, such as the over-indebted, students, unemployed, migrants and are developed both at European Union level and at national level.

The European Commission has been active in the promotion of financial education since the 2008 crisis. Indeed, the Communication from the European Commission on financial education COM(2007) 808 underlines the need to provide financial education within the European Union to citizens of all stages of life and points out the potential economic and social benefits deriving from it. In the documents, several basic principles for the provision of high-quality financial education schemes are set out, which includes the fact the financial education should be available and actively promoted at all stages of life on a continuous basis and that consumers should be educated in economic and financial matters beginning at school. Dolceta ('Developing On-Line Consumer Education and Training for Adults') represents one of the main initial steps by the European Union to address financial education. It was a website, translated into all Community languages and adapted to the specific characteristics of each national market, which included modules dedicated to financial services consumer credit, mortgages, means of payment and investments, targeted at helping teachers incorporating financial issues into the school curriculum but also directly accessible by any individuals.

Behind EU policy responses, several national strategies have been developed over years across European countries, showing a certain degree of heterogeneity in terms of the role of public authorities in the national strategies, the direct or indirect involvement of private and not-for-profit stakeholders, policy priorities and target groups.

For example, Spain is one of the countries that have already implemented and revised a national strategy. Indeed, the Bank of Spain, together with the stock market authority (Comision Nacional de Mercado de Valores) and several collaboration agreements with the banking industry association and consumer associations, implemented in 2008 the first financial education plan targeted at the general population (Plan de Educacion Financiera) subsequently revised in 2013 with specific instruments for young people. A website[62] was developed for disseminating information on managing basic and household economics and a brand logo (Finanzasparatodos) helped the exposure and visibility of the programme. A pilot programme targeted at the young in collaboration with the Ministry of the Education was introduced in the 2010 academic year. It had the aim to teach personal finance and basic concepts such

---

[61] European Economic and Social Committee (2014); OECD (2016).
[62] www.finanzasparatodos.es

as savings, responsible consumption, means of payments and the value of money. Nowadays, financial education programmes are included both in primary school and secondary school. The website also provides teachers with resources, games and other tools to teach financial education at school.

The United Kingdom also implemented a comprehensive national strategy, which was initially overseen by the Financial Service Authority and later by the Money Advice Service, an independent body set up by the government and responsible for financial education and consumer advice.[63] The financial capability strategy includes several actions such as the campaign about the pension scheme reforms, education programmes for vulnerable groups, including migrants, training programmes for teachers together with teaching materials, and also a "divorce calculator", which is aimed at calculating the costs associated with divorce and help to plan finances in the new circumstances and a "mortgage affordability calculator" to estimate the amount to borrow given income and other outgoings. The coverage of the national strategy also includes specific programmes targeted at expectant mothers, with basic concepts regarding household finance, parent's guide to money distributed for the birth of a child, and awareness-raising videos produced using real cases which illustrate everyday life situations relating to finances.

The financial sector is also indirectly involved in the UK's national strategy through mandatory financial support. More in general, direct and indirect involvement of private and not-for-profit-institutions alongside public ones is quite common across countries. In the Netherlands, the MoneyWise Platform,[64] developed by the Ministry of Finance together with the central bank, the stock market authority, the banking and the insurance association, includes also more than 40 partners from the financial sector and consumers associations involved in the implementation of the national strategy. Similarly, in the Czech Republic the working group on financial education consists on representatives of the government, professional associations and consumer associations.[65]

As already pointed out, financial education programmes are also targeted at specific group of individuals like vulnerable people, those in low income, migrants, the unemployed. For example, the Danish Money and Pension panel[66] delivers teaching materials on budgeting and loans which is distributed at all jobcentres, while the Microfinance Centre in Poland provides financial education programmes for low-income households across Eastern Europe.[67]

---

[63] www.moneyadviceservice.org.uk/en
[64] www.wijzeringeldzaken.nl
[65] www.mfcr.cz
[66] www.finanstilsynet.dk
[67] mfc.org.pl

4.9.3 Behavioural Factors and Financial Education

Whereas it seems plausible and intuitive that financial education programmes or other public policy measures adopted to improve individuals' understanding of basic concepts in finance would be beneficial, existing studies offer mixed evidence on the effectiveness of such interventions. A crucial but often neglected point is that such educational programmes may be effective or not depending on certain behavioural characteristics of the user. A growing body of literature is focusing on this issue.

Gathergood (2012), in examining how financial literacy and self-control relate to consumer over-indebtedness, shows that both poor financial literacy and self-control problems are positively associated with over-indebtedness, but the second plays a more statistically significant role in the model. A plausible reason might be that consumers with self-control problems are more likely to use forms of credit that facilitate impulse-driven purchases (quick access to funds, close to point of purchase), which usually bear higher cost of credit. Along the same lines, Meier and Sprenger (2013) analyse time preferences and financial information acquisitions, concluding that impatient individuals are a critical group since they heavily discount the benefits of being financially literate and, as a consequence, are less likely to participate in credit counselling programmes even though those programmes are provided for free. Other studies offer mixed evidence on the effectiveness of financial education programmes or other public policy measures adopted to improve individuals' understanding of basic concepts in finance.[68]

Besides, on the basis of the financial education received, individuals may also overrate their ability to evaluate correctly the risk and subsequent impact, for instance, of taking out a loan,[69] while many researches on biases in judgement and decision-making have shown that individuals tend to display overconfidence about their ability to manage resources but also overconfidence about their knowledge. Due to overconfidence, people often believe that they know more than they actually do, and this can have negative consequences since it affects decision-making because individuals overestimate their own judgements relative to other input, that is for example all the technical information provided by financial education programmes.

As for debt counselling services designed to raise awareness about the implications of debt, Hung and Yoon (2010) find that expanding access to advice can have positive effects, particularly for the less financially literate. Besides, debt advice agencies are helpful since they also offer ex post support for the management of situations of difficulty when these emerge, to help households to get their finances back on track.[70] At the same time, more extensive compulsory programmes of financial

---

[68] Fernandes et al. (2014); Willis (2011).
[69] Willis (2008).
[70] Measures range from simple advice services to more complex help with out-of-court agreements and formal debt settlement procedures, as well as access to special rate consolidation loans. Networks of

counselling may be ultimately ineffective if the target population, despite lacking the necessary skills, is not inherently prepared to take advice.

The next section contributes to this relatively new field of research with an empirical analysis that investigates the relationship among impulsivity, financial education and debt decision.

4.9.4 Over-Indebtedness, Financial Literacy and Impulsivity: an Empirical Analysis

The empirical literature reported in the previous sections highlighted two relevant findings which work in two opposite directions:

- among personal traits impulsivity is one of the major driver of over-indebtedness, in particular when consumer credit is concerned;
- financial literacy supports informed decisions and reduces the risk of over-indebtedness.

Therefore, it is relevant to investigate the extent to which impulsivity plays any role in weakening the positive impact of financial literacy on household debt decisions and debt burden.

This empirical analysis is based on a sample of 445 individuals: 348 men and 97 women who underwent a series of questions about demographic-socio-economic information (e.g. household composition, demographic data, real and financial wealth, personal financial choices) and the Barratt Impulsiveness Scale (BIS–11),[71] which is a measure of impulsivity.[72]

A financial literacy indicator was created ad hoc to take into account several components such as knowledge about different types of financial product (i.e. from simple to more sophisticated products), time dedicated to read and understand financial information, awareness about the payoff of financial investments and the dynamics of the cost of indebtedness. The indicator was created to fill a gap, as there

---

counselling agencies are not equally developed in Europe; they are well established in the north of Europe, while in other countries they are at an early stage of development or still unavailable, such as Hungary, Lithuania, Romania, Slovakia. A good example of publicly funded debt advice service is the Money Advice Service in the UK. In other countries (e.g. Finland and the Netherlands), there is a statutory obligation for local authorities to provide debt advice. Funding is considered a key issue for the effectiveness of this service, in order to meet demand in a timely manner and to provide the comprehensive geographical coverage that many Member States lacked. A detailed analysis of debt advice provision in Europe is in Civic Consulting (2013).

[71] Patton et al. (1995).
[72] The BIS–11 is a validated measure of impulsivity that has been extensively used in impulsivity-related research for over fifty years. The BIS–11 consists of thirty items that are answered on a 4-point scale ranging from rarely–never to almost always–always. It provides a total score and separate scores for three subscales measuring different aspects of impulsiveness: motor (acting without thinking; e.g. 'I do things without thinking'), non-planning (lack of future orientation or forethought; e.g. 'I plan for job security'), and attentional impulsiveness (inability to focus attention or concentrate; e.g. 'I don't pay attention').

are currently no standardised instruments to measure financial literacy and the definition of financial literacy metrics is still an open issue. Specifically, as underlined in Huston (2010) there are still three barriers to creating a successful measure of financial literacy: the lack of conceptualisation and definition of financial literacy; the lack of a comprehensive measure of financial literacy; the lack of clarity for measurement interpretation. In fact, the strength of the above-mentioned ad hoc indicator is that it jointly analyses – among available information – different features and profiles of household financial literacy. The principal component analysis is then used in order to compact, from a statistical viewpoint, the dimensionality of the problem and check for a reduced number of appropriate combinations of the original variables.[73] A variable with a higher score is associated with a higher level of financial literacy and vice versa. From a descriptive point of view, the financial literacy indicator was characterised by a mean value of 7.42 (2.35) and ranged from 0 to 10.

A hierarchical regression analysis was then conducted to test for the role of financial literacy (Model 1), and impulsivity (Model 2) in the prediction of debt burden, controlling for the traditional socio-economic predictors (age, family size, financial wealth; Model 3). The debt-service-to-income ratio (debt burden) served as the dependent variable. This ratio provides an indicator of the burden that debt holdings represent to current income and reflects more the significance of short-term commitments.

The following model was computed:

$$\text{debtburden}_i = \beta_0 + \beta_1 \text{finlit}_i + \beta_2 \text{impuls}_i + \beta_3 \text{control}_i + \beta_i + \varepsilon_i$$

where finlit_i (financial literacy score) measures the impact of financial literacy on debt burden, impuls_i (Barratt Impulsiveness Scale) refers to impulsivity, control_i is a vector of control variables, β's are the related coefficient, and ε_i is the residual term. All the estimates were performed by OLS with standard errors robust to heteroscedasticity.

Intercorrelations between the key variables of the present study are illustrated in Table 4.6.

As shown in Table 4.7, Model 1 in the hierarchical regression analysis indicates that financial literacy is a significant predictor of debt burden (p = 0.05). Interestingly, in Model 2, impulsivity resulted as a significant predictor (p = 0.01) but its inclusion made financial literacy no longer significant (p = 0.16). The inclusion of traditional socio-economic predictors did not change the role of impulsivity as a significant predictor (p = 0.02). None of the traditional socio-economic predictors appeared to be a significant predictor in Model 3 (ps > 0.1). The absence of excessive multi-collinearity was suggested by variance inflating factors not substantially greater than 1 and tolerance well above 0.2.

---

[73] See Ottaviani and Vandone (2018) for a detailed explanation of the index and interpretation of the components derived from PCA.

TABLE 4.6 *Correlation matrix between key variables of the study*

	1	2	3	4	5	6
1. Debt burden	1	.07	−.11*	−.08***	.20**	−.12*
2. Family size		1	.16**	.25**	.03	−.02
3. Financial wealth			1	.10*	−.08	.22**
4. Age				1	−.02	−.12
5. Impulsivity					1	−.17**
6. Financial literacy						1

Source: authors' elaborations
Notes: *$p < .05$; **$p < .01$; ***$p < .06$

TABLE 4.7 *Hierarchical regression analysis for the prediction of debt burden*

	Model 1			Model 2			Model 3		
	B	SE	β	B	SE	β	B	SE	β
Financial literacy score	−.14	.08	−.12*	−.11	.08	−.09	−.09	.08	−.08
Impulsivity				.06	.02	.17**	.06	.02	.16**
Age							.03	.02	.11
Family size							−.03	.10	−.02
Financial wealth (log)							−.05	.21	−.02
R^2	.014			.041			.051		

Source: authors' elaborations
Notes: *$p < .05$; **$p < .01$. B = unstandardised regression coefficient; SE = standard error; β = standardised regression coefficient.

Finally, for a better understanding of the role of impulsivity in the relationship between financial literacy and debt burden, a bootstrapping test of mediation using the Preacher and Hayes (2008) process macro with 5,000 bootstrap samples was performed with debt burden as the dependent variable, financial literacy as the independent variable, and impulsivity as the intermediary variable.

Mediation analysis has the interrelationship between the examined variables as a prerequisite. As already established in the literature, financial illiteracy is positively related to debt burden,[74] while impulsivity is positively related to debt burden,[75] and negatively related to financial literacy.[76] Therefore, the question arises whether the

---

[74] Disney and Gathergood (2013); Lusardi and Tufano (2015).
[75] Henegar et al. (2013); Limerick and Peltier (2014); Meier and Sprenger (2010); Ottaviani and Vandone (2011); Verplanken and Sato (2011).
[76] Meier and Sprenger (2013).

inclusion of impulsivity drops the relationship between the independent variable and the dependent variable.

Among the traditional predictors (age, family size, financial wealth), those that resulted significantly correlated with our dependent variables were included as covariates in the mediation model. A confidence interval for the size of the indirect path is generated (i.e. the reduction of the effect of the causal variable on the outcome due to the mediator) and, if the values between the upper and lower confidence limits do not include zero, this indicates a statistically significant mediation effect. This approach provides standardised betas for the indirect effect estimates (reflecting the amount of mediation), and the corresponding 95 per cent bias-corrected and accelerated confidence intervals.

As depicted in Figure 4.1, mediation analysis showed that impulsivity was a significant mediator of the impact of financial literacy on debt ($\beta = 0.06$, 95% CI [0.01; 0.10]; Sobel $z = -1.73$, $p = 0.05$). Moreover, after including impulsivity as a mediator, the direct effect of financial literacy on debt became non-significant ($\beta = -0.11$, 95% CI [−0.26; 0.04]) indicating full mediation. Approximately 4 per cent of the variance in debt burden was accounted for by the predictors ($R_2 = 0.04$; $p = 0.01$). Financial wealth did not play a significant role as a covariate in this analysis.

Overall, empirical evidence highlights that poor financial literacy and impulsivity are both positively associated with debt. This means that if these two characteristics are taken into account individually, they both play a significant role in determining debt burden. However, when both are simultaneously considered, impulsivity appears to be a full mediator of the relationship between financial literacy and debt burden. In other words, the effect of financial literacy on debt vanishes when impulsivity is taken into account. Interestingly, impulsivity also resulted negatively correlated with financial literacy: impulsive individuals have poorer levels of financial literacy. Similarly, Meier and Sprengen (2013), provide compelling evidence for an association between time preferences and the decision to acquire financial information. The authors show that acquiring financial information does not represent an attractive investment for impatient (impulsive) individuals, suggesting that these individuals do not participate in financial education programmes. Here, those findings are taken a step further, showing that impulsivity neutralises the positive effects of financial literacy on debt.

Therefore, although financial education initiatives and services provided by debt counselling agencies certainly help to improve individuals' ability to borrow responsibly, for groups of individuals with specific personal traits, financial education may be ineffective because these individuals may in any case not be able to alter significantly behaviour patterns that lead them to over-borrow.

These results call for the need to either target specific financial education programmes to impulsive individuals or to associate them with effective ways of

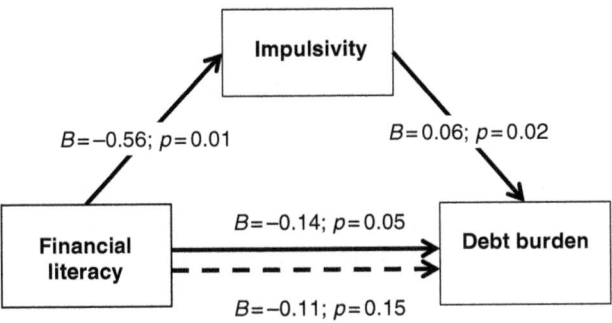

FIGURE 4.1 The mediation analysis
Source: authors' elaborations

reducing impulsive behaviours (e.g. cognitive-behavioural practices). Indeed, it seems clear that 'one-size-fits-all' programmes are unlikely to be effective, since they may not have significant effects on the most vulnerable subjects. If this were the case, lack of self-control instead of lack of financial literacy would be the key ingredient in credit decisions. In fact, if trait dispositions expose individuals to the risk of financial vulnerability and, at the same time, impair them to fully benefit from 'ordinary' financial education programmes, policymakers should think of designing financial programmes that are attractive to this specific and vulnerable target population.

4.10 REMARKS

Overall, several aspects emerge from the empirical analysis of the characteristics of over-indebted consumers. In fact, although the median values of debt burden indicators are below the threshold usually adopted to identify situation of over-indebtedness, the variation across country is considerable. Besides, when moving from measures of central tendency to the right tail of the distribution, where households with higher levels of burden are concentrated, the value of the ratios reflects situation of worrisome financial fragility. In particular, statistical analysis highlights that over-indebtedness mainly affects the economically and socially weakest members of society. Indeed, low-income households and the unemployed are the most financially fragile and exposed to the risk of holding unmanageable debts, as well as the younger and large-sized families. Behavioural traits, in particular impulsivity, may also exacerbate the phenomenon by pushing consumers to opt for buy-now-pay-later solutions regardless of the burden of debt. Furthermore, exogenous macro-economic factors – above all job loss – may easily turn a situation of manageable debt into financial distress.[77]

---

[77] Vandone (2009); Vandone and Anderloni (2016).

Over-indebtedness is therefore a multifaceted phenomenon, caused by a combination of economic, social, behavioural, cultural and institutional factors which need to be tackled with multidimensional and integrated government policy responses, with the aim of preventing and resolving over-indebtedness, not just alleviating or managing it. This is particularly relevant in light of the fact that, since the 2008 crisis, exogenous shocks have negatively affected real income of the majority of consumers. Not only because of higher levels of unemployment, but also for austerity measures in response to the 2011 sovereign debt crisis in most European countries, which have included, among others, cuts in social benefits, tax increases, reduction of wages in some sectors, like the public sector. All these changes may have exacerbated the financial difficulties of those already in difficulty or push previously solvent households into over-indebtedness. The situation need to be addressed by policymakers and governments for the repercussions that over-indebtedness can have at the micro level in terms of social and financial exclusion, as well as mental and physical health,[78] on the stability of the financial system[79] and on the well-being of society as a whole.[80]

---

[78] Brown et al. (2005); Drentea and Reynolds (2012); Hojman et al. (2016); Meltzer et al. (2011); Sweet et al. (2013).
[79] Ampudia et al. (2014); Albeceite and Lindner (2013); Zavadil Messner (2014).
[80] Chmelar (2012).

5

EU Policy and Law for the Prevention and Management of Over-Indebtedness

5.1 THE COMPETENCE OF THE EU VIS-À-VIS NATIONAL COMPETENCE

Regulatory measures adopted to tackle over-indebtedness can be typically categorised into preventive and curative. Preventive measures are aimed at preventing situations of solvency turning into financial distress; they can be further classified into 'responsible credit' measure to include both responsible lending and responsible borrowing behaviours. Curative measures are various *ex post* responses to default, such as debt management and restructuring schemes, debt settlement procedures or legal procedures for the discharge of debt – collectively referred as personal insolvency measures. Both sets of measures have dual aims: on one hand, to avoid active over-indebtedness; on the other, to prevent or reduce the seriousness of either active or passive over-indebtedness by offering advice and legal solutions that allow consumers to manage more effectively the effects of adverse shocks that can negatively impact their financial situation.

Generally, it has long been disputed to what extent it is the task of the EU legislator instead of national ones to intervene with regulation to tackle consumer over-indebtedness and stem private debt problems.

Until the Maastricht Treaty in 1993 and the establishment of the single market, over-indebtedness was perceived as a purely internal matter to be addressed by national authorities. By the late 1980s there were already a number of national initiatives introducing personal bankruptcy or debt counselling services to seek solutions to household debt problems. They represented the response to the consequences of the rapid increase in the volume and variety of credit services in some Member States, especially in northern Europe, reflecting a significant gap in the use and pattern of consumer borrowing across the then European Community (now Union).

However, following the opening-up and integration of national credit markets under EU impetus, an increasing number of reports and literature have started pointing to the adoption of common principles or convergence towards a European approach to the over-indebtedness of consumers. Such scholarship is often directed towards debt restructuring or consumer insolvency regimes to capture common traits or trends towards possible convergence[1]

At the same time, debates over of the division of competences between the EU and the national policymakers, alongside issues of subsidiarity, have cast doubts over the appropriate level of responses.[2]

Nevertheless, at least pragmatically it has to be acknowledged that consumers are key economic agents of credit markets inevitably encapsulated in the process of integration under EU law. In this framework, the EU has already affirmed competence in the areas of consumer credit and mortgages.[3]

In line with the efforts to achieve a single market in credit for consumers, the EU policy response to over-indebtedness has been limited in terms of preventively delivering a credit market that is 'responsible'. The main objective of EU measures to achieve a responsible internal market points to the creation of a regime which encourages vigorous competition, innovation and choice within a trusty framework that favours access to credit and rejects unfair and irresponsible practices.[4] The main drive remains the economic one of enabling consumers and businesses to take full advantage of the single market.[5]

By contrast, the intertwined situation of consumer defaults and debt solutions have not been included in such policies and legal responses. Many studies have stressed that national legal traditions, local institutional structures or cultural

---

[1] e.g. see Braucher (2006); Micklitz (2013a); Ramsay (2012a). For a complete overview of EU-commissioned studies, see Kilborn (August 2010). See also European Economic and Social Committee, *Opinion of the Economic and Social Committee on 'Household over-indebtedness'* (2002/c 149/01); *Opinion of the Economic and Social Committee on 'Consumer protection and appropriate treatment of over-indebtedness to prevent social exclusion'* (Exploratory opinion), INT/726 (Brussels, 29 April 2014).

[2] e.g. see Comparato (2015); Loos (2010); Weatherill (2010).

[3] See Directive 2008/48/EC of the European Parliament and of the Council of 23 April 2008 on credit agreements for consumers and repealing Council Directive 87/102/EEC, L 133/66; Directive 2014/17/EU of the European Parliament and of the Council of 4 February 2014 on credit agreements for consumers relating to residential immovable property and amending Directives 2008/48/EC and 2013/36/EU and Regulation (EU) No. 1093/2010, L 60/34.

[4] See European Commission, *Communication of the European Commission to the European Council of 4 March 2009 'Driving European Recovery'*, COM(2009) 114 and the *Public Consultation on Responsible Lending and Borrowing*, at http://ec.europa.eu/internal ... /responsible_lending/consultation_en.pdf

[5] See e.g. European Commission, *Discussion Paper for the Amendment of Directive 87/102/EEC concerning consumer credit* (2001); see also the Recitals of the Consumer Credit Directive (Directive 2008/48/EC of the European Parliament and of the Council of 23 April 2008 on credit agreements for consumers and repealing Council Directive 87/102/EEC, L 133/66) and the Mortgage Credit Directive (Directive 2014/17/EU of the European Parliament and of the Council of 4 February 2014 on credit agreements for consumers relating to residential immovable property and amending Directives 2008/48/EC and 2013/36/EU and Regulation (EU) No. 1093/2010, L 60/34). A late example is the European Commission *Green Paper on Financial Services and Insurance. Better products, more choice, and greater opportunities for consumers and businesses*, COM(2015) 630 final.

attitudes of consumer insolvency laws are barriers to EU action.[6] At the same time, however, it has been shown how empirical evidence provides little support for such contentions.[7] Undeniably, personal insolvency laws are only one part of broader ideologies, policies and other legislation in which over-indebtedness fit in – e.g. the role of national welfare systems, as well as supply-and-demand market structures.[8] Yet, these are deep political issues which suggest obstacles that surpass the imputation of cultures and traditions. If anything, over the years the latter have already gone through radical transformations in terms of openness towards credit, mass accessibility and changing moral attitudes towards indebtedness.

Arguments may be developed to justify the EU multilevel governance which attributes market issues at a supranational level, while leaving to national law welfare and social concerns such as those generated by debt problems and the procedures to alleviate them. These are politically sensitive claims.

However, the interdependency of the two makes such a division unattainable. Access to the market and financial inclusion go hand in hand with social inclusion and the deterrence of degradation.[9] If in the past, the goals of insolvency law were ideologically parted between the cure of a market failure versus that of a social problem;[10] arguably such a division has been challenged by the latest financial and economic crisis which has exposed the inseparable nature of the two.

Possible justifications have been identified over issues of subsidiarity and proportionality underpinning EU law, which in areas of non-exclusive competence justify EU action only if a certain area is better and more efficiently regulated at that level to internalise negative externalities, as well as proportionate.

In the case in hand, this element has appeared doubtful for the limited outreach of vulnerable consumers outside their national boundaries.[11] But if this may have been the case in the past, the increasing level of labour and citizen mobility in the EU along with related personal debts, especially as a result of the economic crisis, may suggest otherwise. Likewise, even if European cross-border personal insolvency is still in its infancy, Member States have started to pay attention to the issue.[12]

It appears that the combination of political resistance and subsidiarity claims explains – but probably no longer justifies – an attribution of competences where the promotion of financial inclusion and the empowerment of consumers as efficient economic actors become policy and legal tools for market functionalisation, but social inclusion and protection remain a local problem at the margins of EU action.[13]

---

[6] Niemi (2009); Ramsay (2012a); Ziegel (2006).
[7] Spooner (2013).
[8] Braucher (2006); Ramsay (2012a).
[9] Comparato (2015).
[10] Niemi (1999).
[11] Ramsay (2012a).
[12] Linna (2014).
[13] See Comparato (2015).

5.2 PREVENTION: CREDIT LAWS; RESPONSIBLE CREDIT AND CREDITWORTHINESS ASSESSMENT

According to internationally set principles, policy and legal interventions aiming at addressing over-indebtedness consist essentially of two main pillars:

(a) measures for the prevention of over-indebtedness and the legislative implementation of a broadly formulated policy under the principle of 'responsible credit'; and
(b) measures to address over-indebtedness *ex post*, i.e. insolvency proceedings of the debtor natural person and his/her reintegration into the economic and social life.[14]

In aiming for a single market in credit for consumers, the EU policy response to over-indebtedness has been to preventively deliver a credit market that is 'responsible'; where responsible measures entail a raft of responsibilities on the parties of a credit agreement assigning them a role in avoiding borrowers getting into financial distress.

The main objective of EU measures to achieve the internal market point to the creation of a regime which encourages vigorous competition, innovation and choice within a trusty framework that rejects unfair and irresponsible practices. In any event, the main drive remains the economic one of enabling consumers and businesses to take full advantage of the single market.[15]

By contrast, as it will be more clearly shown later in this Chapter, despite consumer over-indebtedness having long been recognised as a major problem affecting the credit markets of the Member States, until now the EU has shown little action in the area of debt solutions.

EU policy measures or legal instruments that directly cover personal financial difficulty holistically have been scarce. Until recently, the handful of documents that the EU has produced are mostly a pre-financial crisis Council Recommendation[16] and two Opinions of the Economic and Social Committee.[17] These are declarations of intent regarding the need for prevention, alleviation and rehabilitation with measures

---

[14] Consumers International (2013); Financial Stability Board (2012); FinCoNet (2014); G20/OECD Task Force on Financial Consumer Protection (2014); International Monetary Fund (2012); OECD (2011); World Bank (2013).
[15] See e.g. European Commission, *Discussion Paper for the Amendment of Directive 87/102/EEC concerning consumer credit* (2001), at http://ec.europa.eu/consumers/cons_int/fina_serv/cons_direc tive/cons_cred1a_en.pdf; recitals of the Consumer Credit Directive and the Mortgage Credit Directive.
[16] Recommendation CM/Rec(2007)8 of the Committee of Ministers to member states on legal solutions to debt problems (20 June 2007).
[17] European Economic Social Committee (2002, 2014). There is also a sketchy mention of over-indebtedness in the European Commission's *Green Paper on Mortgage Credit in the EU* COM (2005) 327 final, which is limited to the observation that 'there is a huge social and human dimension attached to housing and credit, including aspects such as over-indebtedness. Any policy in this area must take that dimension into proper consideration.'

such as monitoring, financial education counselling, responsible credit practices, balanced debt enforcement measures and the promotion of debt adjustment procedures. Leaving aside the non-binding nature of these instruments, Johanna Niemi has noticed that in reality the EU has had no programmes in place relating to consumer over-indebtedness and the matter did not even appear in the Consumer Policy strategy 2007–2013.[18] Equally, all that the European Consumer Agenda has done in the following period is a generic reference to 'households' over-indebtedness is also worrying' anticipating EU-commissioned studies.[19] Yet problem-debt merits no explicit mention in the EU multiannual consumer programme for the years 2014–2020.[20]

It is true that in the aftermath of the latest economic crisis the European Commission has stressed the importance of Member States having 'measures to *prevent* over-indebtedness and maintain access to financial services'.[21] Nonetheless, the declared goal has been to deliver responsible and reliable financial markets for the future announcing that to ensure that European investors, consumers and SMEs can be confident about their savings, access to credit and their rights as concerns financial products, the Commission will come forward with ... *measures on responsible lending and borrowing*.[22]

From all the policy measures produced to date it appears evident how the creation of trust in the market is dominant and how to some extent the prevention of over-indebtedness – but not its treatment – has remained hidden in the quest for the promotion of the internal market. Along these lines, over-indebtedness has become part of the 'responsible lending and borrowing' rhetoric as an introduction of best market practices to be achieved by means of public intervention on the behaviour of the contracting parties of credit agreements. The emphasis is on behavioural grounds of active over-indebtedness which, as noted in Chapter 4, are not its main causes.

Policy documents reveal that responsible lending makes reference to the delivery of responsible and reliable markets, where consumer confidence is restored and credit products are appropriate for consumers' needs and tailored to their ability to repay their debts. It envisages a framework that could ensure that all lenders and intermediaries act in a fair, honest and professional manner before, during and after the lending transaction. Similarly, for responsible borrowing, it is expected that, to

---

[18] Niemi (2012); EU Consumer Policy Strategy 2007–13: Empowering consumers, enhancing their welfare, effectively protecting them, COM(2007) 99 final.

[19] European Commission, *Communication from the Commission to the European Parliament, the Council, the Economic and Social Committee and the Committee of the Regions*, 'A European Consumer Agenda – Boosting Confidence and Growth', COM(2012) 225 final.

[20] Regulation (EU) No. 254/2014 of the European Parliament and of the Council of 26 February 2014 on a multiannual consumer programme for the years 2014–20 and repealing Decision No. 1926/2006/EC, L 84/42.

[21] European Commission, *Communication for the Spring European Council, Driving European Recovery*, COM(2009) 114 final, 4 and 7 (emphasis added; note that there is no reference to a 'cure' for the problem).

[22] *Ibid.*, 7 (emphasis added).

obtain credit, consumers provide relevant, complete and accurate information on their finances. They are also encouraged to make informed and sustainable borrowing decisions.[23]

A consultation conducted by the European Commission provides a more concrete illustration of this concept. It explicitly targets measures to adequately assess, by all appropriate means, borrowers' creditworthiness before granting them a loan, thus attempting to tackle over-indebtedness. The consultation covered, among other things, the advertising and marketing of credit products, the information to be provided to borrowers prior to granting any loans, ways to assess product suitability and borrower creditworthiness, advice standards, responsible borrowing and issues relating to the framework for credit intermediaries (e.g. disclosures, registration, licensing and supervision).[24]

Conceptually, it may not be straightforward why such a duty should be imposed on party autonomy for what already appears to be in their self-interest: *prima facie*, lenders have no self-interest in giving credit irresponsibly (i.e. lending money unlikely to be repaid). Moreover, the economic literature has long explained that the credit industry is traditionally risk-averse.[25] Likewise, with the exclusion of the disproportionately fewer cases of fraud, it may be unclear why someone would borrow money knowing that they cannot repay it, with all the dire consequences that that entails.

Yet, financial markets have demonstrated distortions in such basic principles.

Moreover, recent experience has shown how lenders have devised instruments to pass on the risk of default to third parties, ultimately creating dangerous financial products for consumers, discouraging the former from acting responsibly towards their original interest.[26]

Also, in a very competitive market the costs of properly assessing the risks of default through individualised controls, coupled with the pressure to gain market share and acquire new customers approving quickly credit applications, may encourage financial institutions to factor in the losses of defaults in the cost of credit, passing this onto consumers. Likewise, false economic assumptions of the ever rising value of collaterals such as property may induce lenders to exceed limits. Again, sale structures via intermediaries who earn their fees through commission incentivise the latter to conclude as many credit agreements as they can.[27] These behaviours are driven by competition and in a way they open a further debate as to what extent competition

---

[23] See European Commission, *Communication of the European Commission to the European Council of 4 March 2009 'Driving European Recovery'*, COM(2009) 114 and the *Public Consultation on Responsible Lending and Borrowing*, available at http://ec.europa.eu/internal ... /responsible_lending/consultation_en.pdf.

[24] *Public Consultation on Responsible Lending and Borrowing*, available at http://ec.europa.eu/internal ... /responsible_lending/consultation_en.pdf.

[25] e.g. see Admati and Pfleiderer (2000); Akerlof (1970); Diamond (1991); Stiglitz and Weiss (1981).

[26] See e.g. Engel and McCoy (2011).

[27] Europe Economics (2009).

and consumer protection in the financial marketplace can be compatible. This exceeds the purpose of this study but it shows how competition, alongside 'predatory' – yet not 'fraudulent' – business models may take advantage of consumers being in debt.[28] These practices, not infrequent, may provide market failures of 'irresponsible' behaviour to be corrected.

Moreover, even conceptually, in money lending the interest of lenders in repayment may not be considered equivalent to that of borrowers. Creditors have certainly an interest in the ability of debtors to repay under the credit agreement, but they not may be concerned about the sustainability of the new debt in relation to other financial arrangements that debtors have with other parties. This aspect also differentiates credit risk analysis undertaken in the interest of lenders from the creditworthiness assessment in the interest of consumers (see Chapter 6).

By the same token, as far as responsible borrowing is concerned, behavioural economics have demonstrated that borrowers are not rational maximisers of their resources and they may well take wrong borrowing decisions even if they are provided with adequate information.[29]

The above are market failures that justify the intervention of public measures of responsible credit. The restoration of the contractual balance between the parties of a credit agreement, redistributive justice and paternalism may be additional rationales. Others have identified a further justification as a broader public function to prevent citizens from falling below a minimum welfare level in a healthy free market economy, thus protecting social welfare.[30]

5.3 RESPONSIBLE LENDING, THE RESPONSIBLE CREDITOR AND PRIVATE LAW

From a legal perspective, responsible lending and borrowing are relatively novel but controversial notions that to some extent are at odds with traditional contract law principles, which in turn have already been eroded by consumer law.

In many respects, contracts regulated by private law are the lifeline of the market economy under the principles of freedom of contract and party autonomy. Nonetheless, it is well known that markets require public regulation to the extent that private law alone is incapable of achieving a free and fair market. This is the case of the bulk of consumer law where the legislator intervenes to correct recognised market failures of power imbalance, unfair practices or redistribute rights and resources.[31]

---

[28] See e.g. the sweatbox business model of credit cards or payday lending (Mann (2007); McAteer and Beddows (2014); Pottow (2007)).
[29] Howells (2005); Ramsay (2005); Sunstein (2006).
[30] Atamer (2011); Posner (1995).
[31] Cartwright (2004); Howells and Weatherill (2005).

No doubt credit agreements are the expression of a private law relationship and no overarching right to credit exists. In many instances, consumer law has already affected the legal principle of *caveat emptor* – let the buyer beware – typical of traditional contract law theory of the Member States. But while responsible borrowing and certain aspects of responsible lending with their disclosure duties may be seen as a form of pre-contractual responsibility or an expression of good faith in the pre-contractual phase of civil law systems, other elements of responsible lending seem to depart even further from a traditional consumer law perspective. In holding lenders in principle responsible for delivering products that best suit the needs of the individual consumer, and accountable during all phases of the contractual relationship, some have seen the addition of an atypical fiduciary element to the commercial contract that is normally reserved for agency law or other fiduciary relationships.[32] Likewise, the obligation to undertake a creditworthiness assessment of the borrower seems to exceed traditional freedom of contract and party autonomy in the risk-taking typical of any contract.

From another angle, it may also be argued that in principle it intrudes even further in the individual responsibility of one party of the contract introducing new duties of looking after, or taking responsibility for, the other party – thus shifting paternalism from the state to the former contracting party and/or raising questions over commercial entities becoming to a degree social actors beyond their duties and functions.

To exemplify some of these issues, Federico Ferretti and Christina Livada report that:

> [t]he principle of responsible lending is not limited to the creditworthiness assessment requirement. It also includes … an approach of strong intervention with regard to the conclusion of the credit agreement, focusing on the responsible creditor.
>
> [For example], the approach of the *Crowther Report* of 1971 [in the UK], on which the British legislation for consumer credit was based, seems to have been abandoned at the European level. According to this Report, 'the first principle of social policy should be to treat the users of consumer credit as adults who are fully capable of managing their own financial affairs and not to restrict their freedom of access to it in order to protect the relatively small minority who get into difficulties'. Instead, the assumption made at present has the vulnerable consumer as a point of reference, who – even when he receives sufficient information – is not able to either manage efficiently the risks he takes or to calculate appropriately his economic capabilities. Thus, he is in need of increased protection.
>
> At the same time, it is accepted that the credit risk to which the creditor is exposed may – under normal circumstances – be manageable and controllable, owing to sufficient diversification of his portfolio or to his ability to ensure his profitability in alternative ways. Moreover, a creditor's aggressive commercial policy or the conditions of competition prevailing in the market may result in a lack of sufficient incentive not to grant credit to persons with a high risk of over-indebtedness. The crucial question arising

---

[32] Kondgen (2011).

in this case is whether the creditor, even when he himself is not at risk, should not grant credit to a consumer because of the risk of over-indebtedness for the latter and, in any case, whether the creditor is obliged to take certain preventive measures in this respect, and, if so, to what extent.[33]

Regardless of philosophical questions and debates over how much paternalism society is ready to accept or the 'social' function of commercial entities, the significance of responsible lending and borrowing remains contingent on its method of legal implementation,[34] which is where the EU approaches towards over-indebtedness in general, and responsible lending and borrowing in particular, may need further attention.

5.4 THE CONSUMER CREDIT DIRECTIVE

It has already been pointed out how this far the EU has been concerned primarily with the creation of an integrated internal credit market with a focus on competition, innovation and consumer choice. The Consumer Credit Directive (CCD)[35] provides a clear example of a full harmonising measure attempting to extend the internal market for financial services to the specific field of consumer credit. As extensively recognised by many commentators, it does not mention explicitly over-indebtedness,[36] nor does it include any specific provision on responsible lending.[37] This is remarkable not only because of the frustration of the previous recognition of over-indebtedness as a European problem and of the ensuing policy impetus on responsible lending, but also for the emphasis given to such a policy in the earlier drafts of the CCD that was not retained in the final version.

Peter Rott offers a detailed account of the legislative history of the CCD showing how the European Commission originally aimed at avoiding the consumer's over-indebtedness by evading unreasonable credit contracts, introducing duties on lenders to assess and advise consumers on the risks of default and holding lenders responsible during all phases of the contractual relationship.[38] Instead, the final version of the CCD remains anchored on the usual paradigm of transparency and information requirements by both lenders and borrowers, adding a focus on an undetermined requirement of creditworthiness assessment.[39]

---

[33] Ferretti and Livada (2016), pp. 15–16.
[34] Ramsay (2010), esp. p. 395.
[35] Directive 2008/48/EC of the European Parliament and of the Council of 23 April 2008 on credit agreements for consumers and repealing Council Directive 87/102/EEC, L 133/66.
[36] The only sketchy mention to over-indebtedness is in Recital 26 of the CCD about 'warnings [to be given to consumers] about the risks attaching to default on payment and to over-indebtedness'.
[37] Atamer (2011); Fairweather (2012); Ramsay (2010); Rott (2014).
[38] Rott (2014).
[39] See Arts. 4–6 of the CCD. Recital 26 of the CCD generically affirms that 'in the expanding credit market, in particular, it is important that creditors should not engage in irresponsible lending or give out credit without prior assessment of creditworthiness, and the Member States should carry out the

Thus, in the view of the EU legislator of the CCD, the significance of responsible lending is limited to duties to explain and disclose, and an obligation to assess the creditworthiness of consumers. In particular, Article 8 of the CCD states that creditors have to make such an assessment on the basis of sufficient information obtained from the consumer and, where necessary, by consulting the relevant database.[40] The CCD further allows Member States whose legislation requires creditors to consult databases to maintain this obligation, often a requirement that may be imposed by central banks for purposes of financial stability (see further Chapter 6). At the same time, for competition purposes, Article 9 of the CCD is concerned that access to databases used in another Member State, if any, is ensured on a non-discriminatory basis for creditors from other Member States (see Chapter 4).

For a long time, it was unclear in whose interest the creditworthiness assessment should have been carried out. Importantly, far later in time from the passing of the CCD, the CJEU has clarified in *LCL (Le Crédit Lyonnais)*[41] that the aim of the obligation to assess the creditworthiness of the borrower is that of protecting consumers against the risk of over-indebtedness and insolvency. In *Consumer Finance*[42] it was corroborated that all the above obligations deriving from responsible lending are pre-contractual in nature.

These judgments are significant in making clear in whose interest the creditworthiness assessment should be undertaken and the private law nature of the duty. But they leave unanswered questions as to the remedies available to consumers if the creditor does not comply with such a duty and the extent of the remaining enforcement duties under public law.

If to a large extent the limited understanding of responsible lending focuses on the obligations of the creditor, who carries the main responsibility to assess the creditworthiness, the CCD establishes limited obligations on the borrower. However, according to the majority of views, the concept of responsible lending cannot but also include to some extent the responsible borrower.[43]

As Federico Ferretti and Christina Livada contend:

---

necessary supervision to avoid such behaviour and should determine the necessary means to sanction creditors in the event of their doing so'.

[40] For interpretation of Art. 8(1) of the CCD, see *CA Consumer Finance SA v. Ingrid Bakkaus, Charline Bonato, née Savary, Florian Bonato* (Case C-449/13) of 18 December 2014, according to which it 'must be interpreted to the effect that, first, it does not preclude the consumer's creditworthiness assessment from being carried out solely on the basis of information supplied by the consumer, provided that that information is sufficient and that mere declarations by the consumer are also accompanied by supporting evidence and, secondly, that it does not require the creditor to carry out systematic checks of the veracity of the information supplied by the consumer'.

[41] *LCL (Le Crédit Lyonnais) SA v. Fesih Kalhan* (Case C-565/12) [2014], ECLI:EU:C:2014:190.

[42] *CA Consumer Finance SA v. Ingrid Bakkaus and others* (Case C-449/13) [2014], ECLI:EU:C:2014:2464.

[43] See Ryder et al. (2012), esp. p. 509; FinCoNet (2012). On issues regarding the responsible borrower, see Chapter 4.

in the provisions of Directive 2008/48/EC, in which the obligation of creditworthiness assessment was adopted for the first time at the European level, there is no reference to the borrower's obligations except from recital 26, where it is mentioned that 'Consumers should also act with prudence and respect their contractual obligations'. Therefore, no [real] obligation is established; there is only a light suggestion that the borrower should also be prudent on his part, i.e. regarding the planning of his family budget, avoiding undertaking credit that he cannot afford and being diligent concerning his obligations. The suggestion to respect his contractual obligations does not concern responsible lending but an obligation he has under the general provisions.[44]

Significantly, the CCD does not provide directly for legal obligations to deny credit in case of breach of lenders' duties, particularly as regards the creditworthiness assessment, but it delegates sanctions to Member States.[45]

In general, the CCD has been criticised not only for not incorporating responsible lending in its provisions but especially for insisting on relying on the ability of informed, confident and rational consumers as drivers of economic efficiency,[46] without caring about socially and financially vulnerable consumers[47] such as those who become over-indebted.

5.5 THE MORTGAGE CREDIT DIRECTIVE

The adoption of the Mortgage Credit Directive (MCD)[48] – which has been designed against the backdrop of the financial crisis and as another effort to create a transparent, efficient and competitive internal market for mortgage credit[49] – may be considered a step in the direction of a closer legal transposition of responsible lending.

To some degree, the MCD insists and reproduces the information and transparency model of the CCD in the advertising, marketing, product specifications, pre-contractual and contractual information (including intermediaries and representatives), etc.[50]

The novelty is the introduction of a number of norms that in principle may better correspond to the concept of responsible credit explicated in the policies. These include the following provisions:

---

[44] Ferretti and Livada (2016), p. 21.
[45] Art. 23 of the CCD. On the suitability of national measures, see *LCL (Le Crédit Lyonnais) SA v. Fesih Kalhan*.
[46] Nield (2010); Micklitz (2013).
[47] Micklitz (2013).
[48] Directive 2014/17/EU of the European Parliament and of the Council of 4 February 2014 on credit agreements for consumers relating to residential immovable property and amending Directives 2008/48/EC and 2013/36/EU and Regulation (EU) No. 1093/2010, L 60/34.
[49] See Recital 6 and Art. 1 of the MCD.
[50] See Arts. 8, 10, 11, 13–16 of the MCD.

- the financial education of consumers in relation to responsible borrowing and debt management, including guidance to consumers in the credit granting process;[51]
- conduct of business obligations and product suitability more tailored to individual circumstances, including methods of incentives or remuneration for staff or intermediaries;[52]
- methods for calculating interest rates transparently.[53]

The creditworthiness assessment of consumers features strongly in the MCD as the most reliable tool capable of fostering responsible lending. The EU legislator believes that imposing such a duty will enable lenders to determine the ability of consumers to meet their obligations under the credit agreement, and thus a tool to detect or prevent the over-indebtedness of consumers. After the lessons learned from the financial crisis, such an assessment 'shall not rely predominantly on the value of the residential immovable property exceeding the amount of the credit or the assumption that the residential immovable property will increase in value'.[54] On the contrary, it should be based on information contained in databases alongside income, expenditures, savings, assets and other circumstances about the consumer.[55]

What may appear unclear about this provision is that mainstream lenders already availed themselves of solvency databases well before the financial crisis and the passing of the MCD, and they have always demanded relevant information from applicants. But, arguably, the creation of the internal market and competition suggested that access to such information should be mandated on a non-discriminatory basis (on solvency data, see Chapter 6).

Pursuant to Article 18 of the MCD, the creditor shall make a thorough assessment of the consumer's creditworthiness, taking appropriate account of factors relevant to verifying the prospect of the consumer to meet his obligations under the credit agreement.[56]

In essence, Member States shall ensure that:

[51] Art. 6 of the MCD.
[52] Art. 7 of the MCD.
[53] Art. 17 of the MCD.
[54] Art. 18(3) of the MCD.
[55] Arts. 18–20 of the MCD. On the belief of the usefulness of solvency databases, see Recital 59 of the MCD. On the suggested good practices for the creditworthiness assessment, see also European Banking Authority, *Opinion of the European Banking Authority on Good Practices for Responsible Mortgage Lending* (London, 13 June 2013).
[56] Art. 18 para. 1 and Recital 55 of the MCD according to which:

> In particular, the consumer's ability to service and fully repay the credit should include consideration of future payments or payment increases needed due to negative amortisation or deferred payments of principal or interest and should be considered in the light of other regular expenditure, debts and other financial commitments as well as income, savings and assets. Reasonable allowance should be made for future events during the term of the proposed credit agreement such as a reduction in income where the credit term lasts into retirement or, where applicable, an increase in the borrowing rate or negative change in the exchange rate.

- the procedures and information on which the assessment is based are established, documented and maintained; and
- the assessment of creditworthiness shall not rely predominantly on the value of the residential immovable property exceeding the amount of the credit or the assumption that the residential immovable property will increase in value unless the purpose of the credit agreement is to construct or renovate the residential immovable property.[57] The purpose of this provision is to ensure that the creditor does not rely solely on the value of the immovable property given as collateral for the credit, if the consumer does not possess any other means sufficient for the repayment of his loan.[58]

Article 18(5) of the MCD introduces a nominal 'duty to deny credit' but the nature of this provision appears unclear or open to different readings. According to the norm, the creditor makes the credit available to the consumer only where the result of the creditworthiness assessment indicates that the obligations resulting from the credit agreement are likely to be met in the manner required under that agreement.[59] Therefore, if the outcome of the assessment is negative, indicating that the consumer is not likely to be able to repay his loan, the creditor should not grant the credit.[60] Moreover, should the case arise, the creditor must also be able to invoke the specific indications he took into account for the assessment of the consumer's ability to repay the loan.[61]

Under this interpretation, the intention of the European legislator is to impose on Member States the introduction of a 'duty to deny credit', thus intervening in the freedom of the contractual parties, whereas it could have opted to proceed to the conclusion of the credit agreement despite the negative assessment.[62]

A critique is that to the extent that the interest of lenders is to enlarge their customer base and engage in profitable business, this may not coincide with the provision of suitable products in the interest of borrowers. If creditors have a duty to verify the ability of debtors to repay under a credit agreement, nevertheless they do not have a duty to ensure the sustainability of the new debt on other financial arrangements that the borrower has with other parties.

On a reverse reading of such a duty, the establishment of such an obligation should not mean that a positive creditworthiness assessment obliges lenders to provide the credit. This is expressly provided for in the relevant recital of the Directive.[63] This

---

[57] Art. 18 of the MCD, paras. 2–3.
[58] Recital 55 of the MCD. See also Fairweather (2012), esp. pp. 91–2; Nield (2012), esp. p. 173.
[59] See also Recital 57 of the MCD.
[60] An obligation to deny credit has existed under Swiss law for consumer credit since 2003 (*Loi sur le crédit à la consommation*), even if not directly, but by combining the relevant provisions (Arts. 28–32 of the law). Moreover, heavy sanctions are imposed in case of substantive infringement of said obligation (Stauder and Favre-Bulle (2004), esp. p. 188).
[61] Ferretti and Livada (2016).
[62] *Ibid.*
[63] Recital 57 of the MCD.

seems to be explained by the legislator's intervention in the general principle of the freedom of contract which requires an express legislative provision justified by reasons of superior public interest.

In any event, questions arise as to the public or a private nature of the obligation, as well as of the resulting sanctions and enforcement. All what the MCD does is a reference to sanctions to be set-up by the Member States individually. There is an argument among scholars about the legal nature of the lender's obligation to carry out a creditworthiness assessment.

At least until recently it was the majority's opinion that this obligation is a public law duty.[64] As a result, a breach of such a duty could only trigger remedies laid down in the underlying sanctioning system of the national law providing for it.

By contrast, the view of what at least until recently was seen as a minority is that the duty to carry out the creditworthiness assessment is a duty owed to the debtor, so it is by nature either a private law duty or a duty with both public and private law character.[65] According to this view, breach of this duty entitles the debtor to damages. As a result, the creditor would have to put the debtor in the situation he would have been in had the duty not been breached. According to this view, the debtor could claim that, had the creditor carried out the creditworthiness assessment (properly), either the creditor or the debtor would not have entered into the loan agreement. Hence the creditor would have to pay for every loss suffered by the debtor as a result of having entered into the contract. This includes not only costs and interest but can extend to the loan itself. Also, if the debtor became insolvent as a consequence of taking out the loan, the creditor would have to pay for any loss resulting from the insolvency.[66]

All in all, however, what appears doubtful is the extent to which the provision is capable of tackling the problem of over-indebtedness, since its violation cannot lead to a debt cancellation without immediate repayment of the capital borrowed.

As noted earlier, in the consumer loan case under the CCD *LCL (Le Crédit Lyonnais)*[67] the CJEU maintained that the aim of the obligation to assess the creditworthiness of the borrower is that of protecting consumers against the risk of over-indebtedness and insolvency. In *Consumer Finance*,[68] which is another case under the CCD and not the MCD, it was held that all the above obligations deriving from responsible lending are pre-contractual in nature. These judgments under the CCD may be considered significant in clarifying the private law nature of the duty, but they leave unanswered questions as to the remedies available to consumers.

---

[64] See Ferretti et al. (2016) and the literature there cited.
[65] Ibid.
[66] Ibid.
[67] LCL (Le Crédit Lyonnais) SA v. Fesih Kalhan.
[68] CA Consumer Finance SA v. Ingrid Bakkaus and others.

In any case, it remains unclear in the case of mortgages what consequences there would be, given the substantial amount of capital advanced by lenders and enduring problems with its restitution or repayment.

All in all, the provision may raise a number of problematic legal issues that leave doubts over the extent to which such a measure could have any effect on the real financial difficulties of consumers. For the difficulties in transposing analogically the judgments of the CJEU on the CCD on the MCD, separate legal analyses will have to take place following case law deriving from the national implementations of the MCD.

Unlike the CCD, the MCD introduces limited obligations on the borrower, urging the consumer to provide the creditor with the information needed for the assessment of his creditworthiness.

The following excerpt from Federico Ferretti and Christina Livada (2016) is exemplificatory:

> In Directive 2014/17/EU, the European legislator focuses on the need for the consumer's participation in the process of his creditworthiness assessment, in the sense that he should provide the creditor with the information required for this purpose. According to Article 20 paragraph 3 of the Directive, the creditor should specify in a clear and straightforward way, at the pre-contractual stage, the necessary information and independently verifiable evidence that the consumer needs to provide, and the timeframe within which the consumer needs to provide it. In this framework, the consumer should be aware that he needs to provide information that is correct and as complete as possible. Furthermore, the creditor and, where applicable, the credit intermediary or the appointed representative shall warn the consumer that where the creditor is unable to carry out an assessment of creditworthiness because the consumer chooses not to provide the information or verification necessary for this assessment, credit cannot be granted.
>
> In case it is proven that the consumer knowingly withheld or falsified information he provided to the creditor, the latter is allowed to renounce the credit agreement.
>
> Thus, the creditor is responsible for determining the data and information needed from the consumer in order to assess his creditworthiness – without prejudice to Directive 95/46/EC – and the consumer is responsible for providing the creditor with correct, complete and precise information.
>
> Considering that the creditworthiness assessment of the consumer is carried out on the basis of information provided by the consumer and, where applicable, internal or external sources of the creditor including databases, with regard to the first part of the information the creditor depends to a great extent on the soundness of information provided by the consumer.
>
> In parallel, the consumer, in order to receive the credit he wants, often tends to be over-optimistic as to the affordability of the credit, or he is unable to understand the risks inherent in the conclusion of the credit agreement; as a result, sometimes, he does not provide – intentionally or by negligence – the creditor with the correct information for the assessment of his creditworthiness.

Therefore, the obligation of the consumer to provide correct and complete information in the process of his application for credit, the warning – as mentioned above – to the consumer concerning the consequences in case he does not collaborate with the creditor, and the right of the creditor to renounce the credit agreement if the consumer knowingly provided falsified or incorrect information contribute, without doubt, to the encouragement of his active participation in the process of his creditworthiness assessment and the demonstration of responsible behaviour on his part in this stage of the process.

In other words, it is expected that the establishment of these obligations for the consumer shall contribute to him exhibiting diligence as a 'responsible borrower' when he concludes a credit agreement and avoiding undertaking obligations that he knows, or should know, that he is not able to meet. At the same time, in this way the important role of both parties in the implementation of the responsible lending principle is highlighted, in the sense that this principle undoubtedly presupposes the contribution of both contractual parties. Consequently, Directive 2014/17/EU is considered quite positive, although in need of further enhancement to achieve a responsible behaviour by the consumer during the lending process.[69]

Unlike under the CCD, in the MCD the establishment of the Member States' obligation to promote measures supporting the financial education of consumers is expected to play a significant part.[70] Likewise, when providing advisory services at a pre-contractual stage, the MCD introduces an obligation on the creditor to recommend suitable credit agreements to the consumer based on the latter's personal and financial situation, preferences and objectives.[71]

Financial education is considered key to the consumer's being able to make informed decisions to the extent that s/he becomes familiar with financial products and acquires the knowledge to be able to manage his debt appropriately.[72] The provision of information to a consumer, who does not possess the knowledge to comprehend it, is not considered to be adequate for the consumer in order to make conscious decisions; this consideration may explain why the recent policy trend is towards an increasing emphasis on the promotion and encouragement of financial education. In short, financial education becomes functional to the information paradigm which dominates the law.

On the other hand, the obligation to propose suitable credit agreements to the consumer, under the condition of the provision of advisory services, is different from the obligation of creditworthiness assessment, since it aims to identify appropriate credit products for the consumer, independently of his ability to repay them.

---

[69] Ferretti and Livada (2016), pp. 21–3.
[70] Art. 6 of the MCD and Recital 29 of the MCD. In the CCD, there is only one reference to financial education in Recital 26.
[71] Art. 22 of the MCD. Advisory services may also be provided under the conditions set out in Art. 22 from the credit intermediary and the appointed representative.
[72] See Pearson (2008); esp. pp. 53–7; Ryder et al. (2012), esp. p. 509; FinCoNet (2014); Gortsos (2016).

Hence, as concluded by Federico Ferretti and Christina Livada:

it may happen that a consumer may receive a positive assessment with regard to his income for more than one credit product; however, one of them may not be suitable for the consumer on the basis of his educational profile or the absence of his familiarity with certain transactions.

Moreover, taking into account the obligation of the creditor to refuse the credit in case of negative creditworthiness assessment and that one of the criteria that should be considered is the financial situation of the consumer, it is clear that products for which the consumer has a negative assessment are not suitable for him.

This obligation is similar to the one established in European capital markets law concerning the conduct of appropriateness or suitability testing depending on the investment service provided each time; however, the appropriateness or suitability test is mandatory before the provision of investment services and free of charge, while the provision of advisory services in the framework of the Mortgage Credit Directive takes place only upon the consumer's request and is a paid service.

In this sense, it is more similar, in terms of its content, to the investment service of investment advice, i.e. the provision of personalised recommendations to a customer, either upon his request or on the initiative of the investment firm, regarding one or more transactions relating to financial instruments on the basis of his personal and financial situation.

Pursuant to Article 22 paragraph 5 of Directive 2014/17/EU, it is left to the discretion of the Member States to provide for an obligation for the creditor to warn the consumer when, considering his financial situation, a credit agreement may induce a specific risk for him. Therefore, if the consumer has a negative assessment of his creditworthiness, Article 18 paragraph 5 shall apply, and the creditor shall not grant the credit. On the other hand, if the consumer receives a positive assessment – and under the condition that the creditor also provides advisory services and the national legislator has made use of the above-mentioned option – the creditor should warn him about the specific risk the credit agreement may induce for him. According to the relevant provisions of capital markets law, if in the opinion of the provider of the investment services the product or service is not suitable for the customer, he should also warn him about this.

One of the issues arising in this regard is the extent of the creditor's liability in this case. The obligation and liability of the credit institution must end with the issuing of the warning, where applicable, to the consumer, who will be responsible for any loss he may suffer if he chooses the offered credit product despite the warning that it was not suitable for him. Respectively, the consumer takes the risk of an unsuitable product offered to him by the credit institution because of his having provided insufficient or no information to it.[73]

What probably represents the most innovative institution of the MCD is the enactment of high-level principles on arrears and foreclosures. This is the first attempt to

---

[73] Ferretti and Livada (2016), pp. 24–6.

introduce a sort of curative, as opposed to preventive, measure under EU law. In its Preamble, the MCD acknowledges that foreclosure can have significant consequences on consumers and it asserts that it is appropriate to encourage creditors to deal proactively with emerging credit risk at an early stage. It considers it important to have in place the necessary measures to ensure that lenders exercise reasonable forbearance and make reasonable attempts to resolve the situation through other means before foreclosure proceedings are initiated.[74] Article 28 of the MCD sets out provisions on arrears and foreclosure, and specifically requires that Member States adopt measures to encourage creditors to exercise reasonable forbearance before foreclosure proceedings are initiated.

Once again, the nature of this provision appears questionable and it unlikely to harmonise the laws of the Member States. Nevertheless, it appears to be a principle aimed at introducing debt solutions that penetrates into EU law and that may justify or pave the way for additional 'curative' legal measures.

5.6 THE GUIDELINES OF THE EUROPEAN BANKING AUTHORITY

To ensure that provisions of the MCD on responsible lending are implemented and supervised consistently across the Member States, the European Banking Authority (EBA) – the new independent EU authority in charge of prudential regulation and supervision across the European banking sector[75] – has issued guidelines on the way in which the creditworthiness assessment should be conducted. These guidelines entered into effect in March 2016, with the exception of the information requirements, which apply from the first day following the date of publication in the official languages of the Member States.[76]

By way of illustration according to the EBA's guidelines, the creditor – when verifying a consumer's prospect to meet his obligations under a credit agreement as referred to in Article 18 of the MCD:

> should make reasonable enquiries and take reasonable steps to verify the consumer's underlying income capacity, the consumer's income history and any variability over time. In the case of consumers that are self-employed or have seasonal or

---

[74] Recital 27 of the MCD.
[75] See Regulation 1093/2010/EU establishing a European Supervisory Authority (European Banking Authority) OJ L 331/12. The EBA was established on 1 January 2011 as part of the European System of Financial Supervision (ESFS) which is made up of three supervisory authorities: the European Securities and Markets Authorities (ESMA), the EBA and the European Insurance and Occupational Pensions Authority (EIOPA). The system also comprises the European Systemic Risk Board (ESRB) as well as the Joint Committee of the European Supervisory Authorities and the national supervisory authorities. National supervisory authorities remain in charge of supervising individual financial institutions; the objective of the European supervisory authorities is to improve the functioning of the internal market by ensuring appropriate, efficient and harmonised European regulation and supervision. See www.eba.europa.eu/about-us
[76] European Banking Authority, *Final Report. Guidelines on creditworthiness assessment* (EBA/GL/2015/11).

other irregular income, the creditor should make reasonable enquiries and take reasonable steps to verify information that is related to the consumer's ability to meet his/her obligations under the credit agreement, including profit capacity and third-party verification documenting such income.[77]

However, according to Federico Ferretti and Christina Livada:

> there is no guidance, for example, as to whether the income includes only the net individual income and/or the family income, the period of time for which data should be gathered – particularly in the case of consumers with variable income depending on various parameters such as the profitability of the enterprise where they are employed or the market conditions – and what applies for the calculation of the income in the case of consumers who will retire within the duration of the credit agreement and whose income will thus be reduced.
>
> The precise determination of several of those elements that should be checked by the creditor is objectively quite difficult, since their configuration depends on many different factors varying per category of borrower and the market of each Member State. Moreover, taking into account the long average duration of home loans, the assessment process is quite complex and cannot but end up in assumptions and indications. This is exactly why in Article 18, paragraph 5 of the Directive, reference is made to the terms 'likely to be met', as it is impossible to have certainty, particularly in periods of financial instability or crisis.[78]

Equally, to ensure that the high-level provisions on arrears and foreclosure will be implemented and supervised consistently across Member States and in support of their transposition into Member State domestic law, the EBA has issued a consultation on draft guidelines that aims at providing in greater detail how lenders should give effect to the provisions of Article 28 of the MCD.[79]

These guidelines request that lenders establish policies and procedures to detect and handle consumers in financial difficulty, actively engage with consumers and provide an undefined form of support alongside basic information as to the status of payments, consequences of failure to repay and the existence of public schemes or support. As it concerns the resolution process, the guidelines contain a limited obligation on the creditor having to take into account the individual circumstances of the consumer and his interests (including the ability to repay) when deciding on which steps or forbearance measures to take. The listed concessions to the consumer include a total or partial refinancing of a credit agreement and/or a modification of the previous terms and conditions of a credit agreement (such as extension of the term of the mortgage; change of

---

[77] Ibid., at 1.1–1.2, 10.
[78] Ferretti and Livada (2016), p. 20.
[79] European Banking Authority, *Consultation Paper on Draft Guidelines on Arrears and Foreclosure* EBA/CP/2014/43 (12 December 2014).

the type of the mortgage; deferral of payment of all or part of the instalment repayment for a period; change of the interest rate; or offer of a payment holiday).[80]

Unfortunately, this soft law instrument and its content, though a step in a novel direction, clearly appear insufficient to deal with the complex problem of over-indebtedness as portrayed by the same EU policymaker[81] and so far examined.

---

[80] Ibid.
[81] e.g. see Civic Consulting (2014).

6

The Role and Function of Solvency Data and Financial Technologies (Fintech and Big Data)

6.1 SOLVENCY DATA IN THE ECONOMY

6.1.1 *Classic Economic Theory*

6.1.1.1 The Reduction of Information Asymmetry and Risk Management

The sharing of consumers' solvency data finds its roots in conventional economic theory and the study of risk in finance. This economic literature focuses on credit risk analysis.

Classical economic theory views the sharing of consumer solvency data in the financial system as a tool to meet the problem of asymmetrical information between borrowers and lenders, as well as problems of bad selection of customers, and the risk which arises from the characteristics of prospective borrowers that may increases the possibility of an economic loss.

Economists have identified asymmetrical information as being the problem where one party does not have the same information as the other party relative to the risk-related to the performance of the contract by such other party. In a nutshell, one party knows less than the other, a situation which is different from the one where a party has less information than the ideal, known as 'imperfect information'. In finance, this may be seen as the different knowledge or level of information than the demand side, i.e. customers, has either on financial products or the market behaviour of providers. By the same token, from the perspective of the supply side of the relationship – i.e. the credit industry – this difference of knowledge or information relates to the payment behaviour of customers. In a credit relationship, lenders want to avoid lending money that will not be repaid. If they do not have the same information as borrowers have on their ability or willingness to repay a debt, they will incur a higher risk of making bad business. This risk, in turn, poses problems of bad debts and adverse selection, i.e. the selection of the wrong customers. This explains why economic theory has traditionally emphasised the importance of information in credit markets.[1]

From the supply side, the reduction of asymmetric information and adverse selection of customers encompass several elements relating to market structure and marketing activities of the participants in the retail finance marketplace.

The theory suggests that the lack of information on borrowers can prevent the efficient allocation of credit in a market, and that one way that lenders can improve their knowledge of borrowers is through their observation of clients over time.[2]

In turn, the reduction of asymmetric information affects many aspects of the lending business: risk management and pricing through the assessment of uncertainties about the ability and/or willingness of a debtor to repay, market entry and competition, customers' creditworthiness, application processing and screening, customers' segmentation and product specialisation, and improvement of the credit portfolio.[3]

6.1.1.2 Moral Hazard and Reputation Collateral

All financial transactions in general – and credit transactions in particular – involve risks or uncertainties. Among these, an important one concerns the ability and/or the willingness of the debtor to repay the debt. At the time of contracting, lenders want to assess whether borrowers are creditworthy, i.e. if they have the ability to pay when the repayment is due back, and/or that they have the willingness and incentive to pay back their debt. These are two different types of risk: some people may be able to pay but are unwilling to do so; or, vice versa, they want to pay but due to unexpected changes in their circumstances are unable to do so.

The unwillingness to repay is known as 'moral hazard'. It refers to the risk which arises from personal, as distinct from physical, characteristics of a borrower that increases the possibility of an economic loss. It is a phenomenon normally associated with business credit: it occurs when entrepreneurs have incentives to invest in riskier projects and a larger proportion of the cost is financed by a lender. If the project is successful, they have much to gain from any excess return, but if the project fails their losses would be limited by bankruptcy. Hence, in this circumstance, as lenders will suffer much of the actual economic losses, borrowers do not have incentives to act prudently and exceed in risk-taking in the attempt to maximise returns. Investments, by contrast, are deemed to become capable of being safer if entrepreneurs have more to lose, in particular if they are forced to bear a portion of the risk.[4]

---

[1] Admati and Pfleiderer (2000); Akerlof (1970); Berger and Udell (1995); Diamond (1991); Stiglitz and Weiss (1981).
[2] Ibid.
[3] Ibid.
[4] Bertola et al. (2006).

Moral hazard is now considered directly relevant also for the behaviour of consumers in the use of mortgage or consumptive credit every time that a repayment reflects the willingness, not the ability, to honour one's debts. In credit to consumers, individuals do not make risky investments but they use credit to consume or buy a property.[5] As the theory explains, when deciding to repay, a rational agent weighs the gain of failing to repay vis-à-vis the punishment for default. Since small-size debts are not be cost-effective to recover by lenders, and debtors may receive no or little punishment by the law; a number of consumers may become prone to moral-hazard, i.e. they may willingly decide not to repay their debts.[6]

Similarly, economic theory also explains that information exchanges among lenders play a pivotal role as a borrower's discipline device, as the latter know that a delay or a default in repayment compromises their reputation with all the other potential lenders on the market, resulting in more costly credit or in being cut off from credit entirely.[7] Therefore, information exchanges among lenders would strengthen borrower discipline and reduce moral hazard, since late payment or failure to repay a debt with one institution would result in sanctions by all or many others. According to Miller, a borrower's 'good name', i.e. his or her reputation collateral, should provide 'an incentive to meet commitments much the same way as does a pledge of physical collateral, thus reducing moral hazard'.[8]

From this perspective, some have gone as far as suggesting that information exchanges maintain accountability and honesty in society.[9]

6.1.1.3 Cost-efficiency

Typically, the process of granting credit begins when a prospective customer approaches a credit provider and applies for credit or services/goods to be paid at a later stage. In the event the latter agrees to enter the financing or credit agreement, then, such a relationship ends when the last statement of the credit line is paid back in accordance with the same agreement or, in the worst-case scenario, when the credit is unrecoverable and/or disregarded following a debt recovery proceeding and a judicial procedure, or in some jurisdictions the judicial declaration of insolvency of the borrower. The recourse to debt collection procedures and legal actions,

---

[5] High levels of indebtedness are risky for consumers who may be exposed to economic shocks and over-indebtedness. For example, this is why Sweden proposed new legislation forcing amortisation requirements which demands mortgage holders to repay more than they currently do, especially if they have borrowed high percentages of the purchase price of their home. See the official website of the Swedish central administrative body in charge of monitoring and analysing the trends in the financial market (*Finansinspektionen*), at www.fi.se/upload/90_English/80_Press_office/2014/measures-household-indebtedness-eng.pdf

[6] Bertola et al. (2006).
[7] Admati and Pfleiderer (2000); Diamond (1991); Jappelli and Pagano (2002, 2006).
[8] Miller (2003a, esp. p. 2; 2003b).
[9] Klein (1992, 1997).

however, does not guarantee recovery of the debt and, in any event, they are considered an instrument of last resort as they are perceived to be both costly and time-consuming.[10]

Thus, risk assessment and applicant screening have become particularly important for the consumer credit industry which has to deal with a large number of small-sum (often unsecured) credit lines. It is widely agreed, in fact, that in this sector profitability is only achieved by minimising the risk while ensuring that a sizeable volume of credit lines is granted. Hence, credit grantors consider information about borrowers vital for their risk-assessment purposes. Along these lines, one of the best predictors of future behaviour is considered to be past behaviour. Therefore, information on how a potential borrower has met obligations in the past enables lenders to more accurately evaluate credit risk, easing adverse selection problems.[11]

Moreover, the small or medium size of loans to consumers means that it is not cost-efficient to assess consumers on a case-by-case basis. Traditionally, when lenders evaluate borrowers to determine their creditworthiness for credit risk assessment and management, they interview the applicants and ask them directly for personal information together with the relevant supporting documents. At the same time, they seek and gather information from their own databases developed through years of experience and business practice in the credit market. Such a source of information, however, is incomplete as it covers a lender's own past and present customers, but it does not contain data about the same customers' past and/or present relationship with other financial institutions nor, from a competition perspective, information about new or prospective customers and their past and/or present relationship with other providers. Thus, it is with a view to supplementing comprehensive information about these customers that information exchanges among lenders and sophisticated centralised databases were developed over the past few decades.[12]

6.1.2 Data and Banking Competition

As far as competition is concerned, the exchange of information on customer relationships or applicants reduces the information monopoly of individual lenders and the competitive advantage of large financial institutions. Although lenders lose the exclusivity of data in terms of competition one versus the other, they would ultimately gain by sharing information as this additional accumulation of data enables them to distinguish the good borrowers from the bad ones. Information sharing would serve as a tool to predict the future payment behaviour of applicants allowing lenders to attract creditworthy borrowers and offering them better terms and conditions, thus promoting market competition that could ultimately result in

---

[10] Riestra (2002), esp. p. 4; Bertola et al. (2006).
[11] Miller (2003a, esp. p. 2; 2003b).
[12] Bertola et al. (2006); Riestra (2002). However, in some countries (e.g. Germany) credit bureaus have existed for a longer time (see section 6.3).

benefits to those 'good consumers'.[13] Hence, the adverse selection problem identified by the economic literature indicates that should lenders fail to distinguish the good borrowers from the bad ones, all accepted borrowers would be charged at a higher rate an average interest rate that mirrors their pooled experience.[14] Therefore, the distinction between good and bad borrowers allows lenders on the one hand to offer more advantageous prices to lower-risk borrowers while, on the other hand, higher-risk borrowers are offered higher interest rates or can be rationed out of the market because of lenders' unwillingness to offer these borrowers accommodating rates or any credit at all.[15]

The problem of asymmetric information and adverse selection becomes greater for new market entrants, particularly foreign lenders. This is particularly the case in the context of the creation of the EU single market and cross-border entry or cross-border provision of financial services. In addition to competitive disadvantages in relation to incurring greater risks of incorrectly estimating a borrower's credit risk, without relevant information on borrowers new market entrants would be likely to attract precisely those who were rejected by existing lenders in the market.[16] This circumstance has induced recent literature to conclude that information sharing, market structure and competitive conduct are intrinsically intertwined in the financial services market and, from the standpoint of industrial organisation, the availability of information shared by the sector can affect foreign lenders' choice not only of whether to entry another jurisdiction but also the mode of doing it, i.e. whether through the cross-border provision of services, the setting-up of branches or subsidiaries, or through mergers and acquisitions.[17]

Therefore, on the one hand such strategies may well have the potential to influence the intensity of competition in national markets and among national providers. On the other hand, however, this is an indication that the behaviour of one or few market players – particularly existing lenders – influences and drives the behaviour of others, especially new entrants, which will decide their strategies on the experience, or market intelligence, of existing ones.

Prima facie, considerations of the like may have the effect of casting doubt on whether or to what extent in actual fact this may constitute a concerted practice or simply a reduction of market uncertainty.[18]

Also, to the extent that information monopoly of individual lenders is reduced, this is transferred to those third-party subjects who become the providers of information and manage the corresponding databases, i.e. the credit bureaus. This, in turn, may raise new concerns over market competition and power which are beyond the

---

[13] European Commission (2009).
[14] Alary and Gollier (2001).
[15] Barron and Staten (2000, 2003).
[16] Giannetti et al. (2010).
[17] Ibid.
[18] Ferretti (2014).

scope of this work.[19] Nonetheless, as far as consumer protection is concerned, the monopoly or oligopoly in the centralisation of information into national siloes risks tying consumers in preconceived solvency schemes according to the local designs of the databases.

6.1.3 The Limits of Classic Economic Theory

It is not within the scope of this contribution to challenge or discredit the economic theories and rationale for the use of solvency data and the sharing of same.

Nonetheless, it cannot be underestimated how the traditional economic theories suffer from not being universally accepted. One of the most apparent limitations lies in the neo-classical understanding or bias of the consumer borrower as purely a *homo economicus*. These theories, in fact, seem to envision a commercial relationship where consumers are perfectly rational, informed, vigilant and alert. For example, they know and understand how the data sharing works, as well as the value and meaning given to the data; they appreciate the association of the data with other information; they are capable of regularly identifying and disputing errors, etc. In short, the economic behaviour of consumers is explained as if they were fully rational, narrowly self-interested actors who have the ability to make judgements towards their subjectively defined ends; consumers who maximise their own utility and make intelligent and conscious choices, free of external events biasing or forcing their behaviour.[20]

Such an economic interpretation appears inconsistent with the findings and increasing acceptance of the behavioural literature which attempts to explain relevant features of human behaviour and consumers' cognitive limitations that cannot be explained under standard economic assumptions. It challenges economic assumptions by using a number of alternative social sciences or disciplines such as psychology, sociology, neurosciences to explore the real behaviour of human beings and how economic decisions are taken or dictated in the economic, cultural and social context where they live.[21]

Moreover, solvency data may only give a partial or fragmented picture of the borrower story or situation. They may present a distorted impression of individuals, not because the data are incorrect but for presenting a piecemeal picture making it seem incomplete and incorrect. In simple language, it is like taking a few slivers of a person and presenting that as the whole person.

---

[19] See *ibid.*, where these issues have been addressed.
[20] Becker (1976); Osovsky (2013); Staten and Cate (2004).
[21] The literature on behavioural economics is copious, see e.g. Camerer et al. (2003); Diamond and Vartiainen (2007); Hansen and Kysar (1999); Jolls et al. (1998). For literature specifically relevant to borrowers' behaviour, see e.g. Agarwal and Zhang (2015); Lea [no date]; Tooth (2012); Wright (2007); Xiao (2015).

Also, the economics of giving a second chance to consumers has been underexplored.

Many other questions may arise on the viability and assessment of those who are not in the databases. Arguably, those who are not in the databases for not having incurred into any financing operation are not negligible in numbers. The problem seems to be that there are no fixed rules in the industry or the literature as to what constitutes a good credit risk. Assuming that a good credit risk is someone with immaculate repayment behaviour, the system seems to penalise those with a weaker credit history notwithstanding their personal circumstances, or ignoring behavioural biases or unstandardised conduct. From this point of view, the resulting theories appear to some extent artificial. The ability of these systems to detect atypical behaviours raises new questions and problems because they also make assumptions about what is normal behaviour, where deviation from the established pattern is seen as undesirable or questionable, with all that that implies. In this respect, the biases behind the classic economic theories go against the foundations of human behaviours as heterogeneous and unpredictable.

The above concerns are exacerbated by the consideration that the reviewed economic literature provides no conclusive or at least empirical evidence – nor a certain relation of cause and effect – as to the connection between the data exchanges and the predictability of human behaviour. In addition, the theory that justifies the rationale for credit bureaus has been criticised for being far from complete. According to Jentzsch, for instance, 'this literature is primarily incoherent because there are different approaches to information ... The economic implications of information are multi-dimensional and no model can integrate them all at once.'[22] Others have begun to question the economic efficiency of giving a memory to the market, advancing the proposition that giving second chances to defaulting debtors may be justified not only on equity grounds but also on economic grounds.[23] This exploration has remained at its infancy but it tells that other routes could be explored.

Nevertheless, what seems to be mostly important when considering all such issues is that one should not forget that, unlike public credit bureaus, the use of private or commercial credit bureaus is not mandatory by law.

6.1.4 Expanding Uses of Solvency Data Sharing

6.1.4.1 Credit Scoring

Credit scoring is a related, yet distinct, use of solvency data that avails itself of ad hoc technologies which add additional features and integrate the data with other data

---

[22] Jentzsch (2007), esp. p. 7.
[23] Jappelli and Pagano (2000), esp. p. 15.

sources. Scoring models are mathematical algorithms or statistical programmes that determine the probable repayments of debts by consumers, assigning a score to an individual based on the information processed from a number of data sources and categorising credit applicants according to risk classes. Thus, the resulting credit score is the numerical expression based on a statistical formula to evaluate an individual's financial health and creditworthiness at a given point in time.[24] They involve data-mining techniques which include statistics, artificial intelligence, machine learning and other fields aiming at getting knowledge from large databases of solvency data.[25]

Scoring has been subject to several criticisms for its numerous fallacies, particularly for introducing new biases, or for making assumptions that lack universal acceptance or that may work on large numbers but not for individual cases.[26]

In the end, scoring is essentially a classification and profiling technique, a way of recognising different groups in a population according to certain features expressed by a combination of personal financial and other non-personal data, differentiating consumers on grounds of parameters and classifications set a priori from statistics for a predictive purpose. It is an analysis of customer behaviour having the objective of classifying them in two or more groups based on a predictive outcome associated with each customer. The probability of given events, such as for example a default in the repayment of a loan, is assumed to depend on a number of characteristics of the individuals.[27] The factors relevant for such a classification purpose are usually determined through an analysis of consumers' past payment history together with other descriptive information provided in the credit application form and other personal and non-personal data from a number of different public sources.

In short, a goal of credit scoring systems in the lending process is that of predicting the risk or assessing through automated means the creditworthiness of consumers, as well as the profitability of lenders over each one of them. It is now used for all consumer credit operations, in issuing credit cards and managing accounts, as well as in mortgage origination and securitisation operations of consumer loans. Although credit scoring was originally employed to seek to minimise the percentage of consumers who default, lenders are now using it to identify the customers who are most profitable and to maximise profits through risk-based pricing according to their profile thus obtained, blurring all this with direct marketing activities.[28]

For example, the existence of scores reduces the incentive of lenders to assess the data in the credit register where the main motive is the automatisation of decision-making. This is usually the case for most small- and middle-sized loans.

---

[24] Abdou and Pointon (2011), esp. p. 62.
[25] See e.g. Bigus (1996); Desai et al. (1997); Handzic et al. (2003); Jensen (1992); Yobas and Crook (2000).
[26] For all see e.g. Poulton (1994).
[27] Fractal Analytics (2003).
[28] Thomas (2000).

In such a process, to avoid a selection bias, account has to be taken not only of the characteristics of borrowers who were granted credit but also of those who were denied it.[29]

Computer scientists believe that the reasons for the poor judgemental capabilities of humans are: (1) the subjectivity and large grey area where the decision is up to the officers; (2) humans being prone to bias, for instance in presence of a physical or emotional condition which may affect the decision-making process; (3) personal acquaintances with applicants distorting the decision-making process; (4) humans considering the evidence sequentially rather than simultaneously; (5) the difficulty for humans of discovering useful relationships or patterns from data and the knowledge hidden in the same data.[30] Moreover, humans are costly and time-consuming.[31]

A problematic aspect is the lack of transparency in the scoring process. The methodology is usually not disclosed, while it is not clear who has access to the scoring data. Scoring makes the solvency data more tradable. It could thus be seen as tipping the conflict of interest between the prevention of over-indebtedness vis-à-vis sales acceleration towards the latter. Proprietary algorithms are considered trade secrets and therefore the exact scoring methods are protected. Secrecy over the methods and opacity over their uses are justified as a means to keep competitors from learning how lenders select and price their customers. Therefore, it is not possible to know how the systems are built and operated. Moreover, opacity is justified as a means to prevent scored individuals from deceiving the lender by falsifying their applications to reach a desired score.

For the problems that it raises, previous scholarship has pointed out the need of addressing consumer rights and transparency in the credit scoring of consumers. For example, the opacity surrounding the scoring methods can be criticised for preventing consumers from knowing why their applications have been turned down, challenging existing scoring models and avoiding new adverse data from being added for future applications.[32] From this perspective, to some extent Germany has been a precursor in enacting specific legal measures. For the first time in Germany and largely in the EU, the law altering the German Data Protection Act of 29 May 2009 deals specifically with consumer-related scoring.[33] In turn, the German Supreme Court (Bundesgerichtshof) has confirmed that credit scoring qualifies for meeting legal requirements under data protection legislation, but has affirmed that the underlying mathematical and statistical calculation method can be protected as a trade secret. Thus, it remains open to question to what extent

---

[29] Mester (1997).
[30] Glorfeld and Hardgrave (1996); Yobas and Crook (2000).
[31] Jensen (1992).
[32] Ferretti (2009).
[33] Metz (2012).

transparency can be guaranteed to consumers, which is a matter now under the consideration of the German Constitutional Court.[34]

Clearly, no scoring system, even the most sophisticated ones, may predict with certainty any individual repayment performance or situations of future over-indebtedness.[35]

6.1.4.2 Securitisation

Information pooling and sharing can be used for the securitisation on lenders' portfolios of consumer loans, including mortgages.

In its simplest form, securitisation is a financial operation used by a financial institution on the receiving end of credit repayments from customers who have taken out financing. It bundles its loans repackaging the monthly loan payments into securities rated by rating agencies, and it backs them using the underlying loans as collaterals. It then transfers or sells such securities on to investors in order to receive funding which can be used to issue more loans.

According to financial theory, investors in asset-backed securities need information on the quality of the underlying assets. Without such information, investors would not risk investing or they would require a risk premium which would signify higher refinancing costs for lenders, ultimately being passed onto consumers with higher borrowing costs. Therefore, financial institutions involved in the process of securitisation avail themselves of the services of credit rating agencies such as Standard & Poor's, Moody's and Fitch (to mention just three of the most well-known big rating agencies) which grade or score the repackaged loans on the credit risk associated with those securities. In such rating of securities for the calculation of the risk of default, the agencies need to rely on data on the underlying loans from the information providers organising the exchange of information among the competing lenders. However, they do not have access to the data and they need to rely on the credit score assigned by the same information providers.[36] Thus, the whole process mostly relies on a double scoring or rating from different intermediaries.

---

[34] See Bundesgerichtshof, press release, at http://juris.bundesgerichtshof.de/cgi-bin/rechtsprechung/document.py?Gericht=bgh&Art=en&sid=2ef8cefa03b7d0493f54c1bc71ee0a53&anz=1&pos=0&nr=66583&linked=pm&Blank=1. Schufa, Germany's leading credit bureau was sued by a German individual over the lack of transparency of its credit scoring methods. The plaintiff had been denied credit, and Schufa had already provided him with information as required by law. However, the company did not provide the underlying method, which it regarded as a trade secret. The court held that while credit bureaus must disclose all personal data as prescribed in the Federal German Data Protection Act, they do not have to disclose how the underlying scoring algorithm weighed the various factors or how the reference groups arrive at a credit score. Following this decision of the Supreme Court, the matter has been brought before the German Constitutional Court and a decision is awaited as to the balancing of the fundamental rights of privacy and data protection vis-à-vis the safeguard of trade secrets (German Constitutional Court, Case no. 1 BvR 756/2014).
[35] Mester (1997).
[36] Keys et al. (2008); Engel and McCoy (2011); European Commission (2009).

Securitisation has the effect of transferring credit risks to investors, releasing lenders from concerns over defaults, and ultimately resulting in more reckless credit for consumers as well as dangers for the health and stability of the financial system. Securitisation was identified as one of the biggest factors contributing to the subprime lending boom and bust which led to 'the great financial crisis' that erupted in 2008. Such discussion, however, is beyond the scope of this contribution, and has been analysed elsewhere in great detail.[37]

6.1.4.3 Identity Verification

Traditionally, undertaking the identity check of an applicant has involved lenders requiring individuals to produce documentary evidence, such as a passport, an identity card, a driving licence, or in countries like the United Kingdom even utility bills. Such documents, then, were examined by a lender's officer in order to establish that documents were genuine and they truly related to the individual making the application. Officers, finally, needed to take the evidence of the identity check by photocopying and filing the documents.

The use of databases is said by the industry to enable lenders to check on several sources, thus forming the so-called 'electronic footprint' of every individual, which is used to match against the personal data supplied by the applicant.

In a way, identity verification challenges the role of the state, which is the only one which can determine the identity documents and true identity of individuals. Once more, cost saving is the main driver for such an additional use. But in those countries where such tools are used, the cost of credit does not appear to be lower for consumers (e.g. France and Belgium).[38]

6.1.4.4 Marketing

Solvency data are increasingly used to segment and classify customers, and to price loans accordingly. Yet, those consumers who are a higher risk in the terms of the credit industry are those who pay more for credit. This is certainly not a use for the pursuit of responsible lending policies and over-indebtedness prevention. A trend, for example, is that of setting up businesses whose core activity is that of lending at higher rates to borrowers with poor credit records, also known as 'subprime lending'.[39]

Solvency data are also used for marketing other banking products. Many private credit bureaus do not have predefined and strict conditions under which the data

---

[37] For a detailed account of the securitisation of consumer loans, see e.g. Engel and McCoy (2011).
[38] See e.g. Eurobarometers available from http://ec.europa.eu/public_opinion/archives/ebs/ebs_321_en.pdf; http://ec.europa.eu/public_opinion/archives/ebs/ebs_355_en.pdf
[39] See e.g. in the UK, Callcredit, at www.callcredit.co.uk/products-and-services/consumer-marketing-data/segmentation-analysis; for reading, see e.g. Engel and McCoy (2011).

may be checked (e.g. request of the consumer for a credit offer, payment difficulties). And, even more important, one of the main uses of scores is that they can be sold to other goods/services providers.

Other marketing activities resulting from the use of data are product development for the profitability of the industry and geo-marketing.[40]

6.1.4.5 Fraud Prevention

Consumer solvency data can be used alongside the application-processing systems to compare a current credit application with previous ones over a number of years by matching the application details. Thus, it would be possible to look for discrepancies and detect omissions, the data an applicant would like not to disclose, or inaccurate or untrue details within the applicant's history. Similarly, these databases would be used to detect multiple applications in the applicant's name within the same time frame, misleadingly including consumers shopping around for quotes, or the use by applicants of different names for the same banking details or other patterns of (alleged) fraudulent behaviour.

Databases, in this way, become substitutes of lengthier and more complete documentation in the interest of the credit industry. However, empirical evidence of the incidence of fraud vis-à-vis all loan applications is largely missing, as it is evidence that solvency databases are the appropriate tool to prevent it. Arguably, further research in this area is necessary. If anything, reliance on databases erodes the principle of 'know your customers', where it means acquiring a proper and more individualised knowledge of customers.

6.1.4.6 Fight against Identity Theft

There are two most commonly known types of identity theft: (1) 'account takeover' occurs when the fraudster acquires someone else's credit account information and purchases products and/or services using that person's existing accounts. Victims normally learn of the account takeover when checking their account statements; (2) 'application fraud' occurs when the impostor uses someone else's identifying information to open new accounts in that person's name. In this case, victims usually do not learn of the fraud for some time as the account statements are normally mailed to addresses used by the identity thief and there is no record on the accounts effectively in use.

Thus, databases can be used as real-time identity fraud detection and prevention automated tools, by matching key personal data provided on credit applications by

---

[40] See e.g. the websites of the major credit bureaus: Experian, at www.experian.co.uk/marketing-services/index.html; Equifax, at www.equifax.com/consumer/marketing; CRIF, at www.crif.com/site/en/Pages/default.aspx; Schufa, at www.schufa.de/en/en/produkteundservices_en/produkteservices_1.jsp

real-time access into a range of powerful market leading data sets, including directories and other independent data sources.[41]

The credit industry believes that the practice described above may prevent the 'account takeover' type of identity theft.

In the fight against 'application fraud', by contrast, the use of credit reports requires the active involvement of customers. Thus, a number of credit bureaus have seized the opportunity to develop a new service to the consumer market by offering credit reports for a fee, thus allowing and encouraging individuals, who are motivated by their anxiety, to check their own report regularly and catch possible frauds committed in their name.[42]

By contrast, it can be argued that increasing reliance on databases increments identity theft and makes it possible. Moreover, because of the reliance on databases, consumers who fall victim to identity theft have to go through hurdles to have their files cleaned and suffer the consequences of the theft for long time.

6.1.4.7 Emerging Trends

Increasingly, solvency data are becoming the gateway for other economic sectors such as telecoms or utilities. According to the survey carried out by the information suppliers' trade association (ACCIS), in some countries, utility companies, telecoms, TV and Internet providers have actively started to use solvency data provided by credit bureaus. In ACCIS's view, there is potential for greater supply of data from utility providers and telecommunication companies and for these companies to use the services provided by the credit bureaus.[43]

In some jurisdictions, such as in the UK, solvency data are used by estate agencies and landlords for granting tenancy agreements. Similarly, such data may now be used to screen job applicants. Consumer solvency data, therefore, risk becoming increasingly more a tool of economic and social inclusion or exclusion.

Agencies of non-commercial nature are starting to use solvency data too. For example, in the last few years in the UK, government agencies have started to make use of credit bureau databases to overcome contingent situations, such as measures directed to tackle terrorism or other forms of organised crime (notwithstanding how controversial these remedies may seem to many), as well as to maximise the enforcement of, or give execution to, orders issued under the rule of law. It has also been reported that in the attempt to thwart bogus applications for UK passports in an effort to fight terrorism, 'the data sharing provisions of the draft identity cards bill are to allow the UK Passport Service to tap into the databases of credit bureaus and other commercial organisations'.[44] In the

---

[41] Experian (www.experian.co.uk); Equifax (www.equifax.co.uk).
[42] *Ibid.*; Callcredit, at www.callcredit.co.uk
[43] ACCIS (2015).
[44] 'Topic: Confidence and Data Protection – News and Views', *Privacy and Data Protection* (11 March 2004).

recent past, the use of credit reference data has been a part of the dismissed proposal to set up a national ID card scheme, and an integral element of 'biographical footprint checking' of applications. To this purpose, the UK Passport Service has engaged in a data-sharing project with a credit bureau, the Home Office immigration and nationality department, the Department of Work and Pension and the Driver and Vehicle Licensing Agency.[45] Local governments review council tax payments and entitlements using information that is held on their records and data from commercial credit bureaus.[46]

Even the Department for Constitutional Affairs in the UK, which also has access to the UK Police National Computer to locate defaulters, has signed a contract to use the database of a credit bureau to track fine-dodgers. According to a report, magistrates have used the 500-million records kept by such credit bureaus to pursue a total of £276 million British Pounds in unpaid court fines in England and Wales.[47]

Again, 48 per cent of governments or central banks have access to the data held by credit reference agencies (CRAs) for monitoring and economic policy purposes. For instance, some government departments (e.g. tax authorities) and law enforcement agencies (e.g. police) are allowed access as an exception to the reciprocity rule.[48]

6.1.4.8 New Consumer Services

A number of commercial credit bureaus have developed services for consumers, selling them the credit report to verify whether they qualify for credit and the amount that they may be able to obtain.[49]

However, concerns have been expressed that the credit reports sold to consumers are not the same as those sold to financial institutions, where they have at their disposal much more in-depth data and detail. In the end, consumers do not buy what the credit industry really uses.[50]

In this way, the solvency data system has created new needs for consumers to know if and how they qualify for credit, and how financial institutions value them. This may have the potential to nudge consumers towards the financial behaviour envisaged by the credit industry.

However, it is questionable to what extent it is legitimate or appropriate to sell information to consumers about themselves. Under data protection law, as implemented in the national laws of the Member States, data subjects (i.e. consumers)

---

[45] *Ibid.* See also Secretary of State for the Home Department by Command of Her Majesty, 'Legislation on Identity Cards, a Consultation' (April 2004), at www.privacyinternational.org/issues/idcard/uk/id-card-draft-404.pdf, 21; Home Office, 'Identity Cards Bill Regulatory Impact Assessment', at www.homeofficeqsi.gov.uk; Molloy (2004).

[46] See e.g. Capacitygrid, a commercial company offering on-demand business services to local authorities across the UK, supporting them with review services, at www.capacitygrid.com

[47] 'News', *New Law Journal* (8 October 2004), 154.

[48] ACCIS (2015).

[49] See e.g. Experian, at www.experian.co.uk/consumer

[50] See e.g. Consumer Financial Protection Bureau (2012).

have the legal right to access data regarding themselves. With the emerging provision of this kind of services the solvency data industry may be selling what in fact is a right of access, which by law is usually free of charge or, in the UK, it costs a minimal fee of £2.

6.2 SOLVENCY DATA IN THE POLICY AND LEGAL CONTEXT

6.2.1 Responsible Lending, Creditworthiness Assessment and Over-Indebtedness

As noted in previous chapters, the market for loans available to consumers has grown rapidly in the last decade across the EU and it is increasingly sophisticated. However, with the development of the retail and mortgage credit markets European consumers are becoming increasingly indebted. The growth of over-indebtedness is becoming a concern for national and EU policymakers alike. Besides, the financial crisis has raised important issues regarding the protection of consumers in financial markets and the need for additional safeguards to stem the social problems that it has exacerbated.[51] Therefore, alongside the advancement of measures for the cross-border provision of credit and the abolition of obstacles for further integration, the promotion of responsible lending and borrowing policies to limit the over-indebtedness of European consumers is high on the EU agenda, at least in principle. Likewise, the importance of the relationship between borrowers and financial institutions is under the close scrutiny of European policymakers.

6.2.1.1 The Consumer Credit Directive

As far as solvency data are concerned, the relevant provisions are contained in Articles 8 and 9 of the CCD. The CCD is not explicit and it is to some extent unclear on the exchange of consumer information, at least as far as the obligation to share information is concerned. Article 8 of the CCD states that creditors have to assess the consumer's creditworthiness on the basis of sufficient information obtained from the consumer, not through information exchanges. Only where it is *necessary*, financial institutions have to make such assessment on the basis of a consultation of the relevant database, such circumstance occurring in those Member States whose legislation requires them to consult databases, usually a requirement that may be imposed by central banks for purposes of financial stability (see sections 6.2.1.2 and 6.2.1.3).

---

[51] See European Commission, *Staff Working Paper on National Measures and Practices aimed at Avoiding Foreclosure Procedures for Residential Mortgage Loans* SEC(2011) 357 final, which pointed to the severe consequences for individual homeowners losing their homes in a foreclosure procedure, but also for society as a whole, considering the impact on financial and social stability.

At the same time, Article 9 the CCD is concerned that for competition purposes access is ensured on a non-discriminatory basis for creditors from other Member States to databases used in another Member State, if any.

6.2.1.2 The Mortgage Credit Directive

In the creditworthiness assessment, therefore, the MCD requires that creditors take appropriate account of a number of relevant factors, requiring financial institutions to obtain information directly from the consumer, with the addition of relevant internal or external sources but without mandating or explicating information exchanges among lenders as the necessary 'external source' to be used. Relevant factors include income, savings, assets, expenses, features of the loan of offer, etc. Solvency data are one of many possible sources of information for the assessment of creditworthiness.[52]

What may appear unclear about this provision is that mainstream lenders already availed themselves of solvency databases well before the financial crisis and the passing of the MCD, and they have always demanded relevant information of the applicants. But, arguably, the creation of the internal market and competition suggested that access to such information should be mandated on a non-discriminatory basis.

Indeed, like the CCD, the MCD looks at the competition side of the market and it provides for the non-discriminatory access of creditors to the databases used in another Member States via the exchange of information among the competing creditors, specifying that such databases comprise databases operated by private information providers as well as public registers.[53]

The focus on competition of the MCD is clear from the Recitals:

> to prevent any distortion of competition among creditors, it should be ensured that all creditors, including credit institutions or non-credit institutions providing credit agreements relating to residential immovable property, have access to all public and private credit databases concerning consumers under non-discriminatory conditions.[54]

6.2.1.3 Credit Laws and Solvency Data

When it comes to solvency data, it appears clear that while they are considered as a possible tool to assess consumer creditworthiness, their use is not a mandatory requirement by law. If used, however, non-discriminatory access to all lenders should be guaranteed in order to avoid distortions of competition – this, however, is not a measure of consumer protection.

---

[52] See Arts. 18 and 20 of the MCD.
[53] See Art. 21 of the MCD; see also European Banking Authority (2013).
[54] Recital 60 of the MCD.

In addition, the guidelines of the European Banking Authority (EBA) on creditworthiness assessment do not make reference on the use of solvency data.[55] By contrast, EBA has only started recently to investigate the possible advantages and/or disadvantages of the use of consumer data by financial institutions.[56]

At any rate, it is important to stress that both the CCD and the MCD state that the provisions mentioning the use of solvency data are without prejudice to the application of the EU data protection law on the protection of individuals with regard to the processing of personal data and on the free movement of such data, whose provisions must be respected, particularly as far as the requirements of 'necessity' and 'proportionality' of the processing are concerned[57] (on solvency data in relation to data protection, see Chapter 7).

Only recently, in its thrust towards the creation of a true European market for retail financial services, the European Commission have identified the issue of what solvency data should be necessary for the creditworthiness assessment and whether the increased use of personal financial and non-financial data by firms (including traditionally non-financial firms) require further action to facilitate provision of services or ensure consumer protection.[58] The concern arises from the above analysed provisions of the CCD and MCD where creditors have the right to consult credit databases in other Member States on a non-discriminatory basis to assess the creditworthiness of potential customers. Accordingly, however, lenders still face problems when attempting to use data as the techniques for their collection, distribution and use are still very diverse across the EU, and opinions vary on what data is relevant for creditworthiness assessments. This means that accessing and using these data by creditors in other Member States is problematic and they are unable to provide their services cross-border competitively. At the same time, there is the recognition that private credit bureaus often collect more data than necessary for the purposes of a creditworthiness assessment, or data which might be of questionable relevance to a creditworthiness assessment.[59]

Against such policy and legal context, it can be argued that on the one hand the exchange of solvency data may be regarded as a tool that in the end should be to the benefit of consumers. On the other hand, however, it remains open to debate whether or the extent to which the type of data used and the design of databases is proportionate to the policy goals to be achieved, and whether or the extent to which the level of aggregation or detail of information exceeds the purpose for its sharing. In turn, the first issue raises debates over duties and social responsibilities and the

---

[55] European Banking Authority (2015a).
[56] European Banking Authority (2016); see also the Joint Committee of the European Supervisory Authorities (2016).
[57] See Art. 9(4) of the CCD, and Recitals 59, 61 and 62 of the MCD.
[58] European Commission, Green Paper on Retail Financial Services, COM(2015) 630 final (Brussels, 10 December 2015).
[59] Ibid.

institutions which should be entrusted with the exercise of the social function of controlling over-indebtedness in the interest of consumers, as well as the oversight of these systems.[60]

6.2.2 Prudential Supervision

Information exchanges among competing lenders may be justified and used for the supervision of the financial system as a whole and assist in preserving financial stability. Under certain national systems, solvency data are part of a broader information centralisation system managed by national central banks for the purpose of oversight of the financial system as a whole, i.e. they are an instrument for the macro-prudential supervision of the banking system. But credit risk data may also become a tool for the micro-prudential supervision if used to oversight and safeguard individual financial institutions from excessive risk-taking.[61]

Financial prudential supervision encompasses a number of complex issues and elements that are beyond the scope of this work. But, among the tools to achieve it, there is the need for the authorities in charge of this public function to have adequate and timely information about the behaviour, leverage and condition of banks vis-à-vis the whole system. Among the many types of information needed by the authorities – such as asset quality, capital adequacy, liquidity, internal systems of control and security, income and dividends, foreign operations, and so on – is included the regular reporting on past due loans and non-performing loans. This not only allows supervisors to be in control and have the information on the condition and performance of the supervisees to intervene in time in case of problems, but it also constitutes an instrument to promote transparency to favour greater reliance on market discipline. The information available to financial supervisors also allows them to produce macro statistics and perform a number of analyses. For example, in Spain credit risk data are used for the stress testing of banks.[62]

In addition, access to solvency data by public authorities may provide them with the tools to study credit conditions and so support the decisions of monetary and other macroeconomic policymakers. According to the Bank of England, a key use of such data would be to improve the understanding of the transmission mechanism for monetary policy and to assess its impact upon both the availability of credit and bank risk-taking.[63]

In turn, under a limited number of mechanisms supervisors provide feedback loops to the banks that provide the data.

---

[60] Ferretti (2010).
[61] For the institutional arrangements in the various EU Member States, see the tables in this chapter.
[62] See e.g. European Banking Authority (2014b).
[63] Bank of England (2014).

According to this prudential model, banks benefit from supervision in that they are provided with the instruments to control the quality of their loans in their daily operations. To favour this, in a number of Member States centralised databases managed by public authorities provide banks and supervisors with aggregate or granular information (depending on national regulation) about the level of indebtedness of borrowers vis-à-vis the whole system, including natural persons. In these jurisdictions, information sharing by supervised banks is mandated by law, usually a national banking act.[64]

This mechanism relies on information exchanges among financial institutions where the public authority acts as the third-party pooling, aggregating and elaborating the information exchanged, as well as the organisation setting the rules of the information exchanges.

The exchange of private financial information in this context may become clearer in the discussion of the information providers and their role which, in turn, will be helpful for matters of competition law and policy (see section 6.3).

6.3 THE LEGAL FORM AND FUNCTIONS OF CREDIT BUREAUS IN THE EU

Credit bureaus are the major data channels for a number of different purposes in the Member States. Credit bureaus now exist in all EU Member States with the exception of Luxembourg, but their legal form or institutional structure varies depending on different policy or other objectives, and the function that they perform in the economy and society. Databases are organised and the types of information are provided depending on the pursuit of defined policy objectives or other private interests that they are meant to address. The different role of credit information providers reveals a key distinction between public and private or commercial organisations. While the former is normally a part of a national central bank or supervisory authority, and institutionally and legally designed to address the stability of the financial system and the monitoring of the indebtedness of consumer households, the latter offers to the market risk-management and market intelligence tools to enhance economic efficiency and the profitability of financial institutions irrespective of whether these are banks that lending the money of depositors or any other entity doing business through the provision of credit in return for profit (e.g. specialist credit providers).[65]

6.3.1 *Private or Commercial Credit Bureaus*

These are fully fledged privately owned companies working for profit (see e.g. commercial companies in the UK, Germany, Italy) or for the benefit of banks (see

---

[64] Brealey et al. (2001), esp. ch. 2; Cartwright (2004), esp. pp. 31–4; Ferretti (2008); Jappelli and Pagano (2000, 2003, 2006); Lastra (1996); Lastra and Shams (2001).
[65] Ferretti (2008); Jappelli and Pagano (2000, 2003, 2006).

e.g. not-for-profit entities designed to make the interest of commercial ventures such as banks in Slovenia or Poland) that are no more controlled, monitored or influenced by state-controlled organisations or other public bodies than any other privately owned organisation or business. Nor are they accountable to public bodies, central banks or other financial service regulators. They are subject to the same rules and regulations as every business in the marketplace. Their job is to provide services to the financial services industry compiling databases. Even looking at the websites of these companies, they clearly state that they provide decision-making tools or marketing intelligence to the credit industry. They do not claim to have social tasks to prevent consumer over-indebtedness and they are not held accountable for the decisions taken by the credit industry.

They can have a broad range of client members depending on the jurisdiction, from banks to non-bank lenders. In addition to traditional financing firms that are not banks, other less obvious examples may include telecommunication companies, utility companies, mail order companies and/or any other business advancing goods or services to consumers paying for them at a later stage. Consultation of their databases is not mandatory by law prior to the underwriting of credit and is carried out on a voluntary basis (the exception is Slovenia where banks have to use such bank-owned databases, but other non-bank lenders are not obliged to subscribe to them). As participation by lenders in a privately owned consumer credit information system is not compulsory, the rules relating to the functioning of the system are not imposed by law or regulation but are governed by contract law.[66]

In some jurisdictions, these databases are supplemented with non-solvency data collected from other sources. Thus, financial and non-financial entities may have access to consumer information across different economic segments. In this way, accessibility to full credit and other non-solvency data may affect the inclusion, exclusion or sorting in different economic spheres of the consumers. Moreover, this leads to the problem of incomplete or missing data on one's credit profile, possibly resulting in an inaccurate picture on the consumer's finances and wrong scoring assumptions. This is a problem unique to private credit registers. As commercial ventures, they integrate their services with consumer risk scoring (which includes both behavioural and sociological customer scoring), loan or mortgage rating, risk screening, monitoring, propensity modelling, debtor tracking and support to debt collection.

6.3.2 *Public Credit Bureaus*

These are institutions typical of continental Europe, where they first originated and developed with the objective of providing an information system for supervisors to analyse banks' portfolios and monitor the health and soundness of the overall

---

[66] Ferretti (2008).

financial system of a country, as well as the level of indebtedness of borrowers, both legal and natural persons.

Generally, they exercise a public function by furthering the general stability of the banking and payment system.

This requires the monitoring of the safety and soundness of banks, which includes the monitoring of the amount of exposure of each bank towards legal persons and individuals who, consequently, undergo checks over their levels of indebtedness.

Only banks participate in the system and are subject to the underlying rules, unlike private registries that are conceived as open systems with the incentive of bringing an increasing number of subscribers and information into play.[67]

Another key difference is that financial institutions that are under the supervision of a country's central bank or supervisory authority are required to report certain solvency data on a regular basis by law or other regulation. As participation in the system is compulsory, its rules are imposed by law or regulation and not under contract. This compulsory nature also means that public bureaus have complete coverage of the financial institutions of a country, and no bank lenders are left out as may happen when parties are free to negotiate whether to take part in a system or not, or which system to be part of if more than one exists.[68]

Equally, public authorities have a legal basis for demanding that reporting lenders remedy possible inaccuracies or make available missing data. Failure to comply can result in sanctions that may be imposed by law, such as penalty fees followed by supervisory actions.[69]

It is undisputable from all the features discussed above that private or commercial credit bureaus on the one side, and public credit bureaus on the other side cannot be reciprocally substitutes to the extent that the latter exercise functions in the public interest that the former are not entitled to and do not perform. Public providers, however, can substitute for private/commercial ventures to the extent that the lenders' debt provisioning remains tightly controlled and the amount of overdue or defaulted debt is controlled. Lenders are entitled and do use these databases for risk-management purposes.

In sum, as Tables 6.1 and 6.2 show, the picture in the EU is fragmented. There are profound differences in the legal form and structure in the various Member States, the different roles of credit bureaus and the various types of data exchanged. The tables summarise the above discussion of the legal form of credit bureaus in terms of private versus public ownership and function. In the case of private or commercial credit bureaus, it emerges clearly the self-interest pursued by the credit industry and the bureaus. On the contrary, the

---

[67] Jappelli and Pagano (2003); Ferretti (2008).
[68] Ibid.
[69] Miller (2003b).

TABLE 6.1 *Legal form and structure of credit bureaus in EU Member States*

Country	Public credit register	No. of private credit bureaus			Ownership structure		
		For profit	Not for profit	Not ownership by creditors	≤ 50% ownership by creditors	≥ 50% ownership by creditors	Other
Austria	Yes	1					1
Belgium	Yes						
Bulgaria	Yes	1					
Cyprus	No	1		1		1	
Czech Rep.	Yes	1			1		
Denmark	No	2		2			
Estonia	No	1		1			
Finland	No	1		1			
France	Yes						
Germany	Yes	1			1		
Greece	No	1			1		
Hungary	No	1			1		
Ireland	No	1			1		
Italy	Yes	2	1	1		1	1
Latvia	Yes						
Lithuania	Yes	1				1	
Luxembourg	No						
Malta	No	1				1	
Netherlands	No	1	1	1			1
Poland	No	1			1		
Portugal	Yes	2				1	
Romania	Yes	2		1	1		
Slovakia	Yes	2		1	1		
Slovenia	Yes		1				1
Spain	Yes	2		1		1	
Sweden	No	6		5	1		
United Kingdom	No	3		3			

NB: The Table below should be corrected as regards Romania. The number of private credit bureaus is 1 (instead of 2), and the ownership structure is >50% ownership by creditors – in fact it is 100% (instead of <50% ownership by creditors).
Ireland is underway in establishing a public credit bureau leaving an open question as regards the future of private sector credit bureaus.
(*sources*: European Commission 2009; European Parliament 2011)

goals, role and function of databases controlled by public authorities show the pursuit of the general interest.

6.4 DATA SOURCES

All credit bureaus process data on individual consumers. In addition, the large majority processes data on sole traders and small- and medium-sized enterprises (SMEs).[70]

[70] ACCIS (2015).

TABLE 6.2 *Role and structure of private/commercial and public credit bureaus*

	Credit bureau	Public credit register
Ownership structure	Private/commercial entity	Central bank or supervisory authority
Clients structure	Mainly creditors but sometimes also other services providers	Financial institutions authorised to grant credit
Scope	Credit assessment and monitoring	• Banking supervision, building statistics, financial stability studies • Monitoring and preventing over-indebtedness • Credit assessment • Fostering credit institutions prudent management
Creditors' participation	Generally voluntary	Mandatory by law
Principle of reciprocity/ non-discriminatory access	Yes	Yes
Type of data stored	• Full credit data (positive and negative data • Often also non-credit data	• Credit data from financial institutions authorised to grant credit (including both positive and negative data in a majority of cases) • Data on bankruptcy of natural and legal persons
Additional services provided to creditors	• Mainly: • Credit scoring based on the whole CB data set • Software applications • Portfolio management services • Fraud prevention systems • Authentication products	None
Use of thresholds	Yes, but generally low	Yes
Degree of detail of the information provided	Detailed information on each individual loan. In some countries, credit information merged with other data (e.g. from public sources)	Information sometimes in a consolidated form (giving the total loan exposure of each borrower). In some public credit registers (Belgium, Italy, Portugal or Spain), the information is also given in a detailed form.
Coverage	Depends on the legislation, length of service provided, financial culture, etc.	Universal coverage

(*source:* European Commission 2009)

The data sources vary depending on the type of data typically processed by the credit bureaus and then used by the credit industry for the purposes outlined above. Most credit bureaus collect and then collate data from more than one source. The most common ones are the lenders themselves and the consumers (via the lenders). Public sources are also used for certain types of publicly available data to be then integrated with the other data furnished by the lenders. Examples are the electoral registers for identity data verification and the courts for insolvencies and other court data.

The most relevant data providers are the lenders themselves. However, in the context of credit to consumers the term 'lender' has a very broad significance. Depending on the jurisdictions, it may comprise any organisations that have the potential to provide credit facilities to consumers in the form of loans, mortgages, hire purchase, supply of goods and/or services billed upon use, etc. They include, for example, banks, building societies, finance houses, leasing and other retail credit companies, telecom and Internet service providers, high street retailers, credit card issuers, the home shopping sector, utility companies, estate agents, etc. In short, any legal persons that advance resources to natural persons which will be (re)paid at a later stage.

Credit bureaus often claim that the information is supplied by the lenders on a reciprocal basis, i.e. the lenders are able to access the databases only if they contribute to it for the benefit of all the other contributing member lenders.[71] This mechanism – based on what has been called the 'reciprocity principle' – in most cases relies on private law agreements between the credit bureaus and the lenders save for those jurisdictions where the data sharing is mandated by law (see further below).

Other commonly used characterisations for the data used are those making reference to the breath and the depth of the data. The breadth of data refers to the level of credit product coverage in the databases of the credit bureaus. This is also determined by the type of lenders taking part in the system.

Once again, the detail of the type of information collected and disseminated by credit bureaus varies from country to country. In general terms, it may be synthesised that credit bureaus store, process and disseminate consumers' files containing data on their previous and existing accounts, which normally include detailed information about mortgages, bank accounts, store cards, charge cards, credit cards, loan accounts and in many jurisdictions even mail order accounts as well as telecom and other utilities accounts.

Table 6.4 provides a synthesis of the type of data processed by country. A major problem at EU level is that there is no uniformity or common understanding regarding the terminologies used and there is no accepted use of the breadth of information.

---

[71] Experian, available at www.experian.co.uk; Equifax, cit. at 4; Callcredit, Official Website, available at www.callcredit.co.uk

TABLE 6.3 *Synoptic view of 'data provider lenders' types by country*

	AT	BE	HR	CY	CZ	DK	FI	DE	EL	HU	IT	NL	PL	XK	RO	RU	RS	SK	SI	SE	CH	GB
Banks																						
Credit unions																						
Debt collectors/debt purchasers																						
Leasing																						
Credit card suppliers																						
Retail credit suppliers																						
Health insurance																						
Other insurers																						
Energy (electricity, gas, other fuel)																						
Water																						
Telecommunication companies																						
Television suppliers (cable/satellite TV)																						
Internet providers (Broadband)																						
Mortgage providers																						
Home rental companies																						
Brokers/Intermediars																						
Courts																						
Governments departments																						
Crowd-funding platforms																						
Payment services providers																						
Tax authorities																						
Police																						
Central Banks																						
Acquirers of credit portfolios																						
Investors																						
Others																						

■ Yes, organisation supply data to the CRA   ■ In discussions
□ No, organisation doesn't supply data to the CRA   □ Not answered

Country codes for the EU Member States: AT: Austria; BE: Belgium; HR: Croatia; CY: Cyprus; CZ: Czech Republic; DK: Denmark; FI: Finland; DE: Germany; EL: Greece; HU: Hungary; IT: Italy; PL: Poland; RO: Romania; SK: Slovakia; SI: Slovenia; SE: Sweden; NL: The Netherlands; GB: United Kingdom
Note: Greece debt collectors do not supply data but debt purchasers do; in Finland data is not provided directly to the credit bureaus. The number of organisations providing data to credit bureaus is normally a function of the level of development of credit reporting in the particular country (ACCIS 2015).
(*source*: ACCIS 2015)

The depth of the data refers to the amount of information held about a specific credit agreement.

An important distinction to be drawn is the one between the so-called 'negative' information and 'positive' information.

'Negative' information usually refers to negative consumer data (information about defaults on payments, delays, delinquencies, bankruptcies, etc.). That is, information with a negative connotation on the payment history and the financial behaviour of the data subject.

'Positive' information, by contrast, refers to positive consumer data, i.e. information about the financial standing, payments and other details which do not indicate a default or a late payment.

TABLE 6.4 *Synoptic view of type of data processed by country*

	AT	BE	HR	CY	CZ	FI	DE	EL	HU	IT	NL	PL	XK	RO	RU	RS	SK	SI	SE	CH	GB
Mortgage																					
Consumer Loans																					
Credit and store card																					
Mail order																					
Point of sale credit																					
Energy (electricity, gas, oil)																					
Water																					
Education loans																					
Credit line on current account																					
Internet service provider																					
Satellite/cable TV																					
Fixed line Telecoms*																					
Telecoms - mobile																					
Payday loans /SMS loans																					
Home rent																					
Leasing																					
Health insurance																					
Other insurances																					
Others																					

■ Yes □ No □ Not answered

*includes satellite and cable TV, broadband

(*source*: ACCIS 2015)

Attempts have also been made to classify semi-negative or semi-positive information, which would refer to data on accounts which demonstrate some signs of problems but have not yet proceeded to the state of being 'negative', i.e. accounts which are in acceptable time arrears with no warning to the customer being yet issued by the lender.[72]

At EU level, there is no commonly accepted use of the depth of information. As Table 6.5 shows, some countries make use of both positive and negative information while others prescribe that only negative information can be used. In France, a proposed law allowing the use of positive data was held unconstitutional.[73] Once more, it exposes a great difference in the type and usage across the EU and a jeopardised infrastructure at EU level.

Each credit bureau file may contain the name of the borrower, his/her date of birth, current address, previous addresses if any, linked addresses, marital and employment status, number of accounts, amounts, types, stage (loans under approval, withdrawn,

---

[72] Howells (1995), esp. p. 344.
[73] See Conseil Constitutionnel (Constitutional Court) Decision no. 2014-690 DC of 13 March 2014. In 2010, France proposed legislation implementing the EU Consumer Credit Directive 2008 recommending a positive credit reporting system operated by the Bank of France. It was included within the *Loi Hamon* which introduced a number of consumer protections. However, the relevant provisions on the establishment of a positive solvency database were referred to the Conseil Constitutionnel which declared them unconstitutional as a disproportionate intrusion on the constitutional right of privacy which was not outweighed by possible benefits related to credit decision-making.

TABLE 6.5 *Data stored by credit data brokers*

Country	Data structure				Threshold [€]		CBS operations			
	PCR		CB							
	Positive & negative	Negative only	Positive & negative	Negative only	PCR	CB	For creditors only	For creditors & other service providers	For credit assessment only	For other purposes
Austria	•				35,000		•		•	•
Belgium	•				200		•		•	•
Bulgaria	•		•							
Cyprus			•			1				
Czech Rep.	•		•		1		•		•	
Denmark				•					•	
Estonia			•							
Finland				•			•		•	•
France		•			500					
Germany			•		1.5m	100	•		•	•
Greece			•				•		•	
Hungary			•				•		•	
Ireland			•				•		•	
Italy	•		•		30,000**		•		•	
Latvia	•				150					
Lithuania	•		•							
Luxembourg			•							
Malta	•									
Netherlands			•			125	•		•	
Poland			•				•		•	

(continued)

TABLE 6.5 (continued)

Country	Data structure				Threshold [C]		CBS operations			
	PCR		CB		PCR	CB	For creditors only	For creditors & other service providers	For credit assessment only	For other purposes
	Positive & negative	Negative only	Positive & negative	Negative only						
Portugal			•		50					
Romania				•			•		•	
Slovakia		•	•				•			
Slovenia	•		•				•	•	•	
Spain			•		6,000		•		•	
Sweden			•				•	•	•	•
United Kingdom			•				•	•	•	•

NB: The table should be corrected as regards Romania. CBs operations: there are operations for creditors only (not for other service providers – telecom, gas, water companies, etc.). In the category of creditors there are not only banks, but also non-banking lenders. Also note that Ireland is establishing a public credit bureau leaving an open question as regards the future of private sector credit bureaus.

(*sources*: European Commission 2009; European Parliament 2011)

denied) and terms of the accounts, amount of monthly instalments, amount of residual instalments, historical data, number of defaults, amount of arrears, name of granting institutions, payment history (both regulars and in default), dates. In addition, most of the time, information relating to people that have a financial relationship with him/her are included (including, but not limited to, credit guarantors).[74]

Each personal file, then, usually has status codes assigned to it by the lender, showing whether it is up to date, in arrears, by how much in arrears, if the account is in default and how many times the repayment has been late. Closed accounts show the status codes for a variable amount of time prior to closure.[75]

A survey carried out by the World Bank indicates that a large majority of credit bureaus worldwide also collect information on taxpayer IDs (75 per cent), loan rating data (70 per cent), and type and value of collateral used to secure loans (around 50 per cent).[76]

According to the latest ACCIS survey of its members, most credit bureaus hold information on mortgages, consumer loans, and credit and store cards. Elven out of thirty-one respondent members hold data on mobile telecommunications and low-value loans, where mainly negative data is covered.[77]

The depth of the data on 'mainstream' lending products such as consumer loans, credit and store cards, mortgages and overdrafts, is the highest in terms of both negative and positive data. Credit application, portfolio monitoring and identity checking are the most frequently used services by clients of credit bureaus. Banks, leasing companies, credit card and retail credit suppliers as well as mortgage providers and credit unions are the most advanced users of credit bureaus' services. In some countries, however, utility companies, TV and Internet providers are starting actively to use data provided by credit bureaus.[78]

In many cases, on the consumer's credit files there is also a record of the searches, including the dates and the reason for the search.

In addition, credit bureaus normally collect and make use of 'public record information' obtainable by law from public sources to integrate each consumer's file.

Such information usually includes data from the following sources (which most of the time are not visible or are known to consumers):

1. the electoral or voters' roll, as well as other national directories (which are used to match the address on it with the address provided in the current and previous applications, thus verifying in addition how long the applicant has lived at a given address for);

---

[74] See e.g. Credit Report, Equifax, from www.econsumer.equifax.co.uk. See also Credit Reports, Experian, from www.experian.co.uk; Callcredit, from www.callcredit.co.uk; CRIF, from www.crif.com
[75] Ibid. In the UK, for example, such amount of time extends up to three years.
[76] Miller (2003b), esp. 43.
[77] ACCIS (2015).
[78] Ibid.

2. national or county court judgments or decrees (as the case may be) entered for sums of money in the courts or other competent authorities in the relevant country – in most cases credit bureaus are informed about judgments as soon as they are entered by the courts;
3. bankruptcies; and
4. court administration orders.[79]

Table 6.6 summarises the types of data collected by selected credit bureaus in a surveyed number of Member States. It shows the divergences in the type of data shared.

In some European jurisdictions credit bureaus also make financial connections between separate individuals. The databases may contain in the file of a given consumer additional information about one or more persons other than the relevant individual. The circumstances in which information about another person(s) may appear on someone's credit reference file relate to situations where:

1. the names is the same or similar and the address is the same;
2. the credit bureau knows beforehand that such other person's information applies to such individual;
3. such other person has the same surname as such individual and they have been living at the same time either at the current or at any other previous address contained in such individual's file (this aggregate information enables credit bureaus to include information on the applicant about family members and their payment history).[80]

It is worthy of note that it is the duty of the individual to request the credit bureaus to eventually create a dissociation if a financial connection does not in fact exist.

6.5 CROSS-BORDER EXCHANGE OF DATA AND THE INTEGRATION OF CREDIT MARKETS

As seen earlier, the CCD and the MCD provide that foreign lenders shall not be discriminated against in the participation in such a system.

However, unfair or discriminatory access conditions for foreign lenders may take place in several other circumstances. Foreign lenders may be newly set-up institutions establishing a physical presence or institutions that establish a branch in another Member State. But, at EU level there are other emerging modes of providing credit which are necessary for market integration. Other possible forms of market integration in the sector are the cross-border provision of services, including Internet banking or e-commerce, where lenders are based in one Member State and do business with consumers in another

---

[79] Credit Report, Equifax; See also UK Information Commissioner's Office, 'Credit Explained', at https://ico.org.uk/Global/~/media/documents/library/Data_Protection/Practical_application/credit-explained-dp-guidance.pdf

[80] See e.g. in the UK Callcredit, www.callcredit.co.uk; Experian, www.experian.co.uk; Equifax, www.equifax.co.uk

TABLE 6.6 *Consumer identity, income–asset, bankruptcy–court data*

	AT	BE	HR	CY	CZ	DK	FI	DE	EL	HU	IT	NL	PL	RO	SK	SI	SE	GB
Consumer/borrower identity data																		
Name	x	x	x	x	x	x	x	x	x	x	x	x	x	x	x	x	x	x
Other or previous name	x		x		x		x	x		x	x		x	x	x	x	x	x
Taxpayer or other unique identification number	x	x	x	x	x	x	x		x		x	x	x	x	x	x	x	x
Date of birth	x	x	x	x	x	x	x	x		x	x	x	x	x	x	x	x	x
Place of birth			x	x	x			x		x	x		x	x	x	x	x	x
Gender	x	x	x	x	x			x			x	x	x	x	x		x	x
Addresses	x	x	x	x	x	x	x	x	x	x	x	x	x	x	x	x	x	x
Family group data	x			x					x	x		x	x					
Others	x		x					x	x	x		x	x					x
Consumer/borrower income–asset data																		
Income						x					x		x				x	x
Assets e.g. shares, property, savings	x																	
Employer identity			x		x						x		x	x				x
Consumer/borrower bankruptcy/insolvency court data																		
Bankruptcy/insolvency data	x	x		x		x	x	x	x		x		x			x	x	x
Court judgments	x	x		x		x	x	x	x		x			x		x	x	x

x = data held in/accessed by credit bureau database
(*source: ACCIS 2015*)

Member State. The latest policy initiatives of the Capital Market Union[81] and the creation of a true European market for financial services[82] go in this direction.

Europeans are becoming increasingly mobile under the free movement of persons rights.

In principle, however, under the current system non-established financial institutions do not have access to all existing credit bureaus in the EU, and they would not be able to provide information to all of them every time they establish a financial relationship with a consumer.

This is because lenders from a Member State are unlikely to have or establish an ongoing contractual relationship with a private or commercial credit bureau in another Member State.

Moreover, the business model of reciprocity would prove hard to satisfy, where foreign lenders would be in the impractical situation of providing their data portfolio to the credit bureau of another country, in addition in the type and breadth of data required by such a different system. At the same time, in a commercial environment, the existing national participants may be averse to share their data portfolios with foreign players and allow competition on their market from abroad on a basis that is not reciprocal.

The MCD is of little help in this respect, as it recognises that 'access conditions, such as the costs of accessing the database or requirements to provide information to the database on the basis of reciprocity should continue to apply. Member States should be free to determine whether, within their jurisdictions, credit intermediaries may have access to such databases.'[83]

Likewise, in the case of public credit bureaus, foreign lenders do not have to abide by the national rules of another Member State if not physically established there (provided they qualify as 'banks').

Finally, credit bureaus across the EU make use of different type of information, which makes the exchange within the EU not possible.

If EU law provides for the integration of credit markets via the CCD and the MCD, on the other hand the underlying information markets have remained national, which risk rendering the provisions of EU law ineffective in practice. The CCD and the MCD are likely to be prevented from enhancing cross-border credit, either as cross-border provision of services, consumer consumption abroad or EU migration and access to host Member State services. If foreign lenders are allowed to consult databases on a non-discriminatory basis but there remain barriers for a European exchange of information, information markets will remain jeopardised into national markets and the underlying credit markets will be prevented from integrating.

Indeed, the new thrust of the European Commission in this area is the facilitation of cross-border credit. Under this view, the creditworthiness assessment embedded in

---

[81] European Commission, *Green Paper on Building a Capital Markets Union*, COM(2015) 63 final (Brussels, 18 February 2015).
[82] *Ibid.*
[83] Recital 60 of the MCD.

EU law under the CCD and the MCD is a key requirement that demands common assessment standards and principles for consumer lending. As seen above, however, credit providers face difficulties in the creditworthiness assessment of borrowers from other Member States as they rely on solvency data that are not comparable or equally available from jurisdiction to jurisdiction. Thus, the new European Action Plan sets out the further steps that the European Commission considers necessary to achieve a single market for retail financial services. Under Action 9 the European Commission undertakes to develop a minimum set of data to be exchanged between credit registries in cross-border creditworthiness assessments.[84]

However, a question that should be answered unequivocally is whether the EU is ready for cross-border data exchange without a proper mapping and understanding of the typologies of consumer groups that are more likely to default in the Member States. Little research has been undertaken and the one available indicates that consumer groups that are most likely to default differ considerably from jurisdiction to jurisdiction.[85]

6.6 COMPETITION IN THE CREDIT INFORMATION INDUSTRY

As noted earlier, traditionally consumer credit information exchanges are assessed vis-à-vis the competitive or anti-competitive object or effect on those making use of the information in the market for consumer loans, not on those providing information.

Clearly, there is the element of the competition among lenders; yet, this involves not only the covered horizontal relations between the lenders themselves, but also the vertical relation between the lenders and the credit bureaus. Moreover, when commercial entities are involved, horizontal competition between information providers may become relevant.

However, to the extent that information is turned into a tradable commodity of commercial value, competition issues have not yet been addressed.[86]

Traditionally, information exchanges among competitors have been treated as 'hub and spoke' agreements. These are ordinary vertical agreements but with potential horizontal anti-competitive effects. Precisely as in the case in hand, they involve an exchange of information between two or more undertakings operating at the same level of the production or distribution chain (i.e. the lenders) via a common contractual partner operating at a different level of the chain (i.e. the credit bureau).[87]

---

[84] European Commission, *Communication from the Commission to the European Parliament, the Council, the European Central Bank, the European Economic and Social Committee and the Committee of the Regions – Consumer Financial Services Action Plan: Better Products, More Choice* (Brussels, 23 March 2017), COM(2017) 139 final.
[85] Reisch and Gwozdz (2010).
[86] Ferretti (2014).
[87] Odudu (2011).

But, as outlined earlier in this work, information providers become active market players, especially when private commercial actors are the suppliers, influencing and impacting on the underlying consumer markets in terms of lenders' entry and behaviour, transparency, pricing of loans and consumers access to financial services.

Some economic literature has already shown awareness of anti-competitive problems relating to such a vertical or hub-and-spoke relationship in consumer financial markets beyond the traditional analysis: it has been demonstrated how credit bureaus may well be used by dominant lenders as concerted practices to raise rivals' costs either downstream for new market players, or upstream for possible rival credit bureaus that cannot obtain data from lenders.[88]

This is what happens in several EU Member States where only one credit bureau at national level pools consumer financial data,[89] which risks having the undesirable effect of financial institutions becoming vertically integrated with one credit bureau, often of a commercial nature. This is so because participation, coverage and accuracy are intertwined in the same essence of an information system, which would not make any sense if incomplete, i.e. when participation and coverage are not universal, in turn translating into inaccuracy.

From this point of view, competition in the information industry within the EU is almost absent.

While public authorities are exempted from this, it is an anomaly that commercial credit bureaus do not face competition in the relevant market of solvency data, which remains at national level. Yet, the relevant market for credit for consumers is, or should be, the EU market.

Credit bureaus operate through a network structure. They are natural monopolies in that the extension of a system's coverage itself enhances its effectiveness. In fact, they are dependent on that network structures within which information is traded, where the participants that share the information constitute such a network.[90]

The achievement of economies of scale is essential for coverage, where scale and scope effects affect coverage which has the propensity to universality, thus concentration. Historically, for example, the need to achieve economies of scale with nationwide market coverage was the main reason behind the concentration process that occurred in the US after an initial period of numerous credit bureaus spread over the nation's territory to serve local business communities.[91]

Economic research describes such networks as a form of industrial organisation and market governance, where they can influence market structure, and the behaviour of firms and their performance, hence competition. Accordingly, in credit reporting

---

[88] Giannetti et al. (2010).
[89] European Commission, 'Report on the Retail Banking Sector Inquiry', *Commission Staff Working Document accompanying the Communication from the Commission – Sector Inquiry under Art 17 of Regulation 1/2003 on retail banking (Final Report)* (COM(2007) 33 final) SEC(2007) 106; European Commission (2009).
[90] Pagano and Jappelli (1993).
[91] Olegario (2003).

markets, the information flows among agencies, information suppliers and consumers constitute a network of information whose value increases as more lenders are connected to it. Consequently, the more the network of one credit bureau increases, the more attractive it becomes for potential participants or participants to other networks. Therefore, to the extent that scale and scope effects also affect coverage, the more sources are connected to the network, the more detailed becomes the credit report and knowledge, and the more precise they may become for risk-management purposes.[92]

In short, the very nature of the consumer financial information business demands that the success of the system depends on its universal extension; otherwise it would be of little or no use.

Arguably, a new stream of research is necessary in this area. Competition law is usually investigated in the reference credit market but the market for consumer data (i.e. the market of information suppliers) is understudied. Also, in the area of information pertaining to consumers, many areas of law intersect one with the other. The relationship between competition law and its goals and the interest of consumers under consumer protection law needs to be looked at closer, especially in an area which is dominated by fundamental rights such as data protection law.[93]

6.7 BIG DATA AND FINTECH IN THE AGE OF ALGORITHMIC CONSUMER FINANCE

As seen above, consumer solvency data processing is the instrument most extensively used by the lending industry to underwrite financial decisions, including the prevention of over-indebtedness.

At the same time, data processing for risk analysis is also capable of transforming the way financial products and services are provided. The more data are available, the more the lending industry is able to assess risks. As the financial services industry embraces digitalisation, traditional lenders and other emerging financial services firms (e.g. peer-to-peer lending) use increasing data analysis to target customers and offer them customised products with personalised risk pricing.

The growth and development of lending to consumers via new technological platforms are expanding significantly in the EU,[94] although their volume varies across jurisdictions.[95] Technological innovation is the key aspect of new models for the provision of personal finance. Technologically enabled financial innovation in financial services to consumers ('fintech') capable of making use of large data sets from various unrelated sources ('big data') are one facet of recent innovations that is

---

[92] Jentzsch (2003, 2006).
[93] See Ferretti (2014).
[94] e.g. according to Zhang et al. (2015), the total European online alternative finance market, which includes crowdfunding, peer-to-peer lending and other activities, grew by 92 per cent to reach €5,431m in 2015.
[95] Financial Stability Board and Bank for International Settlements (22 May 2017).

generating significant interest in retail financial markets for its possible disruptive effects in the sector.[96]

Broadly conceived, the term fintech abbreviates 'financial technologies' to deliver financial solutions.[97] Many fintech developments are based on proprietary artificial intelligence (AI) systems and associated innovative uses of data. AI embraces different forms of computer systems that are able to learn from the data and their own experiences to solve complex problems or uncover patterns to predict future data or perform decision-making tasks (also known as machine-learning powered by mathematical algorithms able to create further algorithms based on accumulated data).[98] There is no single methodology to design such systems and they are likely to differ one from the other, closely guarded as trade secrets.[99]

As the financial services industry embraces digitalisation, lenders use increasing data analysis to target customers and offer them customised products with personalised risk pricing. The rise of big data – i.e. large data collection and processing obtained from diverse and unrelated sources – has created vast digital catalogues of personal information that can be continually analysed and categorised with AI.

Fintech should not be understood to refer to a specific scene of start-up legal entities disrupting finance with innovation. More comprehensively, it focuses on the products/services offered to end users, and it is therefore activity or services based. It is finance enabled by, or provided via, new technologies where the value chain increasingly includes alternative providers to the traditional ones. For example, common actors are new start-up platforms, non-mainstream lenders, crowdfunding and peer-to-peer lenders[100] or technological firms (TechFin, like Internet giants, social media companies, online retailers), alongside traditional financial institutions. All together, they make an alternative finance industry that records a substantive expansion and is increasingly gaining a significant market share.[101] At the same time, an increasing number of mainstream banks and credit card companies have started building new proprietary risk models and algorithms that use big data to engage with new market segments at lower costs.[102]

As noted earlier, in mature financial markets the common approach to risk has been that past behaviour is predictive of future behaviour. As a result, assessment tools that make use of data about previous or existing credit lines (i.e. solvency data

---

[96] European Banking Authority (2015a, 2016); Financial Inclusion Centre (2018).
[97] Arner et al. (2016).
[98] De Mooy (2017); Landau (2016); Murphy (2012).
[99] Richards (2013).
[100] *Financial Times*, 'P2P Consumer Loans Given Landmark Rating' (28 January 2015), www.ft.com/content/a22edbe0-a749-11e4-b6bd-00144feab7de
[101] See e.g. Zhang et al. (2016).
[102] See e.g. *Financial Times*, 'Psychometric Testing on the Rise in Emerging Markets' (1 February 2015), http://next.ft.com/content/bf27f8c2-a586-11e4-8636-00144feab7de. According to L. Twardy, Santander and Scotiabank are among mainstream banks availing themselves of non-traditional data ('Alternative Data Usage by FinTech Lenders', *Lending Times* (20 June 2016), http://lending-times.com/2016/06/20/over-12000-variables-of-alternative-data-for-36-billion-in-alternative-loans/).

taken from traditional sources) have been developed on a large scale and in an increasingly automated way. These are early correlations, in many ways the ancestors of big data correlations.

As credit underwriting and technologies evolve, and standards and appetite for credit adapt to changing economic cycles and shifting demographics, a wider array of new data are now available in the credit risk analysis of lenders. These so-called 'non-traditional' or 'alternative' data are those (big) data gathered from diverse sources outside the standard credit reports that lenders use to evaluate consumer borrowers. Their volume is greater than that of the traditional sources as they are usually taken from several data points mined from consumers' offline and online activities. Big data can now assemble data from where consumers shop, Internet browsing, social media, digital data brokers and other online trails to mathematically determine the creditworthiness or credit risk of consumers. In this way, even if such big data are not intuitively related to creditworthiness or credit risk, all data become solvency data with an open nature as to their sources.

These innovative techniques are capable of reshaping business models, underwriting criteria and customer experiences. Their innovations associate the commoditisation of big data analytics with an understanding of demographic changes, borrower needs and how to connect to borrowers through new technological channels.[103] Reportedly, the 2008 financial crisis also played an accelerating role marking the impetus and arrival of new market players pushing for competition over innovation to lower costs and gain market share.[104]

These new business models are the first to recognise the limits of traditional solvency data. As credit underwriting and technologies evolve, and credit adapts to changing economic cycles and demographics, lenders want to target customers that may habitually have no or short credit history in the traditional sense – who may be termed the 'invisible' or 'unscorable' customers. A limit of traditional data is that they are largely of historical nature. As they make use of a limited number of categories of data relating to payment and debt histories to pursue new credit, they do not provide a reliable picture of the many factors that can lead someone to fall short of payments or high debt levels.[105] Again, the traditional model requires borrowers to take on debt before obtaining a credit score, leaving a large number of potentially creditworthy or profitable individuals who cannot be scored by the traditional system. These may include the growing phenomenon of consumers migrated from other countries. In the EU, there are nationals of other Member States who take advantage of EU free movement provisions but who are unknown in the host Member State. As seen earlier, traditional data are 'siloed' in individual Member States. The same can be more markedly the case for non-EU migrants. Moreover, traditional credit risk analysis and assessment methods are less effective in

[103] PricewaterhouseCoopers (2015).
[104] Zetzsche et al. (2017).
[105] See e.g. Leimgruber et al. (4 September 2017).

those economies where past data are not available, and especially where there are large segments of low-income or unbanked consumers.[106] Traditional data portray how reliable someone may be at spending with debt, presupposing that this person is a frequent debtor, incentivising the building of a credit history.[107] Therefore, these kinds of customer profiling remain incomplete.

Another case in point is that of young generations. They are users of new technologies and connected to social media. Although they have not yet amassed wealth and have no or little credit history, they represent an important market segment. Moreover, the generational effects of the economic downturn that erupted in the last decade combined with high levels of youth unemployment may have delayed major purchases and prolonged the time it takes for young generations to establish a credit history.[108]

Other significant market segments exist which traditional data are unable to serve. These are not only the unbanked or under-banked consumers. Many households may have temporarily impaired financial capabilities. For example, consumers with otherwise immaculate or sufficient credit histories may experience hardship associated with the economic downturn.[109]

All these examples show how traditional data sources are an imperfect indicator of credit risk analysis or creditworthiness assessment. From their side, the fintech industry considers that traditional data may easily fail in identifying large segments of consumers, in detecting isolated versus recurring credit issues, or in providing more insight into consumer behaviour. Hence, the big idea of big data where fintech makes the correlations. Lenders source alternative data to target not only traditional customers with the added value of a more accurate profiling, but also customers that may habitually have no credit or short credit histories. Big data offer a more accurate profiling and are more predictive.[110]

Illustrations of non-traditional data are emerging daily. The explosion of social media and professional networks provide unprecedented amounts of information that can be used to support decisions about an applicant's credit risk. People post large amounts of personal information that can be captured. For example, to establish an estimated earning potential for borrowers with short job histories, lenders may consider information such as the education history, student loans and the majors studied. A reported case is that of a law graduate with a limited credit history, where the assessment of social media indicates whether s/he has connections with prestigious law firms as well as professors from the law school or other successful lawyers. In addition, if those 'socially' or 'professionally' connected with an applicant are responsible borrowers with stable employment and good credit histories, this

---

[106] See e.g. Ramos et al. (2016).
[107] Guzelian et al. (2015).
[108] See e.g. Equality and Human Rights Commission (2015).
[109] See e.g. Civic Consulting (2014).
[110] Zetzsche et al. (2017).

may support the probability that the applicant him/herself is also a responsible borrower. The age of their social media accounts and the volume of activity within them can indicate an applicant's interconnectedness and stability with their network. Some lenders apply similar concepts to an applicant's professional networks. The individual's job and the jobs their connections hold may provide insights into the strength of the applicant's job stability.[111] Analysing social networks may allow lenders to understand other information such as race, socioeconomic status and their comparative customer loyalty.[112]

New data sources that can be included in the assessment of a borrower may range from phone and utilities bills. Customers can be asked to sign over permission to access personal emails, bank accounts, social media accounts, shipping data, their monthly cash flow over bank accounts and online financial accounts such as PayPal, Amazon, eBay or else. Heavy activity on these sites may suggest a healthy cash flow. Also, spending patterns may give indications of the frequency someone loses control of finances. Similarly, probing the way applicants click through web pages can give suggestions about some of their character traits such as impulsiveness or attitude towards risk-taking.[113]

Any data that may align with default rates can quickly be incorporated into the assessment. Stories are starting to surface. One well-known UK online lender claims up to 8,000 data points to automatically assess a consumer's creditworthiness.[114] Some lenders are starting to look at customers with gym memberships as they were found to be more reliable than those without.[115] A credit card company has decided to cut someone's credit limit for shopping at stores frequented by people deemed by the company to have a poor repayment history.[116] Systems have been set up to detect unsettling patterns that are indicative of higher risk such as expenses for marriage therapy for possible problems leading to separation or divorce, thus lowering credit lines or setting higher interest rates.[117] Even web searches for the applicant's name combined with keywords chosen by the lender may provide information.[118] Accounts of smart devices provide other detailed data, e.g. they generate calls and text messages over given periods of time, each carrying a rich data set including the time the call was made (this may indicate having a more or less fixed job), the location of the caller at the time of the call, the receiver of the call, the type of information accessed via text messaging, and the types and number of payment

---

[111] PricewaterhouseCoopers (2015).
[112] *Financial Times*, 'Big Data: Credit Where Credit's Due' (4 February 2015), www.ft.com/content/7933792e-a2e6-11e4-9c06-00144feab7de
[113] Ibid.
[114] *The Guardian*, 'With Wonga, Your Prosperity Could Count on an Algorithm' (16 October 2011), www.theguardian.com/money/2011/oct/16/wonga-algorithm-lending-debt-data
[115] Ibid.
[116] *Financial Times*, 'Big Data' (see n. 112).
[117] *New York Times*, 'What Does Your Credit-Card Company Know about You?' (12 May 2009), www.nytimes.com/2009/05/17/magazine/17credit-t.html?pagewanted=all
[118] *The Guardian*, 'Wonga' (see n. 114).

transactions made through such devices. For those customers who consent to the sharing of their data in order to access credit, prepaid-minute or Internet traffic purchase patterns can indicate a steady or uneven cash flow. Retailer loyalty cards can provide important insights into consumers' income, spending habits and family structure.[119]

All the above illustrations show the limitless potential of big data in personal finance and the financialisation of the private lives of consumers.

6.8 OPPORTUNITIES AND RISKS OF ALGORITHMIC FINANCE

As at last acknowledged by European policymakers,[120] big data and fintech have a competitive EU market dimension. However, alongside opportunities they may raise concerns for consumers.

6.8.1 *Opportunities*

Fintech and big data have been magnified for facilitating credit access and promoting financial inclusion.[121] As noted earlier, in principle it may indeed offer opportunities to reach more underserved consumers and reduce prices with the benefit of accelerating assessments and the availability of finance.

Some supporting literature is starting to emerge, in relation to small firms. The main findings emphasise situations where creditworthy borrowers had succeeded in accessing credit via fintech where others with similar characteristics were denied credit in the mainstream banking market.[122] Likewise, some point out price reductions, speed in the granting process and enhanced efficiency through lower operating costs,[123] although the extent to which fintech lenders pass the savings on to borrowers with lower credit costs remains unclear.[124] Others see the personalisation of the financial relationship and pricing positively, as it is attuned to individuals' more accurate risk profile.[125]

An advantage for consumers may be that fintech challenges the centralisation of information and the traditional near-monopoly of solvency data intermediaries in the Member States. To the extent that solvency data are turned into a tradable commodity of commercial value, competition issues in the financial data markets have not yet been addressed.[126] However, information providers such as credit bureaus are active market players influencing and impacting on the underlying

---

[119] Baer et al. (2013).
[120] European Commission, *Green Paper* (see n. 58).
[121] Zetzsche et al. (2017).
[122] Desai and Meekings (2016); Schweitzer and Barkley (2017).
[123] De Roure et al. (2016); Morse (2015).
[124] Morse (2015)
[125] Zetzsche et al. (2017).
[126] Ferretti (2014).

consumer markets in terms of lenders' entry and behaviour, transparency, pricing of loans and consumers' access to financial services. Some economic literature has shown awareness of anti-competitive problems relating to a vertical or hub-and-spoke relationship between information intermediaries and lenders in consumer financial markets: it has been demonstrated how the former may be used by dominant lenders as concerted practices to raise rivals' costs either downstream for new market players, or upstream for possible rival credit bureaus that cannot obtain data from lenders.[127] This is what happens in several EU Member States where only one or few database pool consumer financial data.[128] This risks having the undesirable effect of financial institutions becoming vertically integrated with the information provider. This is so because participation, coverage and accuracy are intertwined in the information system, which would not make any sense if incomplete, i.e. when participation and coverage are not universal, in turn translating into inaccuracy. Solvency databases operate through a network structure. They are natural monopolies in that the extension of a system's coverage itself enhances its effectiveness. They are dependent on the network structures within which information is traded, where the participants that share the information constitute such a network.[129] In short, the success of the system depends on its universal extension, otherwise it would be of little or no use.

Fintech and big data, bringing into play many more actors with proprietary algorithms and accessing data from diverse sources, are likely to challenge national dominance over traditional financial databases and break the information siloes that occur at national level. Moreover, if used properly, they could allow a more cost-effective information analysis to be passed on to consumers.[130]

6.8.2 Risks

Alongside the potential of serving a larger customer base and lower prices, a number of opposite concerns for consumers can be anticipated.

As for traditional data, recall that expanded data processing is mostly done in the interest of the lenders for their own risk and price assessments, and ultimately their profitability. It remains questionable the extent to which credit risk analysis and marketing (in the broadest sense) may coincide with responsible lending or creditworthiness assessment.[131] In *LCL (Le Crédit Lyonnais)* the CJEU made clear that the

---

[127] Giannetti et al. (2010).
[128] European Commission, 'Report on the Retail Banking Sector Inquiry', *Commission Staff Working Document accompanying the Communication from the Commission – Sector Inquiry under Art 17 of Regulation 1/2003 on retail banking (Final Report)* (COM(2007) 33 final) SEC(2007) 106; European Commission (2009).
[129] Pagano and Jappelli (1993).
[130] Financial Inclusion Centre (2018).
[131] Policy documents reveal that responsible lending makes reference to the delivery of responsible and reliable markets, where consumer confidence is restored and credit products are appropriate for consumers' needs and tailored to their ability to repay their debts. See Communication of the

creditworthiness assessment should be done in the interest of consumers to prevent irresponsible lending practices and over-indebtedness.[132] To the extent that the interest of lenders is to enlarge the customer base and profitability, these interests may not coincide with the provision of suitable products in the interest of borrowers in terms of provision of financial services at affordable costs to those who need and qualify for them. Creditors have certainly an interest in the ability of debtors to repay under the credit agreement, but they are not concerned about the sustainability of the new debt on other financial arrangements with other parties. Moreover, the higher the risk for the creditor, the higher the price of the loan. In this context, there is neither clarity nor certainty that big data could in fact be used to identify and target vulnerable consumers with high-cost or unsuitable products.[133]

A question is whether borrowers' creditworthiness could be achieved through correlations or associations, bearing in mind that they are not causation. Likewise, prediction is not the same as knowledge. Unlike the latter, the former is not neutral and it is used to determine the future. Therefore, the risk is that fintech will create a more complex and fragmented financial environment where data analytics may exploit or manipulate consumer behaviour or biases.

The problem is that these systems are overly complex, not transparent and there are no mechanisms to safeguard against abuses and mistakes – generally known as the 'black box' problem.[134]

The complications and opaqueness of algorithms is that they transform numerous bits of apparently neutral or unrelated information about a consumer into straight numerical scores that determine the outcome and/or price of applications with all the following implications. Most of the time not only the logics/biases of the algorithms remain secret, but also the data sources used by the individual lenders are undisclosed. As a consequence, consumers have limited means to identify and contest lenders' decisions and undertake the necessary steps to improve their chances.[135] Arguably, it is very difficult to determine how the data are correlated and whether the variety of unrelated data operate as proxies for personal features – also of sensitive nature – targeting vulnerable individuals or behavioural biases.

Big data may dig up protected information. For instance, they may reveal information that could not otherwise be obtained in any credit application, e.g. shopping lists may reveal medical information or the health status of a person.[136]

European Commission to the European Council of 4 March 2009 'Driving European Recovery', COM(2009) 114 and the Public Consultation on Responsible Lending and Borrowing, available at http://ec.europa.eu/internal . . . /responsible_lending/consultation_en.pdf. See also http://europa.eu/rapid/press-release_IP-09-922_en.htm

[132] *LCL (Le Crédit Lyonnais) SA* v. *Fesih Kalhan* (Case C-565/12) [2014], ECLI:EU:C:2014:190.
[133] Hurley and Adebayo (2016).
[134] Pasquale (2015).
[135] Hurley and Adebayo (2016).
[136] Ibid.

An indiscriminate use of data may easily lead to increased stereotypical decisions. They may respond to schemes concluding that certain groups of the population pose greater credit risks than others, so lenders decide to refrain from allowing access to financial services to those groups of consumers (e.g. young families with children). In short, big data and fintech allow lenders too much access into their customers' personal life and they can create or ruin reputations.[137]

All the above can be exacerbated by inaccuracies in the data, the speed of their dissemination or pre-existing biases. Big data can become a real problem for consumers who will not be able to determine where an error or a bias are. If under the traditional credit assessment system they may be able to identify wrong or partial information in relation to a credit line or credit history, big data make it impossible to know where the error or bias are because too many unrelated data from too many sources come into play. Equally, big data can well frustrate the legal right individuals have to correct their data.[138]

The above difficulties could have additional counterproductive effects if a number of consumers become untrustworthy of their data being processed properly. Sections of the population may become averse to share information for fear of having their personal integrity violated. This, in a vicious circle, poses challenges to the commercial use of the data that will leave them behind or excluded. Ultimately, it may even impinge on people's freedom of speech for limiting or directing what and where to share data to avoid future adverse consequences.[139] People may start changing the way they communicate or behave to the point of removing honesty if they think that it might affect their financial standing. Indirectly, this can become a form of social control.

Relatedly, there are risks for those segments of the population who are un-networked or have no or limited digital presence. With fintech development, increasing concerns are expressed by groups of consumers who face difficulties in accessing information, or buy and pay for goods/services in the digital domain. These include elderly persons who for various reasons do not use technologies, persons with disabilities or persons in poverty. The causes for these difficulties may be diverse and range from a lack of digital literacy, lack of accessibility to the digital devices supporting the financial services or lack of trust in digitalised services (e.g. fear around fraudulent use of identity, difficulty to identify misuse and claim redress).[140] As a result, significant numbers of consumers could be denied access to financial services.

In any event, the concern may not be limited to those who are not digitalised. The broader question, affecting everyone, is the extent to which people remain with the liberty of being un-networked or offline, with the safeguard of not attracting

---

[137] Sandage (2005).
[138] Art. 15 General Data Protection Regulation (GDPR), on which, see Chapter 7 in this volume.
[139] Datatilsynet (2018).
[140] Central Bank of Ireland (June 2017); OECD (2017).

negative consequences in case personal data are not available digitally, such as on social media or else.[141]

All in all, these risks not only expose an increasing intrusion in people's private lives but they also raise debates and concerns over the financialisation of their lives and the shaping and conforming of behaviours beyond that of repayment.

6.9 ANACREDIT

At the proposal stage of the MCD the European Commission had included provisions that would have allowed for the harmonisation of at least some key terms used in solvency databases (terms such as 'defaults', 'arrears') and to define uniform credit registration criteria, as well as data processing conditions to be applied to solvency databases (e.g. the registration thresholds), in order to increase reliability of information contained in databases, facilitate creditworthiness assessments and in the long run promote cross-border supply of credit. But these provisions were dropped during negotiations and from the final text of the directive.[142]

Nevertheless, as outlined above, the EU internal market and the integration of credit markets for consumers raise questions of how to measure over-indebtedness and assess household creditworthiness. Likewise, the establishment of a level playing field for the competition of financial institutions may demand that they are equipped with similar tools and that there are no restrictions or barriers in Member States. In turn, this means that credit risk data may require standardisation or a harmonised measurement system for the EU and its market players. As shown earlier, however, this is far from being the situation of a jeopardised system of national solvency data sharing.

This study has already outlined that other public policy goals are associated with the use of solvency data, especially as regards the databases operated by national central banks containing loan-level or borrower-level information to supervise the national financial system. Solvency data also serve the purpose for statistical and economic analysis.

The free movement of capital and economic and monetary union within the EU demand the adoption of an economic policy which is based on the close

[141] Packin and Aretz (2016).
[142] Commission adoption of a proposal for a Directive on credit agreements relating to residential property, COM(2011)142. The following provisions were deleted during the negotiations between the Council and the European Parliament:
Art. 14(5) – 'Powers are delegated to the Commission ... to specify and amend the criteria to be considered in the conduct of a creditworthiness assessment as laid down in paragraph 1 of this Article and in ensuring that credit products are not unsuitable for the consumer as laid down in paragraph 4 of this Article'.
Art. 16(2) – 'Powers are delegated to the Commission ... to define uniform credit registration criteria and data processing conditions to be applied to the databases referred to in paragraph 1 of this Article. In particular, such delegated acts shall define the registration thresholds to be applied to such databases and shall provide for agreed definitions for key terms used by such databases.'

coordination of Member States' economic policies, on the internal market and on the definition of common objectives. Price stability, sound public finances and monetary conditions, and a sustainable balance of payments are goals of the EU to pursue its objectives set out in Article 3 TEU.[143]

A major euro-area response to the 2008 financial and economic crisis has been the deeper integration – or ever closer union – of its banking system, which culminated in the making of the Banking Union (BU).[144] In the rhetoric of the EU, this is an important step towards a genuine economic and monetary union which could allow for the consistent application of EU banking rules in the participating Member States, and which could be equipped to tackle those problems caused by the crises and the close relationship between public finances and the banking sector.[145]

One important goal of the BU is the pursuit of a number of initiatives to create a safer and sounder financial sector for the single market. One such initiative includes a common stronger prudential framework for financial institutions through the establishment of a single supervisory mechanism (SSM) for banks.

The European Central Bank (ECB) is the European institution in charge of Europe's single currency, monetary policy and price stability alongside the European System of Central Banks (ESCB).[146] In addition to these tasks, the SSM places the ECB as the new central prudential supervisor. On the basis of Article 127(6) of the Treaty on the Functioning of the European Union (TFEU) and of the Council Regulation (EC) No. 1023/2013 (the 'SSM Regulation'),[147] the ECB is the institution responsible for specific tasks concerning the prudential supervision of credit institutions established in participating Member States. It carries out these tasks alongside the national competent authorities, where the ECB directly supervises the largest banks while national supervisors continue to oversee the remaining smaller financial institutions. As supervisors, the main task of the ECB and the national authorities is to work closely together within an integrated system to make sure that banks comply with the rules of the EU and to early intervene in case of detection of problems.[148]

To achieve their goals in the framework of the SSM, supervisors need the tools to perform their newly assigned task. Among these tools, the ECB is promoting the setting-up of a centralised infrastructure for the collection and sharing of granular

---

[143] See Arts. 119 and 127 TFEU.
[144] Non-euro-area countries are entitled to join.
[145] See the official website of the ECB at www.bankingsupervision.europa.eu/about/incontext/bankingunion/html/index.en.html
[146] Arts. 127 and 282 TFEU.
[147] Council Regulation (EU) No. 1024/2013 of 15 October 2013 conferring specific tasks on the European Central Bank concerning policies relating to the prudential supervision of credit institutions, OJ L287/63 29.10.2013, pp. 63–89.
[148] See the official websites of the ECB at www.ecb.europa.eu/ecb/tasks/html/index.en.html and www.bankingsupervision.europa.eu/home/html/index.en.html

credit risk data within the banking sector on an EU-wide scale, called analytical credit data set ('AnaCredit').

The idea of centralising credit risk data for risk management and/or supervisory purposes is not new and already existed in a number of Member States in the form of national credit registries, i.e. information systems providing central banks or other regulatory bodies and banks with data about the indebtedness of firms and individuals vis-à-vis the whole banking system.[149] However, not all Member States share the same regulatory and institutional experience of having national credit registries and in some countries the latter do not exist, having data centralisation systems set up for different credit management purposes in the interest of the credit industry (i.e. credit bureaus or CRAs).

Yet, for coordination at EU level, the ESCB has long been exploring the potential statistical use of the data contained in national credit registries for macroeconomic and financial stability purposes. Even before the outbreak of the crisis national authorities had finalised a plan for a pan-European data exchange among the registries of Belgium, Germany, France, Italy, Austria, Portugal and Spain, as well as representatives of the ECB (later extended to Bulgaria, Czech Republic, Latvia, Lithuania, Romania, Slovenia and Slovakia). The plan consisted in the creation of a reporting system allowing data exchange on a regular basis on borrowers who also have debt in other European countries. The envisaged cross-border exchange was not intended for the consumer sector but to provide information to financial institutions across Europe about the indebtedness of their corporate customers. Also, the information exchange could provide useful additional information to supervisory authorities on credit concentration. For supervisory purposes, the growing internationalisation of lending to companies within the European Union, as well as the introduction of the single currency, required an exchange of information among national authorities in order to maintain the value of information contained in their databases.[150]

The reporting to central national credit registries has proved its analytical usefulness but it has also outlined the absence of homogeneity and the differences at national level of the data in terms of coverage, attributes and content. This lack of standardisation and comparable measurements has pointed to the need for

---

[149] Reportedly, Germany established the first National Credit Registry in 1934, followed by France in 1946, Italy and Spain in 1962, and Belgium in 1967. See Miller (2003b).

[150] As explicitly documented by the Deutsche Bundesbank (the Central Bank chairing the Working Group on Credit Registries), in fact, 'data on the total amount of loans taken up will be available for each of the participating countries as well as on an aggregated basis. The data will also provide a breakdown into asset items and off balance-sheet transactions. *There will be no cross-border exchange of information on loans to individuals*' (emphasis added). See Deutsche Bundesbank, press release, 7 June 2005, emphasis added), www.bundesbank.de/Redaktion/EN/Downloads/Press/Pressenotizen/2005/2005_06_07_credit_registers.pdf?__blob=publicationFile. See also European Central Bank (2010).

harmonisation in concepts and definitions, as well as for convergence in time, coverage and content of the data.[151]

However, the recent financial crisis and the impact of defaults of both business and personal loans on the banking system have exacerbated the desirability for more credit risk data to allow the ECB and the ESCB to perform their responsibilities of monetary policy, price stability, the development and production of analyses and statistics, and – last but not least – for micro-prudential supervisory purposes.

Hence, the ECB and ESCB have accelerated the exploration of the potentials of credit risk data and they are working towards their collection and standardisation in order to be able to have common grounds to engage in EU-wide credit analysis, and measure levels of indebtedness and over-indebtedness in the financial system.

In a nutshell, with the ultimate goal of addressing both micro- and macro-prudential issues in the supervision of the EU banking system alongside monetary policy, the ECB and ESCB have launched the 'AnaCredit' project with the mandate of:

1. Identifying a core set of data to meet the main users' needs and elaborate on their scope;
2. Further analysing and considering harmonised concepts and definitions, and methodological enhancements of the data;
3. Estimating the costs to be incurred by the ESCB to set up a sharing system and that of the reporting agents; and
4. Considering the governance, as well as the legal and confidentiality issues for a centralised data sharing system, and preparing the appropriate legal instrument.[152]

It is with the view of setting up such a data set containing detailed information on individual bank loans harmonised across the Member States that the ECB has issued a regulation on the collection of granular credit and credit risk data (the 'AnaCredit Regulation')[153] regarding the issue of technical rules, procedures and reporting thresholds. EU Member States which are not part of the Eurosystem are also invited to participate. For example, Denmark and Sweden have initiated activities to create similar databases.

The expectation is of implementing a practical application of 'AnaCredit' by 2018 and have in place a 'Eurosystem' database of standardised deposit and loan-by-loan data on credit granted of or above €25,000 to legal entities, including SMEs and sole traders/proprietors. According to Recital 12 of the AnaCredit Regulation, personal data will not be collected in the first stage of the reporting. The prospect is that of comprising also the data relating to the credits to consumers, in particular mortgage

---

[151] De Almeida and Damia (2014).
[152] Damia and Israel (2014).
[153] Regulation (EU) 2016/867 of the European Central Bank of 18 May 2016 on the collection of granular credit and credit risk data (ECB/2016/13), OJ L 144/44.

loans and the evolution of indebtedness and defaults rates at national level. The same Recital 12 of the AnaCredit Regulation, in fact, clearly provides for the possibility of extending it in subsequent stages, in which case it commits to ensuring the protection of the rights of natural persons with regard to the collection and processing of their personal data. Even more, the broadening of the scope of AnaCredit to the data on consumer credits is a specific proposal of the European Commission, which aims to potentially involve all lenders and not only banks to enable it to monitor the performance of the consumer credit market and fulfil the obligations set by the Consumer Credit Directive 2008/48/EC covering overdrafts, credit cards, credit lines and other consumer credits.[154] A further expansion of the credit data collection is subject to a decision by the governing council, which shall be taken two years prior to the implementation of additional stages (Recital 10 of the AnaCredit Regulation).

For the purpose of this study, AnaCredit may have an important impact on the function and activities of credit bureaus, especially the private or commercial ones. The standardisation of the measurement of over-indebtedness and the way to conduct creditworthiness assessment represent a back-door interference of the way lenders share solvency data, credit bureaus conduct their business and the type of data they supply. European lenders will need to accommodate future changes in market practices and regulations. The new setup, in fact, reflects a paradigm shift in the statistical reporting from a template-based reporting of summary statistics to the reporting of entire harmonised and granular credit registers. AnaCredit underlines the ECB's intention of a more quantitative supervisory approach that will allow increasing the link between monetary policy, financial stability and banking supervision and the usage of additional preventive measures in prudential regulation. However, for European lenders the granularity of the data required by the new system will result in changes in reporting systems, solvency databases and processes, as well as the ensuing data collection to provide the requested data. A collection of data without standardised and coherent planning is likely to lead to higher operational costs in achieving regulatory compliance and they can cause errors. From a data risk-management perspective, this means that comprehensive data structures should only be organised once and in a way that enables lenders to capture all relevant data across different business lines in a consistent and definite new database structure.

Arguably, therefore, AnaCredit will force lenders and credit bureaus to adapt or rebuild their databases in order to remain up to date with regulatory requirements and/or competitive in the market. The efforts to harmonise the type of solvency data that credit bureaus currently report may force them to use the same set of indicators and uniform definitions allowing for a European comparison of the levels of

---

[154] See European Commission, Opinion of 7 August 2015 on the Draft Regulation of the ECB concerning the collection of granular credit and credit risk data (2015/C 261/01).

indebtedness. Even though the current coverage of AnaCredit does not allow for a complete analysis of the indebtedness of individuals because of the high reporting threshold of €25,000, it nevertheless introduces the reporting standards that lenders and credit bureaus in the euro area will be obliged to follow. An extreme argument may thus consider credit bureaus redundant to the extent that their role and functions may be substituted by the public authorities.

The bottom line is that the ECB intervention, if and when implemented in step-by-step stages, has the potential to have a major impact on the solvency data usage, to the point of forcing credit bureaus to evolve or risk their own continued existence. The latter circumstance, for example, could materialise if the coverage of AnaCredit is extended to individuals with all types of loans and the reporting threshold is lowered to below the currently planned one of €25,000 or eliminated altogether for individual loans.

7

Credit Risk Analysis and Creditworthiness in Relation to EU Data Protection Legislation

7.1 DATA PROTECTION AND ITS VALUES

The processing of financial and non-financial personal data is subjected to the general provisions of data protection legislation in the absence of specific sectorial or derogating legislation that may exist in national banking laws (especially for public credit registries or in the national banking acts). In some Member States, specific provisions complementing or altering data protection acts exist.[1]

Before assessing the extent of the legitimacy of data-processing operations in personal finance or the adequacy of data protection law to stem possible consumer concerns, it is worth summarising the values behind protecting personal data and the rationales for regulation.

The literature on data protection law is extensive, albeit scholarship specific on the new legal framework established by the General Data Protection Regulation (GDPR)[2] is starting to emerge only now for its very recent enactment.[3]

At the same time, the GDPR represents more an evolution than a revolution of the existing law. Most of its underlying rules and principles have stayed the same as the preceding legal framework set by Directive 95/46/EC.[4] These have been studied for years. The elaborate legal structures in response to new complex technologies, as well as the increasing amount of case law over the years, have given rise to a bourgeoning of legal scholarship.[5]

---

[1] e.g. in Germany see § 28b and 34 Bundesdatenschutzgesetz (BDSG); in Italy see Garante per la Protezione dei Dati Personali (2004); in the UK see Information Commissioner Office (2006).

[2] Regulation (EU) 2016/679, OJ 2016 L 119, pp. 1–88.

[3] e.g. De Hert and Papakonstantinou (2016); Gellert (2015); Gutwirth et al. (2016); Lynskey (2015); Putrova (2014); Voss (2014).

[4] OJ 1995 L 281 pp. 0031–0050.

[5] This is testified by the large and growing list of specialised writings on the many legal issues of data protection/privacy. Specialist law journals in the field have emerged (e.g. the *Computer Law & Security Review*, *International Data Privacy Law* and the *European Data Protection Law Review* among European peer-reviewed international journals). The SSRN eJournal library for data protection/privacy alone has over 3,500 papers, and this figure excludes books, pre-internet works and

Data protection is a complex and multifaceted concept both from a societal and a legal point of view. Traditionally, its primary objective has been identified with the protection of personal privacy within the context of processing operations involving personal data. The considerable body of literature and many debates on privacy exemplify the difficulty in delineating what remains a broad and at times ambiguous concept.[6] Scholarly debates have helped to accept to a large degree that, in its most general acceptation, privacy protection is a legal way of drawing a line at how far society or other individual subjects may intrude into a person's own affairs. It entails that such a person should be left able to conduct their personal legitimate affairs relatively free from unwanted intrusion. Nonetheless, the considerable body of literature on the concept of privacy exemplifies the difficulty in defining with precision what remains a broad and at times ambiguous term, but it also helps to set the basis for distinguishing 'data protection' from 'privacy'.

Personal data protection is a distinctive European innovation in law that over the years has been gaining a mixed fortune outside the EU. The horrors of last-century European history and the subsequent international conventions played an important role in the development of data protection laws across Europe and, ultimately, in the adoption of the Data Protection Directive 95/46/EC. Two other factors, however, proved decisive for its enactment under the remit of the EU: (1) the progressive development in information technologies transcending national borders; and (2) the need for the free movement of personal data within the EU to enable trade and prevent conflicts arising from separate national regimes (Recitals

---

scholarship from non-legal fields. See SSRN eLibrary Information Privacy Law eJournal, at https://papers.ssrn.com/sol3/JELJOUR_Results.cfm?form_name=journalbrowse&journal_id=1125502

[6] See e.g. Bloustein (1964); Paul et al. (2000); Pennock and Chapman (1971); Rachels (1975); Stromholm (1967); Warren and Brandeis (1890). Other narrower views of privacy see it as self-determination, intimacy or a meaningful aspect of interpersonal relationships, personal expression and choice. See e.g. DeCew (1997); Fried (1970); Gavison (1980); Gerstein (1978); Inness (1992); Moore (1998); Parent (1983); Schoeman (1984); Westin (1967). Such an individualistic approach to privacy has been criticised by scholarship arguing that greater recognition should be given to the broader social importance of privacy: other than a common value in which individuals enjoy some degree of it, privacy is seen as a public and collective value vis-à-vis technological developments and market forces, requiring minimal levels of privacy for all (Regan (1995)). There exists a number of works critical of privacy, too. The so-called 'reductionist approach', e.g. takes the view that the right to privacy is derivative, meaning that it can be explained in the context of other rights without deserving any separate attention. As such, it can be protected through other rights without any explicit protection of its own. Any privacy violation would be better understood as the violation of other more basic rights: ultimately, the right to privacy would merely be a cluster of rights, where these rights are always overlapped by property rights or rights over the person such as bodily security (Thomson (1975)). For another strong critique of privacy, see Bork (1990). These 'reductionist approaches' have been criticised by a number of commentators: Johnson (1994); Scanlon (1975). Another well-known contribution to the 'reductionist approach' is that of Posner (1981) who took an economic, cost-benefit analysis of privacy. He argues that the types of interests protected under privacy are not distinctive. Most of all, nevertheless, the central proposition is that privacy protection is economically inefficient. Protection of individual privacy would be difficult to defend because it does not maximise wealth. On this line of argument, Posner defends organisational or corporate privacy as more valuable than personal privacy, the reason being that the former is likely to improve economic efficiency.

1–11 of Directive 95/46/EC). Indeed, the real aims and scope of Directive 95/46/EC were both the protection of fundamental rights and freedoms of European citizens, and the achievement of the internal market. Both objectives were equally important, even though the jurisdiction of the EU on this subject rested on internal market grounds, having its legal basis in Article 100a of the EC Treaty (now Art. 114 TFEU).

All the same, as documented in the literature, the EU legislator consistently took a rigorous 'fundamental human rights' approach.[7]

This position has been made explicit lately by Article 16 TFEU which elevates the provision on data protection to a 'provision of general application' under Title II alongside other fundamental principles of the EU. Equally, with the Treaty of Lisbon, the Charter of Fundamental Rights of the EU has become binding, and in its Article 8 it recognises the protection of personal data as an autonomous right distinguished from that of 'privacy' recognised in Article 7.

Indeed, data protection refers to the protection through regulation of personal information pertaining to an identified or identifiable individual (data subject). Individuals do not own information about themselves. Information does not exist prior to its expression or disclosure but it is always to some extent constructed or created by more than one agent.[8] Normatively, no proprietary rights exist on personal information. It pertains to an individual but it does not belong to him or her in a proprietary sense. Those who process personal data (data controllers) have the right to process those data as long as such processing is in compliance with procedural rules set by law. The objective of data protection law is to protect individuals not against data processing per se, but against unjustified collection, storage, use and dissemination of the data pertaining to them.[9] As persuasively shown by Paul De Hert and Serge Gutwirth, data protection cannot be reduced to a late privacy spin-off echoing a privacy right with regard to personal data, but it formulates the conditions under which information processing is legitimate.[10]

At least under EU law, the two have become distinct, yet complementary, fundamental legal rights which derive their normative force from values that – although at times coincidental and interacting in many ways – may be conceptualised independently. While privacy laws derive their normative force from the need to protect the legitimate opacity of the individual through prohibitive measures, data protection law formulates the conditions under which information processing is legitimate by forcing the transparency of the processing of the data, thus enabling its full control by the data subjects where the processing is not authorised by the law itself as necessary for societal reasons. In short, data protection law focuses on the activities

---

[7] Heisenberg (2005); Mayer-Schonberger (1997); Simitis (1995); contra, on the utilitarian approach of the UK, see Kenyon and Richardson (2006: 1–10).
[8] Rouvroy and Poullet (2009: 45–76).
[9] On discussions about individuals not owning information about themselves, see Kang and Bunter (2004); Rouvroy and Poullet (2009).
[10] De Hert and Gutwirth (2009).

of the processors and their accountability, thus regulating an accepted exercise of power.[11] Both privacy and data protection regimes (i.e. seclusion and legitimate opacity on the one side, and inclusion and participation on the other side) represent a bundle of legal protections to pursue the common goal of a free and democratic society where citizens develop their personality freely and autonomously through individual reflexive self-determination.[12] Granting to individuals control over their personal data is not only a tool to allow them control over the *persona* they project in society free from unreasonable or unjustified associations, manipulations, distortions, misrepresentations, alterations or constraints. It is also a fundamental value pertaining to humans to keep and develop their personality in a manner that allows them to fully participate in society without having to conform their thoughts, beliefs, behaviours or preferences to those of the majority; or to have those set from above by the industry for commercial interests.[13] The rights conferred by data protection law become participatory rights of self-determination.

It is in light of the significance of the above values that one should read the new European legislation set by the GDPR and the processing of personal data by lenders.

7.2 NOTICE AND LEGITIMATE GROUNDS FOR DATA PROCESSING

Establishing whether data processing in personal financial transactions truly abide by the law may be problematic.

There can be concerns about the necessity, adequacy and relevance of the type and amount of data involved vis-à-vis the assumptions upon which they work. Of interest are determinations on the predictability of individual human behaviour, and the real financial capability of borrowers via correlations or associations with other aspects of the same subjects. In particular, doubts may arise as to the legal compliance of the notice to be given to data subjects required by Articles 13 and 14 GDPR, and the further demand that they must be provided 'in a concise, transparent, intelligible and easily accessible form, using clear and plain language' (Art. 12 GDPR). Under the GDPR, the notice to data subjects includes the legitimate interests pursued by the controller or by a third party when this is a ground for processing.[14]

The general objectives of transparency and informational self-determination set by the GDPR seem compromised by the amount and vagueness of information that should be provided to data subjects, the indefinite number of actors involved in a spill-over data dissemination and the secondary uses of the data.

---

[11] Davis (1997); De Hert and Gutwirth (2009); Rouvroy and Poullet (2009).
[12] Rouvroy and Poullet (2009).
[13] Ibid.
[14] See Arts. 13(1)(d) and 14(2)(b) GDPR.

A critical element of fintech is that for competition concerns lenders may not disclose the type and amount of data used, the impact of data on the assessment, the criteria and data-mining techniques employed in data processing, or the criteria used in decision-making. Information about the proprietary algorithm may reveal commercial secrets or breach intellectual property rights, which under the GDPR should not be adversely affected.[15]

The GDPR sets the legal requirements for a valid basis for legitimate data processing. A data controller must be able to provide a base for the processing activity only if it can claim that the processing relies on one of the criteria established by law. The set of criteria is exhaustive, so that if a data controller is unable to rely on one of them the processing is unlawful. These are expressed in Article 6 GDPR:

(a) the data subject has (unambiguously) given his/her consent;
(b) the data processing is necessary for the performance of a contract to which the data subject is party or in order to take steps at the request of the data subject prior to entering into a contract;
(c) the data processing is necessary for compliance with a legal obligation to which the data controller is subject;
(d) the data processing is necessary in order to protect the vital interests of the data subject;
(e) the data processing is necessary for the performance of a task carried out in the public interest or in the exercise of official authority vested in the controller or in a third party to whom the data are disclosed;
(f) the processing is necessary for the purposes of the legitimate interests pursued by the controller or by a third party, except where such interests are overridden by the interests or fundamental rights and freedoms of the data subject which require protection of personal data, in particular where the data subject is a child.[16]

As far as these requirements are concerned – alongside the processing purposes, adequacy and relevance of data, accuracy or data-retention periods – ultimately, the whole solvency data system seems to rely predominantly on two grounds of legitimacy: (a) consent and (f) the legitimate interest of data controllers. Fintech and big data, instead, have to rely on consent only. This is because fintech reuses previously retrieved data most of the time processed for purposes incompatible with the original one (e.g. social media, credit card purchases) under the terms of Article 5 GDPR.[17] Therefore, the data subject must consent to information being reused by the lender in connection with the loan application, also in order to ensure that the processing is conducted under the principle of purpose limitation.[18]

---

[15] Recital 63 GDPR.
[16] Art. 6 GDPR.
[17] According to these provisions, personal data shall be collected for specified, explicit and legitimate purposes and not further processed in a manner that is incompatible with those purposes.
[18] See also Datailsynet (2018).

The lawful base set by (b) 'performance of a contract' is not applicable to traditional solvency data or big data because a financing agreement can well be underwritten without processing such data of other unrelated credit lines or data from other sources as the latter fall out of the scope for which data was originally collected, that is for the conclusion of a pre-existing contract.

In order to be able to process solvency data, data intermediaries such as commercial credit bureaus mostly rely on (f) the legitimate interest clause as the most favoured base. According to ACCIS (2015), in fact, 55 per cent of their members stated that all or part of their data was shared on the basis of legitimate interests of the data controllers and that the data subject is notified that data will be shared if they proceed with the conclusion of a contract.[19]

In data protection legislation, the legitimate interest of data controllers or that of third parties is known as the 'balance of interest' clause, where data controllers can process personal data lawfully without meeting the tight conditions provided by the other bases.

Under this condition, the processing must be necessary for the purpose, which must be a legitimate interest of the controller or a third party to whom the data is disclosed, provided that such legitimate interests do not impinge upon the fundamental rights and freedoms of individuals.

Under the previous regime of Directive 95/46/EC, the room for manoeuvre intentionally left by the balance of interest test to national implementation complicated the interpretation and application of the norm, leading to considerable divergences in the Member States. These inconsistencies went in different directions. For example, the choice of the subject in charge of making the assessment of the test had been left in some Member States to the determination of the data controllers, while in others this was for previous specification by the national supervisory authority. Similarly, some countries had provided indications while others have provided none.[20] If anything, Recital 30 of Directive 95/46/EC complicated the picture, as it stated that 'in order to maintain a balance between the interests involved while guaranteeing effective competition, Member States may determine the circumstances in which personal data may be used or disclosed to a third party in the context of the legitimate ordinary business activities of companies and other bodies'.

In one case involving solvency data, the CJEU intervened to declare as contrary to EU law the national law restricting the application of the balance of interest criterion only to data in public sources, affirming *inter alia* the direct effect of Article 7(f) of Directive 95/46/EC in case of non-compliance by national law.[21]

---

[19] ACCIS (2015).
[20] See Balboni et al. (2013).
[21] *ASNEF and FECEMD* v. *Administración del Estado* (Joined Cases C-468 and C- 469/10) [2011], ECLI:EU:C:2011:777.

The flexibility of the principle was later confirmed in a judgment concerning the collection of IP addresses.[22]

However, despite the affirmation of the direct applicability of the legitimate interest test of Directive 95/46/EC, the provision failed in its goal to create a harmonised legal framework for data processing in the EU. The GDPR, precisely as it is a regulation and does not require national implementation, is meant to correct the anomaly and create a level playing field within the EU.

The GDPR presents once again the test, providing for few changes in the wording but maintaining the substance of the current norm. However, in its Recital 47 it clarifies that the legitimate interests of a controller, including those of a controller to which the personal data may be disclosed or of a third party, may provide a legitimate basis for processing when it meets the reasonable expectations of data subjects based on their relationship with the controller. The provision explicitly exemplifies that such legitimate interest could exist where there is a relevant and appropriate relationship between the data subject and the controller in situations such as where the data subject is a client or in the service of the controller, such as in a credit relationship with a lender. At any rate, the existence of the legitimate interest would need careful assessment including whether a data subject can reasonably expect at the time and in the context of the collection of the personal data that processing for that purpose may take place. Under any lending process, lenders may easily claim that this is the case. The interests and fundamental rights of the data subject could override the interest of the lenders only where personal data are processed in circumstances where data subjects do not reasonably expect further processing, but this will hardly be a demonstrable circumstance in view of the existing traditional lending practices.

If anything, however, the legitimate interest clause is now hardly justifiable in the case of non-traditional data sources used by big data and fintech. Moreover, the new data analytics technologies increasingly use large data sets obtained from diverse unrelated sources (the definition of 'big data') which make the fulfilment of this legal basis unsustainable and impracticable.

That said, even within the range of traditional solvency data sources, distinctions should be made. As seen in Chapter 6, in fact, the depth and breadth of solvency data is inconsistent and differs greatly among the Member States. This poses problems of interpretation as to which data would fall within the scope of the legitimate interest clause and which would not. This is especially the case since the GDPR is meant to apply uniformly within the EU.

Crucially, the last limb of Recital 47 of the GDPR affirms that the processing of personal data strictly necessary for the purposes of preventing fraud also constitutes a legitimate interest of the data controller concerned. Likewise – to give an idea of how loose the legitimate interest base may be – under the Recital even the

---

[22] *Patrick Breyer v. Bundesrepublik Deutschland* (Case C-582/14) [2016], ECLI:EU:C:2016:779.

processing of personal data for direct marketing purposes may be regarded as carried out for a legitimate interest.[23]

The doubt that remains, however, is what counts as 'strictly necessary' and who makes such a determination. For example, in the case of traditional solvency data, lenders and credit bureaus have unilaterally decided that one of the purposes of their processing is to prevent fraud in credit applications.

Moreover, following the introduction in the GDPR of an accountability principle,[24] it appears that the data controller will be left with the determination of whether it has a legitimate interest to justify the processing, and whether its interest overrides the fundamental rights and freedoms of the data subject. Nonetheless, in providing further input on the data protection reform discussions, the Article 29 Working Party argued that additional guidance is essential in order to have a common understanding of the provision, especially as regards the very concept of legitimate interest and where such interest may override the fundamental rights and freedoms of data subjects. Such guidance should occur at EU level, because leaving further regulation to national law through the use of delegated acts would create discrepancies across the Union where data controllers would not be able to process data on the same grounds or following the same rules.[25]

Looking back at the case law of the CJEU under Directive 95/46/EC, the decision in *ASNEF and FECEMD v. Administración del Estado*[26] supports a liberal notion of processing of data, having the effect of giving way to the credit industry in the processing of negative financial data of consumers on grounds of their legitimate interest. However, it is important to stress that it is only negative data, not positive, that fall within the scope of the decision. The case was about national law which qualified the legitimate interest requirement by adding extra conditions, such as that the data should appear in public sources, and thereby excluding, in a categorical and generalised way, any processing of data not appearing in such sources; the CJEU ruled that such national law was precluded.[27] However, the CJEU had the opportunity to touch upon the significance of the legitimate interest where it recognised that the processing of data appearing in non-public sources necessarily implies that personal data is known by the controller, acknowledging that this more serious infringement of the data subject's rights enshrined in the Charter of Fundamental Rights of the EU must be taken into account when balanced against the legitimate interest of the controller.[28] However, it missed the opportunity to make such a balance in the specific case, limiting its analysis to the illegitimacy of the more restrictive criteria imposed by national law. As a result, since the national law in

---

[23] The last limb of Recital 47 GDPR explicitly states that 'The processing of personal data for direct marketing purposes may be regarded as carried out for a legitimate interest.'
[24] Art. 5(2) GDPR.
[25] Art. 29 Working Party (2012).
[26] *ASNEF and FECEMD v. Administración del Estado* (Joined Cases C-468 and C-469/10) [2011], ECLI:EU:C:2011:777.
[27] Ibid.
[28] Ibid., paras. 45–6.

question prevented commercial credit bureaus from using the legitimate interest clause to process and disseminate negative consumer financial data within the industry in Spain, the judgment had the factual effect of legitimising such a practice.

Finally, it is worth noting that Article 40 GDPR provides for the establishment of 'Codes of Conduct' whereby data controllers are encouraged to draw up codes of conduct intended to contribute to the proper application of the GDPR, taking account of the specific features of the various processing sectors. Under this norm, associations and other bodies representing categories of controllers or processors (in the case at study, for example, ACCIS) may prepare codes of conduct, or amend or extend such codes, for the purpose of specifying the application of the GDPR, in particular including fair and transparent processing and the legitimate interests pursued by controllers in specific contexts.

The question whether and to what extent data controllers should be entrusted with the determination of which of their own interests should prevail, albeit forcing them to provide a justification, remains controversial. Likewise, the effort of levelling the imbalance of power between data controllers and data subjects pursued by the GDPR could remain frustrated. Arguably, until now one of the most questionable aspects has been the lack of involvement or co-participation of civil society or consumer organisations in the co-determination of such codes of conduct.

In sum, the use of the 'legitimate interest' legal basis for the processing of traditional solvency data is not without controversy. At any rate, its use should remain limited to only a few types of data whose use is universally accepted within the EU, although the tide does not seem to go in that way.

7.3 DATA SUBJECT'S CONSENT

For the inclusion of broader data sources in their processing operations and less obvious controversy, (a) the consent of the data subjects is the most reliable legal basis in use. Credit bureaus and lenders need to rely on the informed consent of data subjects who unequivocally agree to all the 'game rules' set by the credit industry, notwithstanding whether these are set unilaterally and the degree of transparency.

Consent, as conceived by the law, is a key element that permits the processing of personal data by data controllers that would otherwise be forbidden. When a data subject gives valid consent, data controllers are released from the restrictions provided by law in a fashion that can be described as an opt-in system. In other words, the processing becomes lawful from the moment consent is unambiguously expressed. However, despite the apparently robust legal protection afforded to data subjects, consent may be obtained by a number of methods and has proved problematic as a basis for personal data processing because it can be easily abused, confused or conflated.[29]

---

[29] In theory, consent that does not meet the requirements of the law or is vitiated should be regarded as void, and should invalidate all data processing *ex tunc* – from the outset. See Art. 29 Working Party (2011).

The complexities of both the solvency data sharing and (even more) the fintech business models, data-collection practices, vendor–customer relationships, or technological applications may make them impossible for consumers to understand. Alternatively, these complexities may in practice render consumers unable to freely and actively decide to accept the consequences of consenting to data processing, particularly when faced with a perceived immediate economic benefit. For example, under the previous regime of Directive 95/46/EC it was not infrequent to notice these occurrences in the inclusion of a notice to consent to data processing within the standard contractual terms for credit. However, treating consent as a transactional moment using standard-form agreements constitutes a mechanical or perfunctory means of obtaining overarching consent for data processing.[30]

The inclusion of data-processing consent in the general terms and conditions of a credit application can be a common yet elusive method of obtaining consumer consent. A central tenet of an agreement is that one agrees voluntarily; consent becomes therefore associated with the legal paradigm of contract. Moreover, the lending contractual relationship is a situation with a clear imbalance between the consumer and the business counterpart. Consumers do not have much choice but to abide by the rules of the credit bureaus, lenders or fintech if they wish to receive credit. A consumer's consent regarding the credit bureaus' use of databases or fintech usage of big data is either mandatory or assumed. Lenders claim that lack of consent would impede them from taking the credit application any further. The same occurs for the use of credit scoring. In the end, concerns regarding the suitability of the law to address consumer credit reporting and scoring result in a number of undesirable phenomena: economic and social classification; profiling; generalisation; segmentation; and consumer sorting. These actualities may lead to various types of economic discrimination – from pricing to access and inclusion – with possible repercussions in the social sphere. Big data invite reflections over the financialisation of the private lives of individuals.

Consent is again a core tenet of the GDPR, which reinforces its concept providing for new stricter conditions. As before, it must be 'freely given, specific, informed and unambiguous' ex Article 4(11) GDPR. However, the law now mandates affirmative consent requiring the data subject to signal agreement by 'a statement or a clear affirmative action' (Art. 4(11) GDPR).

At the same time, the GDPR continues to distinguish between 'explicit' consent if the data in question is sensitive personal data (i.e. relates to any of the categories of sensitive data listed in Art. 9(1) GDPR, such as physical or mental health data, racial or ethnic origin) and 'unambiguous' consent for data considered of non-sensitive nature, i.e. all the other personal data (Art. 6 GDPR combined with Art. 4 GDPR).

The issue of what standard of consent should apply under the GDPR was the subject matter of intense debates and negotiations at the lengthy proposal stage of

---

[30] See Brownsword (2009).

the GDPR. The legislative history of the GDPD demonstrates that the final drafting was intentional in maintaining different qualifiers of consent and making the explicit distinction between unambiguous and explicit consent depending on the ordinary or sensitive nature of the data to be processed.

To the extent that the GDPR makes clear that 'explicit' and 'unambiguous' consent are not the same, the boundaries of what is 'unambiguous' remain unclear, with the additional complication that the law now states that it must be given by an affirmative action. For example, it is unclear to what extent implied consent remains possible.

While the GDPR provides that 'silence, pre-ticked boxes or inactivity should not ... constitute consent',[31] it also states that consent can be given through 'another statement or conduct which clearly indicates in this context the data subject's acceptance of the proposed processing of his or her personal data'.[32] The distinction between 'explicit' and 'unambiguous' consent matters in practice as long as different models of consent translate into very different engineered solutions within products and services, especially online. In the 'explicit' consent model an 'opt-in tick box' or declaratory consent statement will be clearly necessary. However, in the 'unambiguous' consent model that dominates commercial services a prominent notice together with an 'affirmative action' may suffice to obtain an implied consent without the need for an opt-in box or declaratory consent.

This can make a substantial difference in terms of the way consent is collected from consumers or the interface presented to them, and the way in which they interact with the product or service provider in question. Ultimately, this also makes a difference as to the real knowledge and control that consumers may have on the processing of their personal data, and the uses that can be made with the data.

In the end, consent must rely on transparency and 'affirmative action' (whether explicitly given or inferred through conduct) but how this will be translated in practice remains to be seen, especially within the complexities of financial transactions.

The GDPR also establishes explicitly that data subjects have a subsequent right of withdrawal of consent (or an opt-out). The data subject may withdraw consent at any time and this must be as practical as granting consent. Clearly, the withdrawal of consent shall not affect the lawfulness of processing based on consent before its withdrawal.[33]

Overall, it remains unclear how these aspirations are to be effectively reconciled with the realities of solvency data-sharing systems or fintech and big data. First, there seem to be tensions in the legislation: on the one hand, consent must be informed; on the other, consent 'should cover all processing activities carried out for the same

---

[31] Recital 32 GDPR.
[32] *Ibid.*
[33] Art. 7(3) GDPR.

purpose or purposes' and when 'the processing has multiple purposes, consent should be given for all of them'.[34]

Thus, if consent is the legal basis to rely upon, theoretically it would have to be given and renewed at a number of different stages, not only at the time of making a credit application but also to the processing of each piece of data generated through a search on databases, including information relating to having secured a credit line, having been refused credit, etc. However, 'consent is presumed not to be freely given if it does not allow separate consent to be given to different personal data processing operations despite it being appropriate in the individual case'.[35] Likewise, consent is presumed not to be freely given 'if the performance of a contract, including the provision of a service, is dependent on the consent despite such consent not being necessary for such performance'.[36]

The picture regarding solvency data and big data becomes more confused where the GDPR further intends to protect the data subject stating that consent should not be regarded as freely given if the data subject 'is unable to refuse or withdraw consent without detriment'[37] or 'where there is a clear imbalance between the data subject and the controller'.[38]

The problem is that an effective right to withhold consent to the processing of personal data for the purposes of calculating credit risk would undermine the entire *raison d'être* of the industry by removing debtors or bits of information from the overall data pool of the databases, thus causing incomplete market coverage which in turn would diminish the accuracy of the databases themselves.[39] By pre-empting consumers of the possible negative effects of the withdrawal of consent under the GDPR, the solvency data or fintech industries not only confirm this analysis but they also provide a more imbalanced scenario. If a consumer is able to exercise his or her right to withdrawal or erasure of personal data, ACCIS warns that such an action will lead to an incomplete credit file and the data subject would 'join a potential group of financially excluded consumers who would have amended files ... [This] may make attaining credit extremely difficult in the future for [the consumer], and lenders would lack certainty on what has or hasn't been deleted'.[40]

Therefore, what remains doubtful and of concern for consumers is the effect that the right of withdrawal of consent may have on their future financial relationships, given that the latter are increasingly dependent on the completeness of solvency data or big data coverage. Almost certainly, the right of withdrawal of consent for the processing of these data will not mean that those who exercise it are exempted from all credit risk analysis across the board. The suspicion, by contrast, is that they will be

---

[34] Recital 32 GDPR.
[35] Recital 43 GDPR.
[36] Ibid.
[37] Recital 42 GDPR.
[38] Recital 43 GDPR.
[39] Ferretti (2008).
[40] ACCIS [no date] also retrieved in ACCIS (2016).

excluded altogether for not being in the databases, not having a credit history or being un-networked.

Last but not least, recent studies show that in order to gain specific transactional and personal advantages most consumers willingly disclose information about themselves and their social activities without thinking about the effects of their disclosures, thus making consent de facto ineffective. Yet very few consumers understand the significant consequences of this trade-off, including how data controllers will use their personal data. Not only can data processing be very complex and non-transparent, but most consumers lack both the information and the skills to properly evaluate their own decision to consent.[41]

In the end, it remains unclear how the aspirations of the law are to be effectively reconciled with the reality of solvency data sharing, big data and fintech.

7.4 AUTOMATED DECISION-MAKING AND PROFILING

The GDPR regulates the automated decision-making and profiling through the processing of personal data. As seen above, these methods are largely used in the financial services industry with the use of credit scoring alongside the credit reports, or the fintech artificial intelligence systems.

Directive 95/46/EC already contained a specific provision designed for credit scoring. Article 15 on automated individual decisions provided that in certain cases, including the evaluation of a person's creditworthiness, data subjects had the right not to be subject to a decision based solely on the automatic processing of data. Nevertheless, Member States were given the ability to provide that a person could have been subjected to an automated decision as long as the decision was 'taken in the course of the entering into or performance of a contract, provided the request for the entering into or the performance of the contract has been satisfied or that there are suitable measures to safeguard his legitimate interests, such as arrangements allowing him to put his point of view'.[42] Member States could allow automated decision-making if authorised by a law that also laid out measures to safeguard a data subject's legitimate interests.[43]

For example, for the first time in Germany, the law altering the German Data Protection Act of 29 May 2009 dealt specifically with consumer-related scoring.[44] In turn, the German Supreme Court (Bundesgerichtshof) has confirmed that credit scoring qualifies for meeting legal requirements under data protection legislation, but it has affirmed that the underlying mathematical and statistical calculation method can be protected as a trade secret. Thus, it remains open to question to

---

[41] Frank (1988); Pasquale (2015); Peppet (2011).
[42] Art. 15 of Directive 95/46/EC.
[43] Ibid.
[44] Metz (2012).

what extent transparency can be guaranteed to consumers, which is a matter now under the consideration of the German Constitutional Court.[45]

At least, the GDPR attempts to provide more transparency to data subjects as regards the existence of automated decision-making, including profiling. In these cases, under Articles 13(f), 14(g) and 15(h) GDPR data controllers should provide 'meaningful information about the logic involved, as well as the significance and the envisaged consequences of such processing for the data subject'. Nonetheless, it remains unclear the extent to which data controllers will have to disclose full details of scoring or fintech logics and see their interests or rights for trade secrecy and competition compromised. Likewise, it remains to be seen the extent to which consumers will be able to understand the complex techniques behind the making of profiling and the logics of algorithms. The suspicion is that information about the logics employed will remain at a general level not allowing a full understanding of how algorithms work and how the new generations of intelligent machines learn and generate evolving results.

In the absence of this type of law, under Directive 95/46/EC Article 15(2)(a) applied. Interestingly, the key terms *satisfied* and *legitimate interests* had not been specifically defined, leaving uncertainty, especially if one considers that the right to data protection should have been satisfied in the first place. One must consider, however, that credit scoring is built on solvency data processing. Therefore, before the application of Article 15, the data used to generate a score would have been processed according to the other provisions of Directive 95/46.

Once again, the GDPR attempts to reinforce the protection of data subjects by stating that they shall have the right to object, on grounds relating to his or her particular situation, at any time to processing of personal data concerning him or her which is based on profiling. However, the data controller may still process such data if it demonstrates compelling legitimate grounds for the processing which override the interests, rights and freedoms of the data subject or for the establishment, exercise or defence of legal claims (Art. 21 GDPR). This means that once more data controllers are called upon a balancing exercise. In the case at hand, the usual justifications regarding the protection of credit or the over-indebtedness of consumers are likely to be used or, depending on the point of view, abused. In the case of fintech, big data constitute the business model, and the usual justification that otherwise the application cannot be taken further is likely to be used.

At first sight, according to Article 22 GDPR, consumers shall have the right not to be subject to a decision based solely on scoring (the GDPR refers to 'automated

---

[45] See Supreme Court ruling on information access to scoring practices by consumer: http://juris.bundesgerichtshof.de/cgi-bin/rechtsprechung/document.py?Gericht=bgh&Art=pm&Datum=2014&Sort=3&nr=66583&pos=1&anz=17; see the press release of the judgement at http://juris.bundesgerichtshof.de/cgi-bin/rechtsprechung/document.py?Gericht=bgh&Art=en&sid=2ef8cefa03b7d0493f54c1bc71ee0a53&anz=1&pos=0&nr=66583&linked=pm&Blank=1; see Chapter 6, n. 34, for detail and discussion of this case.

processing, including profiling'). However, the provision does not apply if the decision is necessary for entering into or performing an agreement (e.g. the credit contract). Again, this may give leeway to the credit industry which claims that the use of credit scoring is necessary to make a decision on the opening of a credit line to consumers, despite the fact that such decisions may well be taken without scoring consumers. Or, again, this may give leeway to the fintech industry whose business model is made of the necessary usage of big data. Likewise, the right not to be subjected by automated decision processing does not apply if it is authorised by other EU or national law (e.g. specific provisions altering data protection act such as in the case of German law or Italian law, or the banking act of a Member State), making the fundamental right of data protection of consumers succumb to financial services legislation.

Finally, automated decision-making and profiling can take place if it is based on the data subject's explicit consent – therefore all the above considerations on 'consent' and its weaknesses to protect consumers apply *mutatis mutandis*.

The only safeguard that the law offers to consumers is that they will have the right to obtain human intervention on the part of the controller, to express his or her point of view and to contest the decision. However, it remains an open question how and to what extent in practice lenders (and their employees in particular) will be ready to overturn the results of a credit score. Under the tenets of the GDPR, this will happen with the correction of inaccuracies, and provided that explicit discriminatory effects are prevented on the basis of racial or ethnic origin, political opinion, religion or beliefs, trade union membership, genetic or health status or sexual orientation, or that result in measures having such an effect.[46]

Nonetheless, especially but not exclusively for fintech and big data, it may be very difficult to trace errors in the past data or be able to claim hidden biases. Also, the problem may be that it may prove impossible to demonstrate the extent to which scoring may conceal forms of discrimination that it may generate, especially indirectly by not using such sensitive data. Arguably, it is impossible for a consumer to demonstrate a cause-and-effect relationship on an individual basis, between the data used, the data-mining technique employed and the discriminatory decision affecting an entire group.

7.5 RELIABILITY AND PROPORTIONALITY OF DATA TO ACHIEVE POLICY OBJECTIVES

Overall, an effective protection of consumers' personal data is particularly important in the financial services sector. If the values upheld by data protection law are considered, it becomes apparent how solvency data may raise issues of consumer classification, standardisation, simplification, sorting, economic discrimination and

---

[46] Recital 71 GDPR.

financial inclusion of some and exclusion of others. Generally, consumer solvency data are capable of driving the conforming of consumer behaviours to the economic needs of the credit industry under market tenets of the neo-liberal ideology.[47] All these undesirable outcomes can be direct consequences of solvency data processing, which comprise any form of automated processing of personal data intended to analyse or predict economic situations or behaviours.[48]

The issue of selecting qualitative in addition to quantitative data can also pose the problem of unintentional or even intentional discrimination (e.g. by cherry-picking certain borrowers and manage default rates that increase profitability), especially since their choice reflect biased human decisions. Obviously, such a decision-making does not overtly discriminate on the basis of factors such as race, gender or age that are caught by anti-discrimination laws.[49] Nevertheless, it may instead use correlated information to build an in-depth profile of a particular customer and make other types of discriminations not explicitly covered by the law, e.g. discriminations based on behaviours, culture or wealth. Some instances of these discriminations can be reconducted to traits of race, gender or age but they will be very hard – if not impossible – to prove.

An indiscriminate use of data may also easily lead to increased stereotypical decisions. If data protection can be problematic for traditional data, this is exacerbated by the use of big data and by allowing lenders too much access into their customer's personal life.

These situations have to be contextualised with the complications and opaqueness of algorithms that transform numerous bits of apparently neutral or unrelated information about a consumer into a straight numerical score that determines the outcome and/or price of applications with all the following implications. Most of the time not only the logics of the algorithms remain secret, but also the data sources used by the individual lenders are undisclosed.

In the end, when balancing the fundamental right of data protection, one of the main issues remains the determination of what data and data sources are necessary to achieve policy goals for the creditworthiness assessment and the prudential supervision of the financial system. Likewise, in the absence of legislative or other regulatory indications, it is also critical to determine who makes such a decision as to the necessity of the types of data to be processed.

---

[47] In particular those advanced by the Chicago School: see Bork (1993); see also Harvey (2005). On a late account on the persistence of the neo-liberal ideology in financial markets, see Williams (2013: ch. 2).
[48] Art. 29 Working Party (2013).
[49] e.g. see Council Directive 2000/43/EC of 29 June 2000 implementing the principle of equal treatment between persons irrespective of racial or ethnic origin, OJ L 180/22; Council Directive 2004/113/EC of 13 December 2004 implementing the principle of equal treatment between men and women in the access to and supply of goods and services, OJ L 373/37. See also *Association Belge des Consommateurs Test-Achats ASBL and others v. Conseil des ministers* (Case C-236/09) [2011], ECLI:EU:C:2011:100, where the CJEU ruled that insurers can no longer take gender into account when calculating insurance premiums.

It is important that the data used are only those necessary to achieve policy or other important goals, ensuring that they are reliable and proportionate.

As shown above, the exchange of consumers' financial information and the use of centralised databases are now regarded not only as a risk management tool in the interest of the credit industry, but also a form of creditworthiness assessment and a tool to identify the over-indebtedness of individuals.

However, it is helpful to recall that in the case LCL (Le Crédit Lyonnais) the CJEU has made clear that the creditworthiness assessment should be done in the interest of consumers to prevent irresponsible lending and over-indebtedness,[50] and the use of solvency data is regarded as one possible – though non-exclusive – tool to make such an assessment.

If on the one hand this point of view may support an argument for the exchange of information in the general interest of consumers, on the other hand it remains open to debate whether the design of databases is proportionate to the policy goals to be achieved, and whether the type and the level of aggregation or detail of information exceeds the purpose for its sharing.

Solvency data or big data – with the uncertainty of which data sources would be necessary – may capture existing or likely debt problems if further credit is taken, but they cannot address the most frequent causes of consumer over-indebtedness, such as lifetime events or poor market conditions, when repayment difficulties emerge at a later stage. Certainly, behavioural factors may have a role in consumers becoming over-indebted. However, solvency data can sanction or penalise failures to repay or repay late. But the large majority of consumers fail to repay their debts or pay them back late (with profitable interests for the industry) for the occurrence of events that are not predictable at the time of contracting a loan and that solvency data cannot foresee. Poor macroeconomic conditions, job losses, divorces, illnesses, family deaths cannot be anticipated but solvency data give a memory to the system, potentially and possibly penalising the affected consumers even further.[51] On the contrary, market deregulation – coupled with incomplete social safety nets – is often recognised as the structural condition that leads to an environment hospitable to financial difficulty.[52] This consideration should be contextualised with the findings of recent studies confirming the nature and causes of over-indebtedness, which reveal empirically how this is not limited to the issue of debts stemming from financial credits but includes all consumer essential outgoings, and is tied to income and other expenditures relating to taxation and cuts in social welfare. Consumers are considered over-indebted if they are having – on an ongoing basis – difficulties meeting (or falling behind with) their commitments, whether these relate to

---

[50] LCL (Le Crédit Lyonnais) SA v. Fesih Kalhan (Case C-565/12) [2014], ECLI:EU:C:2014:190.
[51] On the causes of defaulting see e.g. Balmer et al. (2006); Berthoud and Kempson (1992); Caplovitz (1963); Dominy and Kempson (2003); Hoermann (1986); Niemi (1999); Ramsay (2007: 578–80, esp.); Vandone (2009).
[52] Braucher (2006).

servicing secured or unsecured borrowing or to payment of rent, utility or other household bills.[53] The major causes of consumer over-indebtedness have been confirmed to be external lifetime events or accidents of life exacerbated by poor macroeconomic factors, the increasing costs of living and the over-reliance on consumptive credit as an economic model for growth.[54] The findings reveal that people who lose their jobs and incomes have a higher probability to default and become entrapped in unsustainable debt, as do people confronted with accidents of life no one can anticipate. Behavioural factors, such as poor financial choices, mismanagement of resources or irresponsible lending practices, seem to have a limited bearing. Yet a reading of the major causes behind problem debt could be a conjuncture of external events with behavioural factors, where consumers do not effectively adjust their budgets to the external changes.[55]

These situations cannot be caught or resolved by solvency data and their exchange. All that data may do is make an abstract representation of unique or circumstantiated situations without distinguishing the causes, and they retrieve and give a memory to such representations that become accessible to all other market players, thus *inter alia* raising doubts as to their ability to predict whether the same consumer will repay loaned money in the absence of those lifetime events that once originated the data themselves.

All things considered, it becomes apparent that the nature of the problem is rooted in a number of economic soils that are beyond the remit or control of what solvency data can do. This ultimately questions the reliability and proportionality of solvency data to reach such policy goals, as also confirmed by a study of experts advising the European Commission in the field of financial services from the perspective of users which found no evidence that their increased availability has helped prevent over-indebtedness, support prudential regulation or facilitate access to affordable credit.[56]

Arguably, moreover, giving a second chance to consumers may well be in the consumer interest and it may even be economically efficient. In this context, a second chance is intended as not retrieving information which could have negative consequences on consumers, especially under those circumstances that are not tied or linked to the original negative information. The same may be put forward for the case of personal insolvencies under the law of the Member States in order to avoid the perpetration of the stigma attached to such procedures.[57] The examples of countries where only public credit bureaus exist such as Belgium and France (where *inter alia* only negative data are allowed) corroborate this stance and further question the role and effectiveness of private credit bureaus. In these countries, for

---

[53] Civic Consulting (2014).
[54] Ibid.
[55] e.g. Banque de France (September 2014).
[56] Financial Services User Group (2015).
[57] Personal insolvency laws in the EU raise difficult issues and questions that are beyond the scope of this work. For a thorough discussion, see e.g. Micklitz (2012); Niemi (2012); Ramsay (2012a).

example, the levels of consumer over-indebtedness are not higher than in the other Member States where there is an extensive sharing of consumer data.[58] Likewise, in these two Member States the cost of credit for consumers does not appear to be higher than in other Member States.[59]

Therefore, in the end it is argued that extensive, expansive or indiscriminate use of solvency data is disproportionate to the policy goals to be achieved. Only negative data in aggregate form can provide a partial static picture of the consumer financial exposure and their state of financial difficulty. Moreover, the types of data used must be reliable – a circumstance that cannot be left to the sole determination of the credit industry.

7.6 SOLVENCY DATA AND BIG DATA AS THE GATEWAY OF THE ECONOMIC AND SOCIAL LIFE OF CONSUMERS

Solvency data sharing by commercial credit bureaus and the uses made by lenders raise questions of possible economic discrimination, classifications, sorting, standardisation of behaviours and the need to build a financial curriculum vitae as dictated by the industry. These issues may easily translate into inclusion or exclusion from mainstream financial services, and they have the potential of ultimately affecting the social sphere of consumers in addition to their dignity and liberty as human beings.

In addition, the idea that the conforming of behaviours may be dictated by the financial industry can be a problematic scenario for society that many are not ready to accept. Consumers adapt their behaviours to what the industry demands, becoming aware that failure to play by their rules may translate in exclusion from mainstream services. An expanded use of personal data can easily turn them into the gateway for other economic and social aspects of the lives of people, which makes personal financial data a potentially harming tool for consumers and a threat for societies resting on values of social inclusion and welfare. For example, recently it has been reported that in the Netherlands consumers were asked to pay large deposits of hundreds of euros for their utilities on the basis of solvency data processing.[60] Consumers may be turned down from telecom contracts and be forced to buy more costly pay-as-you-go packages – or vice versa they may pay more for their mortgages for missed payments of telecom bills of little value.[61]

---

[58] See Civic Consulting (2014).
[59] See e.g. Eurobarometers, http://ec.europa.eu/public_opinion/archives/ebs/ebs_321_en.pdf; http://ec.europa.eu/public_opinion/archives/ebs/ebs_355_en.pdf; for literature comparing the use of consumer credit in France and in the UK, see Ramsay (2012b). Trumbull (2014) puts forward that America's credit culture emerged from an evolving coalition of lenders seeking to make their business socially acceptable and NGOs that pushed the idea of credit as welfare-enhancing to promote labour and minority rights. By contrast, the author argues that in France, where a similar coalition did not emerge, consumer credit continued to be perceived as economically regressive and socially risky.
[60] See www.consumentenbond.nl/nieuws/2016/tientallen-klachten-op-meldpunt-dupe-van-je-data
[61] See http://plug-n-score.com/blog/credit-scoring-methods-for-telecom-financiers.htm and www.theguardian.com/money/2011/feb/19/credit-score-mobile-phone-mortgage. See also Turner and Walker (2015).

Moreover, it is disputed that also those who are not in the databases for not having a credit history may face negative consequences in the access of mainstream services, so that everyone becomes induced to build his/her financial CV for not becoming penalised at a later stage. This is what already happens in the US where the market is more mature than in the EU.[62] Moreover, the rise in usage of non-traditional data opens further questions as regards other behaviours of individuals in a free society, e.g. whether there is or there should be an explicit right to be un-networked,[63] thus safeguarding people against attracting negative consequences in case personal data are not available on social media or elsewhere.

It is suggested that empirical research is needed to assess whether or to what extent solvency data, the scoring of consumers and big data act to exclude low-income, vulnerable or non-conforming consumers from markets. As the use of solvency and big data or scoring can turn into classification, categorising and sorting mechanisms, financially vulnerable consumers may be easily recognised, classified and excluded. Until now, very little is known about the relationship between the use of consumers' data as a method of selection or credit pricing, as well as exclusion of those members of society who do not qualify under the standards set by the lenders. For example, more knowledge is needed to understand the credit behaviour of those who are not eligible to take credit by mainstream lenders and have a poor credit rating retrieved by the data. Likewise, more knowledge is important regarding the needs and conditions of those who are not in the databases or the young generations who are unlikely to have a substantial credit history. Open questions are the extent to which they are likely to recourse to subprime lenders, as well as whether and how other economic segments could be affected (e.g. tenancies, telephone and utility contracts).

It is warned that the increased processing of solvency data, the scoring of individuals across different economic segments and big data usage may lead to situations where credit risk can be used as a proxy for other types of risks – insurance claims, workplace trustworthiness, rent payment, telecommunications or utilities pricing. This use of solvency and big data may create the additional concern – so far unresolved by the law – regarding the extent to which data sharing across industries may lead to exclusion from non-financial services or wider economic and social discrimination or marginalisation.

These issues are even more important in a voluntary system because there is no requirement, either legal or natural, to justify the unilateral sharing of data for the performance of a contract that is the core of the lending business.

Lending money in exchange for profit is perfectly possible and probably lucrative even without the expansion of data processing. At most, increased data sharing is useful and more profitable in the same manner as using personal data for marketing purposes is useful and profitable. Certainly, one may reasonably think that data

---

[62] Hendricks (2004); Mierzwinski and Chester (2013).
[63] See Packin and Aretz (2016).

induce an increased volume of lending, thus indirectly providing important benefits to those with 'good' or 'conforming' profiles. Accordingly, it would be reasonable to expect that increased lender profits unequivocally result in more favourable credit conditions for those who fall within the classification of 'good' or 'conforming' consumers. This presumption reflects the view that there is relative equivalence between pursuing lenders' self-interest in maximising profits and promoting the general interest resulting in lower prices for consumers. This is an idea dating back to Adam Smith and his notion of the 'invisible hand'. The economic assumption implied is that in perfectly competitive markets, marginal private benefits equal marginal social benefits, and marginal private costs equal marginal social costs. Accordingly, self-interest always promotes the interest of the community even though it is not part of the original intention.[64] The traditional assumptions of Smith's perfect-competition theory, however, are that all market actors act rationally in their own self-interest with good and full information, that all goods and resources are freely transferable, that all markets permit free and easy entry and exit, and that prior distributions of wealth and resources do not unfairly impact competition.[65] It is well accepted today that such assumptions practically never hold true in the real world, a circumstance of which Adam Smith was aware.[66]

Economic arguments on this subject are numerous and they touch upon contentious areas. The economic advantages appear to be for some consumers only – the 'conforming' ones – while others would be excluded or penalised by paying more. These 'other' consumers do not qualify as 'good' or 'conforming' consumers because they do not fit into predefined criteria, and they would ultimately have more difficulty repaying their debts and avoiding default. At any rate, whether extensive data processing really serve the interest of debtors seems inconsequential if one embraces the idea that economic efficiency does not stand in isolation, but that there are greater social concerns relating to the position of individuals in society. Namely, where they are not merely equated to consumers but valued as citizens in a free and democratic society.

As it stands, the law does not resolve the question of how far consumers should be forced to sacrifice their own rights in the interest of the credit industry, bearing in mind that the 'utilitarian' concerns of the credit industry cannot necessarily prevail over civil liberties and fundamental-rights concerns.

Therefore, it remains open to debate whether the institutional form of credit bureaus, the design of their databases or fintech systems advance the desired policy goals, or whether the level of aggregation and the type of information exceeds the purpose for which it is shared, especially with respect to EU citizens' fundamental rights.

---

[64] See generally Smith (1776).
[65] See generally Malloy (2004).
[66] See generally Smith (1759); Stiglitz (2007).

At the same time, the sharing of solvency data raises debates over social duties and social responsibilities of the credit industry or the data intermediaries as social actors, prudential supervision, and the institutions which should be entrusted with the exercise of such a social function. The credit industries, as well as the data providers, are not social actors or institutions designed to work in the public interest. They are commercial or private entities whose mission is to make the interest of shareholders and generate profits or, when not-for-profit in the context of banking associations, they are designed to make the interest of the associated commercial ventures. In these cases, there seems to be a conflict of interest which prevents possible arguments that they may work in the interest of consumers.[67]

The picture may be different when public institutions are involved under the legitimacy of the rule of law. For example, unlike for the creditworthiness assessment and over-indebtedness, the use of solvency data for the prudential supervision of the financial system has addressed the institutional nature and regulation of the organisations entrusted with such a public duty.

7.7 ALTERNATIVE DATA PROTECTION-FRIENDLY DATA ANALYSIS: A SEMI-SERIOUS PROPOSAL

As noted earlier in this work, several studies have shown that, in most cases, loan defaults are due to an unexpected drop in income, not to a bad payer behaviour that could be detected in advance as most of the credit bureaus or fintech systems pretend to do. In addition, the drop in income is often inconsequential to a change that solvency databases or fintech can anticipate regardless of the level of sophistication of their tools: for example, divorce, job loss, illness or the effects of an economic recession. It also been proved that the vast majority of borrowers facing income losses try to fulfil their repayment obligations by delaying the payment of other debts and/or trying to borrow more to repay previous loans. These behaviours – or 'tactics' – are rarely efficacious and often lead to over-indebtedness (see Chapter 4). This also means that for the vast majority of borrowers, there seems to be a real commitment or at least willingness to meet their financial obligations at all costs.

Arguably, the simple worthwhile creditworthiness assessment could be whether the borrower has sufficient resources to meet her/his repayments at the time of the granting of credit and over the term of the contract. The relevant data for performing such an assessment are her/his income and expenses. To assess the creditworthiness of any consumer, there is a single source of information that is relevant and reliable,

---

[67] There are considerable differences in size, turnover, volume of activities and public engagement of credit bureaus across Europe. Some credit bureaus engage in social activities of financial education or other socially helpful activities. All the same, the duty of commercial credit bureaus is towards their shareholders and socially helpful activities remain within the sphere of publicity or enhancing their commercial reputation.

and contains all that is arguably needed to assess the financial situation of a consumer, namely his/her bank account. All the information on income and expenses necessary for creditworthiness assessment may be found on the consumer's bank/payment account statements. This information is objective and should allow the lender to conclude whether the borrower has sufficient and stable income, whether the level of the loan-to-income ratio is appropriate, whether the consumer already has other pending mortgage credit, personal loans or payment arrears, as well as all other financial and non-financial commitments (e.g. rent, utility bills, insurances) that may give rise to situations of repayment difficulty and, ultimately, unsustainable debt problems leading to over-indebtedness.

A preliminary work of defining what data is necessary and sufficient to assess the borrower's ability to repay a loan should be carried out.

As an illustration, the following information in an aggregated format could prove sufficient and proportionate:

- the expenses-to-income ratio;
- outstanding loans (if any), including use of authorised/non-authorised overdraft facilities;
- account regularly or temporarily in negative or positive balance, or frequency of overdraft usages;
- penalties for arrears (if any); and
- saving capacity.

It should also be defined who has the right to access or produce the assessment data, i.e. whether the consumer her/himself (e.g. by downloading his bank statement), or a trusted third party to which the consumer would give access to his/her bank accounts (a most suitable solution for multiple bank accounts in different banks).

Arguably, the main benefits would be the following:

- little or reduced risk of incorrect data as it may be too often the case with solvency databases or big data;[68]
- those that do not need credit are not subject to any centralisation of their records or personal data in databases;
- data would be controlled by the consumer;
- it may hinder the development of fintech systems collecting data from the most varied unrelated sources that lead to the financialisation of the private lives of consumers;

---

[68] See e.g. the last in a series of scandals caused by a major commercial credit bureau concerning data breaches and the violation of the data of millions of consumers at www.consumer.ftc.gov/blog/2017/09/equifax-data-breach-what-do, www.nytimes.com/2017/09/23/business/equifax-data-breach.html and www.telegraph.co.uk/technology/2017/09/08/equifax-hack-britons-data-watchdog-investigates-ukimpact-major. For examples of precedents, see e.g. www.tripwire.com/state-of-security/security-data-protection/4-credit-bureau-data-breaches-predate-2017-equifax-hack

- it would comply with far less controversy with the objective of data minimisation and the proportionality principle of the GDPR;
- it would fit with the principle of data portability that is a key novelty brought in data protection legislation by the GDPR. By contrast, the model represented by commercial credit bureaus may make it difficult to allow such a right to consumers;[69]
- it may increase financial inclusion: those who are excluded from the credit market because they do not fit into the predetermined category of risks (e.g. low-income people, people in some types of jobs, residents in stigmatised neighbourhoods) could demonstrate that they are managing their budget appropriately and they have even savings capacity; and
- it may increase budget management skills: those who are not skilled in managing their budget could be encouraged to do better if they want to get a positive assessment to convince prospective lenders.

---

[69] The right to data portability is one of eight rights enforced by the GDPR. Under Art. 13(2)(b), 'the controller shall, at the time when personal data are obtained, provide the data subject with the following further information necessary to ensure fair and transparent processing ... the existence of the right to request from the controller access to and rectification or erasure of personal data or restriction of processing concerning the data subject or to object to processing as well as the right to data portability'. Article 20 GDPR provides that:

1. The data subject shall have the right to receive the personal data concerning him or her, which he or she has provided to a controller, in a structured, commonly used and machine-readable format and have the right to transmit those data to another controller without hindrance from the controller to which the personal data have been provided, where:
   (a) the processing is based on consent pursuant to point (a) of Article 6(1) or point (a) of Article 9(2) or on a contract pursuant to point (b) of Article 6(1); and
   (b) the processing is carried out by automated means.
2. In exercising his or her right to data portability pursuant to paragraph 1, the data subject shall have the right to have the personal data transmitted directly from one controller to another, where technically feasible.
3. The exercise of the right referred to in paragraph 1 of this Article shall be without prejudice to Article 17 (the right to erasure or 'right to be forgotten'). That right shall not apply to processing necessary for the performance of a task carried out in the public interest or in the exercise of official authority vested in the controller.
4. The right referred to in paragraph 1 shall not adversely affect the rights and freedoms of others.

8

The Treatment of Over-Indebtedness

Towards a Harmonisation of Personal Insolvency Law in a Fragmented EU?

8.1 PERSONAL INSOLVENCY LEGISLATION IN THE EU

8.1.1 *National Law*

What may strike a jurist's attention is the absence of measures to cure or mitigate over-indebtedness at the same level of EU legislation as for the preventive responsible lending measures. Consumer defaults are the other side of the coin, but EU law seems oblivious of the negative economic and social consequences generated by the same financial market that it aims at integrating through harmonisation.

To the extent that the EU focuses on the prevention of behavioural causes of over-indebtedness, it appears clear that it overlooks the externalities that are the main causes of the problem, leaving a vacuum of market functionalism and consumer protection.

On the one hand, it looks evident that the law has limits to solve the unexpected major causes of consumer defaults, which are predominantly matters or wider social and economic policy (see Chapters 4 and 5). On the other hand, nonetheless, the law may address a palpable market failure by providing alleviating measures to repair or restructure the economic situation of the concerned persons, and allow them to return to a financially sustainable or sociably acceptable situation.

However, it may be argued that personal insolvency law has become the 'elephant in the room' in EU credit market law.[1] As briefly hinted earlier in Chapter 5, debt solutions and procedures once consumers become insolvent have been left to the competence of national legislation in a multilevel division of functions between the EU and the Member States, despite the clear interest of the EU in the matter evidenced by the many commissioned reports.

The traditional parochial nature of personal insolvency law is well documented in legal scholarship. Endogenous systems have developed at various times in history

---

[1] Ibid.

depending on local social values, culture and moral codes of conduct.[2] Long gone are the days of banishing or imprisoning defaulting debtors, but different countries have addressed in their own way the long-established contract law principle of *pacta sunt servanda*. Likewise, they have addressed differently the degrees of primacy attached to ensuring that debtors honour their contractual obligations, as well as the stigmatisation of personal failure and/or value given to moral hazard deployed in their systems.

There have been attempts by commentators to classify these different systems, formulated on various approaches and taking into account that some Member States have no tradition/history of personal insolvency law (e.g. Italy, Spain). Iain Ramsay initially divides personal insolvency systems into 'old' and 'new' systems. The former are typical of common law countries traditionally recognising the possibility of non-traders to discharge debts through bankruptcy. The latter, by contrast, belong to continental European jurisdictions which had not recognised until recently the possibility of individual non-traders to having recourse to debt discharge mechanisms.[3] Frequent classifications are those represented by legal traditions: the Nordic model (e.g. in Scandinavian countries) characterised by a common early attitude in accepting the breach of contractual obligations to relieve over-indebtedness and offering formal relief based on a good faith test such as the occurrence of external factors on an otherwise disciplined debtor; or the Germanic model open to all debtors but characterised by firm and sometimes draconian rules to eventually allow a discharge of the obligations (e.g. Germany, Austria, Estonia).[4] Iain Ramsay uses the 'straight' liquidation bankruptcy form vis-à-vis the repayment model, differentiated by a complete discharge of non-exempt assets in a relatively short period of time vis-à-vis the repayment of a proportion of debts in return for a later discharge after a longer period of time.[5] Other types of classifications have focused on market models based on quick discharges and a fresh start for debtors as a form of reallocation or re-equilibrium of risk in credit markets by shifting it from debtors to creditors to increase market efficiency, albeit with economic, political and civil disqualifications and restrictions during and after the insolvency procedure (e.g. the UK); another model is one based on creditor protection and long discharge periods with behavioural obligations for debtors aimed at maximising payments (e.g. Germany and Austria); by contrast, a mercy model is one focusing on the debtor and characterised by the deservingness or good faith of the latter, which concentrates on the abilities of debtors and the discretionary powers of courts or other officials in shaping the proceedings and their outcome (e.g. France, the Benelux countries and the Scandinavian countries).[6] Similar studies have

---

[2] Kilborn (2009); Ramsay (2007).
[3] Ramsay (2017).
[4] Kilborn (2009); Niemi (2009).
[5] Ramsay (2017).
[6] Heuer (2013).

grouped insolvency procedures according to a market-based model encouraging responsible lenders, a rehabilitation model directed at social considerations and deserving debtors, and a liability model with the burden placed on debtors to show good conduct.[7]

Johanna Niemi offers a legislative classification vis-à-vis the social policies of a given country, whereby some Member States have incorporated consumer insolvency provisions within broader corporate bankruptcy codes (e.g. Germany, Austria, Estonia, Portugal, the UK), others have chosen an approach based on broader consumer protection (e.g. France and Belgium), or some other else have focused on rehabilitation as a social policy goal (e.g. the Scandinavian countries).[8]

Whatever classification one may draw, the reality is that with the increase of over-indebtedness in the aftermath of the 2008 economic crisis, many Member States have moved towards brand-new or renovated national regimes for the protection of consumers in financial distress and the treatment of the insolvency of natural persons, with nearly all Member States now having a law in place.[9] However, these appear individual but uncoordinated legal initiatives in the Member States which expose the complete absence of common, harmonised or appropriately resourced strategies at EU level. Each Member State has developed its own legislation with its own features and institutional infrastructure for the implementation of the law (including the availability and training of judges and trustees, administrative capacity, accounting and valuation systems), but whose design has been driven by emergency and purely internal social policy considerations.[10]

The result is that personal insolvency laws in the EU do not appear cohesive.[11] Many substantive differences exist relative to the content-based notion of over-indebtedness, the institutional arrangements, the type of procedures (judicial or administrative), the prerequisites and impediments or exclusions *rationae personae* to access the procedure, the modalities or conditions and time frame for accessing the procedures, the duration of payments and time to grant the discharge, the stay on enforcement actions, the involvement of creditors in the procedures, ranking of creditors' claims, the treatment of secured credit and the costs of the procedure, etc.

8.1.2 EU Law and Mutual Recognition

Within such a fragmented legal framework, the EU has pursued the route of mutual recognition to ensure engagement between the Member States. This principle – which

---

[7] Viavoice (2015).
[8] Niemi (2012).
[9] London Economics (2012).
[10] Liu and Rosenberg (2013).
[11] European Commission, *Report from the Commission to the European Parliament, the Council and the European Economic and Social Committee on the Application of Council Regulation (EC) No. 1346/2000 of 29 May 2000 on insolvency proceedings*, COM(2012) 743 final.

derives from the seminal case *Cassis de Dijon*[12] to give effect to the principles of freedom of movement and obviate the absence of relevant harmonising provisions – holds that a Member State should not apply its domestic law to regulate activities originated in another Member State but it has to recognise the equivalent, albeit different, law in the Member State of origin unless there are special circumstances ('country of origin' principle). This is a common method in the field of corporate law in the provision of a system of order to sidestep diverse laws between the Member States.[13]

The legal instruments which have emanated from the EU concern procedural aspects and jurisdictional rules applicable to cross-border insolvencies mostly in the context of the cognate – yet different – area of business insolvency.

8.1.2.1 Council Regulation 1346/2000

Council Regulation (EC) 1346/2000,[14] though designed for business insolvency, applies also to natural persons as consumers, as long as the national proceedings are listed in its Annex A. The listed national proceedings do not include the large number of national insolvency laws, which have been enacted at a later point in time by Member States. The application of Brussels I(a) Regulation 1215/2012[15] to these uncovered legal instruments is questionable. First, it may apply only to some proceedings as long as these qualify as decisions being issued by a 'court or tribunal', so it does not apply in those jurisdictions where insolvency proceedings are of an administrative nature. Second, but most importantly, it does not apply to 'bankruptcy, proceedings relating to the winding-up of insolvent companies or other legal persons, judicial arrangements, compositions and analogous proceedings',[16] where the 'analogous proceedings' have been interpreted as including personal insolvency ones by analogy.[17]

A drawback of the above combination is that when a payment plan is confirmed by a court in a Member State it is not recognised or enforceable in another Member State, with debtors remaining liable to foreign creditors thus frustrating the aims of the proceedings.[18]

---

[12] *Rewe-Zentral AG v. Bundesmonopolverwaltung für Branntwein* (Case C-120/78) [1979], ECLI:EU:C:1979:42.
[13] Craig and de Búrca (2008), esp. pp. 684–9.
[14] OJ L 160/1.
[15] Regulation (EU) No. 1215/2012 of the European Parliament and of the Council of 12 December 2012 on jurisdiction and the recognition and enforcement of judgments in civil and commercial matters (recast), OJ L 351/1.
[16] Art. 1(2)(b).
[17] Israël (2005); Linna (2014).
[18] The personal insolvency procedures in Annex A are those of Austria, Belgium, the Czech Republic, Cyprus, Germany, Latvia, Malta, the Netherlands, Poland and partly France, Slovenia and the UK. See European Commission, *Report from the Commission to the European Parliament, the Council and the European Economic and Social Committee on the Application of Council Regulation (EC) No. 1346/2000 of 29 May 2000 on Insolvency Proceedings*, COM(2012) 743 final. According to London

In any event, regardless of the (then) scant number of relevant national proceedings for the insolvency of natural persons in the Annex, the Regulation neither regulates substantive insolvency law nor attempts to enforce a common system at EU level. Instead, it deals with matters of jurisdiction, recognition and enforcement, applicable law and cooperation in cross-border proceedings. The principle of mutual recognition is at the heart of the Regulation. The aim is to make sure that insolvency proceedings opened in one Member State are recognised in all other Member States. The Regulation establishes that the domestic law of the country where the case is opened is applicable for the insolvency proceedings and their effects.[19] In theory, as the determination of who qualifies for bankruptcy/insolvency is determined under national law,[20] any European consumer who meets the qualification criteria of a country which does permit consumer insolvency has the ability and right to access this, effectively making their domestic or other legislative position irrelevant.[21] The Regulation further provides that the domestic law of the country where the case is opened is applicable as long as the individual has established a 'centre of main interest' (COMI) in the relevant jurisdiction. The concept of COMI, designed with businesses in mind, corresponds to the place where the debtor conducts the administration of his interests on a regular basis.[22] Incidentally, the Regulation's rules have given rise to forum shopping by a handful of natural persons through abusive COMI relocation. Arguably, however, this is an irrelevant issue for over-indebted consumers, as COMI provisions could be capable of affecting a minority of skilled or well-informed individuals or small traders who are able to take advantage of regulatory arbitrage. On the contrary, they can hardly be applicable to the large majority of millions of people in real financial distress across the EU, i.e. the vulnerable consumers.

8.1.2.2 The Recast Regulation 2015/848

The Recast Regulation 2015/848[23] – which came into effect from 26 June 2017 and only applies to insolvency proceedings opened after that date[24] – builds on the main shortcomings identified under Regulation 1346/2000, namely its scope of application,

---

Economics (2012), many countries have moved or are moving from judicially led to administrative processes because of the high costs of the former when consumers are unable to meet such costs.

[19] Art. 4 Regulation 1346/2000.
[20] *Ibid*. Art. 4.2(a).
[21] London Economics (2012).
[22] Recital 13 Regulation 1346/2000.
[23] Regulation (EU) 2015/848 of the European Parliament and of the Council of 20 May 2015 on Insolvency Proceedings (Recast), OJ L 141/19.
[24] Ahead of that date, Member States will be required under Art. 86 to provide a description of their national insolvency legislation and procedures. In turn, Art. 24(1) – to come into effect on 26 June 2018 – provides for the establishment of publicly available insolvency registers in each Member State, with the European Commission to establish a system for the interconnection of these registers by 26 June 2019.

the exact determination of which Member State is competent to open insolvency proceedings and issues with COMI jurisdiction (forum shopping, above), the opening of secondary proceedings in other Member States, problems with rules on publicity of proceedings and the lodging of claims, and the absence of specific rules dealing with the insolvency of multinational enterprises.[25]

Of interest to this study is the scope of application of the Recast Regulation to include pre-insolvency proceedings for viable debtors and the many personal insolvency proceedings that were enacted only later in Member States. The Recast goes further than the liquidation proceedings of its predecessor, extending to proceedings which provide for the restructuring of a debtor at a stage where there is only a likelihood of insolvency, proceedings which leave the debtor fully or partially in control of his assets and affairs, and proceedings providing for a debt discharge or a debt adjustment of consumers and self-employed persons.

The technique adopted by the legislator is in addition to the pre-existing requirement of proceedings based on laws in which 'a debtor is totally or partially divested of its assets and an insolvency practitioner is appointed'[26] of the alternative of proceedings where 'the assets and affairs of a debtor are subject to control or supervision by a court'.[27] The Recitals reinforce that since consumer proceedings do not necessarily entail the appointment of an insolvency practitioner, they should be covered by the Recast Regulation only if they take place under the control or supervision of a court (including situations where the court only intervenes on appeal by a creditor or other interested parties).[28]

The new law also clarifies that it applies only to proceedings which are based on laws relating to insolvency, thus not only excluding proceedings based on general company law not designed exclusively for insolvency situations, but also specific proceedings in which debts of a natural person of very low income and very low asset value are written off (the so called 'NINA' – no income, no asset consumers – or 'LILA' – little income, little asset consumers), provided that such proceedings do not make provisions for payment to creditors.[29] This excludes the application of proceedings in those Member States where laws have been designed to maximise creditor returns, or to preserve human dignity where access to discharge has been made easier for NINAs/LILAs[30] (who form the majority of over-indebted consumers).

The other novelties under the Recast Regulation applicable to consumers relate to the improvement of the coordination of insolvency proceedings within the EU,

---

[25] See European Commission, Proposal for a Regulation of the European Parliament and of the Council amending Council Regulation (EC) No. 1346/2000 on insolvency proceedings, COM (2012)744 final – followed by the endorsement from the European Parliament's Legal Affairs Committee (JURI) on 17 December 2013 (MEMO/13/1164).
[26] Art. 1(1)(a) Regulation 2015/848.
[27] Ibid. Art. 1(1)(b).
[28] Ibid. Recital 10.
[29] Ibid. Recital 16.
[30] e.g. the proceedings in the France, Sweden, Austria, Germany, Belgium, Estonia and Denmark (Kilborn (2009)).

the equitable treatment of creditors and the minimisation of forum shopping, i.e. the movement of assets from one country to another so as to take advantage of a more favourable legal position.

In particular, for individuals who do not carry on an independent business or professional activity, COMI is to be presumed to be the place of the individual's 'habitual residence', unless this was shifted in the preceding six months. In that case, the presumption does not apply.[31] As explicated in the Recitals, it should be possible to rebut the presumption, for example where the major part of the debtor's assets is located outside the Member State of the debtor's habitual residence, or where it can be established that the principal reason for moving was to file for insolvency proceedings in the new jurisdiction, and where such filing would materially impair the interests of creditors whose dealings with the debtor took place prior to the relocation.[32] Evidence about the location needs to be put forward, as strengthened under Article 4 which requires the court of its own motion to examine whether it has jurisdiction and to specify the grounds on which jurisdiction is based. In any event, the requirements of 'habitual residency' remain unclear, especially where an individual moves to another Member States and the continuity or stability of such a move needs to be determined.

Once more, however, the emphasis given to COMI relocation seems to lie far away from the reality of the millions of European over-indebted vulnerable consumers.

Like its predecessor, moreover, the Recast Regulation does not attempt to harmonise substantive provisions and it does not aim at tackling divergences and inconsistencies between individual proceedings under national law.

Mutual recognition and private international law in the EU have been recognised as being legal tools usually employed when it is difficult for Member States to reach agreement on substantive laws. In this sense, they have been portrayed as a fallback or ancillary position where harmonisation cannot be achieved.[33] As far as personal insolvency legislation is concerned and for what has been discussed so far, it would be difficult to negate such a stance.

However, given the absence of substantive harmonisation, some Member States remain exposed to internal weak systems. Likewise, coordination among legal systems may not always be straightforward.

8.2 CONSUMER PROTECTION AND THE ROLE OF THE EUROPEAN COURTS

The significance of personal insolvency proceedings to promote legitimate social and economic objectives finds a pre-economic crisis recognition in the jurisprudence of

---

[31] Art. 3 Regulation 2015/848.
[32] Ibid. Recital 30.
[33] Mills (2009). See also Council of the European Union, *The Hague Programme: Strengthening Freedom, Security and Justice in the European Union*, available at http://ec.europa.eu/justice_home/doc_centre/doc/hague_programme_en.pdf, 31.

the ECHR in *Bäck* v. *Finland*,³⁴ which takes a human rights perspective vis-à-vis the right of property of the creditor. Although the court stated that there must be limits to safeguard property rights if there is an excessive burden on the creditor, it established that restrictions to property rights are justified by a general public interest served by the national insolvency law. This approach sets an international precedent in affirming a balance between the creditor rights and debt discharge, taking away the individualistic approach of the underlying relationship. Arguably, it is significant for expanding the debtor's position to a broader issue of social welfare and human dignity.

As noted in Chapters 4 and 5, the 2008 economic crisis has exasperated the latter aspect with over-indebtedness growing exponentially.

In its wake, the case law of the Court of Justice of the EU ('CJEU') has shown a surge in litigation grounded in the dated unfair contract terms legislation (UCTD)³⁵ applied to procedures relating to credit agreements of consumers in financial distress – colourfully but meaningfully depicted by Micklitz and Reich as 'Sleeping Beauty awaken by the kiss of the ECJ (CJEU)'.³⁶ Recent literature has further stressed how, until then, the UCTD had not been functionally integrated into the private law discourse and the judicial reasoning of the Member States coping with large increases in consumer over-indebtedness. Equally, national courts did not have suitable substantive and procedural national legal tools to treat the large number of consumers defaulting in their financial obligations.³⁷

An uninterrupted flow of cases claiming the unfairness of contract terms in financial agreements during the enforcement proceedings have reached the CJEU, whose decisions have assisted consumers to deal with their debts.³⁸

The so-called 'Spanish mortgage saga' (from the surge of case law arising from that Member State) takes stock of the situation and the way the UCTD has been used by the CJEU on national procedural law to protect over-indebted consumers through procedural remedies and the effectiveness of their rights. Significantly, Spain did not have legislation in place for debt solutions or the insolvency of individual debtors.

From its jurisprudence in *Océano Grupo*,³⁹ *Penzügyi*⁴⁰ and *Invitel*⁴¹ the CJEU has developed a doctrine of procedural effectiveness of unfair terms obliging national judges to undertake an investigation to assess the effective protection of consumers and effectiveness as a tool to put consumers in a position of exercising their rights. Moreover, since *Invitel* it was clarified that the effects of unfair terms can extend to

---

³⁴ Application no. 37598/97 of 20 July 2004.
³⁵ Directive 93/13/EEC of 5 April 1993 on Unfair Terms in Consumer Contracts, OJ 1993, L 95/29.
³⁶ Micklitz and Reich (2014).
³⁷ Jòzon (2017).
³⁸ Domurath (2017).
³⁹ *Océano Grupo Editorial SA v. Roció Murciano Quintero* (Case C-240/98) and *Salvat Editores SA v. José M. Sánchez Alcón Prades* (Case C-241/98), *José Luis Copano Badillo* (Case C-242/98), *Mohammed Berroane* (Case C-243/98) and *Emilio Viñas Feliú* (Case C-244/98) [2000], ECLI:EU:C:2000:346.
⁴⁰ VB *Pénzügyi Lízing Zrt.* v. *Ferenc Schneider* (Case C-137/08) [2010], ECLI:EU:C:2010:659.
⁴¹ *Nemzeti Fogyasztóvédelmi Hatóság* v. *Invitel Távközlési Zrt* (Case C-472/10) [2012], ECLI:EU:C:2012:242.

consumers not party to the legal proceedings before the court discussing the case, thus penetrating into the collective dimension of consumer protection.[42]

In *Aziz*,[43] concerning a contractual agreement between a financial institution and a consumer unable to repay his debts and under enforcement proceedings, Spanish procedural law was found to breach EU law for failing to provide for the assessment of a court with regard to the unfairness of standard terms in a mortgage contract to offer interim relief. Particular reference was made to the impossibility of suspending mortgage execution proceedings, as a result of which the debtor could have been evicted from his property before a court could give a judgment on the fairness of the lender's standard mortgage terms. As a result, to comply with the CJEU judgment national law was amended to repair the legal flaws concerning the enforcement of mortgage contracts.[44]

Later, in *Sánchez Morcillo*[45] it was held that the amended Spanish procedural law still fell short of the standards required under the UCTD for leaving to the discretion of the national court the assessment of the unfairness of the relevant terms. Moreover, the law did not grant consumers the same procedural defences accorded to lenders by allowing them, but not debtors, to appeal the staying of proceedings and thus giving an unjustified advantage to the former vis-à-vis the latter.

Unicaja Banco and *Caixabank*[46] further confirmed the trend of Member States having to ensure that over-indebted consumers are protected and not bound by unfair clauses in credit agreements. The question referred by the Spanish courts asked whether it should declare void and not binding on the consumer unfair clauses regarding default interest rates higher than those set by law, or whether they should rather adjust the clause to the statutory limits. In fact, Article 6 UCTD provides that unfair terms should not be binding on the consumer who remains nevertheless bound upon the other terms of the contract if this is capable of remaining in existence without the excluded unfair term. At the same time, EU law does not authorise national courts to revise the content of the unfair term. This was affirmed in precedent case law[47] where the CJEU held that the contract containing the term 'must continue in existence, in principle, without any amendment other than that resulting from the deletion of the unfair terms, in so far as, in

---

[42] Domurath (2017).
[43] *Mohamed Aziz v. Caixa d'Estalvis de Catalunya, Tarragona i Manresa (Catalunyacaixa)* (Case C-415/11) [2013], ECLI:EU:C:2013:164.
[44] Lei 1/2013 amending Art. 695 of the Spanish Code of Civil Procedure.
[45] *Juan Carlos Sánchez Morcillo and María del Carmen Abril García v. Banco Bilbao Vizcaya Argentaria SA* (Case C-169/14) [2014], ECLI:EU:C:2014:2099.
[46] *Unicaja Banco, SA v. José Hidalgo Rueda and others and Caixabank SA v. Manuel María Rueda Ledesma and others* (Joined Cases C-482/13, C-484/13, C-485/13 and C-487/13) [2015], ECLI:EU:C:2015:21.
[47] See *Banco Español de Crédito SA v. Joaquín Calderón Camino* (Case C-618/10) [2012], ECLI:EU:C:2012:349 and *Dirk Frederik Asbeek Brusse and Katarina de Man Garabito v. Jahani BV* (Case C-488/11) [2013], ECLI:EU:C:2013:341.

accordance with the rules of domestic law, such continuity of the contract is legally possible'.[48]

However, in *Kasler*,[49] the contract was found to not remain in existence without the unfair clause and, given the negative consequences this would have had on the consumer, the CJEU held that the national court was allowed to replace the unfair term by a supplementary provision of national law. Against this legal background, the referred issue raised difficult questions because the further existence of the mortgage contract might be endangered in case lenders no longer receive interest payments, which may be considered to be an essential part of the mortgage agreement.[50] Nevertheless, the CJEU held that national law is compatible with EU law insofar as it does not interfere with the national courts' duty to hold unfair terms to be not binding on the consumer, without revising the terms' content,[51] effectively offering protection to the affected consumers.

Again, in *BBVA SA v. Lòpez et al.*,[52] the CJEU persisted in the reinforcement of the protection of the over-indebted consumer. With reference to cases in which enforcement proceedings were pending and no unfair terms control had been exerted under the procedural rules in place before the *Aziz* case, the new Spanish law granted consumers a one-month period from its publication to bring an action based on the unfairness of a contractual term. The CJEU found that the transitional provision did not guarantee the effective exercise of the new right.

In *Finanmadrid EFC SA*[53] the opinion of the Advocate General headed in the same direction of protection for the over-indebted consumer. In this case the questions referred for a preliminary ruling also gave the CJEU an opportunity to clarify the relationship between the general principles of effectiveness and equivalence under EU law and Article 47 of the EU Charter of Fundamental Rights of the EU, which safeguards the fundamental right to an effective remedy and a fair trial before a court of law for the violation of rights within the scope of EU law. However, the CJEU did not seize this opportunity but dealt with the case exclusively in the framework of the effectiveness of the UCTD and confirmed that national procedural

---

[48] *Unicaja Banco, SA v. José Hidalgo Rueda and others* and *Caixabank SA v. Manuel María Rueda Ledesma and others* (Joined Cases C-482/13, C-484/13, C-485/13 and C-487/13) [2015], ECLI:EU: C:2015:21, para. 28.

[49] *Árpád Kásler, Hajnalka Káslerné Rábai v. OTP Jelzálogbank Zrt* (Case C-26/13) [2014], ECLI:EU: C:2014:282.

[50] *Unicaja Banco, SA v. José Hidalgo Rueda and others* and *Caixabank SA v. Manuel María Rueda Ledesma and others* (Joined Cases C-482/13, C-484/13, C-485/13 and C-487/13), Conclusions of Advocate General Whal (16 October 2014), ECLI:EU:C:2014:2299.

[51] *Unicaja Banco, SA v. José Hidalgo Rueda and others* and *Caixabank SA v. Manuel María Rueda Ledesma and others* (Joined Cases C-482/13, C-484/13, C-485/13 and C-487/13) [2015], ECLI:EU: C:2015:21.

[52] *BBVA SA v. Pedro Peñalva López and others* (Case C-8/14) [2015], ECLI:EU:C:2015:731.

[53] *Finanmadrid EFC SA v. Jesús Vicente Albán Zambrano and others* (Case C-49/14) [2016], ECLI:EU: C:2016:98. The Advocate General finds it against EU law national legislation not providing for the judge of the execution the possibility to declare *ex officio* abusive clauses void and not binding for the consumer. See Opinion of Advocate General Szpunar (11 November 2015), ECLI:EU:C:2015:74.

arrangements are liable to undermine the effectiveness of the protection that it accords. Effective protection under the UCTD can only be guaranteed if the national procedural system allows the court, either during the order for payment proceedings or before granting leave for execution, to check of its own motion whether the terms of the contract at issue are unfair.[54]

The CJEU has further specified that national law is incompatible with the UCTD where it prevents national courts to proceed with the examination of an individual consumer claim regarding unfair contract terms in those cases where a collective action against such contract terms has been filed by a consumer organisation and is pending, and where the individual consumer may not dissociate himself from this collective action.[55]

Expanding on its previous string of case law, and overruling national case law that limited the temporal effects of the declaration of nullity of an unfair term, the CJEU has further strengthened the judicial protection of consumers in financial difficulty against unfair contract terms. The judgment overturned the Spanish Tribunal Supremo's decision over the unfairness of floor clauses in mortgage agreements to limit the temporal effects of such a judgment after the date of its publication. As a result, the CJEU ruling had an important impact on the banking sector placing them under the obligation to repay very large sums to affected consumers.[56]

In *Banco Primus*[57] the CJEU has specified that consumer protection is not absolute but finds its limits on the principle of *res judicata*. Therefore, national courts shall not set aside domestic procedural rules that confer finality on a court decision, even if the finality of the decision does not allow remedying an infringement of the UCTD. However, if the national final decision was limited to issues examining of its own motion a limited number of terms instead of the contract taken as a whole, the *res judicata* does not cover allegations of unfairness of other terms of the contract. Furthermore, it ruled that whether a term is unfair cannot be contingent on whether that term was actually applied or not in the specific case.

At the same time, it should be stressed that in its latest addition relating to the Spanish mortgage enforcement procedure the CJEU has set the limits of procedural fairness driven by its own case law, excluding proceeding of extrajudicial nature. This is particularly the case where the proceedings are independent of the legal relationship between the creditor and the consumer, and the consumer has not availed herself/himself of the legal remedies provided.[58]

---

[54] Ibid.
[55] *Jorge Sales Sinués and Youssouf Drame Ba v. Caixabank SA and Catalunya Caixa SA (Catalunya Banc SA)* (Joined Cases C-381/14 and C-385/14) [2016], ECLI:EU:C:2016:909.
[56] *Francisco Gutiérrez Naranjo v. Cajasur Banco SAU, Ana María Palacios Martínez v. Banco Bilbao Vizcaya Argentaria SA (BBVA), Banco Popular Español SA v. Emilio Irles López and Teresa Torres Andreu* (Joined Cases C-154/15, C-307/15, and C-308/15) [2016], ECLI:EU:C:2016:980.
[57] *Banco Primus SA v. Jesús Gutiérrez García* (Case C-421/14) [2017], ECLI:EU:C:2017:60.
[58] *Banco Santander SA v. Cristobalina Sánchez López* (Case C-598/15) [2017], ECLI:EU:C:2017:945.

The 'Spanish saga' does not seem to be settled yet, with other preliminary references having already been filed to challenge other aspects of the Spanish procedural law on the same grounds of unfairness,[59] as well as a new stream testing its compatibility with the principle of effective judicial protection affirmed in Article 47 of the Charter of Fundamental Rights of the European Union.[60]

In *Radlinger* v. *Finway*[61] (for once not a Spanish referral) the CJEU recently considered a case of consumer credit secured by a mortgage where the contract established a higher interest rate than anticipated, several penalties for delay or default and an acceleration clause.[62] When the debtors could no longer repay, they filed for personal insolvency under national law. Upon its declaration, the insolvent debtors sought to challenge certain terms in the contract as contrary to public morality, an assessment which was not allowed under the national procedural rules. The CJEU, extending its precedents above on procedures and unfair terms, established that personal insolvency laws barring such an assessment do not comply with the UCTD.

In the absence of legal measures for debt solutions, commentators have put forward that the jurisprudence of the CJEU on unfair terms in consumer financial agreements provides for private law becoming instrumental to the public interest, where the proceduralisation of fairness substitutes for the absence of substantive justice in the Member States. Accordingly, in so doing, 'the CJEU encourages Member States to assume a more active role in defining substantive justice by enacting rules or developing judicial solutions according to the needs of their consumers'.[63]

Despite claims on the fragility of procedural justice,[64] the above case law may suggest what has been defined by scholars as a new constitutional role of the CJEU,[65] where the judiciary takes over from politics and substitutes the legislator in policy and lawmaking: where a Member State and the EU failed to put in place measures to provide for the insolvency of over-indebted consumers, the CJEU has been described as engaging in a form of social engineering which compensates for the deficiencies of the pre-established institutions by law.[66]

---

[59] Request for a preliminary ruling from the Audiencia Provincial de Cantabria (Spain) lodged on 7 August 2015 – *Liberbank SA* v. *Rafael Piris del Campo* (Case C-431/15) [2017], ECLI:EU:C:2017:90.
[60] Request for a preliminary ruling from the Audiencia Provincial de Illes Balears (Spain) lodged on 16 July 2015 – *Francisca Garzón Ramos and José Javier Ramos Martín* v. *Banco de Caja España de Inversiones, Salamanca y Soria, SA, Intercotrans, SL* (Case C-380/15) [2016], ECLI:EU:C:2016:112.
[61] *Ernst Georg Radlinger and Helena Radlingerová* v. *Finway a.s.* (Case C-377/14) [2016], ECLI:EU:C:2016:283.
[62] Acceleration clauses are terms in loan agreements that require the borrower to pay off the loan immediately if certain conditions are met, e.g. if the borrower misses a number of payments or other breaches of the contract occur.
[63] Jòzon (2017), esp. p. 165.
[64] Ibid.
[65] See Gerstenberg (2015); Micklitz (2013b).
[66] Kelemen (2012); Micklitz (2015).

Yet, a harmonised judicial framework under EU law for over-indebted consumers remains elusive.

8.3 TESTING THE SENTIMENT OF EXPERT STAKEHOLDERS

Arguably, to the extent that the EU has to take the treatment of consumer over-indebtedness seriously, at least as an integral element of the internal credit market, it will have to consider resetting as a priority its current policy and legal agenda. A rethinking of the status quo is called for, with reconceptualised and integrated responsible lending and personal insolvency harmonised regimes, where irresponsible lending and borrowing behaviours are punished, but where objective difficulties, good faith and innocent delinquency find protection.

For all that has been reported by the academic literature on the matter, the harmonisation process of debt solutions is not a straightforward route, starting with the initial major challenge of developing common standards on how to assess and screen household debts and over-indebtedness.

However, prevention and cure of the problem should go hand in hand, especially since the former appears a long way from tackling the causes of the phenomenon routed in passive over-indebtedness. Moreover, to the extent that borrowing is not the only financial commitment but over-indebtedness is of such a complex nature that includes causes that are broader than the private law relationship with financial institutions, then curing the problem with legal solutions should become an unavoidable part of EU law no different from responsible lending and borrowing.

The treatment of over-indebtedness may not target its causes directly, but if legal solutions are appropriately designed they can provide a useful tool to fix problems brought in by that neo-liberal model embedded in the creation of the EU single market,[67] at the same time contributing to bridge a social element with the market element in the European model of the social market economy promoted by the Treaties.[68]

A survey carried out by one of the authors under a thematic EU-funded research project[69] indicates that expert stakeholders favour the introduction of a harmonised legal framework for personal insolvency proceedings.

The Survey asked the basic question whether, based on subject experts' knowledge and experience, they would envisage a framework where the European Union take action to harmonise personal insolvency laws across the Member States.

---

[67] Crouch (2011).
[68] Art. 3 TFEU.
[69] 'Consumer Over-Indebtedness, Responsible Lending, and the Insolvency of Natural Persons: the Need for a Comprehensive Reform to Protect Consumers in Financial Difficulty', Research project funded by the EU under the Civil Justice Programme of the EU, Grant Agreement JUST/2013/JCIC/AG/4620. The research project was related to the EU priority that aims to promote the creation of a genuine European area of justice in the area of personal insolvency.

A sample of ninety-two experts from the financial services industry, civil society organisations, insolvency practitioners, lawyers, academics and other experts (e.g. regulators and agencies set up by policymakers) responded to the survey in the numbers and proportion shown in Figure 8.1.

The majority of the respondents expressed the view that EU harmonisation of personal insolvency legislation is 'very desirable' or 'desirable' with an aggregate result of 71 per cent. Only an aggregate of 12 per cent thought that EU action in the field is either 'undesirable' or 'very undesirable'; 17 per cent of respondents had a neutral position (Figure 8.2).

In percentage terms and proportionate to the respondents, the distribution by types of stakeholders or professions among those who favour or disfavour EU harmonisation shows a mixed picture (Figures 8.3, 8.4 and 8.5). Of the 71 per cent who favour harmonisation, civil society organisations appear keener towards the industry, which are next to the majority after academics among the total of 12 per cent of those who find harmonisation undesirable.

A sector-by-sector breakdown reveals that academics are more divided in their views (Figure 8.10). The industry has no middle or neutral position and almost one in three oppose an EU legislative intervention to harmonise the area (Figure 8.6). Civil society organisations, by contrast, despite a 17 per cent neutral position, largely

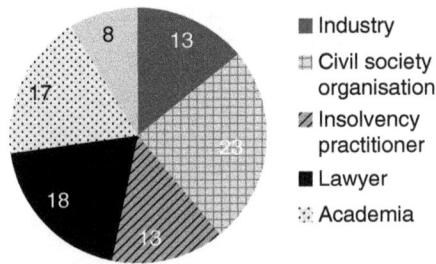

FIGURE 8.1 What sector do you work in?

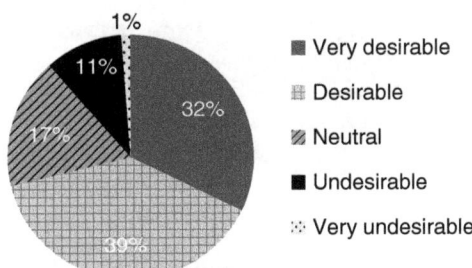

FIGURE 8.2 Based on your knowledge and experience, would you like that the European Union take action to harmonise personal insolvency laws across the Member States?

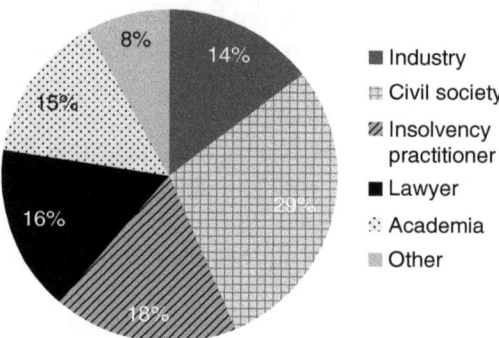

FIGURE 8.3 Very desirable and desirable

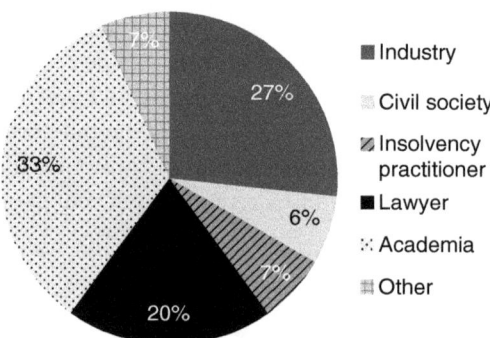

FIGURE 8.4 Undesirable and very undesirable

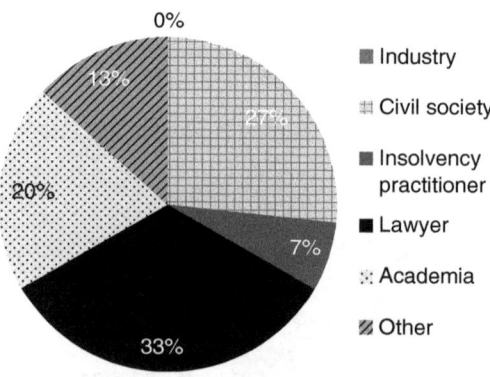

FIGURE 8.5 Neutral

find harmonisation at least desirable (almost four out of five – see Figure 8.7). Insolvency practitioners are those most in favour of harmonisation (Figure 8.8), while lawyers – though mostly in favour – take a more neutral position (Figure 8.9).

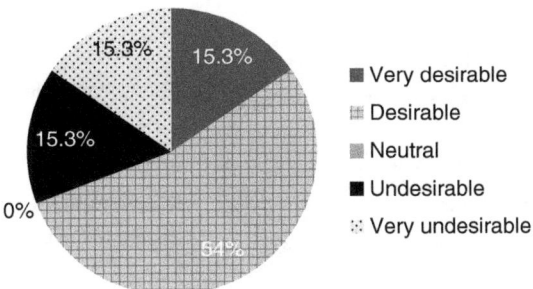

FIGURE 8.6 Industry

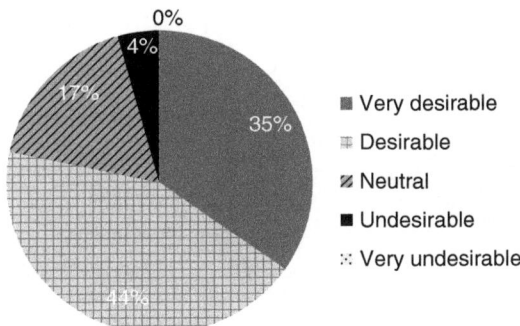

FIGURE 8.7 Civil society organisations

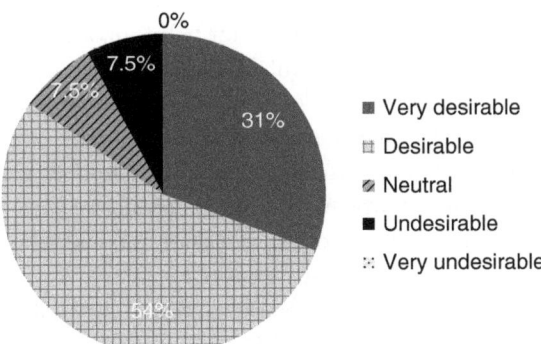

FIGURE 8.8 Insolvency practitioners

Experts were asked to justify or provide reasons for their answers. An analysis of the survey allows a grouping of the answers into five main justifications.

The main arguments in favour of EU harmonisation are as listed below (in order of number of answers starting from the most common justification):

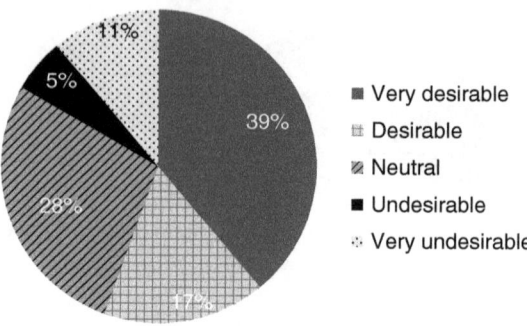

FIGURE 8.9 Lawyers

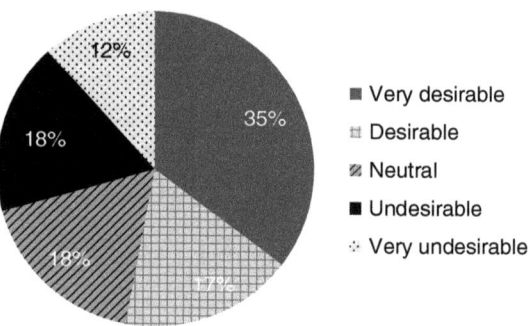

FIGURE 8.10 Academia

1. Internal market grounds: there is a need for harmonisation to give effect to free movement of capital, free movement of financial services, free movement of people, the existence of cross-border creditors and debtors with assets in more Member States. Also, EU harmonisation would be necessary to overcome the problem of disclosure of individual assets in other Member States.
2. Avoidance of bankruptcy tourism or forum shopping.
3. National law not consumer-friendly and/or poor national enforcement.
4. Reduction of transactional costs for creditors.
5. Recognition and promotion of acceptable or shared internationally agreed standards (e.g. standards set by the World Bank and the International Monetary Fund).

By contrast, the main reasons given against EU harmonisation (starting from the most common reason given) can be grouped as follows:

1. Different national traditions/cultures/values/social norms (as a result, some countries are more punitive, others more debtor-friendly, and EU action would soften or harden existing approaches).

2. There is no real EU dimension (subsidiarity) – as a matter of fact, credit markets have remained national and there is no compelling argument for harmonisation.
3. Harmonisation of personal insolvency legislation would require the alignment of other underlining legislation and judicial systems first (e.g. laws of forced execution, immovable property law, movable property law, credit practices), which looks an unrealistic prospect.
4. There is no technical capacity to achieve a workable full or semi-full harmonisation in this area.
5. Traditional insolvency legislation, procedures or methods are not helpful anyway – so why harmonise them?

8.4 OVER-INDEBTEDNESS IN CONTEXT: THE CAPITAL MARKETS UNION AND RETAIL FINANCIAL SERVICES IN THE EU

Although it can be maintained that the EU is moving towards some common basic principles, the significant differences among the substantive insolvency laws of the Member States are likely to create obstacles, difficulties and/or competitive advantages/disadvantages especially for firms with cross-border activities.[70] This angle does not take the view of consumer protection or social welfare, but rather the perspective of integration or strengthening of the internal market. It is more oriented towards a market perspective from the viewpoint of creditors. To a more limited extent, it may also become a market perspective for natural persons functional to the enjoyment of the EU free movement provisions.[71]

It is in this context that the establishment of the Capital Markets Union (CMU)[72] has become a new political priority of the EU. It is an initiative part of, and to give effect to, the free movement of capital which is one of the (often neglected) fundamental freedoms of the EU. Its main aim is the funding of the EU economy through the creation of a single market for capital by removing barriers to cross-border financing and investments.

The achievement of the CMU touches upon many areas of law and it will lead to a potential inundation of harmonisation proposals that could haunt the EU legislator for years. Insolvency law generally, and personal insolvency proceedings in particular, are among them.[73]

---

[70] INSOL Europe (2010).
[71] See the CJEU case *Ulf Kazimierz Radziejewski* v. *Kronofogdemyndigheten i Stockholm* (Case C-461/11) [2012], EU:C:2012:704.
[72] Communication from the Commission to the European Parliament, the Council, the European Economic and Social Committee and the Committee of the Regions, *Action Plan on Building a Capital Markets Union*, COM/2015/0468 final.
[73] European Commission, *Green Paper – Building a Capital Market Union*, COM(2015) 63 final; *European Commission Green Paper on Financial Services and Insurance. Better products, more choice, and greater opportunities for consumers and businesses*, COM(2015) 630 final.

The targets of the CMU are mostly small and medium enterprises (SMEs) but consumers are included. The rhetoric of the European Commission is that a CMU should move towards a situation where SMEs can raise financing as easily as large companies, and lenders are able to provide capital to SMEs and consumers cross-border: seeking or providing funding in another Member State should not be impeded by legal or supervisory barriers. According to this view, effective levels of consumer and investor protection become priorities to ensure trust in capital markets across borders.[74]

In short, the CMU would require the removal of barriers for capital providers to supply credit cross-border, as well as for consumers who should become confident in accessing capital cross-border. Under the current regime, to the extent that consumers may receive the protection afforded by EU law or the law of their home country (depending on the stage and situation of the financing relationship), lenders by contrast are likely to face risks and costs where EU law does not provide a cohesive framework. The diversity – and in some cases the inadequacy – of national insolvency laws would make it difficult for foreign investors to assess the risks and consequences of dealing with twenty-eight different legal systems, a circumstance that would lead to deterring low recovery rates or costly procedures for creditors. Cross-border capital provision and investments by companies would become unattractive and unfeasible, or at least exorbitant.

If the above is to be the case, only the elimination of uncertainties to the supply side through the reduction of divergences would contribute to the emergence of a CMU, in turn benefiting consumers on the demand side. Thus, to the extent that the supply side finds an environment favourable or at least cohesive for debt solutions, it may be encouraged to open up capital access for foreign consumers and SMEs.

From this angle, mutual recognition of insolvency proceedings may be a potential barrier incompatible with an effective CMU as the expression of the fundamental EU principle of free movement of capital. To achieve the institutional goals of the EU, broad-contour principles or the common cores of national laws are likely to lead towards the lowest point of possible convergence among the Member States. Instead, the CMU is likely to reject the use of principles to fill gaps in EU law, and it may require an obligation to achieve legal harmonisation through rules.

Under these circumstances, the real challenge for an effective consumer protection would become the design of the law. Some principles are already there from the common cores, soft law and CJEU jurisprudence outlined earlier. Other guarantees would derive from the Charter of Fundamental Rights which sets out the basic rights that must be respected both by the European Union and the Member States when implementing EU law.

---

[74] Ibid.

8.5 A POLICY AND LEGAL ANALYSIS

8.5.1 *A Critique of the Current Framework*

A criticism that may be made of the EU legal framework set by the Consumer Credit Directive (CCD) and the Mortgage Credit Directive (MCD) is that responsible lending – as translated into EU law – is inadequate to address over-indebtedness for the undetermined nature of its corresponding provisions and the inherent difficulty of their enforcement.

The provisions on financial education, product suitability, conduct of business, remuneration structures, and arrears and foreclosure (alongside their guidelines) take the form of open-texture principles but it is difficult to imagine their enforcement and ensuing sanctions once transposed into national laws. This work is concerned with over-indebtedness, and not with the effective harmonisation of such provisions or the removal of obstacles for the establishment of a single market, but at some point questions will have to be raised as to the market effects of having different implementing measures and practices in the Member States or the use of soft law to give effect to such principled norms.

In any event, however, enforcement will remain a key aspect of an already weak and insufficient focus on responsible lending to combat over-indebtedness.

Arguably, its weakness mainly lies in the perseverance of the creditworthiness assessment as a sort of panacea for the prevention and detection of the problem. Experience shows that in the EU it was a method already in use, and the toxic practices of sub-prime mortgage lending were a US phenomenon almost unknown in the Member States.[75] If anything, excluded consumers from mainstream lending have resorted to other more dangerous forms of legal or illegal credit, and there should be more focus on the practices of creditworthiness assessment in place to properly address the policy goals set by the law.

If financial institutions are to lend responsibly beyond their commercial interest, this is to address the risk of consumers becoming over-indebted. But it has been demonstrated that credit provision is not a main cause of over-indebtedness. This is not to suggest a complete uselessness of creditworthiness assessment. On the contrary, when suitably designed, it may help to detect existing or early signs of debt problems or unaffordability which is something that mainstream lenders have always cared about. But the reality is that over-indebtedness continues to increase. Therefore, after more than a decade of database use by the credit industry as the principal method coupled with other practices, the reasons why the creditworthiness assessment has failed remain largely mysterious unless it is recognised that creditworthiness alone is inadequate.

Proper and responsible lending should include measures of interest-rate caps or limitation of penalties for consumers, as well as measures to guarantee access to

---

[75] Engel and McCoy (2011).

basic or affordable credit.[76] These issues raise further complex political and legal problems in the Member States and exceed the purpose of this analysis. The point is that giving a proper meaning to 'responsible lending' would have an outreach much broader than what EU law provides.

This is why the renovated primary focus on creditworthiness assessment of the MCD induces us to make the same considerations that Stephen Weatherill has advanced in the context of the CCD, that is that behind its thin provisions lies the real debate about the proper reach of EU intervention in this domain, and the continuing opposing thrust of EU policies in opening up credit markets.[77] If the CCD does nothing to tackle over-indebtedness, the MCD does probably too little.

For sure, unfair and predatory practices need to be tackled. Yet again, it is doubtful that information disclosure, transparency and creditworthiness assessment are the solutions. Instead, as seen earlier, in the wake of the financial crisis the case law of the CJEU has demonstrated a surge in litigation grounded in the dated – and until then dormant – unfair contract terms EU legislation[78] applied to credit agreements.

No policy designed to prevent over-indebtedness can on its own address the problem. Preventive measures alone, however designed but without ex-post debt solutions, cannot be conclusive.[79] In analogical terms, it would be like having in place measures to prevent someone from getting injured, but without having the medicine if this occurs – with the aggravation of allowing others to injure the patient even further, possibly finishing him/her off (in the analogy, the various interests/penalties and unregulated debt collection procedures).

A problem is that over-indebtedness seems to have been taken in a static dimension. At EU level, all the legal constructions and measurements make reference to the time when consumers apply for credit. This is clear from the policies and laws which insist on the usual paradigm of information requirements, transparency and the assessment of creditworthiness at the time of the making of the loan. Such measures may capture limited circumstances of existing or likely debt problems if further credit is taken, but they fail to address the real and most frequent causes of consumer over-indebtedness, such as lifetime events, poor market conditions and all the other elements identified by the latest studies on the problem – all having in common that the repayment difficulties emerge at a later stage that responsible lending measures cannot possibly foresee.

By nature, EU responsible lending policies do not offer debt solutions. Therefore, it appears self-evident that the current policy and legal responses are inconsistent and intrinsically unsuitable to deal with a complex multidimensional problem such as consumer over-indebtedness. Arguably, a more dynamic approach tackling the

[76] Consumers International (November 2013); FinCoNet (2014).
[77] On the original consideration on the CCD, see Weatherill (2013), esp. pp. 102–3.
[78] Directive 93/13/EEC of 5 April 1993 on Unfair Terms in Consumer Contracts, OJ 1993, L 95/29.
[79] Vandone (2009).

effects of the real causes and the various stages of financial difficulty is needed. As anticipated earlier, while the former solutions may prove extremely complex and are subject to radical political choices by the Member States, the latter solutions are not new to academic studies and reports. For example, a study managed by the Financial Services User Group (FSUG)[80] on the means to protect European consumers in financial difficulty has presented a variety of suitable debt solutions aiming at allowing them a fresh start by reorganising, reducing or cancelling the debt value.[81]

8.5.2 Responsible Lending

Consumer over-indebtedness is a growing phenomenon in the EU and all Member States seem to show full awareness of the problem, displaying novel legal initiatives to tackle it.

A number of these measures are clearly the result of the impact of EU policies and law, especially as regards the preventive side of financial difficulty in the form of 'responsible credit'. This is not surprising given the relative maturity of EU law in the area of consumer credit. Indeed, according to the European Commission's evaluation, no systematic deficiencies in the transposition of the CCD by Member States have been identified so far.[82] As the CCD is based on full maximum harmonisation, the Member States have been precluded from adopting or retaining different national law provisions within the harmonised areas, other than to the extent permitted by the CCD itself.

Yet, differences still exist and some additional convergence in specific areas may be desirable.

It is true that the Member States have implemented the CCD in similar terms but the extent of official guidelines given is very different.

For example, the UK seems to provide an example of good practice in issuing very detailed guidance to lenders on the meaning of responsible lending and its application, providing a more effective legal environment for consumer protection backed by clear public and private law enforcement. Moreover, it has gone as far as anticipating detailed measures in relation to mortgages despite the fact that the term for implementing the MCD was some way off.[83] In this respect, the UK seems

---

[80] The FSUG is an expert group appointed to advise the Commission in the preparation of legislation or policy initiatives which affect the users of financial services; provide insight, opinion and advice concerning the practical implementation of such policies; proactively seek to identify key financial services issues which affect users of financial services; liaise with and provide information to financial services user representatives and representative bodies at the European Union and national level. See http://ec.europa.eu/internal_market/finservices-retail/fsug/index_en.htm

[81] London Economics (2012).

[82] See European Commission, *Report from the Commission to the European Parliament and the Council on the implementation of Directive 2008/48/EC on credit agreements for consumers*, COM(2014) 259 final (May 2014).

[83] Rowlingson et al. (2016).

to show an approach of particular care and attention towards consumers in line with its traditional 'market economy' model, where consumers are economic agents in an economically imbalanced relationship with suppliers and they need protection or support to sustain, promote, curtail and adjust the structure of a free and competitive market.[84]

By contrast, the failure of issuing guidelines and absence of clarity about the meaning and methods of creditworthiness assessment, the existence of a public vis-à-vis private law dispute and enforcement uncertainty, and generally the lack of clearly defined or light consequences for creditors appear the most marked differences in the implementation of responsible credit provisions in other jurisdictions which remain mostly anchored to a legal tradition grounded in the Roman principle of *caveat emptor* – let the buyer beware.

For example, Germany seems to exhibit a minimal implementation of EU law and low enthusiasm about responsible lending, which appears against the tradition of German case law[85] and represents an opposing thrust to the ideology of the self-responsible consumer. This may also explain the apparent lack of consequences for the creditworthiness assessment whose violation does not lead to prohibition of lending or discharge of the debtor's obligations.[86]

Likewise, to some extent Italy displays a similar attitude of minimal implementation. No guidelines are offered for responsible credit and the assessment of the creditworthiness of consumers. Moreover, the implementation of responsible lending obligations seems to find its home in the pre-contractual responsibility of the creditor whose breach results in the ensuing soft award of damages.[87]

Like Germany and Italy, Greece seems to offer no guidelines for responsible lending and the creditworthiness assessment. Unlike the other two countries, however, it has introduced punitive consequences for the breach of the creditworthiness obligation allowing for the discharge of the total cost of credit and the interests – arguably a measure introduced in the aftermath of the severe economic and social crisis to alleviate the burden on severely over-indebted consumers, as well as a political one driven by the scope and intensity of the crisis.[88]

The different approach in the issuing of guidelines incorporated into national law does not appear a secondary element for a concept of 'responsible credit' that has already been criticised for not being clear and for having failed to be truly absorbed into EU law.[89] Moreover, not only have they the effect of granting a different type of

---

[84] e.g. see Howells and Weatherill (2005), esp. pp. 1–98.
[85] BGH, NJW 1989, 1665.
[86] Sutschet (2016).
[87] Cerini (2016).
[88] Livada (2016).
[89] e.g. Peter Rott (2014) shows the frustration of the emphasis given to such a policy in the earlier drafts of the CCD that was not retained in the final version. The author shows how the Commission originally aimed at avoiding the consumer's over-indebtedness by evading unreasonable credit contracts, introducing duties of lenders to assess and advise consumers on the risks of default and holding

protection to consumers in the various Member States, but they may have major consequences in the way the common market operates in the granting of credit and the behaviour of lenders, where a level playing field does not find its way and regulatory barriers remain in place.

Enforcement may also represent a ground of concern. As an illustration, the UK appears at the forefront where a system of both public and private enforcement exists and which provides for strong measures, indicating that the problem is taken seriously. By contrast, the debate in the other countries over the legal nature of the lenders' obligation to carry out the creditworthiness assessment and acting 'responsibly' carries an element of uncertainty over an effective or efficient enforceability, which once again risks fragmenting the common market.[90]

As noted above, the CJEU may play a role in this area. In *LCL (Le Crédit Lyonnais)*[91] the CJEU has pointed out *incidenter tantum* that 'the creditor's obligation, prior to conclusion of the agreement, to assess the borrower's creditworthiness is intended to protect consumers against the risks of over-indebtedness and bankruptcy'.[92] This passage may be relied on to conclude that the assessment is not exclusively a public law duty but it is also one owed to the borrower, thereby entitling him to private law remedies in case of breach of this obligation.[93] Opposing views, however, may still insist that the creditworthiness assessment remains solely a public law duty, and that the only effect the CJEU decision in *LCL (Le Crédit Lyonnaise)* should have is to reconsider the sanction system under the national laws.[94] At the same time, in *CA Consumer Finance*,[95] the CJEU further ruled that the burden of proof for complying with the obligations of the lender to inform borrowers and undertake the creditworthiness assessment lies with the lender and it cannot be shifted to the consumer through standard terms, otherwise it would deprive consumers of the effectiveness of their rights. Once more, this case appears to suggest a private law obligation owed to the consumer.

Further clarification by the CJEU may be necessary in this area if proper harmonisation has to be achieved. In this respect, to the extent that the EU accepts and pursues the liberalisation of financial markets and an expansion of consumption, the approach taken by the UK seems to lean more towards a consistent harmonised framework.

---

them responsible during all phases of the contractual relationship. Instead, the final version of the CCD remains anchored to the usual paradigm of transparency and information requirements by both lenders and borrowers, adding a focus on an undetermined requirement of creditworthiness assessment.

[90] Ferretti et al. (2016).
[91] *LCL (Le Crédit Lyonnais) SA v. Fesih Kalhan* (Case C-565/12) [2014], ECLI:EU:C:2014:190.
[92] Ibid.
[93] See Ferretti et al. (2016) and Sutschet (2016) and the literature cited there.
[94] Ibid.
[95] *CA Consumer Finance SA v. Ingrid Bakkaus, Charline Bonato, née Savary, Florian Bonato* (Case C-449/13) [2014], ECLI:EU:C:2014:2464.

8.5.3 Debt Solutions

Arguably, one of the most striking features of the EU internal market is that all Member States have moved towards new or renovated national regimes for the protection of consumers in financial distress and the treatment of the insolvency of natural persons.[96] However, the major shortcoming seems to be that these are individual but uncoordinated legal initiatives in the Member States which uncover a complete absence of common, harmonised or appropriately resourced strategies at EU level.

Without the harmonising intervention of the EU – as in the case of the legal transposition of the policies of responsible lending with all its limits – personal insolvency or debt-discharge systems have developed in different ways which still reflect economic, cultural or legal traditions. For example, the UK has an established system of personal bankruptcy laws that it has reformed to adapt to the needs of over-indebted consumers as an inevitable side effect of the free market,[97] whereas other countries such as Italy and Greece – where personal bankruptcy and debt discharge had not traditionally been available for non-business debtors – have introduced consumer debt-relief provisions as a new legal instrument to repair the effects of the liberalisation of markets or following the financial crisis.[98]

The literature has already illustrated how continental European personal insolvency systems differ from the Anglo-Saxon ones. For Germany, it has identified a 'liability model' emphasising the debtor's responsibility for debt repayments.[99] This is confirmed by the general approach taken and by recent measures that only formally aim to reduce the time to obtain a debt relief, but that in practice leave the system unaltered from the past.

Another typical classification within continental Western Europe is that of a 'mercy model' underpinned by social and political notions of 'deservingness', good faith or innocent over-indebtedness, which focuses on the debtor's needs or abilities to repay alongside the granting of broad discretionary powers to bankruptcy officials. Examples are usually the personal insolvency systems of the Scandinavian countries, Belgium and France.[100] While Italy seems to have endorsed this 'mercy model' based on the good faith of the consumer debtor and ample discretionary powers of the judiciary, Greece appears more hybrid, having developed its law from that of Germany and providing for a tighter liability of the debtor and his assets towards the creditors but showing an attitude of increased forgiveness.[101]

---

[96] e.g. see McCormak et al. (2017), ch. 8.
[97] Tribe (2016).
[98] Comparato (2016); Katsas (2016).
[99] Ramsay (1997); Kilborn (2009).
[100] Ibid.; see also Niemi (1999).
[101] Ferretti et al. (2016).

8.6 INCONSISTENCIES IN THE EU LEGAL FRAMEWORK

To the extent that the analysed case law of the CJEU on unfair contract terms contributes towards the provision of remedies for over-indebted consumers at EU level, this occurs via procedural rather than substantive means.

This case law could now be read in conjunction with the case of *Radziejewski*,[102] which is the CJEU's first and so far only jurisprudence on personal insolvency proceedings and the potential negative effects of national remedies on the internal market. The case establishes that national insolvency procedures for natural persons may be restrictive of the fundamental free movement rights of the EU. It dealt with the issue of residency as a requirement for access to the national insolvency procedure and its compatibility with Article 45 TFEU on the free movement of persons. The CJEU, recalling its jurisprudence in *Olympique Lyonnais*,[103] noted that national provisions which preclude or deter someone from leaving his/her country of origin in order to exercise his/her right to freedom of movement constitute restrictions on that freedom, even if they apply without regard to the nationality of the workers concerned. Therefore, the CJEU found that national law which makes the grant of debt relief subject to a condition of residence in that Member State is unlawful under EU law.

This element may have far-reaching consequences, as 'habitual residence' forms the basis of jurisdiction in national insolvency laws and it sits at the heart of the Recast Regulation, as above noted.[104]

To the extent that *Radziejewski* has the effect of changing infringing national law for being contrary to EU law, the impact on the Recast Regulation may be that of frustrating its *ratio* over COMI alongside the EU legislator's principal concern over forum shopping. In the absence of a definition of 'habitual residence', in its former jurisprudence on unrelated EU law the CJEU has affirmed that 'habitual' requires a certain permanence or regularity, making reference to the *ratio* of the Regulation under discussion.[105] Therefore, in the absence of an autonomous interpretation by the CJEU, this impasse is likely to create an inconsistency in the EU legal framework and uncertainty.

In addition, other shortcomings exist in the EU legal framework examined so far.

The CJEU jurisprudence over the procedural control of fairness – though significant in plastering problematic situations emerging from a legal vacuum in the treatment of over-indebtedness – has many limits, especially in the large majority of situations where there are no unfair standard terms to be contested in a condition of over-indebtedness. This is the frequent instance where under the UCTD the

---

[102] *Ulf Kazimierz Radziejewski v. Kronofogdemyndigheten i Stockholm* (Case C-461/11) [2012], EU:C:2012:704.
[103] *Olympique Lyonnais SASP v. Olivier Bernard and Newcastle UFC* (Case C-325/08) [2010], EU:C:2010:143.
[104] Art. 3 of Regulation 2015/848.
[105] *Barbara Mercredi v. Richard Chaffe* (Case C-497/10) [2010], EU:C:2010:829 on Council Regulation 2201/2003 concerning jurisdiction and the recognition of judgments in matrimonial matters and parental responsibilities.

assessment of fairness of a term cannot relate to the definition of the main subject matter of the contract or to the adequacy of the price or remuneration.[106] Such exclusion, for example, made the UCTD powerless to challenge mortgage agreements in foreign currencies that created so many problems in a number of countries, especially in the new Member States. Moreover, consumer protection through procedural means is not easily attainable as it rests on the capacity and resilience of over-indebted consumers to seek enforcement of rights.

Another major gap in the law appears to be the treatment of consumers with little or no assets (the NINAs and LILAs). Arguably, especially – but not exclusively – in the aftermath of an economic downturn, this is often the case with over-indebted consumers, who are in that situation precisely for not having any other means to pay off their debts. However, substantive laws of the Member States are very different. Many countries which focus on creditors' fair treatment and satisfaction exclude this kind of debtor from insolvency proceedings precisely for the impossibility to make a repayment plan. Likewise, the Recast Regulation is explicit in excluding them from its scope, even under legislation allowing for the writing-off of such debts.[107] This exclusion may infringe the free movement of vulnerable consumers who after the economic crisis have shown a tendency to move to other EU countries to escape the lack of jobs or austerity in their home Member State.

8.7 THE SURFACING OF EU PRINCIPLES?

Arguably, despite substantive differences in national laws and reliance on mutual recognition, some broad-contour principles have started to emerge at EU level. This process has been particularly boosted by the emergency caused by the great economic crisis of the recent past.

Soft law instruments of the EU have encouraged Member States to follow basic principles in designing national laws. Also, as the EU and other international organisations such as the IMF and the World Bank have contributed to the framing of national laws of the Member States in need of financial assistance,[108] it can be maintained that some form of alignment of the basic features of modern personal insolvency regimes has started to emerge.

8.7.1 Recommendation CM/Rec(2007)8

Recommendation CM/Rec(2007)8 focuses specifically on consumer over-indebtedness. It acknowledges the development of the consumer credit market and the increased debt problems caused by more lending as a driver of the market

---

[106] Art. 4 UCTD.
[107] Recital 16 of Regulation 2015/848.
[108] e.g. see the IMF involvement in Latvia, Romania, Spain, Greece, Hungary, Ireland and Portugal. The international dimension is comprehensively documented in Ramsay (2015), p. 189.

economy. In recognising the scale of the matter, it addresses the social and health problems of the over-indebted consumers, as well as their social exclusion. At the same time, however, it stresses the responsibility of the Member States for the effects of their economic and social policies.

The Recommendation is explicit in leaving the regulation of consumer debt solutions to the national law of the Member States. Nonetheless, it recommends them to take appropriate measures, among others, to alleviate the effects of the recovery of debt by an efficient and unbiased enforcement system. At the same time, it demands the respect of the debtor's rights and human dignity, and the introduction of enforcement alleviation procedures (e.g. measures that include the protection of the essential assets of the debtor and his basic living needs).[109]

These are principled recommendations that do not attempt to converge the substantive laws of the Member States. For the legal instrument used, they are not binding on the Member States.

In line with Regulation 1346/2000 in force at the time, it confirms the principle of mutual recognition by recommending the recognition and enforcement in Member States of payment judgments and repayment plans emanating from the competent authorities in other Member States.[110]

8.7.2 The 2014 Commission Recommendation

The latest Commission Recommendation[111] on business failure and insolvency generates from the proposal stage of the lengthy process of the reform of Regulation 1346/2000, ending with the later adoption of the Recast Regulation. In this sense, it can be considered an evolution of the latter.

It aims at tackling discrepancies between preventive procedures promoting the rescue of economically viable debtors. Its objective is to ensure that viable enterprises in financial difficulty have access to national legislation enabling them to early restructure, thus giving them a second chance. Officially, it does not apply to situations of consumer over-indebtedness and insolvency. Nevertheless, it invites Member States 'to explore the possibility of applying these recommendations also to consumers, since some of the principles following in this Recommendation may also be relevant for them'.[112]

The rationale behind the Recommendation lies in the inconsistencies between national restructuring frameworks and the national rules that give honest entrepreneurs a second chance. These discrepancies are likely to fragment conditions of

---

[109] Recommendation CM/Rec(2007)8 of the Committee of Ministers to member states on legal solutions to debt problems (Adopted by the Committee of Ministers on 20 June 2007), 3a–c.
[110] Recommendation CM/Rec(2007)8.
[111] Commission Recommendation of 12.3.2014 on a new approach to business failure and insolvency, C (2014) 1500 final.
[112] Ibid. Recital 15.

access to credit and result in different recovery rates for creditors depending on the jurisdiction. This generally leads to increasing costs and uncertainties that disincentivise investments in other Member States or cross-border activities. Therefore, encouraging Member States to put in place national systems for restructuring and put honest entrepreneurs back on the market aim at the creation of a level playing field and a smoother functioning of the internal market.[113] The recommended minimum standards point to the availability of a preventive restructuring framework as soon as it becomes apparent that there is a likelihood of insolvency. They request that a procedure is in place to suspend enforcement actions, facilitate out-of-court negotiations, adopt a restructuring plan later confirmed by a court binding on all creditors, and protect new financing necessary for the implementation of the restructuring plan.[114] The other recommended minimum standards at the second chance are given to entrepreneurs, allowing for the full discharge of the debts included in a bankruptcy procedure after a maximum of three years, with the warning of the inappropriateness of discharges after a longer period. The recommendation concludes with the desirability of having in place stringent provisions that discourage actions carried out dishonestly, in bad faith or non-compliant with the plan.[115]

The chosen soft law instruments do not bind the Member States. In particular, the provisions of the latest Recommendation are of a very general nature. When it comes to consumer over-indebtedness proceedings, they are limited to a Recital with 'an invitation to explore a possibility'. This is still far from suggesting at which stage of the default process EU action is needed and, in the event, what type of action should be taken. Nevertheless, they arguably represent a step further in the definition of common EU macro principles alongside those set by the jurisprudence of the CJEU on procedural respect of fairness and of the ECHR on the public interest served by insolvency law.[116]

What emerges from a general assessment is that modern systems seem to depart from punishing models marked by the enforcement of national moral codes of conduct alongside the obstinate protection of creditors' interests. Instead, they

---

[113] *Ibid.* Recitals 4, 8–11 and Art. I.
[114] *Ibid.* Art. III A–D.
[115] *Ibid.* Art. IV.
[116] According to the European Commission, the Recommendation has provided useful focus for some Member States which have undertaken reforms in the area of insolvency: Spain, Hungary, Croatia and Romania have improved their personal insolvency regime. However, Spain did not follow the Commission's recommendation on limiting the discharge periods for honest debtors. In Lithuania, discussions on the personal insolvency laws are underway, while in others Member States consideration is still being given to whether any specific action is necessary following the Recommendation, e.g. in Sweden a special committee was appointed to look at the need to adapt national legislation in the light of the Recommendation; and in the UK a public consultation has been carried out recently. See Directorate-General Justice & Consumers of the European Commission, *Evaluation of the Implementation of the Commission Recommendation of 12.3.2014 on a New Approach to Business Failure and Insolvency* (30 September 2015), http://ec.europa.eu/justice/civil/commercial/insolvency/index_en.htm

seem to be heading towards a more balanced or equitable allocation of the risk of default between creditors and debtors in a transparent and predictable manner. This is not only directed at innocent debtors returning as viable economic actors after a reasonably short period of three years. To ensure the 'fresh start', it also presupposes a principled automatic and temporary stay on enforcement actions with adequate safeguards of creditor interests, as well as the subsequent establishment of repayment terms that accurately reflect the debtor's capacity to repay.

The establishment of appropriate filing criteria allowing access to fair procedures to innocent debtors and the minimisation of system abuses complete the emergence of the picture, which relies on the principle of mutual recognition of foreign proceedings and cross-border cooperation.[117]

8.7.3 Proposal for a Directive on Preventive Restructuring Frameworks, Second Chance and Measures to Increase the Efficiency of Restructuring, Insolvency and Discharge Procedures

As extensively noted earlier in this chapter, insolvency rules adopted by EU Member States differ considerably. At the same time, the 2014 Recommendation did not have the effects that the European Commission wished for. The *Evaluation* of the 2014 Recommendation[118] reports that the latter 'was useful for Member States that had previously started reforms in this area. At the same time, it was unable to spur coordinated EU-wide insolvency reforms leading to convergence, for instance, in the availability of preventive restructuring procedures or in the area of second chance.'[119] The insolvency was listed among the inefficient proceedings that lead to a high amount of accumulated and increasing private debt.[120]

Nonetheless, as evidenced in the thematic consultation, many investors cite uncertainty over discordant national insolvency laws or the risk of lengthy, complex and unknown insolvency procedures in another Member State as the main reasons for not investing or entering into business in another jurisdiction. Consistent and harmonised insolvency and restructuring procedures are considered as a tool to facilitate greater legal certainty and encourage the timely restructuring of viable businesses in financial difficulty. Therefore, taking forward the 2014 Recommendation, the European Commission

---

[117] See also Liu and Rosenberg (2013).
[118] Directorate-General Justice & Consumers of the European Commission, *Evaluation of the Implementation of the Commission Recommendation of 12.3.2014 on a New Approach to Business Failure and Insolvency* (30 September 2015), available from: http://ec.europa.eu/justice/civil/commercial/insolvency/index_en.htm
[119] European Commission, Directorate-General for Justice and Consumers, *Impact Assessment Study on Policy Options for a New Initiative on Minimum Standards in Insolvency and Restructuring Law*, Contract No. JUST /2015/JCOO/FWCIVI0103 (2017), p. 20. See also University of Leeds, *Study on a New Approach to Business Failure and Insolvency. Comparative Legal Analysis of the Member States' Relevant Provisions and Practices*, Tender No. JUST/2014/JCOO/PR/CIVI/0075 (January 2016).
[120] Ibid.

has proposed a directive on preventive restructuring frameworks, second chance and efficiency measures for entrepreneurs ('Proposal').[121]

Within the framework of the Capital Markets Union, the Proposal's key objective is to reduce barriers to the free flow of capital caused by differences in Member States' restructuring and insolvency frameworks.[122] It aims for all Member States to implement key principles for effective preventive restructuring and second-chance frameworks for honest debtors, as well as measures to improve the quality and efficiency of all types of insolvency procedure by reducing their length and associated costs.[123] It also aims to support efforts to reduce future levels of non-performing loans in the EU.[124]

Critically, the Proposal applies to either legal persons or natural persons engaged in a trade, business or professional activity (entrepreneurs), thus excluding natural persons who are consumers.

The exclusion is first made explicit in Recital 15 of the Proposal:

> Consumer over-indebtedness is a matter of great economic and social concern and is closely related to the reduction of debt overhang. Furthermore, it is often not possible to draw a clear distinction between the consumer and business debts of an entrepreneur. A second chance regime for entrepreneurs would not be effective if the entrepreneur had to go through separate procedures, with different access conditions and discharge periods, to discharge his business personal debts and his non-business personal debts. For these reasons, *although this Directive does not include binding rules on consumer over-indebtedness*, Member States should be able to also apply the discharge provisions to consumers. [emphasis added]

The chosen legislative route is to establish a minimum harmonisation framework for restructuring and second chance for entrepreneurs, with a non-binding provision on second chance for consumers. According to Article 1(2)(g) the Directive shall not apply to procedures that concern debtors who are natural persons who are not entrepreneurs. The Explanatory Memorandum of the Proposal further clarifies that Title I (General provisions) containing provisions on the scope of application *rationae materiae* and *rationae personae*, definitions and a provision on the availability of early-warning tools for debtors, applies to both legal persons or natural persons engaged in a trade, business or professional activity, i.e. it applies to

---

[121] Proposal for a Directive of the European Parliament and of the Council on preventive restructuring frameworks, second chance and measures to increase the efficiency of restructuring, insolvency and discharge procedures and amending Directive 2012/30/EU, COM(2016) 723 final.

[122] Communication from the Commission to the European Parliament, the Council, the European Economic and Social Committee and the Committee of the Regions – Action Plan on Building a Capital Markets Union, COM(2015) 468 final.

[123] Communication from the Commission to the European Parliament, the Council, the European Economic and Social Committee and the Committee of the Regions – Upgrading the Single Market: More Opportunities for People and Business, COM(2015) 550 final.

[124] Outcome of the Council Meeting, 3480th Council meeting, Economic and Financial Affairs (Brussels, 12 July 2016), 11052/16.

entrepreneurs only.¹²⁵ Indeed, under the definitions of Article 2(13), an over-indebted entrepreneur is 'a natural person exercising a trade, business, craft or profession, who is otherwise than temporarily unable to pay debts as they fall due'. In turn, Title II of the Proposal establishes common, core elements for preventive restructuring frameworks to give to either legal or natural person debtors in financial difficulty effective access to procedures facilitating restructuring plans' early negotiation, adoption by creditors and possible confirmation by a judicial or administrative authority.

At the same time, Article 1(3) is explicit is stating that Member States may extend the application of the procedures leading to a discharge of debts incurred by over-indebted entrepreneurs to over-indebted natural persons who are not entrepreneurs.

According to the European Commission, evidence shows that shorter discharge periods have a positive impact on consumers, as they are quicker to re-enter the cycles of consumption, in turn boosting entrepreneurship.¹²⁶ Likewise, it recognises the major economic and social problem represented by the over-indebtedness of natural persons, which is mostly due to unfavourable macroeconomic conditions in the context of the financial and economic crisis (e.g. unemployment) combined with personal circumstances (e.g. divorce, illness). It notes that not all consumers have the same treatment under national insolvency laws, which results in increased costs for Member States' social security arrangements and negative economic consequences such as reduced consumption, labour activity and growth opportunities.¹²⁷

Despite the exclusion of harmonised binding rules on consumers, the recognition that individual entrepreneurs' personal and business debts are often intertwined is significant.¹²⁸ As explained in the Explanatory Memorandum, it is often the case that entrepreneurs, especially SMEs, take out personal loans to start and run their businesses, for example by guaranteeing their business loan with their personal assets. Likewise, it is not infrequent that natural persons use consumer credit to buy resources for their professional activity. Importantly, under the proposal, both types of personal and business debts can be consolidated where incurred by individuals in their entrepreneurial activity.¹²⁹ This represents a novelty in the inclusion in the harmonisation process of insolvency proceedings of over-indebted individuals, not only covering a significant number of affected individuals but also opening up new future prospects for consumer debtors too.

At the same time, in fact, in line with the Recommendation 2014 the Proposal invites Member States to extend the application of the discharge principles also to

---

[125] Ibid.
[126] Explanatory Memorandum, Proposal for a Directive of the European Parliament and of the Council on preventive restructuring frameworks, second chance and measures to increase the efficiency of restructuring, insolvency and discharge procedures and amending Directive 2012/30/EU, COM (2016) 723 final.
[127] Ibid.
[128] Ibid.
[129] Ibid.

natural persons who are not entrepreneurs, i.e. consumers. Although the provisions in Title III on second chance for entrepreneurs are restricted to entrepreneurs, it is explicitly stated that Member States may extend those provisions to all natural persons to ensure consistent treatment of personal debt. Indeed, several Member States do not distinguish between personal debts incurred following a business activity and those incurred outside such activity. The Proposal does not suggest that such a distinction should be made or is appropriate. What it does is invite Member States to apply the same principles to all natural persons.

The Explanatory Memorandum further explains:

> On second chance, since the Recommendation's adoption, several Member States have introduced for the first time a debt discharge regime for natural persons. However, important discrepancies remain over the discharge period's duration. Such differences in Member States' legal frameworks mean continuing legal uncertainty, additional costs for investors in assessing their risks, less developed capital markets and persisting barriers to the efficient restructuring of viable companies in the EU, including cross-border enterprise groups.
>
> ...
>
> Many Member States in recent years have adopted or reformed national laws on consumer insolvency recognising the importance of enabling consumers to discharge of their debts and obtain a second chance. However, not all Member States have such laws and the discharge periods for over-indebted consumers remain very long. Helping consumers back into the economic spending cycle is an important part of good functioning markets and retail financial services. The Commission will continue to look into how Member States have reformed their national frameworks and monitor how they implement this specific second chance provision in the proposal, so as to review the situation of consumer over-indebtedness.[130]

On second chance, to assess the question of subsidiarity, the European Commission distinguishes between natural persons who are entrepreneurs and those who are consumers. The key differentiating point is that entrepreneurs are likely to search for any sources of investment, even cross-border. Unlike the latter, consumers tend instead to receive local financing. Therefore, at this stage the European Commission considers that the problem of consumers' over-indebtedness should be tackled first at national level. At the same time, the financial services industry often indicated diverging national consumer insolvency laws as a barrier to selling retail financial products cross-border.[131]

For the above reasons, the European Commission invites once again Member States to consider the possibility of applying the principles on the discharge of entrepreneurs also to all natural persons including consumers. As the legal technique employed is that of setting up minimum harmonisation, it is designed to enable

---

[130] *Ibid.*, pp. 8 and 14.
[131] At the same time, the banking sector was of the view that EU rules on consumer discharge, if considered, should be covered in a separate legal instrument (*ibid.*).

Member States to go beyond the Directive's provisions, for example by extending its personal scope to cover all natural persons, including consumers.[132]

Finally, Article 29 in Title V on the monitoring of restructuring, insolvency and discharge procedures provides for data collection obligations by the Member States. To have reliable annual statistics, among the number of procedures which were initiated, pending and resolved, the Member States will have also engage in the collection of data at national level on the procedures leading to a full discharge of debt for natural persons. Member States will have to break down such statistics to reflect whether debtors are natural or legal persons and where such distinction is made under national law, whether the procedures concern only entrepreneurs or all natural persons.

---

[132] *Ibid.*

9

Conclusions and Scope for Further Research

9.1 CONCLUDING REMARKS

In the last few decades personal debt in Europe has experienced a strong growth, fuelled by several factors that have increased the demand for debt. These factors may mostly be attributed to changes in sociocultural norms and new spending models that have made personal debt more acceptable, the reduction in intergenerational transfers and a decline in the informal credit market, the retreat of the welfare state and the dismantling of public provision of services such as health, retirement and education which have posed further pressures on debt demand. The supply side has also played a significant role in shaping the evolution of the market. Indeed, over years banks and financial intermediaries have widened and refined their portfolio of products and services, in order to satisfy more effectively existing customer needs and to develop and serve new market niches, such as consumers with thin or no credit history, older age groups and students. Aggressive marketing strategies have also exerted various degrees of influence on consumer credit growth, especially on credit cards. In fact, the economics of personal debt are such that financial intermediaries can derive several sources of income from the business, both in terms of interest revenues from lending funds with double-digit levels of interest rates, and non-interest revenues derived primarily from fees from services on loans-related products.

Although it is well known from traditional economic theories that personal debt may heighten economic welfare by providing individuals greater flexibility over their spending, smoothing consumption over the lifetime and repaying the amount owed with future earnings, it is also undoubted that – especially for certain groups of individuals – paying back debt may turn into a source of problems, causing both financial and non-financial detriments.

Empirical analyses have highlighted that over-indebtedness mainly affects the economically and socially weakest in society. Indeed, low-income households and the unemployed are the most financially fragile and exposed to the risk of holding unmanageable debts, as well as the younger and large-sized families. Behavioural traits, in particular impulsivity, may also exacerbate the phenomenon by pushing consumers to opt for 'buy now and pay later' solutions regardless of the burden of debt. Furthermore, exogenous factors and unexpected events – above all job loss, but also divorce and illness – may negatively impact repayment capacity and make what was once a manageable liability no longer sustainable.

Over-indebtedness is therefore a multifaceted phenomenon, caused by a combination of economic, social, behavioural, cultural and institutional factors which need to be tackle with multidimensional and integrated government policy responses, with the aim of preventing and resolving over-indebtedness as well as alleviating or managing it. The relevance of the phenomenon has come to light especially after the 2008 and the 2011 crises, when exogenous shocks negatively affected the real income of the majority of consumers, reduced by higher levels of unemployment, as well as austerity measures such as cuts in social benefits and tax increases. All these changes may have turned situations of manageable debt into over-indebtedness. The situation needs to be addressed by policy and lawmakers for the consequences that over-indebtedness may have on consumers, in terms of social and financial exclusion, as well as mental and physical health, on the stability of the financial system, and on the economic growth of the society as a whole.

Indeed, consumer over-indebtedness has been a concern for both national and EU policymakers for decades. It is certainly not an entirely new theme, and the role of national as well as EU policymakers and lawmakers has already been discussed for over twenty years.[1]

Yet, the latest findings on the nature and causes of the problem of over-indebted consumers question the policies and law adopted so far. With the increasing liberalisation of financial markets, and the growing role and use of consumer financial services in the modern economy, data on consumer over-indebtedness show that national measures are proving ineffective at tackling the problem.[2] Likewise, despite the established EU dimension, materially little has been ever done at the supranational level. At the same time, in the light of the gravity of the effects of the recession on individuals and the retracting role of states in securing the economic security of their citizens, the issue seems to have turned into one that requires long-term solutions. The harm caused by the financial crisis, alongside the changing role of states, have raised important issues regarding the protection of individuals, the scope, intensity and effectiveness of regulation in financial markets, as well as the need for additional safeguards to alleviate the social problems that market liberalisation has exposed.

A recurring theme of this book is that over-indebtedness is a complex multidimensional problem which results in the excessive level or inability to meet

---

[1] For example, see the writings over twenty years ago of Huls (1993) and the early academic literature and reports that followed, well summarised in Kilborn (2010).
[2] See also Anderson et al. (2016); House of Commons (2017).

financial commitments, even the basic ones. The majority of its causes are not rooted in the private law relationship between lenders and consumers at the time of contracting, but in lifetime events or macroeconomic conditions beyond their control. The pecuniary commitment with financial institutions is certainly affected, and if anything it contributes to make the situation worse once interests, penalties and fees become due, and debt collection procedures begin.

This book has attempted to show that, in principle, preventive measures are desirable but EU responsible lending and borrowing, as designed, are not suited to deal with the complex multidimensional nature of the problem. The information paradigm which imbues the law and the focus on the creditworthiness assessment have been criticised for being ineffective, at least if taken in isolation and without complementary elements of credit that is truly comprehensively responsible, including for example interest-rate caps and access to basic or affordable credit.

One of the major shortcomings seems to lie in the curative side – or treatment – of over-indebtedness in the form of personal insolvency. The majority of EU Member States now have separate legal regimes for corporate and personal insolvency. However, these are national but uncoordinated initiatives that entrench themselves and operate in a limping common market.

Arguably, a more dynamic approach tackling all the causes and the various stages of financial difficulty is needed. But EU law cannot deal with the difficult national macroeconomic policies where most of the causes are embedded. These include unemployment, salary levels and labour markets, provision of social care and assistance etc. These are sensitive political matters to be confronted by Member States.

Nevertheless, a desirable legal regime should cover comprehensively all the stages of the financial difficulty of consumers. These include both preventive and curative measures. Also, a desirable legal regime should recognise that the financial distress of natural persons is intertwined with market as well as social issues.

Arguably, a reformed common system for the treatment of the insolvency of natural persons at EU level, which departs radically from the current approach of mutual recognition, should step in to provide a more complete response to address the over-indebtedness of European consumers, not as a form of social assistance but rather as a social insurance protecting individuals and society from ruin and degradation, as well as counterproductive and destructive debt management and enforcement practices that are also detrimental for creditors. Ultimately, this stance questions the use of mutual recognition in the context of over-indebtedness and the insolvency of natural persons. Mutual recognition and private international law in the EU are used when it is difficult for Member States to reach agreement on the substantive laws.

Besides, the integration of retail financial markets, consumer protection, responsible lending, and social and economic cohesion are derived from the EU Treaties to justify the EU competence for a common, harmonised or resourced strategy at Union level.

As noted earlier in this book, recent scholarship demonstrates how empirical evidence provides little support for arguments grounded in national legal traditions, local institutional structures or cultural attitudes of consumer insolvency laws. Therefore, these should not represent further obstacles for an EU reformed system. Deregulation and integration of financial markets were brought in by the EU regardless of pre-existing national legal traditions, institutions and cultures. By the same token, the EU should not find obstacles to step in with measures to fix the very same market with the treatment of its side effects.

The EU competence on the matter is arguably important to the effective operation of the single market to avoid the fragmentation between the various national jurisdictions when dealing with the effects generated by the very same market. The legal basis for a uniform or harmonised procedure looks solid under Article 38 of the Charter of Fundamental Rights (Consumer Protection), as well as Articles 114 (Establishment and Functioning of the Internal Market) and 81 TFEU (Judicial Cooperation in Civil Matters).

The EU has already affirmed competence in consumer credit and mortgage legislation under the rhetoric of delivering a responsible credit market which encourages competition, innovation and choice. By contrast, dealing with the intertwined situation of consumer defaults and insolvencies – the other side of that same credit market – has been left to the uncoordinated competence of national legislators.

The result is a fragmented EU legal framework with substantive differences in the treatment of over-indebtedness and personal insolvency legislation, where EU law only provides for the legal instrument of mutual recognition to ensure clarity over procedural and jurisdictional rules in cross-border matters.

The combination of traditional moral factors, political resistance and claims of subsidiarity used to explain this multilevel division of competence between the EU and the Member States. Today, this stance is becoming increasingly difficult to justify in light of the interdependency between the market on the one side, and welfare and social concerns on the other. The economic crisis has exposed the inseparable nature between market failure and social concerns. That the same market continues to be regulated inconsistently, despite the intertwined nature of access, inclusion, default, exclusion and the relationships of cause and effect is questionable.

If, in principle, preventive measures are deemed desirable – but the principles of responsible lending and borrowing, as administered throughout the EU, do not seem suited to deal with the complex multidimensional nature of the problem – it seems that a more coherent and holistic approach, dealing with the effects brought about by the major causes of over-indebtedness would be desirable. No policy or law, designed to prevent over-indebtedness without *ex post* debt solutions, can, on its own, address the problem conclusively.

Even though the CJEU has shown significant activism beyond the exercise of its traditional function in developing the protection of consumers in financial difficulty, the legal instruments at its disposal have been and remain limited.

Arguably, the procedures available to consumers who default and become insolvent need the same level of attention, not only for the sake of promoting the internal market and consumer protection, but also in terms of providing access to justice and effective remedies. Otherwise, apparent inconsistencies in the current legal framework may create a deadlock to the detriment of stakeholders, while political resistance may make it difficult to agree on the content of a law.

Nevertheless, the EU may be guided by some basic binding principles, for example in harmonising the scope of the procedure; the duration of the insolvency; the payment period for debtors who can pay; the liquidation of the debtor's non-exempt assets; the prevention of insolvency misuse; essential debtor obligations; restrictions and disqualifications; stay of individual debt enforcement; the treatment of NINA/LILA debtors; and the nature and powers of insolvency officials.

Following the introduction of 'soft' EU law and the involvement of other international organisations in the design of national personal insolvency legislation in Member States, especially those overwhelmed by the financial turmoil, some broad-contour principles are emerging. Likewise, new proposals for the harmonisation of business insolvency now extend to natural persons in their capacity as small entrepreneurs. This represents a novelty in the inclusion in the harmonisation process of insolvency proceedings of over-indebted individuals, not only covering a significant number of affected individuals but also opening up new future prospects for consumer debtors too. Now the question remains about EU full harmonisation in an area of law traditionally sensitive.

To the extent that the increasing integration of EU markets and the economy create mounting pressure for more substantive harmonisation, this is unlikely to occur as a matter of consumer protection. If anything, it may come through the back door, prompted by the EU prioritising the Capital Markets Union and further integration of retail financial services markets. In this context, fragmented national insolvency laws are likely to constitute barriers for the free movement of capital, services and people within the EU. Clearly, for consumer protection, the challenge will lie in the design of the law, and in this respect the Charter of Fundamental Rights of the EU and the principles of procedural fairness developed by the CJEU should assist the legislators. But everything else risks being jeopardised by local interests and concerns of the Member States coming from further afield; for example, the harmonisation of insolvency law would indirectly impact on social security strategies that are at the 'hard core' of Member States' exclusive competence.

9.2 THE WAY FORWARD FOR NEW STREAMS OF RESEARCH

As state responsibility for personal economic security declines, there is an increasing onus on people to engage with the financial services sector. Arguably, more understanding and research are needed about the interconnectedness between consumer finance, unmanageable personal debt problems and labour markets in the EU. In the context of the EU quest for the creation of a 'competitive social market economy' that will 'combat social exclusion and discrimination',[3] proper knowledge is necessary to understand and assess the most appropriate legal measures to support policies for tackling consumer over-indebtedness and reconciling social justice with market liberalisation.

Consumer over-indebtedness is a problem that concerns a significant part of the EU population[4] and it impacts harshly on the lives of those who are affected. Moreover, it carries important social and economic costs for the EU, particularly in terms of both social justice and the integration of markets.

Traditionally, personal debt problems have been associated with financial credit and the relationship between lenders and consumer borrowers, but recent findings reveal empirically how these are not limited to credit-taking but are tied to consumer income and purchasing power. They consist of all consumer essential outgoings, even including expenditures relating to taxation and cuts in social welfare.[5] Moreover, they are intertwined with problems typical of the labour market: for example, market pressures for work flexibility and income instability, job protection and insecurity, level of wages and purchasing power, and technological innovations.[6]

Consumer over-indebtedness has always been a complex phenomenon difficult to analyse. This is because across the EU it is described by several variables and definitions,[7] as well as geographical and demographic distribution.[8] Moreover, until recently the cultural approach, use and extension of consumer loans have varied significantly from one Member State to another. At the same time, consumer and mortgage credit markets are considered crucial for an efficient functioning of the EU financial system, the economy and the realisation of the internal market. Credit availability and open access to credit markets have meant widening participation and financial inclusion to allow as many consumers as possible without discrimination to participate in the credit society and the consumption model of the market economy.[9] Moreover, consumerism has been promoted to reduce class

---

[3] Arts. 3 and 4 of the Treaty on the Functioning of the EU (TFEU).
[4] Eurostat, 'Over-indebtedness and Financial Exclusion Statistics', at http://ec.europa.eu/eurostat/statistics-explained/index.php/Archive:Over-indebtedness_and_financial_exclusion_statistics
[5] Civic Consulting (2014).
[6] Crouch (2015).
[7] Betti et al. (2001); Civic Consulting (2014); OEE Etudes (2008).
[8] Civic Consulting (2014).
[9] Micklitz (2013); Ramsay (2012a).

conflict between capital and labour,[10] as well as the dependence of labour and welfare entitlements to feed demand in the marketplace.[11] The liberalisation and expansion of credit markets alongside the increased availability and sophistication of credit from an increasing variety of lenders have explained the mounting levels over time of consumer debt across societies. On the other hand, if more credit is available and offered to a broader base of consumers, more of them become indebted. Consequently, a proportionally larger number of consumers become unable to meet the contracted obligations.[12]

All these bases may explain why for a long period of time excessive lending/ borrowing has been the focus of consumers becoming over-committed and unable to repay their debts, pushing the policy and legal debate over behavioural issues of creditors or debtors. Irresponsible lending and predatory practices on one side, and irresponsible borrowing decisions, consumption choices and cognitive biases on the other side have for long dominated the attention of scholars and policymakers alike.[13] The emphasis on behavioural causes has often resulted in the attribution of defaults to a responsibility of the creditor or a personal failure of the debtor. Therefore, alongside the advancement of legal measures for the abolition of obstacles for further integration and facilitate competition, the promotion of responsible lending to preventively limit over-indebtedness has dominated the EU agenda as the core policy.[14] The resulting legal instruments have regulated the provision of credit insisting on the paradigm of information requirements and the assessment of creditworthiness at the time of the making of the loan.[15] However, such measures appear inadequate to comprehensively address the problem as they may capture existing or likely debt problems if further credit is taken, but they cannot address the most frequent causes of consumer over-indebtedness when repayment difficulties emerge at a later stage. These have been confirmed to be external lifetime events – predominantly macroeconomic factors like unemployment, declining wages or generally low income vis-à-vis the cost of living. Other important external causes include the impact of illness or divorce on budgets. Behavioural factors alone, such as poor financial choices, mismanagement of resources or irresponsible lending practices, seem to have a limited bearing. A conjuncture of such external events with

---

[10] Whitman (2007).
[11] Schmidt and Thatcher (2013).
[12] Turner (2016).
[13] Micklitz (2013); Ramsay (2012a).
[14] See Communication of the European Commission to the European Council of 4 March 2009 'Driving European Recovery', COM(2009) 114.
[15] They focus on the advertising and marketing of credit products, the information to be provided to borrowers prior to granting any loans, ways to assess product suitability and borrower creditworthiness, advice standards and issues relating to the framework for credit intermediaries (disclosures, registration, licensing and supervision). See Directive 2008/48/EC of 23 April 2008 on credit agreements for consumers and repealing Council Directive 87/102/EEC, L 133/66; Directive 014/17/EU of 4 February 2014 on credit agreements for consumers relating to residential immovable property and amending Directives 2008/48/EC and 2013/36/EU and Regulation (EU) No. 1093/2010, L 60/34.

behavioural factors of consumers not effectively adjusting their budgets to the external changes may provide a more complete picture.[16] Likewise, responsible lending measures cannot anticipate likely debt problems as they are disengaged from those structural conditions that lead to an environment hospitable to financial difficulty, i.e. market deregulation, incomplete or retracting social safety nets, labour market issues or technological innovations.[17]

The late financial and economic crisis has exacerbated the problem and significance of personal debt. Job losses, austerity measures, public cuts and the deterioration of the welfare state, and large-scale inabilities to repay debts have accelerated transnational narratives and policies on insolvency legislation as an alleviating measure. Debt discharge or other settlement procedures point at offering a relief or a 'fresh start' to otherwise bankrupt consumers. Almost all Member States have moved towards national regimes for the protection of consumers in financial distress and the treatment of the insolvency of natural persons.[18] Despite substantive national differences and reliance on mutual recognition of laws, 'soft law' instruments of the EU and international organisations have encouraged Member States to follow basic principles in the enactment or modernisation of national laws.[19] However, personal insolvency laws remain tied to credit liberalisation and market objectives. They aim at the promotion of entrepreneurialism or the reintroduction of consumers in the market as economic agents.[20] Debts may be discharged but these remain incomplete measures if not supported by sufficient income.

Against the above background, social rationales or narratives for the regulation of over-indebtedness remain absent or separated from labour markets and/or the welfare system – and vice-versa. Likewise, legal scholarship has understudied the relevance of financial services for labour markets and relations. Yet, debt problems concern all individuals across societies who are dependent on regular income or affected by raising living standards, diminished spending capacity or purchasing power, i.e. all those in the labour market and their dependants (e.g. not only vulnerable members of society but also all those with a stable and decently paid occupation but all the same at risk of losing their jobs or becoming subject to deteriorating adjustments as a result of unbalanced macroeconomic conditions, austerity measures, public cuts or advances in technologies).[21] A strong connection exists between labour markets, economic policies, income and spending power,

---

[16] e.g. see Banque de France (2014).
[17] Braucher (2006).
[18] e.g. see London Economics (2012).
[19] Recommendation CM/Rec (2007) 8 of the Committee of Ministers to member states on legal solutions to debt problems (Adopted by the Committee of Ministers on 20 June 2007); Commission Recommendation of 12.3.2014 on a new approach to business failure and insolvency, C (2014) 1500 final; e.g. see the IMF involvement in Latvia, Romania, Spain, Greece, Hungary, Ireland and Portugal. The international dimension is comprehensively documented in Ramsay (2015).
[20] McCormack et al. (2017).
[21] Civic Consulting (2014); see also Savage (2015).

personal finance and unmanageable debt problems, and economic and social exclusion. As Crouch identifies, workers rely on financial services to offset increasing labour market uncertainty and past dependence on job protection or robust forms of social security.[22] However, at present, problem debt is regulated at EU level by credit laws and, to a more uneven degree, by national insolvency laws. These are legal instruments apt for sustaining the debt economy, but in so doing the law supports the survival of the present model. Therefore, it does little to effectively tackle the problem and reconcile EU social justice with market liberalisation under the quest for a competitive *social* market economy. Although the reintegration of individuals in society is at stake, debt problems are neither treated as a circumstance falling within the scope of labour or social laws, nor are they an area where measures for their prevention and alleviation are integrated in the conventional social dialogue for the protection from market uncertainty and supported by social partners such as trade unions. Illustrations of key areas to be investigated are: the link between personal finance, over-indebtedness and the labour market, low economic growth, stagnating wages, unemployment and income instability; the role of debt as an instrument used to maintain a stable level of consumption and the intertemporal exchange of debt and income; the importance of financial inclusion and access to finance for labour markets as conditions for decent work and the protection of wages; the integration of financial services with social policies (e.g. employability, re-employment, retirement); the institutional interaction between social partner organisations (e.g. trade unions) and the development of the personal financial system; the involvement and entry points of such social partners in areas of consumer protection, including their involvement in policy choices in domains currently unrelated to the issues of the conventional social dialogue, in preventively intercepting risky situations in labour market crises, and debt advisory and counselling services alongside the other support offered to individuals.

Although the EU has limited competence in social legislation, there is an EU dimension to this. Soft forms of social governance among the Member States have emerged with the increasing impact of EU economic rights (e.g. free movement rights) on national social rights, the ensuing limits on the ability of Member States to regulate their effects, and concerns that the EU should focus more on its social side.[23] In this perspective, the EU may also be able to hold Member States accountable for running convergent and effective social systems designed by the Member States themselves. In short, to the extent that the EU multilevel governance can explain supranational intervention for the market issues of debt problems, while leaving its social concerns at national level, the interdependency of the two makes such a division unattainable. The latest economic crisis has exposed the inseparable

---

[22] Bellofiore and Halevi (2009); Crouch (2015).
[23] Ramsay (2015); Scharpf (2002).

nature of finance, political economy, labour markets, salary levels vis-à-vis the cost of living, and welfare systems on the lives of people regardless of their classification as consumers, workers or otherwise. Arguably, market access and financial inclusion go hand in hand with social inclusion and the deterrence of degradation.[24]

Therefore, consumer over-indebtedness has become a concern for both national and EU policymakers. Yet it is not an entirely new theme, and the role of the EU has already been discussed for over twenty years. However, with the increasing liberalisation of financial markets, and the growing role and use of consumer financial services in the modern economy, data on consumer over-indebtedness show that national measures are proving ineffective to tackle the problem. At the same time, despite the established EU dimension, materially little has been ever done at the supranational level. The harm caused by the financial crisis, alongside the changing role of states, have raised important issues regarding the protection of individuals, the scope, intensity and effectiveness of regulation in financial markets, as well as the need for additional safeguards to alleviate the social problems that market liberalisation has exposed.

So far, however, the scholarship has focused on the role of financial services and the regulation of financial markets or the economic and legal aspects of insolvency laws. In-depth studies linking consumer over-indebtedness with issues of the labour market are lacking. New research should uncover and apply social and labour law concerns to personal financial difficulty. It could involve legal research with interdisciplinary aspects, incorporating insights from disciplines such as economics and the social sciences. Also, within the study of law, scholarship should cross areas traditionally covered separately. Availing itself of the most recent scholarship on the theme as the starting point, such new research should attempt to explore innovative solutions to the problem of consumer over-indebtedness through a holistic approach. It should purport to establish a clear relationship between financial services and personal debt (usually treated as issues of consumer protection and law) with areas of labour or social laws such as income or wages, purchasing power, the role of social partners and social exclusion. In so doing, the overarching theme of the research to be tested would be the interconnectedness between consumer law and labour and/or social law in the age of neo-liberal markets, where personal finance is used as a proxy for assessment. Such an approach requires revisiting – if not reconceptualising – consumer law and social and labour law as a broader 'law of economic subordination', along the lines of recent social sciences and economic scholarship exploring the tensions between consumption and labour, and the ways in which different balances of power affect the ways in which they are resolved. The research could lead to the theoretical result of revisiting or reconceptualising consumer law and labour law in light of contemporary social and economic trends. In so doing, it may have the potential of setting the basis for the development of

---

[24] Comparato (2015).

novel conceptual and coherent normative models to be extended to other areas of economic subordination or vulnerability for supporting the achievement of the policy goal of EU social justice. In sum, it is argued that future research should question the extent to which inroads of labour and/or social law into consumer law may improve consumer protection against over-indebtedness, and if so whether labour relations and social partner organisations could encompass consumer financial protection in the conventional social dialogue to improve social justice in the EU.

Bibliography

Abdou, H. and Pointon, J. (2011) 'Credit scoring, statistical techniques and evaluation criteria: A review of the literature', 18 *Intelligent Systems in Accounting, Finance & Management*, 59–88

ACCIS (2013) *ACCIS Response to Financial Services User Group (FSUG) Position Paper on the London Economics Study on Means to Protect Consumers in Financial Difficulty* (October), at www.accis.eu/uploads/media/ACCIS_Response_to_FSUG_Position_Paper_October_2013.pdf

(2015a) *ACCIS 2015 Survey of Members – An Analysis of Credit Reporting in Europe* (November)

(2015b) *Response to the Proposal for a General Data Protection Regulation – Perspective of Credit Reporting Agencies* (16 November), at www.accis.eu/fileadmin/filestore/position_papers/ACCIS_Position_Paper_16_November_2015.pdf

(2016) *ACCIS Response to the FSUG Position Paper on Assessing the Impact of Credit Data on Preventing Over-Indebtedness, Contributing to Prudential Regulation and Facilitating Access to Affordable and Quality Credit Published by the FSUG*, at www.accis.eu/fileadmin/filestore/position_papers/ACCIS_Response_to_the_FSUG_Final.pdf

[no date] *The Lending Journey*, at www.accis.eu/fileadmin/filestore/position_papers/Accis_-_The_Lending_Journey.pdf

Achtziger, H., Kenning, R. and Reisch, L. (2015) 'Debt out of control: the links between self-control, compulsive buying and real debts', 49 *Journal of Economic Psychology*, 141–9

Acolin, A. et al. (2015) 'Credit market innovations and sustainable homeownership: the case of non-traditional mortgage products', *Working Paper* (April)

Adler, M. and Wozniak, E. (1980) 'The origins and consequences of default – an examination of the impact of diligence', *Research Report no. 6* (Scottish Law Commission)

Admati, R. and Pfleiderer, P. (2000) 'Forcing firms to talk: financial disclosure regulation and externalities', 13 *Review of Financial Studies*, 479–519

Agarwal, S. and Zhang, J. (2015) *A Review of Credit Card Literature: Perspectives from Consumers* (19 October), at www.fca.org.uk/publication/market-studies/review-credit-card-literature.pdf

Akerlof, A. G. (1970) 'The market for "lemons": quality uncertainty and the market mechanism', 28(3) *Quarterly Journal of Economics*, 523–47

Alary, D. and Gollier, C. (2001) *Strategic Default and Penalties on the Credit Market with Potential Judgment Errors*, EUI Working Paper (European University Institute)

Albacete, N. and Lindner, P. (2013) 'Household vulnerability in Austria: a microeconomic analysis based on the household finance and consumption survey', 25 *Oesterreichische Nationalbank, Financial Stability Report*, 57–73

Alder, M. and Wozniak, E. (1980) 'The origins and consequences of default – an examination of the impact of diligence', *Research Report no. 6* (Scottish Law Commission)

Ampudia, M., Vlokhoven, H. and Zochowski, D. (2014) 'Financial fragility of euro area households. European Central Bank', *Working Paper no. 1737*

Anderson, G. et al. (2016) 'The Bank of England/NMG Survey of Household Finances', 37(1) *Fiscal Studies*, 131–52

Arellano, M. and Bover, O. (1995) 'Another look at the instrumental variables estimation of error components models', 68 *Journal of Econometrics*, 29–51

Arner, D. W., Barberis, J. N. and Buckley, R. P. (2016) 'The evolution of fintech: a new post-crisis paradigm?', 47 *Georgetown Journal of International Law*, 1271–319

Article 29 Working Party (2011) *Opinion 15/2011 on the Definition of Consent*, 01197/11/ENWP187 (Brussels, 13 July)
  (2012) *Opinion 08/2012 Providing Further Input on the Data Protection Reform Discussions*, WP 199 (Brussels, 5 October)
  (2013) *Advice Paper on Essential Elements of a Definition and a Provision on Profiling within the EU General Data Protection Regulation* (Brussels, 13 May)

Atamer, Y. M. (2011) 'Duty of responsible lending: should the European Union take action?', in S. Grundmann and Y. M. Atamer (eds.), *Financial Services, Financial Crisis and General European Contract Law* (Kluwer), 179–202

Baer, T., Goland, T. and Schiff, R. (2013) 'New credit-risk models for the unbanked', *McKinsey Quarterly* (April), at www.mckinsey.com/business-functions/risk/our-insights/new-credit-risk-models-for-the-unbanked

Baister, S. (2014) 'Shooting from the hip'. *A chapter delivered to the INSOL Academic Forum* (Istanbul, 8 October)

Baister, S. and Toube, F. (2012) 'All change is not growth, as all movement is not forward!', 25 (4) *Insolvency Intelligence*, 49–54

Balboni, P. et al. (2013) 'Legitimate interest of the data controller. New data protection paradigm: legitimacy grounded on appropriate protection', 3 *International Data Privacy Law*, 244–61

Balmer, N., Pleasence, P., Buck, A. and Walker, H. C. (2006) 'Worried sick: the experience of debt problems and their relationship with health, illness and disability', 5(1) *Social Policy and Society*, 39–51

Bank of England (2010) *Annual Report*
  (2014) 'Should the availability of UK credit data be improved?', *Discussion Paper* (May)

Bank for International Settlement (2018) *Implications of FinTech Developments for Banks and Bank Supervisors* (February)

Banque de France (1996) 'Traitement du surendettement: nouvelles perspectives', *Bulletin 2 trimestre, Supplement Etudes*
  (2014) *Étude des Parcours Menant au Surendettement* (September)
  (2016) *Le surendettement des ménages. Enquete typologique*

Barron, J. M. and Staten, M. (2000) 'The value of comprehensive credit reports: lessons from the US Experience', *Research Paper – Credit Research Centre* (Georgetown University)
  (2003) 'The value of comprehensive credit reports: lessons from the US experience', in M. J. Miller (ed.), *Reporting Systems and the International Economy* (MIT Press), 273–310

Beck, T., Büyükkarabacak, B., Rioja, F. K. and Valev, N. T. (2012) 'Who gets the credit and does it matter? Household vs. firm lending across countries', 12 *BE Journal of Macroeconomics*, 1–46

Beck, T., Demirgüç-Kunt, A. and Levine, R. (2003) 'Law and finance: why does legal origin matter?', 31(4) *Journal of Comparative Economics*, 653–75

Becker, G. S. (1976) *The Economic Approach to Human Behavior* (University of Chicago Press)

Bellofiore, R. and Halevi, J. (2009) 'Deconstructing labor. A Marxian–Kaleckian perspective on what is "new" in contemporary capitalism and economic policies', in C. Gnos et al. (eds.), *Employment, Growth and Development. A Post-Keynesian Approach* (Edward Elgar)

Berger, A. N. and Mester, L. J. (2003) 'Explaining the dramatic changes in the performance of US banks: technological change, deregulation and dynamic changes in competition', 12 *Journal of Financial Intermediation*, 57–95

Berger, A. N. and Udell, G. F. (1995) 'Relationship lending and lines of credit in small firm finance', 68 *Journal of Business*, 351–81

Berthoud, R. and Kempson, E. (1992) *Credit and Debt: The PSI Report* (PSI)

Bertola, G., Disney, R. and Grant, C. (2006) 'The economics of consumer credit demand and supply', in G. Bertola, R. Disney and C. Grant (eds.), *The Economics of Consumer Credit* (MIT Press), 1–26

Betti, G., Dourmashkin, N., Rossi, M. and Ping Yin, Y. (2001) *Study of the Problem of Consumer Indebtedness: Statistical Aspects, Final Report*, at http://ec.europa.eu/consumers/cons_int/fina_serv/cons_directive/fina_servo6_en.pdf

Bianco, M., Jappelli, T. and Pagano, M. (2002) 'Courts and banks: effects of judicial enforcement on credit markets', *CSEF – Centre for Studies in Economics and Finance*, Working paper no. 58

Bigus, J. P. (1996) *Data Mining with Neural Networks: Solving Business Problems from Application Development to Decision Support* (McGraw Hill)

Bishop, T. B. and Shan, H. (2008) 'Reverse mortgages: a closer look at HECM loans', Cambridge: National Bureau of Economic Research

Bloustein, E. J. (1964) 'Privacy as an aspect of human dignity: an answer to Dean Prosser' 39 *New York University Law Review*, 962–1007

Bork, R. (1990) *The Tempting of America: The Political Seduction of the Law* (Simon & Schuster)

  (1993) *The Antitrust Paradox* (Free Press)

Bouyon, S. and Boeri, F. (2014) *ECRI Statistical Package* (ECRI)

Braucher, J. (2006) 'Theories of overindebtedness: interaction of structure and culture', 7 *Theoretical Inquiries in Law*, 323–46

Braunstein, S. and Welch, C. (2002) 'Financial literacy: an overview of practice, research, and policy' 88 *Federal Reserve Bulletin*, 445–57

Brealey, R. et al. (2001) *Financial Stability and Central Banks* (Routledge)

Bridges, S. and Disney, R. (2004) 'Use of credit and arrears on debt among low-income families in the United Kingdom' 25(1) *Fiscal Studies*, 1–25

British Competition Commission (2009) 'Market investigation into payment protection insurance', *Report*

Brown, S., Taylor, K. and Price, S. W. (2005) 'Debt and distress: evaluating the psychological cost of credit' 26 *Journal of Economic Psychology*, 642–63

Brownsword, R. (2009) 'Consent in data protection law: privacy, fair processing and confidentiality', in S. Gutwirth et al. (eds.), *Reinventing Data Protection?* (Springer), 83–110

Camerer, C. et al. (2003) 'Regulation for conservatives: behavioral economics and the case for asymmetric paternalism', 151 *University of Pennsylvania Law Review*, 1211–54
Caplovitz, D. (1963) *The Poor Pay More: Consumer Practices of Low Income Families* (Free Press)
Carbò-Valverde, S. (2017) 'The impact of digitalization on banking and financial stability', 5 *Journal of Financial Markets and Institutions*, 133–40
Cartwright, P. (2004) *Banks, Consumers and Regulation* (Hart)
Cavalletti, B. et al. (2014) 'Consumer debt and financial fragility in Italy', DEMM Working Paper no. 2014-08
Central Bank of Ireland (2017) *Discussion Paper: Consumer Protection Code and the Digitalisation of Financial Services* (June)
Cerini, D. (2016) 'Consumer over-indebtedness and interference with credit contracts: an Italian perspective', in F. Ferretti (ed.), *Comparative Perspectives of Consumer Over-Indebtedness – A View from the UK, Germany, Greece and Italy* (Eleven), 345–70
Chmelar, A. (2012) 'Household debt in Europe's periphery: the danger of a prolonged recession', *ECRI Commentary no. 12* (Brussels)
Christelis, D., Jappelli, T., Paccagnella, O. et al. (2010) 'Income, wealth and financial fragility in Europe', 19(4) *Journal of European Social Policy*, 359–76
Civic Consulting (2013) *The Over-Indebtedness of European Households: Updated Mapping of the Situation, Nature and Causes, Effects and Initiatives for Alleviating its Impact* (Brussels)
Comparato, G. (2015) 'The design of consumer and mortgage credit law in the European system', in H.-W. Micklitz and I. Domurath (eds.), *Consumer Debt and Social Exclusion in Europe* (Ashgate)
  (2016) 'The Italian law against over-indebtedness: fresh start, debt advice and financial education', in F. Ferretti (ed.), *Comparative Perspectives of Consumer Over-Indebtedness – A View from the UK, Germany, Greece and Italy* (Eleven), 371–90.
Consumer Financial Protection Bureau (2012) *Analysis of Differences between Consumer- and Creditor-Purchased Credit Scores* (September), at http://files.consumerfinance.gov/f/201209_Analysis_Differences_Consumer_Credit.pdf
Consumers International (2013) *Responsible Lending: An International Landscape* (November)
Cosma, S. (2016) 'The Italian banking system, consumer credit and the financial crisis: economic perspectives', in F. Ferretti (ed.), *Comparative Perspectives of Consumer Over-Indebtedness – A View from the UK, Germany, Greece and Italy* (Eleven), 315–30
Cox, D. and Jappelli, T. (1993) 'The effect of borrowing constraints on consumer liabilities', 25 (2) *Journal of Money Credit and Banking*, 197–213
Craig, P. and de Búrca, G. (2008) *EU Law* (Oxford University Press)
Credit Agricole (2017) *Overview of Consumer Credit in Europe 2016*
Crook, J. (2005) 'The measurement of household liabilities: conceptual issues and practices', University of Edinburgh, *Credit Research Centre*, Working paper
  (2006) 'Household debt demand and supply', in G. Bertola, R. Disney and C. Grant (eds.), *The Economics of Consumer Credit* (MIT Press), 63–92
Crouch, C. (2011) *The Strange Non-Death of Neoliberalism* (Polity)
  (2015) *Governing Social Risks in Post-Crisis Europe* (Edward Elgar).
Crowther, G. (1971) *Consumer Credit: Report of the Committee* (Department of Trade and Industry)
D'Alessio, G. and Iezzi, S. (2016) 'Household over-indebtedness: definition and measurement with Italian data', *Banca d'Italia, Occasional Paper no. 149*

Damia, V. and Israel, J. M. (2014) *Standardised Granular Credit and Credit Risk Data, Seventh IFC Conference on Indicators to Support Monetary and Financial Stability Analysis: Data Sources and Statistical Methodologies* (Basel, 4–5 September)

Datatilsynet [Norwegian Data Protection Authority] (2018) 'Artificial intelligence and privacy' (January)

Davies, I. (ed.) (2003) *Insolvency and the Enterprise Act 2002* (Jordans)

Davis, S. G. (1997) 'Re-engineering the right to privacy: how privacy has been transformed from a right to a commodity', in P. Agre and M. Rotenberg (eds.), *Technology and Privacy: The New Landscape* (MIT Press), 143–65

De Almeida, A. M. and Damia, V. (2014) 'Challenges and prospects for setting-up a European Union shared system on credit', *IFC Bulletin no. 37* (January)

De Hert, P. and Gutwirth, S. (2009) 'Data protection in the case law of Strasbourg and Luxembourg: constitutionalisation in action', in S. Gutwirth et al. (eds.), *Reinventing Data Protection?* (Springer), 3–44

De Hert, P. and Papakonstantinou, V. (2016) 'The new General Data Protection Regulation: still a sound system for the protection of individuals?', 32(2) *Computer Law & Security Review*, 179–94

De Mooy, M. (2017) *Rethinking Privacy Self-Management and Data Sovereignty in the Age of Big Data* (Bertelsmann Stiftung)

De Roure, C., Pelizzon, L. and Tasca, P. (2016) 'How does P2P lending fit into the consumer credit market?', *Deutsche Bundesbank Discussion Paper no. 30*

de Silva, A. J. et al. (2015) 'The residential mortgage (de)regulation–innovation nexus', *Munich Personal RePec Archive MPRA, Working Paper no. 62549* (November)

Deaton, A. (1992) *Understanding Consumption* (Oxford University Press)

DeCew, J. W. (1997) *In Pursuit of Privacy: Law, Ethics, and the Rise of Technology* (Cornell University Press)

Del Rio, A. and Young, G. (2006) 'The determinants of unsecured borrowing: evidence from the British Household Panel Survey', 15 *Applied Financial Economics*, 1119–44

Demirgüç-Kunt, A. and Huizinga, H. (2000) 'Financial structure and bank profitability', *Policy Research Working Paper Series 2430*, World Bank

Department of Trade and Industry (2003) *Fair, Clear and Competitive, the Consumer Credit Market in the 21st Century*, White Paper

Desai, S. and Meekings, J. (2016) 'Small business loans through funding circle boost UK economy by £2.7 billion', *Centre for Economics and Business Research*

Desai, V. et al. (1997) 'Credit scoring models in the credit union improvement using neural networks and genetic algorithms', 8 *IMA Journal Mathematics Applied in Business and Industry*, 323–46

Deutch, S. (1994) 'Are consumer rights, human rights?', 32 *Osgoode Hall Law Journal*, 537–78

Diamond, D. (1991) 'Monitoring and reputation: the choice between bank loans and directly placed debt', 99(4) *Journal of Political Economy*, 689–721

Diamond, D. and Vartiainen, H. (eds.) (2007) *Introduction to Behavioural Economics and Its Applications* (Princeton University Press)

Disney, R. and Gathergood, J. (2013) 'Financial literacy and consumer credit portfolios', 37 *Journal of Banking & Finance*, 2246–54

Dittmar, H. and Bond, R. (2010) '"I want it and I want it now": using a temporal discounting paradigm to examine predictors of consumer impulsivity', 101 *British Journal of Psychology*, 751–76

Dominy, N. and Kempson, K. (2003) *Can't Pay or Won't Pay? A Review of Creditor and Debtor Approaches to the Non-Payment of Bills* (DCA)

Domurath, I. (2017) *Consumer Vulnerability and Welfare in Mortgage Contracts* (Hart)
Domurath, I., Comparato, G. and Micklitz, H.-W. (eds.) (2014) 'The over-indebtedness of European consumers – a view from six countries', *EUI Working Paper Law 2014/10*)
Drentea, P. and Reynolds, J. R. (2012) 'Neither a borrower nor a lender be: the relative importance of debt and SES for mental health among older adults', 24 *Journal of Aging and Health*, 673–95
Duffy, I. P. H. (1985) *Bankruptcy and Insolvency in London During the Industrial Revolution* (Garland)
Duygan, B. and Grant, C. (2008) 'Household debt repayment behaviour: what role do institutions play?', *FRB of Boston Quantitative Analysis Unit, Working Paper, no. 3*
Dynan, B. and Kohn, G. (2007) 'The rise in U.S. household Indebtedness: causes and consequences', *Board of Governors International Finance Discussion Paper no. 37*
Economist, The (2015) *The Bank in Your Pocket* (9 May)
ECRI Statistical Package (2017) *Lending to households and non-financial corporations in Europe, 1995–2016*
Elliott, A. (2005) *Not Waving But Drowning: Over-Indebtedness by Misjudgment* (CSFI)
Engel, K. C. and McCoy, P. A. (2011) *The Subprime Virus* (Oxford University Press)
Equality and Human Rights Commission (2015) *Is Britain Fairer?*
Eurofinas (2017) *Annual Report*
Europe Economics (2009) *Study on Credit Intermediaries in the Internal Market*, MARKT/2007/14/H (Brussels), at http://ec.europa.eu/finance/finservices-retail/docs/credit/credit_intermediaries_report_en.pdf
European Banking Association (2017) 'EBA's approach to financial technology', *EBA Discussion Paper no. 2*
European Banking Authority (2013) *Opinion of the European Banking Authority on Good Practices for Responsible Mortgage Lending* (London, 13 June)
  (2014a) *Consultation Paper on Draft Guidelines on Arrears and Foreclosure* EBA/CP/2014/43 (London, 12 December)
  (2014b) *Results of the 2014 EU-wide Stress Test* (London, 26 October)
  (2015a) 'EBA guidelines on creditworthiness assessment' *Final Report on Guidelines on Creditworthiness Assessment* (London, 19 August)
  (2015b) *Final Report. Guidelines on creditworthiness assessment*, EBA/GL/2015/11 (London, 1 June)
  (2016) *Discussion Paper on Innovative Uses of Consumer Data by Financial Institutions* (London, 4 May)
  (2017) *Discussion Paper on the EBA's Approach to Financial Technology*
European Central Bank (2005) *Banking Structures in the New EU Member States*, at www.ecb.europa.eu/pub/pdf/other/bankingstructuresnewmemberstatesen.pdf
  (2010) *Memorandum of Understanding on the Exchange of Information Among National Central Credit Registers for the Purpose of Passing It on to Reporting Institutions* (April)
  (2011) *Annual Report*
  (2017) *Manual on MFI Interest Rate Statistics* (January)
  (2018) *Supervisory Banking Statistics*
European Commission (2008) *Towards a Common Operational European Definition of Over-Indebtedness* (Brussels)
  (2009) *Report of the Expert Group on Credit Histories* (Brussels)
European Economic and Social Committee (2014a) *Financial education for all*
  (2014b) *Opinion of the Economic and Social Committee on 'Household over-indebtedness'*
  (2002/c 149/01); *Opinion of the Economic and Social Committee on 'Consumer protection*

and appropriate treatment of over-indebtedness to prevent social exclusion' (*Exploratory opinion*), INT/726 (Brussels, 29 April)
European Parliament (2011) *Responsible Lending – Barriers to Competition*, DG For Internal Policies, Economic and Monetary Affairs, IP/A/ECON/ST/2011–05, Brussels: European Parliament (Brussels, June)
Fabbri, D. and Padula, M. (2004) 'Do poor legal enforcement make households credit constrained?', 28 *Journal of Banking and Finance*, 2369–97
Fairweather, K. (2012) 'The development of responsible lending in the UK consumer credit regime', in J. Devenney and M. Kenny (eds.), *Consumer Credit, Debt and Investment in Europe* (Cambridge University Press), 84–110
Farkas, B. (2012) 'The impact of the global economic crisis in the old and new cohesion member states of the European Union', 57(1) *Public Finance Quarterly*, 53–70
Fernandes, D., Lynch, L. G. and Netemeyer, R. (2014) 'Financial literacy, financial education and downstream financial behaviors', 60 *Management Science*, 1861–83
Ferretti, F. (2008) *The Law and Consumer Credit Reporting Systems in the EC* (Routledge-Cavendish)
  (2009) 'The "credit scoring pandemic" and the European vaccine: making sense of EU data protection legislation', 1 *Journal of Information Law and Technology*, 1–24, at http://go.warwick.ac.uk/jilt/2009_1/ferretti
  (2010) 'A European perspective on consumer loans and the role of credit registries: the need to reconcile data protection, risk management, efficiency, over-indebtedness, and a better prudential supervision of the financial system', 33(1) *Journal of Consumer Policy*, 1–27
  (2014) *EU Competition Law, the Consumer Interest and Data Protection* (Springer)
Ferretti, F. and Livada, C. (2016) 'The over-indebtedness of European consumers under EU policy and law', in F. Ferretti (ed.), *Comparative Perspectives of Consumer Over-Indebtedness – A View from the UK, Germany, Greece and Italy* (Eleven), 11–39
Ferretti, F., Salomone, R., Sutschet, H. and Tsiafoutis, V. (2016) 'The regulatory framework of consumer over-indebtedness in the UK, Germany, Italy, and Greece: comparative profiles of responsible credit and personal insolvency law', 37(2–3) *Business Law Review*, 64–71 (pt I) and 86–93 (pt II)
Ferri, G. and Simon, P. (2010) 'Constrained consumer lending: methods using the survey of consumer finances', *Università di Bari*, Working Paper
Financial Inclusion Centre (2018) 'FinTech – beware of the "geeks" bearing gifts?', a Financial Inclusion Centre Discussion Paper (January)
Financial Services Authority (2010) *Mortgage Market Review: Responsible Lending*
Financial Services User Group (FSUG) (2015) *Assessing the Impact of Credit Data on Preventing Over-Indebtedness, Contributing to Prudential Regulation and Facilitating Access to Affordable and Quality Credit*, at http://ec.europa.eu/finance/finservices-retail/docs/fsug/papers/1512-credit-data_en.pdf
Financial Stability Board (2012) *Principles for Sound Residential Mortgage Underwriting Practices*
Financial Stability Board and Bank for International Settlements (2017) 'FinTech credit', *Report prepared by a Working Group established by the Committee on the Global Financial System and the Financial Stability Board* (22 May)
FinCoNet (2014) *FinCoNet Report on Responsible Lending – Review of Supervisory Tools for Suitable Consumer Lending Practices* (July)
Finlay, S. (2009) *Consumer Credit Fundamentals* (Palgrave Macmillan)
Fletcher, I. (1978) *Law of Bankruptcy* (Macdonald & Evans)

Fractal Analytics (2003) *Comparative Analysis of Classification Techniques, A Fractal White Paper* (September)
Frank R. (1998) *Passions within Reason* (Norton)
Franken, I. H., Van Strien, J. W., Nijs, I. and Muris, P. (2008) 'Impulsivity is associated with behavioral decision-making deficits', 158(2) *Psychiatry Research*, 155–63
Fried, C. (1970) *An Anatomy of Values* (Harvard University Press)
Garante per la Protezione dei Dati Personali (2004) *Balancing of Interests: Data Collection by CRAs without Consent* (Rome, 16 November)
Garcia Porras, C. I. and Van Boom, W. H. (2012) 'Information disclosure in the EU Consumer Credit Directive: opportunities and limitations', in J. Devenney and M. Kenny (eds.), *Consumer Credit, Debt and Investment in Europe* (Cambridge University Press), 21–55
Gathergood, J. (2012) 'Self-control, financial literacy and consumer over indebtedness', 33 *Journal of Economic Psychology*, 590–602
Gathergood, J. and Weber, J. (2017) 'Financial literacy, present bias and alternative mortgage products', 78 *Journal of Banking and Finance*, 58–83
Gavison, R. (1980) 'Privacy and the Limits of the Law', 89 *Yale Law Journal*, 421–71
Gellert, R. (2015) 'Data protection: a risk regulation? Between the risk management of everything and the precautionary alternative', 5 *International Data Privacy Law*, 3–19
Gelpi, R. and Julien-Labruyère, F. (2000) *The History of Consumer Credit* (Macmillan)
Gerhardt, M. (2009) 'Consumer bankruptcy regimes in the US and Europe. Further effects and implications of the crisis' CEPS Working Document no. 318 (July)
Gerstein, R. S. (1978) 'Intimacy and privacy', 89 *Ethics*, 76–81
Gerstenberg, O. (2015) 'Constitutional reasoning in private law: the role of the CJEU in adjudicating unfair terms in consumer contracts', 21(5) *European Law Journal*, 599–621
Giannetti, C., Jentzsch, N. and Spagnolo, G. (2010) *Information-Sharing and Cross-Border Entry in European Banking*, ECRI Research Report no. 11 (Brussels, February)
Glorfeld, L. W. and Hardgrave, B. C. (1996) 'An improved method for developing neural networks: the case of evaluating commercial loan creditworthiness', 23(10) *Computer Operation Research*, 933–44
Gortsos, C. (2008) 'MiFID's investor protection regime: best execution of client orders and related conduct of business rules', in E. Avgouleas (ed.), *The Regulation of Investment Services in Europe under MiFID: Implementation and Practice* (Tottel)
  (2016) 'Financial inclusion: an overview of its various dimensions and the initiatives to enhance its current level' ECEFIL Working Paper Series no. 2016/15, at http://ssrn.com/abstract=2715625
Graeber, D. (2011) *Debt – The First 5,000 Years* (Melville House)
Grant, C. (2003) 'Estimating credit constraints among US households', European University Institute Working Paper (Florence)
Green, M. (2009) 'New Labour: more debt – the political response', in J. Niemi, I. Ramsay and W. C. Whitford (eds.), *Consumer Credit, Debt & Bankruptcy – Comparative and International Perspectives* (Hart), 393–418
Group of Specialists on Seeking Legal Solutions to Debt Problems (Cj-S-Debt) (2007) *Final Activity Report of the Group of Specialists for Legal Solutions to Debt Problems (CJ-S-DEBT)*, CJ-S-DEBT (2006) 6 Final (Strasbourg, 18 January)
G20/OECD Task Force on Financial Consumer Protection (2014) *Effective Approaches to Support the Implementation of the Remaining G20/OECD High-Level Principles on Financial Consumer Protection* (September)
Gutwirth, S., Leenes, R. and De Hert, P. (eds.) (2016) *Data Protection on the Move* (Springer)

Guzelian, C. P., Stein, M. A. and Akiskal, H. S. (2015) 'Credit scores, lending, and psycho-social disability', 95 *Boston University Law Review*, 1807–68

Haffner, M. et al. (2015) 'Mortgage equity withdrawal and institutional settings: an exploratory analysis of six countries', 15(3) *International Journal of Housing Policy*, 235–59

Handzic, M. (2003) 'How neural networks can help loan officers to make better informed application decisions', Informing Science, 97–109

Hansen, J. and Kysar, D. (1999) 'Taking behaviouralism seriously: the problem of market manipulation', 74 *New York University Law Review*, 630–749

Harvey, D. (2005) *A Brief History of Neoliberalism* (Oxford University Press)

Heidhues, P. and Koszegi, B. (2010) 'Exploiting naivete about self-control in the credit market', 100 *American Economic Review*, 2279–303

Heisenberg, D. (2005) *Negotiating Privacy* (Lynne Rienner)

Hendricks, E. (2004) *Credit Scores & Credit Reports – How the System Really Works* (Privacy Times)

Henegar, J. M. et al. (2013) 'Credit card behavior as a function of impulsivity and mother's socialization factors', 24 *Journal of Financial Counseling and Planning*, 37–49

Herrala, R. and Kauko, K. (2007) 'Household loan loss risks in Finland – estimation and simulations with micro data', *Bank of Finland Research Discussion Papers no. 5*

Heuer, J.-O. (2013) Social Inclusion and Exclusion in European Consumer Bankruptcy Systems, *Paper for the conference Shift to Post-Crisis Welfare States in Europe? Long Term and Short Term Perspectives* (Berlin, 4–5 June)

Hlavac, P. et al. (2013) 'Household stress tests using micro data', *Czech National Bank, Financial Stability Report*

HM Treasury (2014) *Improving Access to SME Credit Data: Summary of Responses* (June), at www.gov.uk/government/uploads/system/uploads/attachment_data/file/323318/PU1681_final.pdf

Hoermann, G. (ed.) (1986) *Consumer Credit and Consumer Insolvency: Perspectives for Legal Policy from Europe and the USA* (ZERP)

Hojman, D. A., Miranda, A. and Ruiz-Tagle, J. (2016) 'Debt trajectories and mental health', 167 *Social Science and Medicine*, 54–62

House of Commons (2017) 'Household debt: statistics and impact on the economy', *Briefing Paper no. 7584* (27 April)

Howells, G. G. (1995) 'Data protection, confidentiality, unfair contract terms, consumer protection and credit reference agencies', 4 *Journal of Business Law*, 343–59

  (2005) 'The potential and limits of consumer empowerment by information', 32 *Journal of Law and Society*, 349–70

Howells, G. G. and Weatherill, S. (2005) *Consumer Protection Law* (Ashgate)

Huls, N. (1993) 'Towards a European approach to overindebtedness of consumers', 16 *Journal of Consumer Policy*, 215–34

Huls, N., Reifner, U. and Bourgoinie, T. (1994) *Overindebtedness of Consumers in the EC Member States: Facts and Search for Solutions* (Kluwer)

Hung, A. and Yoong, J. (2010) *Asking for Help: Survey and Experimental Evidence on Financial Advice and Behavior Change* (RAND)

Hurley, M. and Adebayo, J. (2016) 'Credit scoring in the era of big data', 18 *Yale Journal of Law and Technology*, 1–69

Huston, S. J. (2010) 'Measuring financial literacy', 44(2) *Journal of Consumer Affairs*, 296–316

Information Commissioner Office (2006) *Credit Agreements – Data Sharing* (6 November), at www.ico.org.uk/for_organisations/sector_guides/~/media/documents/library/Data_Protection/Practical_application/CREDIT_%20AGREEMENTS%20-%20DATA_%20SHARING.ashx

Inness, J. C. (1992) *Privacy, Intimacy, and Isolation* (Oxford University Press)
INSOL Europe (2010) *Harmonisation of Insolvency Law at EU level* (European Parliament, Directorate General for Internal Policies, Policy Department C: Citizens' Rights and Constitutional Affairs)
International Monetary Fund (2012a) 'Dealing with household debt', *World Economic Outlook* (Washington, DC)
  (2012b) 'Spain: vulnerabilities of private sector balance sheets and risks to the financial sector technical notes', *IMF country Report no. 12/140* (Washington, DC)
  (2013) *Annual Report* (Washington, DC)
  (2017) *FinTech and financial services: initial considerations* (Washington, DC)
Israël, J. (2005) *European Cross-Border Insolvency Regulation* (Intersentia)
IVASS (2016) *PPI – Thematic Review on Policies Linked to Loans: Premiums, Loading and Commissions*
Jappelli, T. and Pagano, M. (2000) 'Information sharing in credit markets: the European experience', *Working Paper no. 35, Centres for Studies in Economics and Finance* (University of Salerno)
  (2002) 'Information sharing, lending and defaults: cross-country evidence', 26(10) *Journal of Banking and Finance*, 2017–45
  (2003) 'Public credit information: a European perspective', in M. Miller (ed.), *Reporting Systems and the International Economy* (MIT Press), 81–114
  (2006) 'The role and effects of credit information sharing', in G. Bertola, R. Disney, and C. Grant (eds.), *The Economics of Consumer Credit* (MIT Press), 347–71
Jensen, H. L. (1992) 'Using neural networks for credit scoring', 18(6) *Managerial Finance*, 15–26
Jentzsch, N. (2003) 'The regulation of financial privacy: the United States vs. Europe', *ECRI Research Report no. 5* (June)
  (2006) *The Economics and Regulation of Financial Privacy* (Physica-Verlag)
  (2007) *Financial Privacy – An International Comparison of Credit Reporting Systems* (Springer)
Jiang, S. S. and Dunn, L. F. (2013) 'New evidence on credit card borrowing and repayment patterns', 51 *Economic Inquiry*, 394–407
Johnson, J. L. (1994) 'Constitutional privacy', 13 *Law and Philosophy*, 161–93
Joint Committee of the European Supervisory Authorities (2016), *Joint Committee Discussion Paper on the Use of Big Data by Financial Institutions JC 2016 86* (19 December)
Jolls, C., Sunstein, C. R. and Thaler, R. (1998) 'A behavioral approach to law and economics', 50 *Stanford Law Review*, 1471–1550
Jones, W. J. (1979) 'The foundations of English bankruptcy: statutes and commissions in the early modern period', 69(3) *Transactions of the American Philosophical Society*, 1–63
Jones, M. A., Reynolds, K. E., Weun, S. and Beatty, S. E. (2003) 'The product-specific nature of impulse buying tendency', 56 *Journal of Business Research*, 505–11
Józon, M. (2017) 'Unfair contract *terms* law in Europe in time of crisis: substantive justice lost in the paradise of proceduralisation of contract fairness', 4 *Journal of European Consumer and Market Law*, 157–66
Kamleitner, B., Hoelzl, E. and Kirchler, E. (2012) 'Credit use: psychological perspectives on a multifaceted phenomenon', 47 *International Journal of Psychology*, 1–27
Kang, J. and Bunter, B. (2004) 'Privacy in Atlantis', 18 *Harvard Journal of Law and Technology*, 230–67
Kant, I. (1785) *Groundwork of the Metaphysics of Morals* [*Grundlegung zur Metaphysik der Sitten*]

Karacimen, E. (2017) 'Financialization in Turkey: the case of consumer debt', 16(2) *Journal of Balkan and Near Eastern Studies*, 161–80
Karlsson, N. et al. (2004) 'Household consumption: influences of aspiration level, social comparison and money management', 25 *Journal of Economic Psychology*, 753–69.
Katsas, T. G. (2016) 'Key elements of the Greek legal framework on insolvency of natural persons', in F. Ferretti (ed.), *Comparative Perspectives of Consumer Over-Indebtedness – A View from the UK, Germany, Greece and Italy* (Eleven), 259–70
Keese, M. (2008) 'Who feels constrained by high debt burdens? Subjective vs objective measures of household debt', 33 *Journal of Economic Psychology*, 125–41.
Kelemen, R. D. (2012) *The Transformation of Law and Regulation in the European Union* (Harvard University Press)
Kempson, E. (2002) *Over-Indebtedness in Britain: A Report to the Department of Trade and Industry* (London, DTI)
Kenyon, A. T. and Richardson, M. (2006) 'New dimensions in privacy: communications technologies, media practices and law', in A. T. Kenyon and M. Richardson (eds.), *New Dimensions in Privacy Law* (Cambridge University Press), 1–10
Keys, B. J. et al. (2008) 'Did securitization lead to lax screening? Evidence from subprime loans', *Working Paper prepared for the European Finance Association*
Khan, H. H. H., Abdullah, H. and Samsudin, S. (2016) 'Modelling, the determinants of Malaysian household debt', 6(4) *International Journal of Economics and Financial Issues*, 1468–73
Kilborn, J. (2005) 'Behavioural economics, overindebtedness and comparative consumer bankruptcy: searching for causes and evaluating solutions', 22 *Bankruptcy Development Journal*, 13–46
  (2009) 'Two decades, three key questions, and evolving answers in European consumer insolvency law. Responsibility, discretion, and sacrifice', in J. Niemi, I. Ramsay and W. C. Whitford (eds.), *Consumer Credit, Debt & Bankruptcy – Comparative and International Perspectives* (Hart), 307–29
  (2010) *Expert Recommendations and the Evolution of European Best Practices for the Treatment of Overindebtedness, 1984–2010* (August), at SSRN: http://ssrn.com/abstract=1663108 or http://dx.doi.org/10.2139/ssrn.1663108
Klein, D. B. (1992) 'Promise keeping in great society: a model of credit information sharing', 4 (2) *Economics and Politics*, 117–36
  (1997), 'Promise keeping in the great society: a model of credit information sharing', in D. B. Klein (ed.), *Reputation: Studies in the Voluntary Elicitation of Good Conduct* (University of Michigan Press), 267–88
Kolenikov, S. and Angeles, G. (2004) 'The use of discrete data in principal component analysis: theory, simulations, and applications to socioeconomic indices', Proceedings of the American Statistical Association
Kondgen, J. (2011) 'Policy responses to the credit crises: does the law of contract provide an answer?', in S. Grundmann and Y. M. Atamer (eds.), *Financial Services, Financial Crisis and General European Contract Law* (Kluwer), 35–59
Koyama, Y. (2010) 'Economic crisis in new EU Member States in Central and Eastern Europe: focusing on Baltic States', 5(3) *Romanian Economic and Business Review*, 31–55
KPMG (2017) *The Pulse of FinTech*
La Porta, R. et al. (1998) 'Law and finance', 106(6) *Journal of Political Economy*, 1113–55
Landau, D. (2016) 'Artificial intelligence and machine learning: how computers learn', *Tech Innovation* (17 August), at https://iq.intel.com/artificial-intelligence-and-machine-learning

Lastra, R. M. (1996) *Central Banking and Banking Regulation* (Financial Markets Group LSE)
Lastra, R. M. and Shams, H. (2001) 'Public accountability in the financial sector', in E. Ferran and C. A. E. Goodhart (eds.), *Regulating Financial Services and Markets in the Twenty First Century* (Hart), 165–88
Lea, S. *Behaviour Change: Personal Debt* [British Psychological Society, no date], at www.bps.org.uk/behaviourchange
Lea, S. and Webley, P. (1995) 'Psychological factors in consumer debt: money management, economic socialization and credit use', 16 *Journal of Economic Psychology*, 681–701
Leimgruber, J., Meier, A. and Backus, J. (2017) 'Decentralized credit scoring powered by Ethereum and IPFS', *Bloom Protocol* (4 September)
Lester, V. M. (1995) *Victorian Insolvency* (Clarendon Press)
Limerick, L. and Peltier, J. W. (2014) 'The effects of self-control failures on risky credit card usage', 24 *Marketing Management Journal*, 149–61
Linna, T. (2014) 'Cross-border debt adjustment – open questions in European insolvency proceedings', 23 *International Insolvency Review*, 20–39
Liu, Y. and Rosenberg, C. (2013) 'Dealing with private debt distress in the wake of the European financial crisis – a review of the economics and legal toolbox', *IMF Working Paper* WP/13/44
Livada, C. (2016) 'The Greek regulatory framework on responsible lending', F. Ferretti (ed.), *Comparative Perspectives of Consumer Over-Indebtedness – A View from the UK, Germany, Greece and Italy* (Eleven), 247–58
London Economics (2012) *Study on means to protect consumers in financial difficulty: Personal bankruptcy, datio in solutum of mortgages, and restrictions on debt collection abusive practices*, Final Report prepared for the Financial Services User Group, Contract No. MARKT/2011/023/B2/ST/FC (December)
Loos, M. (2010) 'Full harmonisation as a regulatory concept and its consequences for the national legal orders: the example of the Consumer Rights Directive', Centre for the Study of European Contract Law Working Paper Series No. 2010/03 (July), at http://ssrn.com/abstract=1639436 or http://dx.doi.org/10.2139/ssrn.1639436
Lusardi, A. and Tufano, P. (2015) 'Debt literacy, financial experiences, and overindebtedness', 14 *Journal of Pension Economics and Finance*, 332–68
Lynskey, O. (2015) *The Foundations of EU Data Protection Law* (Oxford University Press)
McAteer, M. and Beddows, S. (2014) *Fixing a Broken Market* (Report for Association of Chartered Certified Accountants)
McCall, M., Trombetta, J. and Gipe, A. (2004) 'Credit cues and impression management: a preliminary attempt to explain the credit card effect', 95 *Psychological Reports*, 331–7
McCormack, G., Keay, A. and Brown, S. (2017) *European Insolvency Law – Reform and Harmonisation* (Edward Elgar)
McIntyre, S. G. (2017) 'Personal indebtedness, community characteristics and theft crimes', 54 *Urban Studies*, 2395–419
McKinsey (2015) *Global Banking Annual Review*
McMeel, G. (2009) 'Investment firms – retail sector', in M. Blair et al. (eds.), *Financial Services Law* (Oxford University Press), 637–80
Magri, S. (2007) 'Italian households' debt: determinant of demand and supply', 33(3) *Empirical Economics*, 401–26.
Magri, S., Pico, R. and Rampazzi, C. (2011) 'Which households use consumer credit in Europe?', 100 *Questioni di Economia e Finanza* [occasional papers]
Malloy, R. P. (2004) *Law in a Market Context: An Introduction to Market Concepts in Legal Reasoning* (Cambridge University Press).

Mann, R. J. (2007) 'Bankruptcy reform and the "sweatbox" of credit card debt', 1 *University of Illinois Law Review*, 375–403

Martin, L. E. and Potts, G. F. (2009) 'Impulsivity in decision-making: an event-related potential investigation', 46 *Personality and Individual Differences*, 303–8

May, O., Tudela, M. and Young, G. (2004) 'British household indebtedness and financial stress: a household-level picture', *Bank of England, Quarterly Bulletin*

Mayer-Schonberger, V. (1997) 'Generational development of data protection in Europe', in E. Agre and M. Rotenberg (eds.), *Technology and Privacy: The New Landscape* (MIT Press, 1997), 219–41

Meier, S. and Sprenger, C. (2010) 'Present-biased preferences and credit card borrowing', 2(1) *American Economic Journal: Applied Economics*, 193–201.

(2013) 'Discounting financial literacy: time preferences and participation in financial education programs', 95 *Journal of Economic Behavior & Organization*, 159–74

Meltzer, H. et al. (2011) 'Personal debt and suicidal ideation', 41 *Psychological Medicine*, 771–8

Meng, X., Hoang, N. T. and Siriwardana, M. (2013) 'The determinants of Australian household debt: a macro level study', 29 *Journal of Asian Economics*, 80–90

Mentis, G. (2012) *Defense and Release of the Over-Indebted Debtor* (Dikaio kai Oikonomia P. N. Sakkoulas)

(2016) 'The dimensions of the crisis and the response of Greek private law – a general overview', in F. Ferretti (ed.), *Comparative Perspectives of Consumer Over-Indebtedness – A View from the UK, Germany, Greece and Italy* (Eleven), 227–34

Mester, L. J. (1997) 'What's the point of credit scoring?', Business Review Federal Reserve Bank of Philadelphia (September/October).

Metz, R. (2012) 'Scoring: new legislation in Germany', 35(3) *Journal of Consumer Policy*, 297–305

Micklitz, H.-W. (2012a) 'The regulation of over-indebtedness of consumers in Europe', 35(4) *Journal of Consumer Policy*, 417–19

(2012b) 'Do consumers and businesses need a new architecture of consumer law? A thought-provoking impulse', *EUI Working Papers Law 2012/23*

(2013b) 'Unfair contract terms – public interest litigation before European Courts case C-415/11 Mohamed Aziz', in E. Terryn et al. (eds.), *Landmark Cases of EU Consumer Law – In Honour of Jules Stuyck* (Intersentia), 633–52

(2013a) 'Access to, and exclusion of, European consumers from financial markets after the global financial crisis', in T. Wilson (ed.), *International Responses to Issues of Credit and Over-Indebtedness* (Ashgate), 47–77

(2015) 'Conclusions: consumer over-indebtedness and consumer insolvency – from micro to macro', in H.-W. Micklitz and I. Domurath (eds.), *Consumer Debt and Social Exclusion in Europe* (Ashgate), 229–35

Micklitz, H.-W. and Reich, N. (2014) 'The court and Sleeping Beauty: the revival of the Unfair Contract Terms Directive (UCTD)', 51(3) *Common Market Law Review*, 771–808

Mierzwinski, E. and Chester, J. (2013) 'Selling consumers not lists: the new world of digital decision-making and the role of the Fair Credit Reporting Act', 46(3) *Suffolk University Law Review*, 845–80

Miller, M. (2003a) 'Introduction', in M. Miller (ed.), *Reporting Systems and the International Economy* (MIT Press), 1–23

(2003b) 'Credit reporting systems around the globe: the state of the art in public credit registry and private credit reporting firms', in M. Miller (ed.), *Reporting Systems and the International Economy* (MIT Press), 25–79

Mills, A. (2009) *The Confluence of Public and Private International Law* (Cambridge University Press)

Modigliani, F. and Brumberg, R. (1954) 'Utility analysis and the consumption function: an interpretation of cross-section data', in K. K. Kurihana (eds.), *Post-Keynesian Economics* (Rutgers University Press), 388–438
Molloy, T. (2004) 'Fraud in the cross-hairs', 17(3) *Compliance Monitor*, 1
Moloney, N. (2008) *EC Securities Regulation* (Oxford University Press)
Molyneux, P. and Thornton, J. (1992) 'Determinants of European bank profitability: a note', 16 *Journal of Banking and Finance*, 1173–8
Money Advice Service (2016) *A Picture of Over-Indebtedness*
Montgomerie, J. (2013) 'America's debt safety-net', 91 *Public Administration*, 871–88
Moore, A. D. (1998) 'Intangible property: privacy, power, and information control', 35 *American Philosophical Quarterly*, 365–78
Moore, D. L. (2003) 'Survey of financial literacy in Washington State: knowledge, behavior, attitudes, and experiences', *Technical Report 03–39, Social and Economic Sciences Research Center* (Washington State University)
Morgan, B. (2006) 'The North–South politics of necessity: regulating for basic rights between national and international levels', 29 *Journal of Consumer Policy*, 465–87
Morse, A. (2015) 'Peer-to-peer crowdfunding: information and the potential for disruption in consumer lending', *NBER Working Paper*
Moulton, S., Loibl, C. and Haurin, D. (2017) 'Reverse mortgage motivations and outcomes: insights from survey data', 19(1) *Cityscape*, 73–97
Mouzouraki, M. J. (2016) '(Failure to set up an efficient) out of court system to deal with debtors in financial distress in Greece', in F. Ferretti (ed.), *Comparative Perspectives of Consumer Over-Indebtedness – A View from the UK, Germany, Greece and Italy* (Eleven), 235–46
Murphy, K. P. (2012) *Machine Learning: A Probabilistic Perspective* (MIT Press)
Nield, S. (2010) 'Responsible lending and borrowing: whereto low-cost home ownership?', 30 (4) *Legal Studies*, 610–32
  (2012) 'Mortgage finance: who's responsible?', in J. Devenney and M. Kenny (eds.), *Consumer Credit, Debt and Investment in Europe* (Cambridge University Press), 160–81
Niemi, J. (1999) 'Consumer bankruptcy in comparison: do we cure a market failure or a social problem?', 37 *Osgoode Hall Law Journal*, 473–503
  (2012) 'Consumer insolvency in the European legal context', 35 *Journal of Consumer Policy*, 443–59
  'Overindebted households and law: prevention and rehabilitation in Europe', in J. Niemi, I. Ramsay and W. C. Whitford (eds.), *Consumer Credit, Debt & Bankruptcy – Comparative and International Perspectives* (Hart), 91–104
Nogler, L. and Reifner, U. (eds.) (2014) *Life Time Contracts* (Eleven)
Observatoire des crédits aux ménages (2008) *Rapport d'activité FBF* (Paris)
  (2009) *Rapport d'activité FBF* (Paris)
OCR Macro (2001) *Study of the Problem of Consumer Indebtedness: Statistical Aspects*, Report submitted to the Commission of the EU DG Health and Consumer Protection, Contract No. B5-1000/00/000197 (October)
Odudu, O. (2011) 'Indirect information exchange: the constituent elements of hub and spoke collusion', 7(2) *European Competition Journal*, 205–42
OECD (2011) *G-20, High-Level Principles on Financial Consumer Protection* (OECD Publishing, October)
  (2014) 'Household debt', in *OECD Factbook 2014: Economic, Environmental and Social Statistics* (OECD Publishing), at http://dx.doi.org/10.1787/factbook-2014-27-en

(2016) *Financial Education in Europe: Trends and Recent Developments* (OECD Publishing)

(2017) *G20/OECD INFE Report on Ensuring Financial Education and Consumer Protection in the Digital Age* (OECD Publishing)

OEE Etudes (2008) *Towards a Common European Operational Definition of Over-Indebtedness*, Report prepared for the use of the European Commission, Directorate-General for Employment, Social Affairs and Equal Opportunities (February)

Office of Fair Trading (2010) *Consumer Credit Licensing: General Guidance for Licensees and Applicants on Fitness and Requirements* (London)

(2011) *Irresponsible Lending – OFT Guidance for Creditors* (March 2010, updated February)

Oksanen, A., Aaltonene, M. and Rantala, K. (2015) 'Social determinants of debt problems in a Nordic welfare state: a Finnish register-based study', 38 *Journal of Consumer Policy*, 229: 246

Olegario, R. (2003) 'Credit reporting agencies: a historical perspective', in M. J. Miller (ed.), *Reporting Systems and the International Economy* (MIT Press), 115–59

Omar, N. A. et al. (2014) 'Compulsive buying and credit card misuse among credit card holders: the roles of self-esteem, materialism, impulsive buying and budget constraints', 10(1) *Intangible Capital*, 52–74

Ong, R. et al. (2013), 'Channels from housing wealth to consumption', 28(7) *Housing Studies*, 1012–36

Osovsky, A. (2013) 'The misconception of the consumer as a *homo economicus*: a behavioral–economic approach to consumer protection in the credit-reporting system', 46(3) *Suffolk University Law Review*, 881–933

Ottaviani, C. and Vandone, D. (2011) 'Impulsivity and household indebtedness: evidence from real life', 32 *Journal of Economic Psychology*, 754–61

(2018) 'Financial literacy, debt burden, and impulsivity: a mediation analysis', 46 *Economic Notes*, 439–54

Packin, N. G. and Aretz, L. (2016) 'On social credit and the right to be unnetworked', 2 *Columbia Business Law Review*, 339–425

Pagano, M. and Jappelli, T. (1993) 'Information sharing in credit markets', 48(5) *Journal of Finance*, 1693–718

Papastamou and Spyrakos (2013)*The amendments of Law 3869/2010 about the over-indebted individuals' debt settlement by Law 4161/2013* (NoB)

Parent, W. A. (1983) 'Privacy, morality and the law', 12 *Philosophy and Public Affairs*, 269–88

Pasquale, F. (2015) *The Black Box Society* (Harvard University Press)

Patel, A., Balmer, N. J. and Pleasence, P. (2012) 'Debt and disadvantages: the experience of unmanageable debt and financial difficulty in England and Wales', 36 *International Journal of Consumer Studies*, 556–65

Patton, J. H., Stanford, M. S. and Barratt, E. S. (1995) 'Factor structure of the Barratt impulsiveness scale', 51 *Journal of Clinical Psychology*, 768–74

Paul, J. et al. (eds.) (2000) *The Right of Privacy* (Cambridge University Press)

Pearson, G. (2008) 'Financial literacy and the creation of financial citizens, in the future of consumer credit regulation', in M. Kelly-Louw et al. (eds.), *The Future of Consumer Credit Regulation* (Ashgate), 3–28

Pennock, J. R. and Chapman, J. W. (eds.) (1971) *XIII – Privacy* (Nomos)

Peppet, S. R. (2011) 'Unraveling privacy: the personal prospectus and the threat of a full disclosure future', 105(3) *Northwestern University Law Review*, 1153–204

Pirog, S. F. and Roberts, J. A. (2007) 'Personality and credit card misuse among college students: the mediating role of impulsiveness', 15(1) *Journal of Marketing Theory and Practice*, 65–77

Posner, R. A. (1981) *The Economics of Justice* (Harvard University Press)
  (1995) 'contract law in the welfare state: a defense of the unconscionability doctrine, usury laws, and related limitations on the freedom to contract', 24 *Journal of Legal Studies*, 283–319
Pottow, J. A. E. (2007) 'Private liability for reckless consumer lending', 1 *University of Illinois Law Review*, 405–65
Potts, G. F. et al. (2006) 'Reduced punishment sensitivity in neural systems of behavior monitoring in impulsive individuals', 397 *Neuroscience Letters*, 130–4
Poulton, E. C. (1994) *Behavioural Decision Theory* (Cambridge University Press)
Preacher, K. J. and Hayes, A. F. (2008) 'Asymptotic and resampling strategies for assessing and comparing indirect effects in multiple mediator models', 40 *Behavior Research Methods*, 879–91
PricewaterhouseCoopers (2015) 'Is it time for consumer lending to go social?' (February), at www.pwc.lu/en/fintech/docs/pwc-fintech-time-for-consumer-lending-to-go-social.pdf
Psichomanis (2014) *Debt settlement of over-indebted individuals*
Putrova, N. (2014) 'Default entitlements in personal data in the proposed regulation: informational self-determination off the table ... and back on again', 30 *Computer Law and Security Review*, 6–24
Rachels, J. (1975) 'Why privacy is important', 4 *Philosophy and Public Affairs*, 323–33
Ramos, D. et al. (2016) 'Protecting mobile money customer funds in civil law jurisdictions', 65 *International and Comparative Law Quarterly*, 705–39
Ramsay, I. (1997) 'Models of consumer bankruptcy. Implications for research and policy', 20 (2) *Journal of Consumer Policy*, 269–87
  (2003) 'Bankruptcy in transition: the case of England and Wales – the neo-liberal cuckoo in the European bankruptcy nest?', in J. Niemi, I. Ramsay and W. C. Whitford (eds.), *Consumer Credit, Debt & Bankruptcy – Comparative and International Perspectives* (Hart), 205–26
  (2005) 'From truth in lending to responsible lending', in G. Howells et al. (eds.), *Information Rights and Obligations* (Ashgate), 47–65
  (2007a) *Consumer Law and Policy* (Hart)
  (2007b) 'Comparative consumer bankruptcy', 1 *University of Illinois Law Review*, 241–73
  (2010) 'Regulation of consumer credit', in G. Howells et al. (eds.), *Handbook of Research on International Consumer Law* (Edward Elgar), 366–408
  (2012a) 'Between neo-liberalism and the social market: approaches to debt adjustment and consumer insolvency in the EU', 35 *Journal of Consumer Policy*, 421–41
  (2012b) 'A tale of two debtors: responding to the shock of over-indebtedness in France and England – a story from the trente piteuses', 75(2) *Modern Law Review*, 212–48
  (2015) 'Two cheers for Europe: austerity, mortgage foreclosures and personal insolvency policy in the EU', in H.-W. Micklitz and I. Domurath (eds.), *Consumer Debt and Social Exclusion in Europe* (Ashgate), 189–227
  (2017) *Personal Insolvency in the 21st Century* (Hart)
Rasmussen, K. M. and Zenios, S. A. (2007) 'Well ARMed and FiRM: diversification of mortgage loans for homeowners', 10 *Journal of Risk*, 67–84
Regan, P. M. (1995) *Legislating Privacy* (University of North Carolina Press)
Reifner, U. et al. (2003)*Consumer Overindebtedness and Consumer Law in the European Union*, Final Report, Contract Ref. B5-1000/02/000353 (September)
Reisch, L. A. and Gwozdz, W. (2010) 'Financial cultures in Europe: similarities and differences', in H.-W. Micklitz (ed.), *Consumer Loans and the Role of Credit Bureaus in Europe* (EUI Working Papers RSCAS 2010/44), 1–3

Richards, N. M. and King, J. H. (2013) 'Three paradoxes of big data', 66 *Stanford Law Review Online*, 41–6
Riestra, A. S. J. (2002) 'Credit bureaus in today's credit markets', *ECRI Research Report no. 4* (Brussels, September)
Robb, C. (2011) 'Financial knowledge and credit card behavior of college students', 32 *Journal of Family and Economic Issues*, 690–8
Rook, D. W. (1987) 'The buying impulse', 14(2) *Journal of Consumer Research*, 189–99
Rott, P. (2014) 'Consumer credit', in N. Reich et al. (eds.), *European Consumer Law* (Intersentia), 197–238
Rouvroy, A. and Poullet, Y. (2009) 'The right to informational self-determination and the value of self-development: reassessing the importance of privacy for democracy', in S. Gutwirth et al. (eds.), *Reinventing Data Protection?* (Springer), 45–76
Rowlingson, K., Gardner, J. and Appleyard, L. (2016) 'Responsible lending in the UK: what role does the state play?', in F. Ferretti (ed.), *Comparative Perspectives of Consumer Over-Indebtedness – A View from the UK, Germany, Greece and Italy* (Eleven), 105–23
Russell, H., Whelan, C. T. and Maitre, B. (2013) 'Economic vulnerability and severity of debt problems: an analysis of the Irish EU–SILC 2008', 29 *European Sociological Review*, 695–706
Ryder, N., Griffiths, M. and Singh, L. (2012) *Commercial Law: Principles and Policy* (Cambridge University Press)
Salina, K. and Siti Rahayi, H. (2016) 'Do marketing strategies have significant influence on usage of credit cards? Empirical evidence from Malaysia', 24 *Journal of Social Sciences & Humanities*, 179–92
Sandage, S. A. (2005) *Born Losers: A History of Failure in America* (Harvard University Press)
Savage, M. (2015) *Social Class in the 21st Century* (Pelican)
Scanlon, T. (1975) 'Thomson on privacy', 4 *Philosophy and Public Affairs*, 323–33
Scharpf, F. W. (2002) 'The European social model: coping with the challenges of diversity', 40 *Journal of Common Market Studies*, 645–70
Schmidt, V. A. and Thatcher, M. (eds.) (2013) *Resilient Liberalism in Europe's Political Economy* (Cambridge University Press)
Schoeman, D. (ed.) (1984) *Philosophical Dimensions of Privacy: An Anthology* (Cambridge University Press)
Schooley, D. K., Drecnik, D. and Worden, D. D. (2010) 'Fueling the credit crisis: who uses consumer credit and what drives debt burden?', 45(4) *Business Economics*, 266–76
Schweitzer, M. E. and Barkley, B. (2017) 'Is fintech good for small business borrowers? Impacts on firm growth and customer satisfaction', *Federal Reserve Bank of Cleveland Working Paper*
Sealy, L. (2004) 'Publication review – consumer bankruptcy in global perspective', 63(2) *Cambridge Law Journal*, 518–20
Shen, H. and Ziderman, A. (2009) 'Student loans repayment and recovery: international comparisons', 57 *Higher Education*, 315–33
Shui, H. and Ausubel, L. M. (2004) 'Time inconsistency in the credit card market', *14th Annual Utah Winter Finance Conference*
Siemens, J. C. (2007) 'When consumption benefits precede costs: towards an understanding of "buy now, pay later" transactions', 20(5) *Journal of Behavioral Decision Making*, 521–31
Simitis, S. (1995) 'From the market to the polis: the EU Directive on the Protection of Personal Data', 80 *Iowa Law Review*, 445–69
Smith, A. (1976) *The Theory of Moral Sentiments (1759)* (Liberty Classics)
  (1981) *An Inquiry into the Nature and Causes of the Wealth of Nations (1776)* (Liberty Classics)

Spooner, J. (2013) 'Fresh start or stalemate? European consumer insolvency law reform and the politics of household debt', 3 *European Review of Private Law*, 747–94

Staten, M. and Cate, F. (2004) 'Does the Fair Credit Reporting Act promote accurate credit reporting?', *Working Paper Series BABC 04-14*, Joint Center for Housing Studies (Harvard University, February)

Stauder, B. and Favre-Bulle, X. (2004) *Droit de la consommation. Loi sur les voyages à forfait, Code des obligations, articles 40a–40f CO. Loi sur le crédit à la consommation. Commentaire* (Helbing Lichtenhahn)

Stiglitz, J. E. (2007) *Making Globalization Work* (Norton)

Stiglitz, J. E. and Weiss, A. (1981) 'Credit rationing in markets with imperfect information', 71 (3) *American Economic Review*, 393–410

Stromholm, S. (1967) *Right of Privacy and Rights of the Personality* (Norstedt)

Sugawara, N. and Zalduendo, J. (2011) 'Stress-testing Croatian households with debt implications for financial stability', *World Bank Policy Research, Working Paper no. 5906*

Sunstein, C. R. (2006) 'Boundedly rational borrowing', 73 *University of Chicago Law Review*, 249–70

Sutschet, H. (2016) 'An analysis of the German legal framework and the (limited) influence of EU law', in F. Ferretti (ed.), *Comparative Perspectives of Consumer Over-Indebtedness – A View from the UK, Germany, Greece and Italy* (Eleven), 207–23

Sweet, E. et al. (2013) 'The high price of debt: household financial debt and its impact on mental and physical health', 91 *Social Science & Medicine*, 94–100

Szyszczak, E. et al. (eds.) (2011) *Developments in Services of General Interest* (Springer)

Tangney, J. P. et al. (2004) 'High self-control predicts good adjustment, less pathology, better grades, and interpersonal success', 72(2) *Journal of Personality*, 271–324

Tasikas (2011) *The credit institution's obligation for assessment of the consumer's creditworthiness in consumer credit* (NoB)

Thakor, A. V. (2011) 'Incentives to innovate and financial crises', 103(1) *Journal of Financial Economics*, 130–48

Thomas, L. C. (2000) 'A survey of credit and behavioural scoring: forecasting financial risk of lending to consumers', 16(2) *International Journal of Forecasting*, 149–72

Thomson, J. J. (1975) 'The right to privacy', 4 *Philosophy and Public Affairs*, 295–314

Tooth, R. (2012) *Behavioural Economics and the Regulation of Consumer Credit* (New Zealand Law Foundation, August), at www.srgexpert.com/wp-content/uploads/2015/08/Consumer-Credit-Behavioural-Economics-Case-Study-2012-Final.pdf

Tribe, J. (2016) 'Consumer protection problems created by the structure of English personal insolvency law', in F. Ferretti (ed.), *Comparative Perspectives of Consumer Over-Indebtedness – A View from the UK, Germany, Greece and Italy* (Eleven), 125–49

Trumbull, G. (2014) *Consumer Lending in France and America* (Cambridge University Press)

Turinetti, E. and Zhuang, H. (2011) 'Exploring determinants of U.S. household debt', 27(6) *Journal of Applied Business Research*, 85–91

Turner, A. (2016) *Between Debt and the Devil: Money, Credit and Fixing Global Finance* (Princeton University Press)

Turner, M. A. and Varghese, R. (2010) *The Economic Consequences of Consumer Credit Information Sharing: Efficiency, Inclusion, and Privacy* (OECD)

Turner, M. A. and Walker, P. (2015) *Predicting Financial Account Delinquencies with Utility and Telecom Payment Data* (PERC Press, May), at www.perc.net/wp-content/uploads/2015/05/Alt-Data-and-Traditional-Accounts.pdf

Vandone, D. (2001) *L'intervento delle banche italiane nel mercato delle carte di pagamento* (Edizioni ISU)

(2009) *Consumer Credit in Europe: Risks and Opportunities of a Dynamic Industry* (Springer-Verlag)
Vandone, D. and Anderloni, L. (2014) 'Vulnerabilità e benessere delle famiglie italiane', in L. Andriani (ed.), *La fragilità al tempo della crisi: tra vulnerabilità economica e nuove forme di tutela* (Franco Angeli editore), 19–79
   (2016) 'The dimension of over-indebtedness in Italy and the characteristics of the over-indebted households', in F. Ferretti (ed.), *Comparative Perspectives of Consumer Over-indebtedness – A View from the UK, Germany, Greece and Italy* (Eleven), 291–314
Vandone, D., Anderloni, L. and Bacchiocchi, E. (2012) 'Household financial vulnerability: an empirical analysis', 66 *Research in Economics*, 284–96
Venieris, I. and Katsas, T. (2016) *Application of Law 3869/2010 on the Insolvency of Over-Indebted Individuals* (Nomiki Vivliothiki)
Verplanken, B. and Sato, A. (2011) 'The psychology of impulse buying: an integrative self-regulation approach', 34 *Journal of Consumer Policy*, 197–210
Viavoice (2015) *Introductory Report Towards a 'Second Chance' Legislation in Europe* (February)
Voss, G. (2014) 'Looking at European Union data protection law reform through a different prism: the proposed EU General Data Protection Regulation two years later', 17(9) *Journal of Internet Law*, 12–24
Wang, Lu and Malhotra, N. K. (2011) 'Demographics, attitude, personality and credit card features correlate with credit card debt: a view from China', 32 *Journal of Economic Psychology*, 179–93
Warren, S. D. and Brandeis, L. (1890) 'The right to privacy', 4 *Harvard Law Review*, 193–220
Watson, S. (2009) 'Credit card misuse, money attitudes, and compulsive buying behaviors: a comparison of internal and external locus of control (LOC) consumers', 43 *College Student Journal*, 268–75
Weatherill, S. (2010) 'Competence and European private law', in C. Twigg-Flesner (ed.), *The Cambridge Companion to European Private Law* (Cambridge University Press)
   (2013) *EU Consumer Law and Policy* (Edward Elgar)
Weiss, B. (1986) *The Hell of the English: Bankruptcy and the Victorian Novel* (Bicknell University Press)
Westin, A. F. (1967) *Privacy and Freedom* (Atheneum)
Whitman, J. Q. (2007) 'Consumerism versus producerism: a study in comparative law', 117 *Yale Law Journal*, 340–406
Williams, T. (2013) 'Continuity, not rupture: the persistence of neoliberalism in the internationalisation of consumer finance regulation', in T. Wilson (ed.), *International Responses to Issues of Credit and Over-Indebtedness* (Ashgate)
Willis, L. (2008) 'Evidence and ideology in assessing the effectiveness of financial literacy education', *University of Pennsylvania Law School, Research paper no. 8*
   (2011) 'The financial education fallacy', 101 *American Economic Review*, 429–34
Wittmann, M. and Paulus, M. P. (2008) 'Decision making, impulsivity and time perception', 12(1) *Trends in Cognitive Sciences*, 7–12
World Bank (2011) General *Principles for Credit Reporting* http://documents.worldbank.org/curated/en/662161468147557554/General-principles-for-credit-reporting
   (2013) *Responsible Lending – Overview of Regulatory Tools* (October)
   (2014) *Global Financial Development Report 2014: Financial Inclusion*, at https://openknowledge.worldbank.org/handle/10986/16238
Wright, J. D. (2007) 'Behavioral law and economics, paternalism, and consumer contracts: an empirical perspective', 2 *NYU Journal of Law and Liberty*, 470–511

Xiao, J. J. (2015) *Consumer Economic Wellbeing* (Springer)
Yobas, M. B. and Crook, J. N. (2000) 'Credit scoring using neural and evolutionary techniques', 11 *IMA Journal of Mathematics Applied in Business and Industry*, 111–25
Zajaczkowski, S. and Zochowski, D. (2007) 'The distribution and dispersion of debt burden ratios among households in Poland and its implications for financial stability'. 28 *Proceeding of the IFC Conference Measuring the Financial Position of the Household Sector*, 62–74
Zavadil, T. and Messner, T. (2014) 'Regional differences in household wealth across Slovakia', Working and Discussion Papers OP 1/2014 (National Bank of Slovakia)
Zermatten, A. et al. (2005) 'Impulsivity and decision making', 193(10) *Journal of Nervous and Mental Disorders*, 647–50
Zetzsche, D. A. et al. (2017) 'From fintech to techfin: the regulatory challenges of data-driven finance', *EBI Working Paper Series no. 6*
Zhang et al. (2015) *Sustaining Momentum – the 2nd European Alternative Finance Industry Report* (Cambridge University)
  (2016a) *Sustaining Momentum, the 2nd European Alternative Finance Industry Report, Cambridge Centre for Alternative Finance* (Cambridge University)
  (2016b) *The 2015 UK Alternative Finance Industry Report, Cambridge Centre for Alternative Finance* (Cambridge University)
Ziegel, J. S. (1999) 'The philosophy and design of contemporary consumer bankruptcy systems: a Canada–United States comparison', 37 *Osgoode Hall Law Journal*, 205
  (2006) 'Facts on the ground and reconciliation of divergent consumer insolvency philosophies', 7 *Theoretical Inquiries in Law*, 299–322

Index

adverse selection, 107, 108, 110, 111
affordable credit, 173, 200, 216
AI, 142, *See* artificial intelligence
algorithm, 116, 145, 160, 169
Algorithmic Consumer Finance, 141
Algorithmic Finance, 146
algorithms, 114, 115, 142, 147, 148, 169, 171, 229
Anacredit, 150, 152, 153, 154, 155
AnaCredit Regulation, 153
Annual Percentage Rate of Charge, 35
arrears, 8, 9, 51, 55, 57, 63, 103, 105, 132, 135, 150, 178, 199, 227
artificial intelligence, 32, 34, 114, 142, 168
asymmetrical information, 107
austerity, 3, 60, 86, 206, 215, 221
automated decision-making, 168, 169, 170

Banking Union, 9, 151
bankruptcy, 87, 108, 129, 137, 181, 182, 183, 184, 196, 203, 204, 208, 235, 236, 241, 244
Behavioural factors, 71, 80
   economic literature, 80
   impulsivity, 27, 73, 76
   psychological bias, 75
   psychological characteristics, 27
behavioural biases, 113, 148
behavioural causes, 91
big data, 9, 32, 107, 141, 142, 143, 144, 145, 146, 147, 148, 149, 160, 161, 162, 165, 166, 167, 168, 169, 170, 171, 172, 174, 175, 178, 229, 233, 234, 241
black box, 148
BU, 9, 151, *See* Banking Union
business insolvency, 10, 183, 218

Capital Market Union, 1, 10, 138, 197, 210
caveat emptor, 94, 202

CCD, 95, 96, 97, 100, 101, 102, 121, 122, 123, 136, 138, 139, 199, 200, 201, 202, *See* Consumer Credit Directive
Charter of Fundamental Rights, 158, 163, 189, 191, 198, 217, 218
CJEU, 96, 100, 101, 147, 161, 163, 171, 172, 187, 188, 189, 190, 191, 197, 198, 200, 203, 205, 208, 218, 232
Codes of Conduct, 164
COMI
   centre of main interest, 184, 185, 186, 205
Common principles, 88
common standards, 192
competence, 8, 10, 54, 60, 87, 88, 89, 180, 217, 218, 222
competition, 1, 3, 4, 32, 33, 34, 54, 88, 90, 92, 94, 95, 96, 98, 108, 110, 111, 122, 125, 138, 139, 140, 141, 143, 146, 150, 160, 161, 169, 176, 217, 220, 227, 231, 238
competition law, 125, 141
Computer scientists, 115
consent, 146, 160, 164, 165, 166, 167, 168, 170, 179, 232
Consumer credit. *See* personal debt
Consumer Credit Directive, 8, 35, 88, 90, 95, 121, 132, 154, 232
Consumer credit to GDP ratio, 14
consumer law, 3, 6, 8, 93, 94, 223
Consumer Policy strategy, 91
consumer protection, 4, 5, 6, 9, 10, 35, 54, 90, 93, 112, 122, 123, 141, 180, 182, 186, 188, 190, 197, 198, 201, 203, 206, 216, 217, 218, 222, 223, 228, 232, 233, 238, 239, 243
Countries, 13, 18, 22, 37, 38, 66
country of origin, 183, 205
Credit Bureau, 110, 111, 113, 116, 117, 118, 119, 120, 123, 125, 126, 127, 128, 129, 130, 131, 132, 134, 135, 136,

245

138, 139, 140, 146, 147, 152, 154, 155, 161, 163, 164, 165, 169, 173, 174, 176, 177, 178, 179, 240
credit history, 29, 113, 143, 144, 149, 168, 175, 214
credit intermediary, 101, 102
Credit laws, 122
credit risk, 9, 20, 29, 49, 93, 94, 104, 107, 110, 111, 113, 116, 124, 143, 144, 153, 154, 167, 175, 229
Credit Risk Analysis, 156
Credit Scoring, 113, 225, 231, 234, 237, 244
creditworthiness, 8, 9, 62, 90, 92, 93, 94, 95, 96, 97, 98, 99, 100, 101, 102, 103, 104, 108, 110, 114, 121, 122, 123, 138, 143, 144, 145, 147, 148, 150, 154, 156, 168, 171, 172, 177, 199, 200, 202, 203, 216, 220, 230, 232, 242
creditworthiness assessment, 100, 123, 139, 148, 178, 199, 203
cross-border, 1, 6, 89, 111, 121, 123, 136, 138, 139, 150, 152, 183, 184, 196, 197, 198, 208, 209, 212, 217
curative measures, 87, 104, 180, 216

data protection, 6, 9, 115, 116, 119, 120, 123, 141, 149, 156, 157, 158, 161, 163, 168, 169, 170, 171, 177, 179, 225, 226, 227, 229, 231, 232, 233, 236, 237, 241, 243
data protection law, 158
Data sources, 128
database, 12, 41, 96, 98, 101, 110, 111, 113, 114, 117, 118, 119, 120, 121, 122, 123, 125, 126, 127, 128, 130, 132, 136, 137, 138, 147, 150, 152, 153, 154, 165, 167, 168, 172, 175, 176, 177, 178, 199
Debt burden. *See* over-indebtedness
debt cancellation, 100
debt collection, 109, 126, 200, 216, 236
Debt service to income ratio, 56, 66, 71
debt solutions, 7, 10, 29, 30, 35, 62, 89, 90, 104, 180, 187, 191, 192, 198, 200, 207, 217
Debt to asset ratio, 56, 66
Debt to disposable income ratio, 12
Debt to income ratio, 11, 56
defaults, 2, 51, 66, 71, 88, 92, 117, 131, 135, 150, 153, 154, 177, 180, 217, 220
Directive 95/46/EC, 101, 156, 157, 161, 162, 163, 165, 168, 169
discharge, 87, 181, 182, 185, 187, 202, 204, 208, 209, 210, 211, 212, 213, 221
discipline device, 109
Doorstep lenders, 33

EBA, 104, 105, 123, 230, *See* European Banking Authority
ECB, 151, 152, 153, 154, 155, *See* European Central Bank
Economic and Social Committee, 1, 54, 78, 88, 90, 91, 139, 182, 183, 197, 210, 230

economic crisis, 89, 91, 182, 186, 187, 206, 217, 222
economic literature, 22, 62, 92, 107, 111, 113, 140, 147
ECRI Statistical Package, 11
Empirical analysis, 39, 44, 58, 81
enforcement, 91, 96, 100, 119, 182, 183, 184, 187, 188, 189, 190, 196, 199, 201, 202, 203, 206, 207, 208, 216, 218, 227, 231
entrepreneurs, 3, 10, 108, 207, 210, 211, 212, 213, 218
EU dimension, 3, 8, 197, 215, 222, 223
EU law, 8, 10, 61, 88, 89, 104, 138, 139, 158, 161, 180, 182, 188, 189, 192, 198, 199, 200, 201, 202, 205, 216, 217, 218, 228, 242
European Action Plan, 139
European Banking Authority, 8, 34, 98, 104, 105, 122, 123, 124, 142, 230
European Central Bank, 7, 20, 29, 35, 36, 37, 39, 40, 41, 42, 61, 139, 151, 152, 153, 226, 230
exclusion, 4, 51, 53, 86, 88, 92, 119, 126, 171, 174, 175, 206, 207, 210, 211, 215, 217, 219, 222, 223, 231

fees, 32, 34, 35, 36, 38, 61, 77, 92, 127, 214, 216
financial and economic crisis, 2, 10, 89, 151, 211, 221
financial crisis, 3, 6, 12, 51, 60, 65, 90, 97, 98, 117, 121, 122, 143, 153, 200, 204, 215, 223
financial data, 123, 140, 146, 163, 174
financial difficulty, 52, 53, 54, 61, 90, 105, 172, 174, 190, 201, 207, 209, 211, 216, 218, 221, 223, 236, 239
financial education, 4, 8, 25, 76, 77, 78, 80, 81, 84, 91, 98, 102, 177, 199, 230, 231, 237, 239, 243
Financial literacy, 76, 77, 80
financial stability, 66, 96, 121, 124, 129, 152, 154, 228, 242, 244
Financial system stability, 65
Financial Vulnerability Index, 57
Fintech, 7, 9, 29, 34, 50, 107, 141, 142, 144, 146, 147, 148, 149, 160, 162, 165, 166, 167, 168, 169, 170, 176, 177, 178, 226, 231, 234, 235, 241, 243, 244
forbearance, 104, 105
foreclosures, 103
Fraud prevention, 118, 129
fresh start, 181, 201, 209, 221
fundamental rights, 5, 6, 10, 116, 141, 158, 160, 161, 162, 163, 169, 176

GDPR, 9, 149, 156, 159, 160, 162, 163, 164, 165, 166, 167, 168, 169, 170, 179
General Data Protection Regulation. *See* GDPR
Generalized Method of Moments, 44

habitual residence, 186, 205
harmonisation, 3, 9, 10, 35, 153, 180, 186, 192, 193, 194, 195, 196, 197, 198, 199, 203, 210, 211, 212, 218
Hierarchical regression analyses, 82

homo economicus, 112
Household Finance and Consumption Survey, 11, 22, 65, 66
human dignity, 5, 7, 185, 187, 207
human rights, 5, 158, 187

identity theft, 118, 119
Identity verification, 117
imperfect information, 107
Income, 25, 27, 63, 70, 71
Information Asymmetry, 107
information exchanges, 109, 110, 121, 122, 125, 139
information monopoly, 110, 111
Information sharing, 110
insolvency laws, 10, 89, 183, 191, 197, 198, 205, 208, 209, 211, 212, 217, 218, 222, 223
insolvency procedures, 182, 205, 209
insolvency proceedings, 90, 182, 183, 184, 185, 186, 198, 206, 211, 218
interest rate caps, 216
interest rates, 7, 29, 33, 35, 37, 44, 56, 63, 64, 65, 66, 75, 98, 111, 145, 188, 214
interests, 52, 54, 61, 92, 105, 125, 148, 157, 159, 160, 161, 162, 164, 168, 169, 172, 184, 186, 200, 202, 208, 216, 218, 232
internal market, 2, 6, 9, 21, 35, 54, 61, 88, 90, 91, 95, 97, 98, 104, 122, 150, 151, 158, 196, 197, 204, 205, 208, 217, 218, 219, 230
International Monetary Fund, 65
irresponsible borrowing, 2, 220
irresponsible lending, 61, 95, 148, 172, 173, 192, 220

legal persons, 3, 127, 129, 130, 183, 210, 213
legal traditions, 88, 181, 204, 217
legitimate interest, 159, 160, 161, 162, 163, 164, 168, 169
liberalisation, 2, 19, 52, 203, 204, 215, 219, 220, 221, 222, 223
Life-Cycle Theory, 11, 21, 23, 26, 27, 32, 71
LILA, 206, 218
  little income, little asset consumers, 185

Maastricht Treaty, 87
market deregulation, 172, 221
market failure, 3, 4, 6, 89, 93, 180, 217
market integration, 88
Marketing, 117, 236, 241
maximum harmonisation, 201
MCD, 97, 98, 99, 100, 101, 102, 103, 104, 105, 122, 123, 136, 138, 139, 150, 199, 200, 201, *See* Mortgage Credit Directive
Mediation analysis, 83
monopolies, 140, 147
moral hazard, 108, 109, 181

mortgage, 2, 3, 7, 11, 12, 16, 22, 23, 27, 28, 31, 32, 52, 58, 60, 66, 67, 71, 74, 77, 79, 97, 105, 109, 114, 121, 126, 135, 153, 174, 178, 187, 188, 189, 190, 191, 199, 206, 217, 219, 225, 232, 238, 240, 242
Mortgage Credit Directive, 8, 88, 90, 97, 103, 122
Mortgages. *See* personal debt
mutual recognition, 10, 182, 184, 186, 198, 206, 207, 209, 216, 217, 221

National Credit Registries, 152
national law, 89, 100, 161, 163, 170, 184, 186, 188, 189, 190, 191, 201, 202, 205, 207, 213
natural persons, 3, 10, 125, 127, 130, 154, 182, 183, 184, 197, 204, 205, 210, 211, 212, 213, 216, 218, 221, 235
Negative information, 131
NINA, 206, 218
  no income, no asset consumers, 185
Non-mortgage debt. *See* personal debt
Non-performing loans, 38

Orbis Bank Focus, 41
Over-indebtedness
  causes, 59
  consumer characteristics, 62, 68
  definition, 52
  economic literature, 62, 74
  measures, 55
  size, 66

party autonomy, 92, 93, 94
paternalism, 5, 93, 94, 95, 228, 243
Pawnbrokers, 33
penalties, 6, 61, 178, 191, 199, 200, 216
Personal debt
  consumer characteristics, 21, 23, 26
  demand, 20
  economics, 29, 34, 42
  industry, 38, 39, 43, 50
  innovation, 30
  measures, 12, 22, 43
  outstanding amount, 11, 17
  participation in the market, 22, 23
  players, 29, 33
  products, 30
  structural transformations, 19
  supply, 19, 49
personal insolvency, 3, 10, 87, 89, 180, 181, 182, 183, 185, 186, 191, 192, 193, 197, 204, 205, 206, 208, 216, 217, 218, 221, 231
Policy implications, 55, 62, 86
Policy measures, 80
Policy responses, 78
Positive information, 131
preventive measures, 87, 90, 98, 200, 216

privacy, 116, 132, 156, 157, 158, 169, 235
private international law, 186, 216
private law, 8, 52, 62, 93, 94, 96, 100, 130, 187, 191, 192, 201, 202, 203, 216, 237
procedural fairness, 190, 218
procedural rules, 158, 189, 190, 191
profiling, 114, 144, 165, 168, 169, 170
prudential supervision, 9, 124, 151, 171, 177
public interest, 100, 127, 160, 177, 179, 187, 191, 208
public law, 96, 100, 203

rating agencies, 116
repayment, 31, 32, 33, 38, 51, 53, 56, 60, 63, 75, 93, 99, 100, 101, 106, 108, 109, 113, 114, 116, 135, 145, 150, 172, 177, 178, 181, 200, 206, 207, 209, 215, 220, 230, 234
reputation collateral, 108, 109
responsible borrowing, 76, 87, 91, 92, 93, 94, 98
responsible credit, 77, 87, 90, 91, 93, 97, 201, 202, 217, 231
responsible creditor, 8, 93, 94
responsible lending, 8, 9, 10, 87, 90, 91, 93, 94, 95, 96, 97, 98, 100, 102, 104, 117, 121, 147, 180, 192, 199, 200, 201, 202, 204, 216, 217, 220, 236, 238, 241
restitution, 101
restructuring, 10, 87, 88, 185, 207, 209, 210, 211, 212, 213
restructuring procedures, 209
Revolving credit cards, 38
risk assessment, 110
risk management, 107, 108, 152, 172

Salary/retirement-backed loans, 31
second chance, 10, 113, 173, 207, 209, 210, 211, 212
Securitisation, 116, 117

self-determination, 157, 159
Single Supervisory Mechanism, 151
social media, 142, 143, 144, 145, 150, 160, 175
social welfare, 55, 60, 93, 172, 187, 197, 219
soft law, 106, 198, 199, 206, 221
solvency data, 9, 98, 107, 112, 113, 115, 117, 118, 119, 120, 121, 122, 123, 124, 126, 127, 139, 140, 141, 142, 143, 146, 150, 154, 155, 160, 161, 162, 163, 164, 165, 166, 167, 168, 169, 170, 172, 173, 174, 175, 177
Specialised finance company, 30
Specialised financial institutions, 33
Student loans, 31
subsidiarity, 88, 89, 197, 212, 217

telecoms, 119
Treaty of Lisbon, 158

UCTD
  Unfair Contract Terms Directive, 187, 188, 189, 190, 191, 205, 206, 237
unemployment, 20, 56, 60, 63, 65, 66, 86, 144, 211, 215, 216, 220, 222
unfair contract terms, 187, 190, 200, 205
unfair terms, 187, 188, 189, 191
Unmanageable debt. *See* over-indebtedness
Unsecured credit. *See* personal debt
utilities, 57, 60, 63, 119, 130, 145, 174, 175

vulnerable consumers, 89, 97, 148, 175, 184, 186, 206

Wealth, 26, 27, 71
Welfare state, 21

Zero down payment loans, 31

Lightning Source UK Ltd.
Milton Keynes UK
UKHW022041310722
406659UK00017B/385